AF600540

DECENNIAL FACULTIES FOR ORDINARIES IN QUASI-DIOCESES

This dissertation was approved by the Rev. Meletius M. Wojnar, O.S.B.M., S.T.L., J.C.D., as director and by the Very Rev. Clement V. Bastanagel, S.T.L., J.U.D., and the Rev. John Rogg Schmidt, A.B., J.C.D., as readers.

THE CATHOLIC UNIVERSITY OF AMERICA
CANON LAW STUDIES
No. 402

Decennial Faculties for Ordinaries in Quasi-Dioceses

A DISSERTATION

SUBMITTED TO THE FACULTY OF THE SCHOOL OF CANON LAW OF THE CATHOLIC UNIVERSITY OF AMERICA IN PARTIAL FULFILLMENT OF THE REQUIREMENTS FOR THE DEGREE OF DOCTOR OF CANON LAW

BY

THE REV. PETER B. CHYANG, M.A., J.C.L.
THE PRIEST OF THE VICARIATE APOSTOLIC OF TAEGU, KOREA

THE CATHOLIC UNIVERSITY OF AMERICA PRESS
WASHINGTON, D.C.
1961

NIHIL OBSTAT:
Clement V. Bastnagel, S.T.L., J.U.D.
Censor Deputatus
Washington, D.C., May 9, 1960
IMPRIMATUR:
✠ Patrick A. O'Boyle, D.D.
Archbishop of Washington

Washington, D.C., May 9, 1960

The *Nihil obstat* and *imprimatur* are official declarations that a book or pamphlet is free of doctrinal or moral error. No implication is contained therein that those who have granted the *nihil obstat* and *imprimatur* agree with the content, opinions or statements expressed.

Printed by The Abbey Press, St. Meinrad, Indiana, U.S.A.

TO MY FATHER AND MOTHER

AND

TO MY FELLOW MISSIONARIES

FOREWORD

This study consists of two parts: the first, which deals with an investigation of the historical development of the juridical concept of "Faculty," and the second, in which the Decennial Faculties nn. I-XXVIII are to receive a doctrinal comment.

The institution of Apostolic Faculties grew out of the exceptions to the common law of the Church, and it began to exist from the very beginning of the Church itself. For, from the moment when Christ solemnly pronounced the words: "all power in heaven and on earth has been given to me, go, therefore, and make disciples of all nations..., teaching them to observe all that I commanded to you...," "whose sins you shall forgive, they are forgiven them," "many things yet I have to say to you, but you cannot bear them now. But when he, the Spirit of truth, has come, he will teach the truth," etc., the Apostles were vested with the full jurisdiction—legislative, ministerial, and coactive; and the power to make exceptions to the law is but a corollary of the power to make the laws concerned. In the beginning of the history of the Church, and also during the middle ages, those exceptions were made mainly for the sake of facilitating the treatment of problems which arose out of extraordinary needs of individual bishops and groups of missionaries in particular places, especially those who were far removed from the Holy See, while since the seventeenth century Apostolic Faculties were granted in the form of formulas of Apostolic Faculties to bishops and mission prefects. Hence, the development of the legal institution of Apostolic Faculties can be regarded as a corollary of the development of the legal system of the Church. This study, however, deals with an investigation of the historical development of "Faculty" in its characteristics as reflected in the Code of Canon Law.

The Decennial Faculties in *Formula Maior* consist of four major groups of Apostolic Faculties: (1) Faculties concerning Sacraments and Sacred Rites (nn. I-XXI); (2) Faculties concerning the Sacrament of Matrimony (nn. XXII-XXVIII); (3) Faculties concerning Absolutions, Blessings, and Indulgences (nn. XXIX-XXLI); and (4) Faculties for the Ordinary (nn. L-LIII. In this study, however, the Faculties contained in groups (1) and (2) are exclusively to receive a specific doctrinal comment, since these Faculties are of more practical import and have been more affected by the recent legislative activities than the rest of the Faculties in the Formula. As to the method employed for their commentary, in order to clarify the exact mind of the Holy See, which is the author of the Faculties, a commentary on the canons related to a given Decennial Faculty is briefly offered along with a mention of the recent Decrees, Instructions, Decisions, Replies, etc., of the Holy See. This commentary appears under the heading of "*ex iure,*" while the Faculty itself will be studied under the heading of "*ex facultate.*" The Decennial Faculty is furthermore compared with the Quinquennial Faculty, if there be any corresponding Quinquennial Faculty in the Diocesan Quinquennial Faculties, Formula IV.

The writer wishes to avail himself of the opportunity presented here to express his sincere gratitude to his Bishop, the Most Rev. John B. Sye, Ordinary of the Vicariate Apostolic of Taegu, Korea, for graciously granting him the rare privilege of pursuing higher studies at the Catholic University of America; to the Most Rev. Patrick A. O'Boyle, Ordinary of the Archdiocese of Washington, D.C., and the Most Rev. Philip M. Hannan, Auxiliary Bishop and Chancellor of the Archdiocese of Washington, D.C., for graciously granting him a residence at St. Peter's Church, Washington, D.C.; and to the Right Rev. Msgr. Maurice J. King, pastor of St. Peter's Church, Washington, D.C., for offering him the residence and generous assistance.

Grateful acknowledgments are here accorded to the members of the Faculty of the School of Canon Law at the Catholic University of America, Washington, D.C., for their invaluable advice, scholarly guidance, and assistance in the writing of this dissertation; to my benefactors, to my classmates, to the staff of St. Peter's Church, and to all who in any way aided in the completion of this dissertation.

TABLE OF CONTENTS

PART ONE

HISTORICAL SYNOPSIS AND PRELIMINARY NOTES

PART TWO

A COMMENTARY ON THE DECENNIAL FACULTIES NN. I-XXVIII IN THE *FORMULA MAIOR*

SECTION ONE

Faculties Concerning Sacraments and Sacred Rites: The Decennial Faculties NN. I-XXI in the *Formula Maior*

SECTION TWO

Faculties Concerning the Sacrament of Matrimony: The Decennial Faculties NN. XXII-XXVIII In the *Formula Maior*

PART ONE

HISTORICAL SYNOPSIS AND PRELIMINARY NOTES

CHAPTER I

THE JUDICIAL CONCEPT OF *"FACULTAS"*

ARTICLE I. IN ROMAN LAW

In Roman Law, *"facultas"* (or *"facultates"*), for which the English word faculty (or faculties) stands in the Code of Canon Law, has two groups of meanings, i.e., the first: *"potestas"* (power, ability, right, etc.), *"licentia"* (license, permission, etc.), *"libertas"* (liberty, freedom, etc.), *"arbitrium"* (authority, etc.), and the second: *"opes"* (property, substance, wealth, etc.), *"possessiones"* (possessions), *"divitiae"* (wealth, riches, etc.), etc.

In most cases, however, *"facultas"* is used in the meaning of the first group, while *"facultates"* is used in the sense of the second group. Thus, the word *"facultas"* occurs in such phrases as *"facultas agendi," "facultas agendi testamenti," "facultas relinquendi haereditatem," "facultas iudiici," "facultas patrimonii,"* etc., and the word *"facultates"* in phrases such as *"facultates augere," "propter amplissimas facultates,"* etc. When the word is taken in the meaning of the first group, there are sentences such as *"facultas est personae, non rerum quae permittuntur," "libertas est naturalis facultas eius, quod cuique facere libet," "facultas libera intelligitur dummodo iuris ordo servetur,"* etc.[1]

In the eighteenth century, Philip Vicat (†1770) defined *"facultas"* as "[*potestas*] *qua quis iure quid facere, vel non, potest"* (a faculty is a power by virtue of which a person can lawfully do something, or lawfully not do it). He gave

[1] Cf. *Vocabularium Iurisprudentiae Romanae,* auspiciis Instituti Savigniani inchoatum & ex auctoritate Academiae Scientiarum Borussicae compositum (Berolini: Typis et impensis Walter de Gruyter & Co., 1933), Vol. II, coll. 789-791. Bartolus a Saxoferrato, *Gemma Legalis* (11 vols., Venetiis: Apud Iuntas, 1590-1595), Vol. XI, s. v. *"facultas"* and *"facultatis"*; Ioannes Bertachinus Firmanus, *Repertorium* (5 vols., Venetiis: Apud Bevilaquam et Socios, 1570), s. v. *"Facultas,"* Vol. II, 304, coll. 1-2.

examples of such a power, citing the "*facultas accusandi*"[2] the "*facultas abstinendi,*"[3] etc.; he called such power a "*facultas personae.*"[4]

In the light of Roman Law, a modern definition of "*facultas* [*personae*]" has been formulated by Adolf Berger as "the legal ability to conclude an agreement or to accomplish a valid act (a testament)." Berger then explained the "*libera facultas mortis*" as the "permission granted by the emperor to persons condemned to death to evade execution through suicide."[5] Hence it seems that Berger used the word "ability" in the broad sense in such a way that it included permission, license, power, right, liberty, freedom, etc.

A systematic explanation of the juridical meaning of "*facultas*" in secular law was made by a French lawyer, Claude-Joseph de Ferrière (1639-1715). He took the word "*facultas*" only for "*droit*" *or power.* He defined it as "*le droit qu'on a de faire quelque chose,*" or "a power which is possessed by a person to do something," and thus there is a faculty to contract an agreement, a faculty to alienate one's own property, a faculty to make one's own testament, etc.[6]

There are two different sources for such faculties, one, the *ius gentium* or the natural law, and the other, a superior authority. For instance, the faculty to alienate one's own property is one's inherent power in regard to that property, which power is derived from the natural law, whereas the faculty to make one's own testament is derived from

[2] D. (48. 5) (4. 1).

[3] D. (38. 9) 2.

[4] *Vocabularium Iuris Utriusque* (2. ed., auctior atque emendatior, 4 vols., Neapoli: Sumptibus Joannis Grevier, 1760), Vol, II, p. 167.

[5] *Encyclopedic Dictionary of Roman Law,* ed. by The American Philosophical Society (Philadelphia, 1953), p. 567.

[6] *Dictionnaire de Droit et de Pratique* (Contenant l'Explication des Termes de Droit, d'Ordonnances, et Coutûmes et de Pratique avec les Juridictions de France), nouvelle édition, revue, corrigée et augmentée par Claude-Joseph de Ferrière (Paris: Chez Durand Libraire, 1762), fol. 888.

the positive law, as enacted by the public authority. A faculty sometimes denotes a particular power which a person can exercise in virtue of a privilege that he possesses, or as the result of a contract he has made, and such a faculty consists in the doing of something or in the omitting of something. When one's faculty is personal, it does not pass to his heirs at all.[7]

Faculties which have the characteristics of some particular power are divided into three kinds. A faculty of the first kind is that which is purely useful (for example, the faculty to accept or to renounce a succession), and passes to one's heirs or to one's creditors; a faculty of the second kind is that which is purely personal and is neither transmissible nor perishable; and a faculty of the third kind is one which in combining both elements (for example, the faculty to accept an office in a community) is not transmissible to one's own heirs, but is transferable to others. A faculty which comes from an agreement of parties does not last more than thirty years if in the agreement no time was fixed for execution of the faculty; even if the time is fixed, this is not peremptory, since it expires, for at its expiration there can be made a new agreement allowing another term for the execution of the same faculty.[8]

ARTICLE II. IN THE *Decretum* OF GRATIAN AND THE *Decretales* OF GREGORY IX

SECTION 1. IN THE *Decretum* OF GRATIAN

In the *Decretum* of Gratian it is confirmed that the pope

[7] Cf. *loc. cit.*

[8] Cf. *ibid.*, coll. 888-889. Also see "Faculté," in *La Grande Encyclopédie, Inventaire Raisonée des Sciences, des Lettres et des Arts,* par la Société de Savants et de Gens de Lettres (Paris: H. Laminault de Cie, Éditeurs, 1886-1902), Vol. XVI, pp. 1061-1062; John Bouvier, "Faculty," in *Law Dictionary* (3rd rev. ed. by Francis Rawle, 2 vols., Kansas City, Mo.: Vernon Law Book Co., 1914), Vol. I, p. 1178: "In Scotch Law [faculty is] ability or power. The term faculty is more properly applied to a power founded on the consent of the party from whom it springs, and not founded on property; Kames Eq. 504."

has the supreme authority, both legislative and jurisdictional, over the entire Church. The power of the pope to establish laws for the universal Church is set out most systematically in *Distinctio XII,* which emhasizes the subordination of all local churches to Rome, and in *Distinctio XIX,* which is concerned especially with the universal validity of papal decretals.[9] The compiler of the *Decretum* asserted the papal decretals to be of equal authority with the canons of the general councils;[10] that the pope is himself not subject to the canons;[11] that the power of dispensing from the universal laws is a correlative of the universal legislative power, that the power of dispensing from the universal laws of the Church belongs exclusively to the pope,[12] and that the power to establish privileges outside universal laws and privileges contrary to universal laws is reserved to the pope.[13] All these are the essential doctrines upon which the possibility and the legal force of Apostolic Faculties must be based. However, in the *Decretum* of Gratian there are no canons which directly treated Apostolic Faculties.

Nevertheless, two canons in the *Decretum* deserve some consideration here. C. 10, D. XII, reproduces Gregory the

[9] "Nulli vero dubium est, quod apostolica ecclesia mater sit omnium ecclesiarum, a cuius vos regulis nullatenus convenit deviare. . . ."—C. 1, D. XII; ". . . Decretales epistolae Romanorum Pontificum sunt recipiendae, etiamsi non sint codici canonum compaginatae."—C. 1, D. XIX; "Sic omnes apostolicae sedis sanctiones accipiendae sunt, tanquam ipsius voce divina Petri firmatae."—C. 2, D. XIX; "Enimvero, quia in speculum et exemplum Sancta Romana Ecclesia, cui nos Christus preesse voluit, posita est, omnibus, quidquid statuit, quidquid ordinat, perpetuo et irrefragabiliter observandum est."—C. 4, D. XIX; "Nulli fas est vel velle, vel posse transgredi apostolicae sedis praecepta."—C. 5, D. XIX.

[10] "Decretales itaque epistolae canonibus conciliorum pari iure exequantur."—*Dictum* Gratiani ad c. 1, D. XX.

[11] "Sacrosancta Romana Ecclesia ius et auctoritatem sacris canonibus impertit, sed non eis allegatur. . . ."—*Dictum* Gratiani, post c. 16, C. XXV, q. 1.

[12] C. 2, D. XIV. Cf. Brys, *De Dispensatione in Iure Canonico* (Brugis: Beyaert, 1925), pp. 80-81.

[13] Cf. *Dictum* Gratiani post c. 16, C. XXV, q. 1.

Great's answer to the second question of St. Augustine of England; the answer is stated as follows:

> *Novit fraternitas tua Romanae ecclesiae consuetudinem, in qua se meminit nutritam. Sed mihi placet, ut sive in Romana, sive in Gallicorum, seu in qualibet ecclesia invenisti, quod plus omnipotenti Deo possit placere, sollicite eligas, et in Anglorum ecclesia, quae adhuc in fide nova est, institutione precipua, quae de multis ecclesiis collegere potueris, infundas. Non enim pro locis res, sed pro rebus loca amanda sunt. Ex singulis ergo quibusque ecclesiis quae pia, quae religiosa, quae recta sunt, elige, et haec quasi in fasciculum collecta apud Anglorum mentes in consuetudinem depone.*[14]

In virtue of this answer, bishops were empowered to choose from every church those things that were pious, religious, and upright, for the people of their own churches. The other canon is c. 11, D. XII, which repeats the words from the letter of St. Augustine to Januarius, and therein implies this right for the bishops. The words are: "*quod neque contra fidem, neque contra bonos mores esse convincitur, indifferenter* [*est*] *habendum.*" Canons 10 and 11 of *Distinctio XII* are of the same nature: both allow bishops to accept practices of which no mention is made in the law of the Church.

As to the use of the words "*facultas*" and "*facultates*" in the *Decretum* of Gratian, these words did not reflect any degree of divergence from the meaning attaching to these words in the Roman Law. For example, "*facultates*" is used with the meaning of "possessions" in c. 1, C. XIII, q. 2, and c. 2, C. XVI, q. 3.[15]

[14] Cf. Harduin, *Acta Conciliorum et Epistolae Decretales ac Constitutiones Summorum Pontificum* (12 vols., Parisiis: Typographia Regia, 1714-1715), Vol. III, coll. 509-517; Migne, *Patrologiae Cursus Completus, Series Latina* (221 vols., Parisiis, 1844-1855), Vol. XCV, coll. 58-67; Franciscus Wasner, "De Authenticitate 'Libelli Responsionum' Beati Gregorii Magni Papae ad Sanctum Augustinum Angliae Apostolum Animadversiones," *Jus Pontificium*, XVII (1938), 174-185; 293-299.

[15] C. 2, C. XVI, q. 3, is taken from Pope Gelasius' epistle "*Praesulum Nostrorum*," which was written to the people of Sicily on May 15,

SECTION 2. IN THE *Decretales* OF GREGORY IX

The *Decretales* of Gregory IX include a few canons which deal with Apostolic Faculties. In the *Decretales,* there is mention of the fact that a bishop who was to leave to preach the Faith to the pagans asked Pope Clement III (1187-1191) whether he could partake of the foods offered by the infidels. The pope gave his permission to use them through a decretal letter, and in addition granted a concession in virtue of which "worthy clerics" were permitted to join the bishop in the work of preaching the Gospel to the Gentiles, provided that they had obtained permission from their prelates. In this grant the pope used a special expression: "*... qualibet liberam exequendi habeant auctoritate apostolica facultatem,*"[16] which expression came later to denote grants of Apostolic Faculties; no distinction, however, was made between "*facultas*" and "*indulgentia,*" for the introductory rubric reads: "*Ponit duas indulgentias illorum, qui paganis praedicant.*"

The *Decretales* also include a papal bull, in which Pope Honorius III (1216-1227) explained how to interpret the privilege of celebrating Mass on a portable altar, previously given to the Order of the Friars Minor. In the bull the pope declared that such a privilege should be regarded as one of apostolic indulgence, whose interpretation should be "*benigna*" or broad.[17]

As in the *Decretum* of Gratian, so also in the *Decretales* of Gregory IX, no canons deal directly with the doctrine of Apostolic Faculties.[18]

494. C. 1, C. XIII, q. 2, states: "Facultates ecclesiae, nec non et dioeceses, quae ab aliquibus possidentur episcopis, ius sibi vendicent, quod tricennalis lex conclusit. . . ." These words came from the letter of Pope Gelasius, "*Praesulum Nostrorum.*"

[16] C. 10, X, *de haereticis,* V, 6.

[17] C. 30, X. *de privilegiis et excessibus privilegiatorum,* V, 33. Cf. A. Potthast, *Regesta Pontificum Romanorum inde ab anno post Christum natum MCXCVIII ad annum MCCCIV* (2 vols., Berolini, 1874-1875), n. 7467 [hereafter cited Potthast].

[18] Cf. Bartoccetti, "Animadversiones circa Evolutionem Iuris Mis-

Article III. From the Thirteenth Century to the Sixteenth Century

SECTION 1. THE PERIOD OF THE DOMINICAN-FRANCISCAN MISSIONS

During the period from the thirteenth century to the sixteenth century there existed two great groups of missions, i.e., the one, the Dominican-Franciscan missions (from the thirteenth century to the fifteenth century), and the other, the Jèsuit missions (in the sixteenth century).

Since Dominicans and Franciscans launched missionary works in thirteenth century, many Apostolic Faculties were granted to the missionaries through the agency of the papal bull. Oftentimes, indeed, the words *"facultas"* and *"facultates"* were not employed in the papal bulls, but these Apostolic Faculties were generally certified through other phrases and expressions. For example, when Pope Honorius III granted Apostolic Faculties to preach to the Saracens, to baptize converts, to reconcile apostates, to hear confessions, and to absolve from excommunications, to a group of missionaries of the Order of Friars Preacher and those of the Order of Friars Minor, he used the cause: "... [*auctoritate sedis apostolicae*] *concedimus* ... *ut* ... *vobis liceat praecidare, baptiszare Sacracenos,* etc.";[19] Pope Gregory IX (1227-1241) used the clause: *"auctoritate tibi praesentium concedimus potestatem,"* when he granted Apostolic

sionis," *Jus Pontificium,* XIV (1934), 263-265; A. Larraona, "De Iure Missionario," *Commentarium pro Religiosis et Missionariis,* XVII (1936), 85 [hereafter cited as *CpRM*]; Marcel Gérin, *Le Gouvernement des Missions,* Les Thèses Canoniques de Laval, n. 1 (Quebec: Faculté de Droit Canonique, Université Laval, 1944), pp. 12-13.

[19] Potthast, n. 7490; *Bullarium Ordinis Fratrum Praedicatorum* (ed. Th. Ripoli, 8 vols., Romae, 1729-1740), I, 16 (Honorius III, 7 Oct., 1225), n. XXXIII [hereafter cited *B.O.P.*].; *Bullarium Franciscanum* (cura et studio Ioannis Hyacinthi Sbaraleae, O.F.M. Conv., Vols. I-IV, Romae, 1759-1768; continuavit Conradus Eubel, O.F.M. Conv., Vols. V-VII, Romae, 1898-1904), I, 24 (Honorius III, 7 Oct., 1225), n. XXIII [hereafter cited as *Bullarium Franciscanum*]. Cf. Potthast, n. 7429.

Faculties to preach everywhere, to hear confessions, to impart twenty-day indulgences, and to impose penances upon penitents, by means of the Bull *"Descendentibus olim mare."*[20]

In the Bull *"Cum hora undecima,"* the form *"Vobis auctoritate concedimus, ut . . . valeatis. . . ,"* served the confirming of various Apostolic Faculties. This papal bull was the most comprehensive one to date, and the one which was most frequently given to the Dominican-Franciscan missionaries during the thirteenth century. It contained the Apostolic Facutlies to receive converts, to baptize them, to hear confessions, to absolve from excommunication, to dispense from irregularities, to reconcile apostates, to receive sacred orders from any patriarch, archbishop, or bishop, to bless vestments, altars, palls, corporals, etc., and to do whatever was concerned with the glory of God and the salvation of souls, as places and time demanded.[21]

[20] Potthast, n. 7906; *B.O.P.*, I, 19 (Gregorius IX, 16 Maii, 1227), n. IV. Cf. also the Bull *"Cum messis multa,"* in Potthast, nn. 9139, 9196; *Bullarium Franciscanum,* I, 100 (Gregorius IX, 8 Aprilis, 1233), n. XCVII; *ibid.*, I, 103 (17 Maii, 1233), n. CII; Lucien Auvray, *Les Registres de Gregoire IX: Recueil des Bulles de ce Pape, Publiées ou Analysées d'après les Manuscrits Originaux du Vatican,* Vols. I-III (Paris: Librairie Thorin et Fils, 1896-1918), Vol. IV, ed. par Vitte-Clémencet et Louis Carolus-Barré (Paris: E. De Boccard, Éditeur, 1955), I, col. 693, n. 1220; the Bull *"Pro zelo Fidei,"* Potthast, n. 9197 (17 Maii, 1233); *Bullarium Franciscanum,* I, 103, n. CI; the Bull *"Pro zelo Christianae,"* Auvray, *op. cit.*, II, col. 1054 (12 Apr. 1238), n. 4400; Potthast, n. 10569; *Bullarium Franciscanum,* I, 236, n. CCLIV.

[21] Auvray, *op. cit.*, II, col. 1267 (Gregorius IX, 15 Feb. 1235), nn. 2429-2430; Potthast, nn. 9345-9846; *B.O.P.*, I, 73-74. Cf. Potthast, n. 10763; *Bullarium Franciscanum,* I, 269 (11 Iun. 1239), n. CCXCVI. The same bull was given by Pope Innocent IV. See Elie Berger, *Les Registres d'Innocent IV. Originaux des Archives du Vatican et de la Bibliothèque Nationale,* Vols. I-II (Paris: Ernest Thorin, Édit., 1884-1887), Vol. III (Paris: Ancienne Librairie Thorin et Fils, 1897), Vol. IV (Index) (?), I, 208 (23 Iul. 1253), n. 7753; Potthast, n. 15065; *B.O.P.*, I, 310 (27 Iun. 1256), n. CV; *B.O.P.*, VII, 36-37 (13 Feb. 1258), n. CCCVIII; Potthast, n. 17186; *Bullarium Franciscanum,* II, 285 (19 Apr. 1258), n. CDVIII. By Pope Urban IV: *Bullarium*

The word *"facultas"* was used in its proper sense in the Bull *"Patri luminum praestamus"* of Pope Innocent IV, but it had the meaning of *"facultates"* because of the fact that, after having enumerated various Apostolic Faculties for missionaries of the Order of Friars Preacher, the pope stated simply: *"... vobis concedimus facultatem."*[22]

During the thirteenth century another variation in the granting of Apostolic Faculties to missionaries was reflected by Pope Innocent IV who, in 1253, gave Apostolic Faculties, not directly to the missionaries or to their superiors, but to the then Papal Legate Otho (Eudes of Chateauraux), the Cardinal-bishop of Tusculum. The latter, by virtue of the Papal Bull *"Athleta Christi,"* could promote some of the missionaries from the Orders of Friars Preacher and of Friars Minor to the dignity of bishop, and give them the faculty to dispense from the matrimonial impediments of consanguinity and affinity, provided there was question of degrees not prohibited by the divine law, and the faculty to dispense from the law of fast.[23]

From the end of the thirteenth century to the middle of the fifteenth century, there was a foreign missionary institute, called *Societas Peregrinantium pro Christo,* within the Orders of Friars Preacher and Friars Minor.[24] The

Franciscanum, II, 493 (28 Iul. 1263), n. LXXIX; Potthast, n. 18606. By Pope Nicholas IV: *B.O.P.*, II, 154 (23 Oct. 1321), n. XXIII. This papal bull was also given under different titles, such as *"Virtute conspicuos"* (*Bullarum Franciscanum,* II, 298, Alexander IV, 2 Aug, 1258, n. CDXXXVI); *"Cum a Nobis"* (*Bullarium Franciscanum,* II, 446, Urbanus IV, 29 Maii, 1262, n. XXXIV).

[22] Berger, *op. cit.*, I, 99 (22 Martii, 1244), n. 573; Potthast, n. 11297; *B.O.P.*, I, 136-137, n. LVI.

[23] Berger, *op. cit.*, III, 184, n. 6365; Potthast, n. 14886; *B.O.P.*, I, 226, n. CCXCI; *Bullarium Franciscanum,* I, 651, n. CDLVIII.

[24] Before 1456, the *Societas Peregrinantium pro Christo* within the Order of Friars Preacher was suppressed for the first time in 1363 and then was reestablished in 1375. After 1456, it was known as the *Congregation of the Friars Preacher,* and then, from about 1600 to 1857, as the *Congregation of the Orient.* Cf. Raymond Loenertz, "Les Missions Dominicaines en Orient au XIVe Siècle et la Société des Frères Pérégrinants pour le Christ," *Archivum Fratrum Praedica-*

Societas Peregrinantium pro Christo of the Order of Friars Preacher was led by a vicar of the Master-General of the Order, to whom were addressed papal bulls containing Apostolic Faculties for the members of the Society.[25] Among these

torum, II (1932), 1-83; R. Loenertz, *La Société des Frères Pérégrinants: Étude sur l'Orient Dominicain*, Dissertationes Historicae Instituti Historici FF. Praedicatorum, n. 7 (Romae: Institutum Historicum FF. Praedicatorum, 1937); P. Golubovich, "De locis Fratrum Minorum et Praedicatorum in Tartaris," *Archivum Fratrum Praedicatorum*, II (1932), pp. 73-74; Dominicus de Gubernatis, *Orbis Seraphicus: Historia de Tribus Oridinibus a Seraphico Patriarcha S. Francisco Institutis, deque Eorum Progressibus et Honoribus per Quatuor Mundi Patres* (6 vols., Romae: Typis Stephani Caballi, 1682), V, foll. 22-23; Fortunatus Hueber, *Menologium* (Romae: Typis Joannis Straubii, 1698), col. 1498; Lucas Waddingus, *Annales Minorum seu Trium Ordinum a S. Francisco Institutorum* (27 vols., 3. ed., curavit Joseph Maria Fonseca, ad Claras Aquas, Quarrachi, 1931-1935), III (an. 1252, n. XXII), foll. 288-289; Herbert Holzapfel, *The History of the Franciscan Order*, Trans. by Tibesar-Gervase Brinkmann (Teutopolis, Illinois: St. Joseph Seminary, 1948), pp. 12, 193 ff., and 399 ff.; Huber, *A Documented History of the Franciscan Order* (Milwaukee, Wisc. and Washington, D.C.: O.F.M. Conv. Press, 1944), p. 782; Baron Descamps, *Histoire Générale Comparée des Missions* (Paris: Libraire Plon, 1932), p. 271.

[25] Cf. The Bull "*Inter cunctas sollicitudines*" in *B.O.P.*, II, 88-90, n. XVI; Potthast, n. 25370; Ch. Grandjean, *Les Registres de Benoit XI. Recueil des Bulles de ce Pape, Publiées ou Analysées d'après les Manucrits Originaux des Archives du Vatican* (Paris: Albert Fontemoing, 1905), coll. 714-720, n. 1170; *Extravag. Com.* c. 1 *(de privilegiis)*, V. 7. The Bull "*Gratias agimus*" in *B.O.P.*, II, 88-90 (Joannes XXLI, 1 Martii, 1318), n. XI; *ibid.*, II, 184-186. The Bull "*Cum hora undecima*" in *B.O.P.*, II, 154 (Joannes XXII, 23 Octobris, 1321), n. XXII. The Bull "*Fidelium novella plantatio*" in *B.O.P.*, II, 282 (Gregorius XI, 6 Martii, 1374), n. XXVII. The Bull "*Super gregem*" in *B.O.P.*, II, 283 (Gregorius XI, 6 Martii, 1374), n. XXVIII. The Bull "*Cum vos ad Terras Saracenorum*" in *B.O.P.*, II, 281 (Gregorius XI, 6 Martii, 1374), n. XXV. The Bull "*Cum vos ad Terras Armenorum Maioris*" in *B.O.P.*, II, 280 (Gregorius XI, 6 Martii, 1374), n. XXIIV. The Bull "*Sincerus zelus*" in *B.O.P.*, II, 287 (Gregorius XI, 28 Ianuarii, 1375), n. XXXVI. The Bull "*Sincera devotionis*" in *B.O.P.*, II, 300 (Urbanus VI, 13 Aprilis, 1381), n. VIII. The Bull "*Inter cunctas sollicitudines*" in *B.O.P.*, III, 91-92, n. CLXXIX. The Bull "*Plantatus olim*" in *B.O.P.*, III, 109 (Eugenius IV, 12 Aug., 1439), n. CXCVI. The

bulls, the Bull *"Gratiarum agimus"* of Pope John XXII deserves a special attention for its statement on the duration of the Apostolic Faculties. It reads as follows:

> *Ceterum quia expedit vobis Fratres, agentibus in partibus sic remotis, debita cura Vicarii, qui per Magistrum vestri Ordinis, vel ipsius Magistri auctoritate vobis in illis partibus deputatus exstiterit, non carare, Apostolica auctoritate, decernimus, officium eiusdem Vicarii per obitum, vel cessionem, seu amotionem eiusdem Magistri, nullatenus exipare, sed tamdiu durare, donec per sequentem Magistrum, in locum eiusdem Vicarii alius fuerit subrogatus.*[26]

During the period of the Dominican-Franciscan Missions, although there was no development of the concept of *"facultas"* or *"facultates"* by theorists, the practice of the Holy See in granting Apostolic Faculties through papal bulls revealed a definite development in shaping a clearer concept of an Apostolic Faculty. In line with this practice, an Apostolic Faculty meant at that time a power conceded by the Apostolic authority, in virtue of which missionaries could perform lawfully or validly those ecclesiastical functions which they as simple priests were without authority to perform. Apostolic Faculties were necessary for these missionaries both because of the fact that converts in distant regions could not observe all the common laws of the Church, under the conditions in which they lived, and also because of the great distance from Rome, in consequence of which the missionaries could not possibly have recourse to the Holy See, if and when recourse was necessary. With an extension of the meaning of "possessions," *"facultates"* came to be taken as pointing to the particular powers granted by the Holy See in the papal bulls, in which manner most of the Apostolic Faculties were granted in that period.

Bull *"Dum levamus in circuitu"* in *B.O.P.*, III, 431-433 (Pius II, 12 Iunii, 1464), n. LXVII. The Constitution *"Apostolicae servitutis officium"* in *B.O.P.*, III, 498 (Sixtus IV, I Aprilis, 1473), n. XXXI.

[26] *B.O.P.*, II, 186 (1 Oct. 1329), n. LXXII.

SECTION 2. THE PERIOD OF THE JESUIT MISSIONS

In the new world discovered by Columbus, missions were rapidly opened by the Franciscans, Dominicans, and Carmelites, and later also by the Jesuits. These missionaries were sent to those distant lands by the Holy See, by superiors general of the religious orders, or by secular kings under the institution of royal patronage, and were endowed with many privileges, indults, and Apostolic Faculties, in order to be able to fulfill their missions.[27] In addition to the abovementioned religious orders, there were also many other religious orders, congregations, societies, etc., which engaged in the work of conversion of the infidels in distant lands. It can, however, be truly said that the Society of Jesus represented all those missionary institutions during the sixteenth century, in regard to their privileges, indults, exemptions, and particularly Apostolic Faculties, as well as in regard to their missionary activities. In many papal bulls, constitutions, briefs and the like, the afore-mentioned favors were granted directly to the Society; the Society, in turn, shared them with the other missionaries, in consequence simply of the rule which established a common interparticipation in granted privileges.[28]

During the sixteenth century, the meaning of the word "*facultas*" began to point more precisely to the "power" which was granted by the Holy See. For example, the cause: "*plenam et liberam facultatem autcoritate apostolica per praesentes, ad Nostrum et Sedis Apostolicae beneplaci-*

[27] Cf. Joannes Focher, *Itinerarium Catholicum Proficiscentium ad Infideles Convertendos* (Romae: Apud Alfonsum Scribanum, 1574), cap. XI-XII, pp. 18 ff.

[28] Cf. *Litterae Apostolicae, Quibus Institutio, Confirmatio, et Varia Privilegia Continentur Societatis Jesus* (Antverpiae: Apud Ioannem Meursium, 1635) (hereafter cited as *Litterae Apostolicae*); Ramond A. Matulenas, *Communication, A Source of Privilege,* The Catholic University of America Press, 1943); Ralph V. Shuhler, *Privileges of Regulars to Absolve and Dispense,* The Catholic University of America Canon Law Studies, n. 186 (Washington, D.C.: The Catholic University of America Press, 1943), pp. 17-19.

tum, concedimus," served in the granting of Apostolic Faculties to hear confessions, to absolve from reserved sins and censures, etc., in the Constitution *"Cum inter cunctas"* of Pape Paul III, June 3, 1545.[29] Nevertheless, the word *"facultas"* was often used together with the word *"licentia."* For instance, when granting the *Praepositus Generalis* of the Society of Jesus the power to create his coadjutors, who could promote candidates to sacred orders, Pope Paul III (1534-1549) stated in his Bull *"Exponi Nobis"* as follows: *". . . ut . . . creare et deputare libere et licite valeatis, plenam et liberam, apostolica auctoritate, tenore praesentium, concedimus licentiam et facultatem."*[30]

As to some of the new features of *"facultas"* in the sixteenth century, the Constitution *"Licet debitum pastoralis officii"* of Pope Paul III indicated that all the Apostolic Faculties granted to the Society of Jesus could be delegated by the *Praepositus Generalis,* and, further, that they could be subdelegated by his delegates.[31] In the Brief *"Sacrae religionis"* of 1552, Pope Julius III (1550-1555) granted the Founder of the Society of Jesus, Ignatius of Loyola, the faculties, to dispense from the law of fast, to read prohibited books, to anticipate or postpone the Divine Office, to recite it after the celebration of Mass, and for sick missionaries to commute the Divine Office to other pious works, such as short prayers, together with other faculties.[32] Pope Gregory XIII's Constitutions *"Ex sedis apostolicae"* of 1573, *"Exponi Nobis"* of 1575, *"Unigeniti Dei Filii"* of 1576, and

[29] *Institutum Societatis Jesu* (2 vols., Florentiae: Typographia a St. Conceptionis, 1892-1893), I, 10-11. Cf. The Bull *"Exponi Nobis"* of Pope Gregory XIII, January 8, 1575—*ibid.,* I, 55-56; the Bull *"Exponi Nobis"* of April 3, 1582—*ibid.,* I, 80; the Bull *"Ex debito"* of August 5, 1582—*ibid.,* I, 81-84.

[30] *Institutum Societatis Jesu,* I, (5 Iun. 1546), p. 12. See also the Bull *"Decet Romanum Pontificem"* of Pope Gregory XIII, May 3, 1575—*ibid.,* I, 56-60.

[31] *Ibid.,* (18 Oct. 1549), pp. 13-21. This Constitution included the faculty of bination. Cf. *Litterae Apostolicae,* pp. 50-51.

[32] *Litterae Apostolicae,* p. 75; *Institutum Societatis Jesu,* I, (22 Oct. 1552), p. 28.

"*Quanta in vinea Domini*" of 1579,[33] comprised the Apostolic Faculties to recite the divine hours outside the choir, to practice the medical arts, to impart a plenary indulgence once a year in the churches of the Society of Jesus in mission lands, to celebrate Mass within an hour before dawn and an hour after noon, etc.

Among many documents, Pope Gregory XIII's Constitution "*Decet Romanum Pontificem*" of 1575 was probably the one that most comprehensively included Apostolic Faculties granted for the missionaries of the Society of Jesus, and the one that contained rules how to use those granted faculties.[34]

The first general interparticipation of privileges, including the Apostolic Faculties among religious orders, seems to have been effected through Pope Sixtus IV's Constitution "*Dum fructus uberus,*" which was given to the Augustinian Order on February 7, 1474. The Pope made the Augustinian Order a participant in all the privileges theretofore possessed by the Ordesr of Friars Preacher and Friars Minor.[35] Among many other documents, however, the Constitution "*Dum per nos*" of Pope Leo X (1531-1521) effected such a complete intersharing of privileges among the religious orders, that the pope acknowledged the Dominicans, the Franciscans, the Augustinians, the Carmelites, the Servites, and the Minims as holding all their privileges in common.[36]

In consequence of the legal institution of the general interparticipation of privileges among religious institutes, the

[33] *Litterae Apostolicae*, pp. 135; 137-141; 151-152; 184-193 respectively; *Institutum Societatis Jesu*, pp. 54; 55; 60-61; 74-78 respectively.

[34] *Litterae Apostolicae Gregorii Papae XIII, Quibus Gratiae et Facultates Societatis Jesus Declarantur, et Extenduntur, et Aliae de Novo Conceduntur in Forma Brevis* (Rome: Apud Sanctum Petrum, 1575); *Institutum Societatis Jesu*, pp. 56-60.

[35] *Bullarium Ordinis Eremitarum S. Augustini* (ed. L. Empoli, Romae, 1628), p. 347.

[36] *Bullarum Diplomatum et Privilegiorum Sanctorum RR. PP. Editio Taurinensis* (24 vols. et appendix, Augustae Taurinorum, 1857-1872), V, 733 (10 Dec., 1519).

extent of the Apostolic Faculties for missionaries was vast, and practically indefinite. As already pointed out, numerous papal bulls, constitutions, and briefs were given to the individual orders since the thirteenth century, with a view to the granting of privileges and faculties. Since the middle of the fifteenth century many new religious orders, congregations, societies, etc., had come to exist in the Church, each of which was granted privileges and faculties by way of direct concessions. And by way of the general interparticipation of privileges on the part of religious institutes most of the privileges became common to all such institutes, without restriction in their extent, their numbers, and the time period specified for their use. Hence, the Apostolic Faculties for missionaries also became so extensive by the end of the sixteenth century and in the first decades of the seventeenth century, that Raymond Caron (1605-1666) summed up the Apostolic Faculties of the time in the following three points:

1. *Missionarii regulares in locis Roma remotioribus (ubi scil. ad Pontificem non datur pro rei circumstantia accessus vel correspondentia et consolatium animarum urget) habent omnimodam in utroque foro auctoritatem pontificiam; tantum, quantum judicaverint expedire pro conversione infidelium, manutenentia atque profectu illorum in fide Catholica et obedientia Romanae Ecclesiae.*

2. *Dicti missionarii possunt praeterea quaecumque facere, quae ad augmentum Domini nominis et conversionem ipsorum infidelium populorum et ampliationem fidei orthodoxae, pro loco et tempore viderint expedire.*

3. *Missionarii regulares, qui de licentia suorum Superiorum proficiscuntur ad quascumque terras infidelium et ad quamcumque mundi partem, ut eos convertant, sunt tanquam legati et commissarii Papae quoad omnem potestatem in utroque foro, missioni conventientem, cum confirmatione omnium suorum privilegiorum.*[37]

[37] *Apostolus Evangelicus Missionariorum Regularium per Universum Mundum Expositus* (Antverpiae, 1653), pp. 135 ff. cited by Theodorus

ARTICLE IV. FROM THE CREATION OF THE SACRED CONGREGATION FOR THE PROPAGATION OF THE FAITH TO THE PROMULGATION OF THE CODE OF CANON LAW

SECTION 1. THE *Septem Regulae Generales*

For the purpose of entirely revising the various Apostolic Faculties which had been granted to missionaries of the time, Pope Urban VIII (1623-1644) in 1633 appointed a special commission within the Sacred Congregation for the Propagation of the Faith.[38] The said special commission, known as the *Congregatio Urbaniana super Facultatibus Missionariorum,*[39] consisted of five cardinals (two from the Holy Office and three from the Sacred Congregation for the Propagation of the Faith), an Accessor, and a Secretary.

The first undertaking of the said special commission was to compose general formulas of Apostolic Faculties for missionaries, in order to be able to grant the Apostolic Faculties according to their needs, taking into consideration the condition of the people, the time, etc., the distance from the Holy See, the needs of the missions, and the hierarchical positions of the grantees. After having held many sessions, both general and particular,[40] the special commission succeeded in composing the *Septem Regulae Generales* and the *Quinque Typicae Facultatum Formulae,* the principles and the material of which had been contained in the papal bulls, constitutions, briefs, etc., through which Apostolic Faculties had been granted previously to the missionaries of the various religious institutions and to such missionaries as

Grentrup. *Jus Missionarium,* Tom. I (Steyl: Typographia Domus Missionum, a S. Michaele Archang. nuncupatae, 1925), p. 23.

[38] Xaverius Paventi, "Origo Congregationis Urbanianae super Facultatibus Missionariorum," *CpRM,* XXIV (1943), 85-86.

[39] Cf. Paventi, *loc. cit.*

[40] Vermeersch, "De Formulis Facultatum S. C. de Propaganda Fide, De Origine Facultatum," *Periodica de Re Canonica et Morali, Utilia praesertim Religiosis et Missionariis,* XI (1922), (39-(43) [hereafter this article will be cited as "De Formulis Facultatum," and the periodical as *Periodica*]; Paventi, *loc. cit.*

were subject to the Sacred Congregation for the Propagation of the Faith. All prepared rules and formulas were presented to Pope Urban VIII by Cardinal de Cremona in the general session of the commission held on August 4, 1636. The later general sessions were held at the pope's request, on August 12 and September 23 of that year, for the purpose of revising the rules and the formulas. On February 10, 1637, the special commission's final drafts were presented for the pope's consideration by Cardinal de Cremona in a general assembly of twelve cardinals and other officials, and thereupon were approved by the pope through the Constitution *"Operosum."*[41]

The *Septem Regulae Generales* were in substance as follows:

> Rule I. In regions where bishops and parish priests are not rare, the faculty to administer the parochial sacraments, i.e., baptism, matrimony, Holy Communion for the Easter duty, and extreme unction, should not be granted to the missionaries, unless there be fulfilled the cause: *"si in illis non sint Ordinarii vel parochi, vel, si adsint, de eorum licentia."*
>
> Rule II. In regions where the Catholic Faith is practiced freely but not publicly: a) Rule I should be observed in regard to the following three parochial sacraments i.e., baptism, matrimony, and extreme unction; b) Rule I should be observed in regard to the administration of the sacrament of matrimony, in places where the decrees of the Council of Trent have not been promulgated; c) the faculty to administer sacraments other than the three above-mentioned sacraments can be given to missionaries altogether apart from all observances of the clause: *"si in illis non sint Ordinarii vel parochi, vel, si adsint, de eroum licentia."*
>
> Rule III. In regions where the practice of the Catholic Faith either publicly or privately is prohibited, the faculty to administer the parochial

[41] *Collectanea S. Congregationis de Propaganda Fide* (2. ed., 2 vols., Romae: Typographia Polyglotta S. C. de Propaganda Fide, 1907), nn. 88-89 [hereafter cited as *Collectanea*]; cf. Vermeersch, "De Formulis Facultatum," *Periodica*, XI (1922), (41)-(46).

sacraments can be given to missionaries, with or without reference to the clause: *"nisi facile et sine periculo Ordinario vel parocho adiri possint."*

Rule IV. In regions where recourse to the Holy See is difficult for any reason, especially that of great distance, the faculty to absolve from the cases which are reserved to the Holy See should be granted to the missionaries, apart from all references to the clause stated in the previous Rule.

Rule V. In Italy, France, Germany, and Belgium, the faculty to absolve from the reserved cases for those who had been heretics and then became converted to the Faith should for the initial absolution be given to the missionaries; in regions other than the above-enumerated countries, the said faculty should belong simply to the Apostolic Nuncios, who may then subdelegate it for particular cases and places.

VI. The faculty to dispense from matrimonial impediments should be given to missionaries in regions where a hierarchy has not been established, namely in such a way that, if the missionaries did not have bishops, the said faculty would be operative *in utroque foro,* and if they had, then only *in foro conscientiae.*

Rule VII. The *Congregatio Urbaniana super Facultatibus Missionariorum* has the right to neutralize any of the foregoing Rules, if necessary, i.e., in the event that the localities and the attendant circumstances do not reflect the contingencies enumerated in the preceding six Rules.[42]

SECTION 2. THE *Quinque Typicae Facultatum Formulae*

In line with the foregoing *Septem Regulae Generales,* the special commission composed the *Quinque Typicae Facultatum Formulae,* designating them by Roman numerals I to V.[43]

[42] Vermeersch, "De Formulis Facultatum," *Periodica,* XI (1922), (41); cf. George Eagleton, *The Diocesan Quinquennial Faculties, Formula IV,* The Catholic University of America Canon Law Studies, n. 248 (Washington, D.C.: The Catholic University of America Press, 1948), pp. 15-17.

[43] These five formulas of the Apostolic Faculties are transcribed by Vermeersch in *Periodica,* XI (1922), (46)-(61).

Of these, the first three formulas, i.e., *Formula I, Formula II,* and *Formula III,* were composed for bishops, while *Formula IV* was written for mission prefects and other mission superiors who lacked the episcopal character, and *Formula V* for bishops or other mission superiors to whom any of the foregoing four formulas could not be given because of particular circumstances and conditions current in their regions. The last *Formula* was designed also for simple missionaries who were to leave for new missions. Of the formulas for bishops, *Formula I* was written for the bishops of Asia, Africa, and America; *Formula II* for the bishops in those parts of Europe which were under non-Catholic rulers and distant from the Holy See; *Formula III* for Apostolic Nuncios in the neighboring areas of Europe.[44] With the exception of *Formula V,* the formulas of the *Quinque Typicae Facultatum Formulae* remained in use in their original forms, with only a few changes, until December 31, 1919.[45]

Formula I consisted of 29 Articles: eleven (Arts. II-XI and XXVII concerned powers for dispensing from certain ecclesiastical laws, and the majority of them dealt with matrimonial dispensations (Arts. V-XI); two (Arts. XV-XVI) contained a grant of powers for absolving from censures; four Arts. XIV, XVII-XIX) concerned the bestowal of indulgences; nine (Art. I, XII, XX-XXVI) conferred privileges; two (Arts. XIII and XXVIII) dealt with the rules of delegation and communication of the Apostolic Faculties contained in the formula; and the last Article (Art. XXIX) determined the limits of the use of the faculties, along with the added caution that the faculties contained in the formula were to be executed absolutely *gratis.*

[44] *Ibid.,* (41)-(42).

[45] For changes of the faculties in these formulas, see A. Konings-Putzer, *Commentarium in Facultates Apostolicas* (5. ed., Neo-Eboraci-Cincinnati-Chicagiae: Benziger Fratres, 1898), pp. 144-305, *passim;* 174; 226, 268; 439-449, *passim* [hereafter cited as *Commentarium*]. See also Vermeersch, "De Formulis Facultatum," *Periodica,* XI (1922), n. 22. (62)-(65).

However, the twenty-nine Articles in the formula were not necessarily granted in an equal manner to all the bishops of Asia, Africa, and America; when some faculties of the formula were not necessary for certain bishops, such faculties were withdrawn when the formula was given to these bishops.[46]

SECTION 3. FORMULA ACCESSORY TO THE *Quinque Typicae Facultatum Formulae*

At the time when the *Quinque Typicae Facultatum Formulae* were approved and in use, there also existed a number of additional formulas of Apostolic Faculties. These had been written by Ingoli, Secretary of the special commission for the composition of the *Formulae,* in order to show how to draw up formulas for particular regions, with due employment of the *Septem Regulae Generales,* and in accord with the *Quinque Typicae Facultatum Formulae.* Those particular formulas had never been officially approved either in a general or in a particular session of the said special commission, though they were accepted as if they had been.

Four of these particular formulas were numbered with the officially approved *Formulae,* and thus they were called *Formula VI, Formula VII, Formula VIII,* and *Formula IX.* There was also a *Formula X,* which was known as the *Formula Prolixior,* because it was an enlarged edition of *Formula III,* consisting of eleven Articles (I-XI) of *Formula III* plus eight additional Articles. Again, later, possibly between 1782 and 1786, there appeared the *Formula Prolixior Antiqua* and the *Formula Prolixior Ampla,* when Pope Pius VI (1775-1799) enlarged the faculties of Article III and Article XIX of the then existing *Formula Prolixior.*[47] These formulas, i.e., *Formulae VI-X* together with

[46] Cf. The Official Note after Art. XXIX, in Vermeersch, "De Formulis Facultatum," *Periodica,* XI (1922), (50).

[47] Cf. Vermeersch, "De Formulis Facultatum," *Periodica,* XI (1922), (61)-(62). The *Formula Prolixior Ampla* was conceded also to the bishops in Belgium, Holland, Poland, etc.

the *Quinque Typicae Facultatum Formulas* were later called *Formulae Ordinariae.*[48]

In the middle of the nineteenth century, there appeared new formulas of Apostolic Faculties, which were *Formula Extraordinaria A, Formula Extraordinaria B,* etc., *Formula Extraordinaria a, Formula Extraordinaria b,* etc., *Formula Extraordinaria aa, Formula Extraordinaria bb.,* etc.[49] These formulas were not granted in the same way in which the previous formulas were conceded. In addition to this, because of the nature of the faculties contained in them and in view also of their restricted use, these formulas were called the *Formulae Extraordinariae.*

Thus, by 1873 the formulas of the Apostolic Faculties were conceded as follows: (1) *Formula I* was conceded to

[48] Cf. Konings-Putzer, *Commentarium,* pp. 3-4; Van Hove, *De Privilegiis, De Dispensationibus* (Mechliniae-Romae: H. Dessain, 1939), p. 154, note 3 [hereafter cited as *De Privilegiis*]; Cosmas Sartori, *Iuris Missionarii Elementa* (Romae: Secretarii Missionum Ord. F. Minorum, 1947), p. 73; Gommarus Michiels, *Normae Generales Juris Canonici* (2 vols., Parisiis-Tornaci-Romae: Desclée et Socii, 1949), p. 73 [hereafter cited as *Normae Generales*].

[49] *Extr. b. (Formula Extraordinaria b.)* was approved in audience by Pope Gregory XVI, not before the year 1841, for the bishops of the Paris Foreign Mission Society in China, and extended to all ordinaries laboring in the Chinese Empire and her neighboring countries since 1851; *Extr. C. D.* and *E.* were approved in audience by Pope Pius IX on January 26, 1863; July 26, 1863, and March 1, 1864, respectively, and were conceded to all ordinaries in the United States of America. *Extr. P.* was approved in audience in 1859 for the bishops in England; *Extr. R.,* on July 28, 1866, for the vicars apostolic in the East Indies, etc. Cf. Vermeersch, "De Formulis Facultatum," *Periodica,* XI (1922), (62)-(64); Van Hove, *De Privilegiis,* p. 154; Sartori, *loc. cit.;* Eagleton, *The Diocesan Quinquennial Faculties, Formula IV,* pp. 19, 21-22. See "Facultates Extraordinariae Quae Vicariis Apostolicis Sinarum et Regnorum Adiacentium Conceduntur ad Quinquennium," in *Collectanea Constitutionum, Decretorum, Indultorum ac Instructionum Sanctae Sedis ad Usum Operariorum Apostolicorum Societatis Missionum ad Exteros Selecta et Ordine Digesta Cura Moderatorum Seminarii Parisiensis eiusdem Societatis* (Parisiis: Typis Georges Chamerot, 1880), n. 33, pp. 21-24 [hereafter cited as *Collectanea Sanctae Sedis*].

the ordinaries in China, the West and East Indies, Australia, Africa, North and South America; (2) *Formula II,* to the ordinaries in England, Scotland, Greece, Albania, Bosnia, Walachia, Denmark; (3) *Formula III,* to the ordinaries in Prussia, Hungary, Germany, Holland, Belgium, and Russia; (4) *Formula IV,* to the mission prefects throughout the world; (5) *Formula VI,* to the ordinaries in Ireland; (6) *Formula X,* to the ordinaries in France and Switzerland. As to the *Extraordinariae Formulae,* they were issued as follows: (1) *Extr. a. and Extr. aa.,* to the ordinaries in South America; (2) *Extr. b.,* to the ordinaries in the Chinese Empire and her neighboring countries; (3) *Extr. C., D., and E.,* to the bishops in the United States of America; (4) *Extr. F.,* to the bishops in *Nova Scotia;* (5) *Extr. P.,* to the bishops in England; (6) *Extr. Q.,* to the bishops in Holland; (7) *Extr. R.,* to the bishops in the East Indies; (8) *Extr. S.,* to the bishops in Algeria; (9) *Extr. T.,* to the bishops in Canada; (10) *Extr. U.,* to the bishops in Australia.[50]

In addition to these Ordinary and Extraordinary Formulas of Apostolic Faculties, there appeared also during the latter half of the nineteenth century certain formulas of Apostolic Faculties *"pro foro interno,"* which were granted by the Sacred Peneitentiary, and were known as *"Pagellae Facultatum S. Poenitentiariae pro Foro Conscientiae."* There were two distinct formulas, namely, one for the bishops under the title of *"Pagella Facultatum Quinquennalium S. Poenitentiariae pro Episcopis,"* and the other, for simple confessors, under the title of *"Pagella Facultatum S. Poenitentiariae pro Simplicibus Confessariis."*[51]

The *Pagella* which had been issued to the bishops in 1891 and 1892 was conceded for a five-year use by the bishops and their vicars general; some of the faculties contained

[50] Vermeersch, "De Formulis Facultatum," *Periodica,* XI (1922), (67)-(68); *Collectanea,* n. 215; *Collectanea Sanctae Sedis,* n. 42, p. 26; nn. 31-33, pp. 18-24; n. 119, p. 73; Konings-Putzer, *Commentarium,* pp. 426-431.

[51] Konings-Putzer, *Commentarium,* pp. 432-438.

therein could be subdelegated to priests in the dioceses or missions; when recourse was made from a priest in a particular and individual case to the bishops, any of the faculties could be subdelegated; if necessary, these faculties of the *Pagella* could be habitually subdelegated to the canonical penitentiary or the vicars forane. The *Pagella* for simple confessors was conceded directly by the Sacred Penitentiary, if there was a recommendation for this on the part of their ordinaries; otherwise, by their own ordinaries.[52]

SECTION 4. THE ORIGIN OF HABITUAL FACULTIES

Formula I of the *Formulae Ordinariae* was given for a fifteen-year use to the bishops in both the West and East Indies and in North America, for a ten-year use to the bishops in Asia and Africa; *Formula II*, for a seven-year use to the bishops in those parts of Europe which under non-Catholic rulers and distant from the Holy See; *Formula III*, for a five-year use to the Apostolic Nuncios; *Formula IV*, for a fifteen-year use to mission superiors in the West and East Indies, and for a ten-year use to mission superiors in Asia and Africa; *Formula V*, for a five-year use, a seven-year use, or a fifteen-year use, according as the missions were distant, more distant, or most distant from the Holy See.[53]

By virtue of Art. XXVIII in both *Formula I* and *Formula II*, of Art. XXI in *Formula III*, and of Art. XXVI in *Formula IV*, bishops and mission superiors could habitually delegate the faculties in their respective formulas to their missionaries, and these same faculties were to be communicated, *sede vacante*, to the *interim* superiors of their missions and dioceses.[54] For these reasons the faculties con-

[52] *Ibid.*, p. 437.

[53] Cf. Art. XXIX in *Formula I;* Art. XXIV in *Formula II;* Art. XXI in *Formula III;* Art. XXVII in *Formula IV;* Art. XXIV in *Formula V*. Cf. Vermeersch, "De Formulis Facultatum," *Periodica*, XI (1922), (50), (53), (58), and (61), respectively.

[54] Art. XXVIII in *Formula I* and *Formula II*—"Praedictas facultates communicandi, non tamen illas quae requirunt ordinem episco-

tained in the *Formulae Ordinariae* were considered *habitual faculties.*

As to the faculties contained in the *Formulae Extraordinariae,* those of *Extr. C.* were given for a ten-year use (later for a five-year use), and contained no Article or annotation in regard to their communication or subdelegation.[55] The faculties of *Extr. D.* concerned matrimonial dispensations in cases of affinity arising in consequence of illicit intercourse, in cases of disparity of cult, of mixed marriages, and of a *sanatio in radice,* which were given for a ten-year use (later for a five-year use). This formula had an Article concerning the possible delegation of the faculties contained in the formula, but the rule laid down in the Article was not the same as any of the rules applicable for the faculties contained in the *Formulae Ordinariae.* For in *Extr. D.* it was stated that the faculties which were contained in the formula could be subdelegated by the bishop to his vicar general when the former had to leave his residence, or when his see was impeded, and, for a certain number of urgent causes, to two or three of his priests who were laboring in places quite remote from the bishop's residence.[56] The faculties contained in *Extr. E.* all dealt with matrimonial dispensations in impediments of affinity and consanguinity, which were granted for a five-year use. As to their characteristics, each of these faculties was conceded for a number of cases, i.e., ten, thirty, sixty, or one hundred cases,

palem, vel non sine sacrorum oleorum usu exercentur, sacerdotibus idoneis qui in eorum dioecesibus laborabunt, et praesertim tempore sui obitus, ut sede vacante sit qui possit supplere, donec Sedes Apostolica certior facta, quod quamprimum fieri debebit per delegatos, vel per unum ex eis, alio modo provideat, quibus delegatis auctoritate apostolica facultas conceditur sede vacante in casu necessitatis, consecrandi calices, patenas et altaria portatilia sacris oleis ab episcopo tamen benedictis." Cf. Vermeersch, "De Formulis Facultatem," *Periodica,* XI (1922), (50) and (53). Also cf. *ibid.,* pp. (55) and (58).

[55] Konings-Putzer, *Commentarium,* pp. 305-376, *passim.*

[56] Art. VIII of the formula, See *ibid.,* p. 401. For the entire text of *Extr. D,* see *ibid.,* pp. 376-405, *passim.*

and all of them could be subdelegated according to the rule that was stated in Article VIII in *Ext. D.*[57]

Thus the faculties which were contained in the *Formulae Extraordinariae* were not to be subdelegated generally to the priests or missionaries in dioceses or in missions; they were to cease when the see became vacant in any way, and were to expire upon the full use of the allotted cases as also upon the lapse of the time set in the formulas themselves.

In 1888, when asked whether or not the faculties for dispensing from matrimonial impediments, as included in *Extr. D.* and *Extr. E.*, were to be subdelegated to priests for use in urgent cases, the Holy Office referred the question to the pope, who allowed a habitual delegation of these faculties to be made to parish priests only, who were to use these subdelegated faculties only when there would not be sufficient time for approaching the ordinary, and when at the same time danger would arise from any delay.[58] Considering the circumstances of the time, the Holy Office, on November 24, 1897, determined to petition the pope to declare that habitual faculties for dispensing from certain matrimonial impediments as conceded to ordinaries would not cease with the death or loss of office of the ordinary to whom these faculties were addressed, but instead would pass to their successors in office. This petition was granted on November 26, 1897.[59] And the Holy Office made a further declaration on the characteristics of habitual faculties, on May 3, 1899, in answer to the following questions:

> 1. *Utrum sub illis verbis facultates omnes speciales* HABITUALITER A SANCTA SEDE EPISCOPIS ALIO-

[57] Cf. The final Article in *Formula Extr. E.—ibid.*, p. 411. For the whole text of the forumla, see *ibid.*, pp. 406-413, *passim.*

[58] S.C.S. Off., litt. encycl., 20 Febr. 1888—*Acta Sanctae Sedis* (41 vols., 1865-1908), XX (1887-1888), 543-544 [hereafter cited as *ASS*]; *Collectanea*, nn. 1695 and 1698; *Codicis Iuris Canonici Fontes*, cura Emī Petri Card. Gasparri editi (9 vols., Romae, postea Civitate Vaticana: Typis Polyglotiis Vaticanis, 1923-1932); Vols. VII-IX, ed. cura et studio Emī Iustiniani Card. Serédi, 1935-1939), n. 1109 [hereafter cited as *Fontes*].

[59] *Fontes*, n. 1193; *Collectanea*, n. 1985.

RUMQUE LOCORUM ORDINARIIS CONCESSAS[60] *comprehendantur facultates omnes speciales a Sancta Sede Ordinariis concessae, quibus utuntur quoties voluerint, licet ad praefinitum tempus; cuiusmodi sunt Facultates* DE POENITENTIARIA *dictae, reductionis Missarum, etc.*

2. *Utrum Facultas benedicendi et delegandi ad Sacra paramenta benedicanda, quae Episcopis fuerit concessa transeat ob eorum mortem vel a munere cessationem ad successorem Vicarium Capitularem, quamvis Episcopali dignitate non insigntum.*

3. *Utrum sub iisdem verbis Facultates omnes speciales* HABITUALITER A SANCTA SEDE EPISCOPIS . . . CONCESSAS *comprehendantur etiam Facultates, quibus dumtaxat uti valent pro determinato casuum numero, ut sunt Facultates dispensandi a Sacrae Ordinationis titulo, pro definito ordinandorum numero.*

4. *Et, quatenus ad aliquid horum negative, quaenam sit interpretatio illius adverbi* HABITUALITER.

Resp. Ad. 1. 2. et 3. Affirmative:
Ad 4. Provisum in praecendtibus.[61]

As to the mode of subdelegation of habitual faculties, the Constitution *"Apostolicum ministerium"* of Pope Benedict XIV, which was addressed to a vicar apostolic in England, and was dated May 30, 1755, included a rule which the bishop was to employ when he subdelegated his faculties to the priests. According to this rule, subdelegation was to be made to "worthy" (*idonei*) priests, and the bishop was to examine their knowledge and ability to execute the faculties before subdelegating them.[62] In general, the bishop was not necessarily to subdelegate all the faculties he possessed and which he could subdelegate, but, at will, he might subdelegate to his individual priests all his faculties, or he might

[60] This phrase was used in the petition of November 24, 1897, of the Holy Office. Cf. *Fontes*, n. 1193.

[61] These answers were approved by the pope. Cf. *ASS*, XXXII (1899), 60-61; *Fontes*, n. 1223; *Collectanea*, n. 2045.

[62] Cited in Konings-Putzer, *Commentarium*, n. 34, p. 45.

subdelegate only some of them and reserve the rest to himself; he might even subdelegate certain faculties to only certain priests, if there existed a good reason to do so, depending upon the qualifications of the priests, the needs of the faculties on the part of the souls, and the number of cases involved.[63]

The bishop had the right to suspend or revoke whatever faculties he had subdelegated to his priests. In the case of the suspension or the revocation of the subdelegated habitual faculties, the bishop had necessarily to employ great prudence and caution. And, when the bishop subdelegated his faculties to the priests, he was not to add new conditions or any invalidating clauses to the original texts of the faculties in the formulas.[64]

A letter of the Sacred Congregation for the Propagation of the Faith, which was addressed to a vicar apostolic in India on December 8, 1869, instructed the bishop that he must subdelegate the habitual faculties in written form, either manuscript or printed, for the sake of keeping order in his vicariate and for avoiding confusion otherwise likely to arise from the execution of the subdelegated faculties, and that he must clearly indicate the extension of the granted faculties, the determined number of cases, the reserved censures, etc., if necessary, in a letter added to the document of subdelegation of the faculties.[65]

Apostolic Faculties ceased in the same way as other privileges did.[66] For, in the beginning, they were considered practically in the light of personal privileges.[67] Thus the lapse of time, the termination of the number of allotted cases, the loss of office, the revocation and the renunciation

[63] Cf. *loc. cit.*

[64] *Collectanea* (ed. 1893), n. 1488 (16 Martii, 1865).

[65] *Collectanea* (ed. 1893), n. 157.

[66] Van Hove, *De Privilegiis*, pp. 201-287; Michiels, *Normae Generales*, II, 599-651.

[67] Edward Roelker, *Principles of Privilege According to the Code of Canon Law*, The Catholic University of America Canon Law Studies, n. 35 (Washington, D.C.: The Catholic University of America, 1926), p. 147 [hereafter cited *Principles of Privilege*].

of the faculties could effect the cessation of the Apostolic Faculties. The period of time or also the number of cases for which the faculties availed were fixed and determined in the formulas themselves. When a definite number of cases was indicated in the text of the faculties themselves, but at the same time a temporal limit was set in the formula, the faculties, though given for a definite number of cases, expired with the date so set, regardless of whether the number of cases had or had not been called into use for the application of the faculty given.[68]

In instances wherein the faculties expired before a request for their renewal had been submitted, the bishop acted validly if the neglect to petition for their renewal had not been culpable.[69] The Sacred Congregation for the Propagation of the Faith declared to a vicar apostolic in China on July 5, 1841, that extraordinary and special faculties given with a determinate number of cases for their use should be understood as renewed in the same quantity (as to the number of cases) as before, if the vicar apostolic have not received a response from the Holy See for two complete years after they had requested the renewal of the former faculties.[70]

The *resolutio iuris Ordinarii* could occur in several ways, i.e., through his death, his removal, and his renunciation of the office. In any case, with the loss of the ordinary's power, the Ordinary, Extraordinary, and Special Habitual Faculties which he had held passed to his successor in office.[71]

SECTION 5. DEFINITION OF "FACULTY" AND DIVISIONS OF "FACULTIES"

A. Definition of "Faculty"

The similarity between "faculty" and "privilege" was so close that no proper definition seemed to be given for the former until the end of the nineteenth century, when a "fac-

[68] *Collectanea* (ed. 1893), n. 1238.

[69] *ASS*, XXV (1891), 393; *Collectanea* (16 Ian., 1797), n. 633, p. 390.

[70] *Collectanea*, n .923.

[71] Cf. *Fontes*, nn. 1109, 1193, and 1223.

culty" was termed a "special privilege," a "quasi-privilege," or a *"privilegium ad instar"* by canonists before the promulgation of the Code of Canon Law.

Reiffenstuel (1642-1703) contended that a "faculty" was a "special privilege" or "quasi-privilege," because a privilege should, by its very nature, be perpetual, but a faculty had a term fixed to it for its valid and lawful use.[72] To the question: *"Quales episcopi habeant speciales facultates seu quasi-privilegia dispensandi super impedimentis dirimentibus?"* the same author gave the answer that, since such facultaties depended entirely on the free will of the Supreme Pontiff who granted them in such a way that he could revoke, or increase, or diminish them, or grant greater faculties to certain bishops and lesser ones to other bishops, a definite and universally applicable answer for all faculties which were granted to bishops could not possibly be given. However, said he, it should be noted that the Supreme Pontiff used to grant to all bishops who were in regions distant from Rome, more specifically to the Bishops of Germany, a special faculty, besides other privileges, to dispense in both *fora* from certain diriment impediments for the sacrament of matrimony; such a faculty came to the same bishops, not from the common law, but as a special pontifical privilege and *ex mera gratia.*[73] In short, according to Reiffenstuel, there was only a slight difference between privileges and faculties; both of them were in a broad sense *gratiae, favores, indulta, concessiones,* etc.; the two terms were used by him indiscriminately and with also the same meaning.[74]

Credit for the first systematic study on Apostolic Faculties should be given to Konings (1821-1884) and Putzer (1836-1904) in their *Commentarium in Facultates Aposto-*

[72] "De Dispensatione super Impedimentis Matrimonii, etc.," Appendix to *Ius Canonicum Universum* (5 vols. in 7, Parisiis, 1864-1870), Tom. V (ed. 1868), p. 550, n. 33.

[73] *Ibid.*, n. 20, p. 547. Cf. George Eagleton, *The Diocesan Quinquennial Faculties, Formula IV*, p. 30.

[74] *Ibid.*, nn. 20 and 33.

licas. Konings' work was first published in 1884, but it had no general treatises on Apostolic Faculties. It was Putzer who prefixed the general treatises on the notion, the nature, the general rules of interpretation, the communication, the cessation, and the use of Apostolic Faculties, to the extensive commentary on the Ordinary and Extraordinary Faculties done *ex professo* by Konings.[75]

In *the Commentarium in Facultas Apostolicas,* Putzer defined "Faculty" as follows:

> *Facultas in sensu juridico significat quamcumque potestatem in iure proprio sive alieno fundatam aliquid valide aut licite agendi. Strictius vero prout hic praesertim sumitur, facultas denotat potestatem, quam Superior ecclesiasticus jurisdictione in foro externo praeditus cuidam sibi quoquo modo subdito personaliter concedit, aliquid sive in foro conscientiae tantum sive etiam pro foro externo valide aut licite aut saltem tuto agendi.*[76]

In a general way, this definition was followed by authors before and even after the promulgation of the Code of Canon Law, such as Franciscus X. Wernz (1842-1914),[77] Petrus Vidal (1867-1938),[78] Andrew B. Meehan (1867-1932),[79] Ethelred Taunton (1857-1907),[80] etc.

[75] Cf. *op. cit.*, pp. xi-xii and 1-140. Konings-Putzer's first edition appeared in 1893.

[76] *Op. cit.*, n. 1, p. 1.

[77] *Ius Decretalium* (6 vols., *Vols.* I-IV, 2. ed., Romae-Prati, 1906-1913), I, 212.

[78] Wernz-Vidal, *Ius Canonicum ad Normam Codicis Exactum* (7 vols. in 8, Romae: Apud Aedes Universitatis Gregorianae, Vol, I, *Normae Generales*, 2. ed., 1952; Vol. II, *De Personis*, 3. ed., 1943; Vol. III, *De Religiosis*, 1933; Vol. IV, partes I-II, *De Rebus*, 1934-1935; Vol. V, *Ius Matrimoniale*, 3, ed., 1946; Vol. VI, *De Processibus*, 2. ed., 1949; Vol. VII, *Ius Poenale Ecclesiasticum* 2. ed., 1951), I, 442 [hereafter cited as *Normae Generales, De Personis, De Rebus, Ius Matrimoniale, De Processibus, Ius Poenal Ecclesiasticum* respectively].

[79] "Faculty," *The Catholic Encyclopedia* (15 vols. and 2 supplements, New York: Robert Appleton Co., 1907-1922), V, 748.

[80] *The Law of the Church, A Cyclopedia of Canon Law for English*

The Code of Canon Law includes a canon on Apostolic Faculties, i.e., canon 66, and its first paragraph reads as follows: *"Facultates habituales quae concedantur vel in perpetuum vel ad praefinitum tempus aut certum numerum casuum accensentur privilegiis praeter ius."* By this wording, Apostolic Faculties have their status in the Code as *"privilegia praeter ius,"* but this paragraph and two subsequent paragraphs in the same canon do not define Apostolic Faculties, and thus the promulgation of the Code of Canon Law brought no change in the nature of the Apostolic Faculty.

Hence, anuthors follow the definition formulated by Konings-Ptuzer. However, Hubert L. Motry (1884-1952) and Roelker (1897-1957) rewrote the definition because of the fact that, although by virtue of canon 258 the Sacred Penitentiary has no jurisdiction in the external forum, it must be considered as the superior for the internal forum, and thus there is room for the grants in the category of habitual faculties. Accordingly the wording, *"jurisdictione in foro externo praeditus,"* in Konings-Putzer's definition was suggested by Motry and Roelker to be changed into the wording, *"jurisdictione in foro respectivo praeditus."*[81] Michiels, in his turn, at the end of the definition of Koning-Putzer adds an explanatory clause, which reads as follows: [*"... aliquid ... valide aut licite aut saltem tuto agendi*], *quod per se, vel natura sua vel reservatione positiva, ad ipsum Superiorem pertinet."*[82]

Thus, a complete definition of a "faculty" can be rewritten as follows:

> *Facultas est [prout generatim a canonistis et in can. 66 sumitur] potestas, quam Superior ecclesi-*

Speaking Countries (St. Louis, Mo.: B. Herder Co., 1906), pp. 339-340.

[81] Cf. Motry, *Diocesan Faculties According to the Code of Canon Law*, The Catholic University of America Canon Law Studies, n. 16 (Washington, D.C.: The Catholic University of America, 1922), pp. 8-12; Roelker, *Principles of Privilege*, pp. 139-141.

[82] *Normae Generales*, II, 654.

> *asticus jurisdictione in foro respectivo praeditus, cuidam sibi quoquo modo subdito personaliter concedit, aliquid sive in foro conscientiae tantum sive etiam pro foro externo valide aut licite aut saltem tuto agendi, quod per se, vel natura sua vel reservatione positiva, ad ipsum Superiorem pertinet.*[83]

In its nature, a faculty is a participation of the ecclesiastical power of governing, sanctifying, or administering, conceded for the good of the faithful or of the Church, to the one who is not competent for it by law.[84]

Indult and faculty are synonymous terms in the Decree "*Proxima sacra.*"[85] The word "indult" has as yet a still less fixed usage in Canon Law than "faculty." There seems to be attached a modifying quality, which makes the use of the term "indult" usually in instances wherein large numbers of recipients are concerned, as Putzer implied when he stated: *"Si generales sunt* (i.e., *facultates*) *etiam 'Indultorum' nomine cognoscuntur."*[86]

B. Divisions of "Faculties"

Faculties are divisible into various categories: (1) By

[83] This can be translated in English as follows: A faculty can be defined as the power which an ecclesiastic superior, having jurisdiction in the respective *forum,* grants personally to one who is in some way his subject to do something that belongs to the granting superior himself either essentially or by its very nature, or by positive reservation, so that the grantee can do it validly, lawfull, or at least safely, either in the internal *forum* only, or in the external *forum* also. Cf. Van Hove, *De Privilegiis,* n. 153, pp. 148-149; Lucius Rodrigo, *Praelectiones Theologico-Morales Comillenses,* Tom II, *Tractatus de Legibus* (Santander: Sal Terrae, 1944), n. 889, p. 625-626 [hereafter cited as *De Legibus*]; Matthaeus Conte a Coronata, *Institutiones Iuris Canonici* (5 vols., Taurini-Romae: Mariette, Vol. I, *Normae Generales, De Clericis, De Religiosis, De Laicis,* 4. ed., 1950; Vol. II, *De Rebus,* 4. ed., 1951; Vol. III, *De Processibus,* 4. ed., 1956; Vol. IV, *De Delictis et Poenis,* 4. ed., 1955; Vol. V, *Index,* 3. ed., 1951), I, n. 86, pp. 95-96.

[84] Rodrigo, *De Regibus,* n. 890, p. 626.

[85] S. C. Consist., decr., 25 Apr. 1918—*Acta Apostolica Sedis, Commentarium Officiale* (ab anno 1909, Romae, 1909-1928; Civitate Vaticana, 1929-), X (1918), 190 ff. [hereafter cited as *AAS*].

[86] Konings-Putzer, *Comentarium,* p. 2.

reason of the objects to which faculties relate, faculties are either *jurisdictional or non-jurisdictional.* The faculty to absolve from sins and ecclesiastical censures, the faculty to dispense from vows, from irregularities, from matrimonial impediments, etc., are called jurisdictional faculties, since these acts of absolving and dispensing are jurisdictional acts, and the validity of the said acts depends upon the exercise or use of such faculties. On the other hand, an act of anticipating the recitation of the Divine Office, an act of reading prohibited books, an act of binating, etc., are not jurisdictional acts; nevertheless, the legality of these acts (or the element of safety in regard to the legality of these acts) depends upon the exercise or use of faculties which allow ecclesiastics to do such acts. Thus, when the objects of faculties are non-jurisdictional acts, the faculties which permit such acts are called non-jurisdictional faculties.[87]

Some non-jurisdictional faculties involve the power of granting certain favors (*gratiae*) and certain authorization (*licentiae*) necessary for the lawful performing of determined acts, while some of them point simply to precautionary grants (*concessiones ad cautelam*), i.e., assurance to the doubting agent that the determinate acts to be carried out or the omission thereof, as the case may be, receive the approval of authority. Although there are, in proper parlance, not faculties, since they do not imply the possession or use of any power, they are called non-jurisdictional faculties, insofar as they are included in the formulas of Apostolic Faculties. "In certain instances, however, the faculty '*ad cautelam*' or '*ad agendum tuto*' may become a full-fledged faculty, namely, then when objectively the conditions for the validity of an act are wanting, and the faculty granted supplies the deficiency."[88]

(2) By reason of their source, i.e., the grantors, faculties are *apostolic, episcopal,* or *regular.* Faculties are styled *apostolic* or *papal* when they proceed from the Supreme

[87] Michiels, *Normae Generales*, II, 655; Motry, *op. cit.*, p. 20.
[88] Motry, *loc. cit.*

Pontiff directly, or through the ordinary channels of the Sacred Congregations, Offices, and Tribunals of the Holy See and the Sacred Penitentiary; faculties are *episcopal,* if the power or privilege conferred proceeds from a diocesan bishop, by virtue of his own power or ordinary jurisdiction, as, for instance, the faculty of the diocese to hear confessions, to say Mass, to preach in the diocese, etc., granted to priests who labor for the salvation of souls in the diocese; faculties are *regular* or *facultates praelatorum regularium,* when they proceed from the superior of clerical religious orders by reason of their ordinary jurisdiction, or by virtue of extraordinary powers or privileges conceded to them by the Holy See, as, for instance, to establish various confraternities.[89]

(3) By reason of their duration and the mode of their granting, faculties are either *actual* or *habitual.* Actual faculties are granted for use *ad modum actus,* i.e., for one or the other case, or for individually determined cases, or for persons restrictively determined,[90] whereas habitual faculties are granted for use *per modum habitus,* i.e., for indeterminate persons and indeterminate cases, or for certain numbers of indeterminate cases.[91]

(4) By reason of the types of formulas, habitual faculties are either *special* or *general.* General faculties are granted to ordinaries according to the general norms that obtain for the granting of Apostolic Faculties in the form of formulas. Typical of these faculties are the *Quinquennial Faculties* for ordinaries in dioceses, and the *Decennial Faculties* for ordinaries in quasi-dioceses. The former are con-

[89] Michiels, *Normae Generales,* II, 655.

[90] Michiels, *loc. cit.;* Van Hove, *De Privilegiis,* n. 154, p. 149.

[91] Van Hove, *loc. cit.*: "Habitualis facultas definitur illa qua indultarius uti potest quoties voluerit, vel in perpetuum, vel intra tempus definitum, puta quinquennium, decennium, etc., vel in determinato numero casuum, modo casus non sint in individuo determinati, quod ad personas et materias, etiam si bis tantum, indultarius facultate concessa uti possit, immo semel . . . modo non agatur de casu in individuo determinato. Huiusmodi facultas est habitualis, quia impetrans ea uti potest, quando voluerit."

ceded for a five-year use through the Sacred Consistorial Congregation, while the latter are granted for a ten-year use through the Sacred Congregation for the Propagation of the Faith. Both are *ex officio* granted to the respective ordinaries.[92]

Special faculties (or *particular* faculties) are conceded in addition to the Quinquennial Faculties or the Decennial Faculties in the form of indults or rescripts, as their necessity may demand. Ordinaries in Latin America enjoy special Apostolic Faculties.[93] Faculties which are given to the Apostolic Nuncios, Delegates, etc., are particular faculties, different from those which are granted to ordinaries.[94a]

Faculties can be faculties *pro foro interno,* or faculties *pro utroque foro;* they are called *matrimonial* faculties and *non-matrimonial* faculties, according to whether they concern the sacrament of matrimony or not.

Article V. The Juridical Nature of Habitual Faculties in the Code of Canon Law

Section 1. The First Juridical Character of Habitual Faculties

Canon 66, § 1, attributes to Habitual Faculties a definite juridical character and force: *"facultates habituales . . . accensentur privilegiis praetur ius."* By this statement it is

[92] See *infra,* pp. 46-54.

[93] "Facultates Speciales Concessae Ordinariis Americae Latinae Qui Dependent a Sacra Congregatione de Propaganda Fide," see in S.C. Prop. Fid., Prot. 1054/41; Xaverius M. Paventi, *Brevis Commentarius in Facultates S. Congregationis de Propaganda Fide* (Romae: Officium Libri Catholici, 1944), pp. 70-72 [hereafter cited as *Brevis Commentarius*].

[94a] An index of the Apostolic Faculties for the Apostolic Delegates and the Apostolic Nuncios, published by Pope Benedict XV, on March 9, 1919, is found in N. Hilling's *Codicis Juris Canonici Supplementum* (Fiburgi Brisg.: Apud J. Waibel, Bibliopolam, 1925), pp. 26-40; recent editions are found in A. Vermeersch-I. Creusen, *Epitome Iuris Canonici cum Commentariis* (3 vols., Mechliniae-Romae: H. Dessain, Vol. I, 7. ed., 1949; Vol. II, 7. ed., 1954; Vol. III, 6 ed., 1946), I, Appendix I, n. 872, pp. 658-665 [hereafter cited as *Epitome*].

shown that the intent of the legislator assigns Habitual Faculties to the category of *"privilegia praeter ius,"* or of privileges outside the law.[94b] In other words, Habitual Faculties have, in the Code of Canon Law, the force of a privilege, and more specifically the force of a privilege outside the law.

Before the promulgation of the Code of Canon Law, while the *Stylus Curiae* used indiscriminately the terms *"facultates"* and *"privilegia,"*[94c] canonists discussed whether or not *"facultates"* had the juridical force of privileges, inasmuch Habitual Faculties granted by the Holy See could not always be exactly identified with the characteristics of privileges. Authors such as Reiffenstuel, Wernz, etc., termed Habitual Faculties as "privilegia *specialia,"* or *"quasi-privilegia,"* or *concessiones ad instar privilegiorum,"* etc.[95] And then, when they came to determine general norms for the interpretation of Habitual Faculties, they discussed the point whether Habitual Faculties should be considered as *"privilegia praeter ius,"* i.e., as privileges outside the law, or as *"privilegia contra ius,"* i.e., as privileges contrary to the law.

It seems, however, that canonists were trying to define the characteristics of privileges outside the law when they treated of privileges deriving from Habitual Faculties. For instance, according to Reiffenstuel (1642-1703), privileges outside the law were granted, *"quando impsamet materia, seu actus privilegii non est quidem in se iure prohibitus,*

[94b] *"Privilegium praeter ius"* is translated as "privilege outside the law" by John A. Abbo-Jerome D. Hannan, *The Sacred Canons* (2 vols., St. Louis, Mo.: B. Herder Book Co., 1952), I, 63; as "beyond the law" by Roelker, *Principles of Privilege,* p. 31; as "beside the law" by T. L. Bouscaren-A. C. Ellis, *Canon Law* (3. rev. ed., Milwaukee: The Bruce Publishing Co., 1957), p. 62. Roelker defines a *"privilegium praeter ius"* as "a mere favor which does not injure a law."—*loc. cit.*

[94c] Cf. *Collectanea,* I, n. 88; Benedictue XIV, const. *"Apostolicum ministerium,"* 30 Maii, 1753—*Fontes,* n. 425.

[95] Cf. Reiffenstuel, *Ius Canonicum Universum,* V. Appendix, "De Dispensatione super Impedimentis Matrimonii, etc.," nn. 20, 21, and 33. Wernz, *Ius Decretalium,* IV, n. 622, p. 503.

sed tamen non est nisi certis personis concessus";[96] D'Annibale (1815-1892) taught that, when one concedes a power or grants a faculty for the use of which one alone is competent in law, one acts outside the law, but not against it.[97] P. Layman (1574-1635) called a privilege outside the law a power which for the purpose of absolving or of dispensing is conceded to persons who are not competent to do so by the common law.[98] Schmalzgrueber (1663-1735) scarcely went beyond Reiffenstuel's definition of privilege outside the law. Like Reiffenstuel, he added, *"privilegium praeter ius non est stricte privilegium, sed potius dicitur beneficium principis, seu gratia ab ipso concessa."*[99] And Wernz, who censured Hinchius' absolute denial of privileges outside the law,[100] went further by stating that *"multae facultates ... merito dicuntur privilegia, quia constituunt leges privatas concedentes specialem favorem, licet minus strictum."*[101]

The reason behind the theory of the *"beneficium principis,"* the *"gratia,"* or the *"privilegium minus strictum,"* was that the authors above cited were trying to assert a broad interpretation for Habitual Faculties. For, according to the rule of interpretation of privileges: *"Odia restringi et favores convenit ampliari,"*[102] if Habitual Faculties were taken as privileges outside the law, then a broad interpretation was employed for them, while if they were taken as

[96] *Op. cit.*, Lib. V, tit. XXXIII, n. 7.

[97] *Summula Theologiae Moralis* (4 vols., 5. ed., Romae, 1908-1909), I, n. 227, nota 4.

[98] *Theologia Moralis* (2 vols., Venetiis; G. Valentini, 1630), Lib., I, tract. 4, c. 23, n. 5.

[99] *Ius Ecclesiasticum Universum* (5 vols. in 12, Romae, 1843-1845), Lib. V, tit. XXXIII, nn. 57-58. Reiffenstuel, *op. cit.*, Liv. V, tit. XXXIII, n. 8.

[100] *System des katholischen Kirchenrechts* (4 vols., Berlin, 1869-1897), III, p. 808, and nota 5. Cf. also J. F. Schulte, *Die Lehre von den Quellen des katholischen Kirchenrichs* (3 vols., Vol. I, Beriln, 1870), I, 143.

[101] *Ius Decretalium,* I, n. 158, nota 15.

[102] Reg. 15, R. J., in VI°. Cf. Victorius Bartoccetti, *De Regulis Juris Canonici* (Romae: Angelo Belardetti, Editore, 1955), pp. 73-79.

privileges contrary to the law, then the rule for a strict interpretation was applied to them. Furthermore, the *Stylus Curiae* was on the side of a broad interpretation of Habitual Faculties.[103]

On the other hand, viewed from the law itself as to its universal and exclusively binding force, all privileges are in some way contrary to the law. In the laws which concede powers of absolving, or of dispensing, the beneficiaries as holders of powers are determined. Should this power be granted to one not included in the law, then radically the concession is in some way contrary to the law.[104] Nevertheless, if considered in the light of the immediate characteristic of this concession of power, Reiffenstuel's definition of a privilege outside the law can be accepted, since the new beneficiary is not one of those to whom the law itself conceded the power of absolving or of dispensing.[105] Further, the concept of a pure '*beneficium principis*" is easily found in the nature of such concessions as the faculties to bestow special blessings. Hence, it is quite reasonable for practical purposes to group the powers of absolving of dispensing, of bestowing special blessings, and the like, under the heading of privileges outside the law.[106]

Since the promulgation of the Code of Canon Law, however, by virtue of canon 66, § 1, all Habitual Faculties, as to their juridical status, are considered as privileges outside the law, regardless of the fact that some Habitual Faculties might have the juridical characteristics of a simple dispensation, of a license, of a permission, of a privilege contrary to the law, or of a mere delegation of jurisdic-

[103] Cf. Konings-Putzer, *Commentarium*, pp. 11-17.

[104] Cf. Rodrigo, *De Legibus*, n. 855, 1°, p. 600.

[105] Cf. Roelker, *Principles of Privilege*, p. 145.

[106] Compare the definition of a faculty and that of a privilege outside the law. "Privilegium praeter ius concedit quod lege non prohibetur nec imponitur, ita tamen ut necessaria sit concessio auctoritatis, ut quis praerogativa quadam fruatur. . . ."—Van Hove, *De Previlegiis*, n. 33. "Facultas definitur in iure *sensu lato* potestas quaevis aliquid faciendi valide, licite aut tuto, sive potestate propria, sive potestate ab alio accepta."—*Ibid.*, n. 153, p. 148.

tion.[107] As an immediate consequence of being considered privileges outside the law, i.e., as favorable or gracious privileges, Habitual Faculties inherently (*per se*) receive a liberal interpretation, according to the Rule of Law: *"Odia restringi et favores convenit ampliari,"* and the norms of canons 18, 19, 50, 67, and 68. In addition, Habitual Faculties fundamentally (*per se*) should receive a liberal interpretation in virtue of canon 200, § 1, which states: *"Potestas iurisdictionis ordinaria et ad universitatem negotiorum delegata, late interpretanda est; alia quaelibet stricte."* But, a liberal interpretation is excluded when Habitual Faculties infringe on the acquired rights of third parties, or when they refer to ecclesiastical trials. For in both cases Habitual Faculties receive a strict interpretation according to the provisions of canon 68 and 50.[108]

Logically, all the common rules of interpretation of privileges in general[109] must be observed for Habitual Faculties, since, being privileges outside the law, Habitual Faculties are naturally reckoned among privieges; those rules are provided in canon 67, which states that the extent of the privileges must be judged from the wording of the document, and its scope must not be extended or abridged. Roelker offered this comment: "The wording of a privilege is to be taken in its natural, or in its juridical sense; the juridical meaning of a word is to be preferred to the natural meaning, if the two should not coincide."[110]

As to the second part of canon 67: *"nec licet illud extendere aut restringere,"* in the consideration of individual

[107] Cf. Van Hove, *De Privilegiis*, n .157, p. 150; Roelker, *Principles of Privilege*, p. 146; Michiels, *Normae Generales*, II, 662-663.

[108] Cf. Van Hove, *De Privilegiis*, n. 158, p. 152; Michiels, *Normae Generales*, II, 663; Bartoccetti, *De Regulis Juris Canonici*, pp. 73-79.

[109] Cf. Van Hove, *De Privilegiis*, nn. 174-208, pp. 163-195; Rodrigo, *De Legibus*, nn. 880-888, pp. 618-625; Michiels, *Normae Generales*, II, 571-582.

[110] *Principles of Privilege*, p. 77. The author cited Suarez, *De Legibus*, Lib. VIII, c. 28, n. 16, and De Camillis, *Institutiones Iuris Canonici* (Parisiis, 1868), Lib. II, c. I, art. 1, n. 6; Schmalzgrueber, *Ius Ecclesiasticum Universum*, Lib. V, tit. XXXIII, nn. 120-121.

faculties and with reference to the extent of the respective jurisdiction the Sacred Congregation cannot grant what is beyond its own competence; the scope of Habitual Faculties can be judged also by the *Sylus Curiae*:[111] according to canon 66, § 3, Habitual Faculties include also such powers as are necessary for their execution, for instance, the faculty to dispense includes also the power to absolve the ecclesiastical penalties, if such happen to prevent the granting of the dispensation, but this absolution may be given only when it is necessary to permit that dispensation to be received. Necessary conditions are demanded in the light of canon 39. In short, Habitual Faculties, being privileges outside the law, are to be interpreted liberally, that is, in the most comprehensive manner that is compatible with the proper meaning of the text.[112]

SECTION 2. THE SECOND JURIDICAL CHARACTER OF HABITUAL FACULTIES

The second paragraph of canon 66[113] denotes the second character of the nature of Habitual Faculties, namely, Habitual Faculties are inherently (*per se*) to be considered "*privilegia realia,*" or real privileges, and "*privilegia muneralia,*" or muneral privileges.

With reference to the grantees, privileges are called "*privilegia realia,*" if they adhere to some dignity, place, or office, while they are called "*privilegia personalia,*" or personal privileges, if they are conceded directly in favor of

[111] Cf. Konings-Putzer, *Commentarium*, n .12, p. 15.

[112] Cf .Van Hove, *De Privilegiis*, nn. 158-159, pp. 152-153; Michiels, *Normae Generales*, II, 664-665; Eagleton, *The Diocesan Quinquennial Faculties*, p. 41; Konings-Putzer, *Commentarium*, nn. 5-7, 9-11, 13-15.

[113] Canon 66, § 2. Nisi in earum concessione electa fuerit industria personae aut aliud expresse cautum sit, facultates habituales, Episcopo aliisve de quibus in can. 198, § 1, ab Apostolica Sed concessae, non evanescunt, resoluto iure Ordinarii cui concessae sunt, etiamsi ipse eas exequi coeperit, sed transeunt ad Ordinarios qui ipsi in regimine succedunt; item concessae Episcopo competunt quoque Vicario Generali.

a person. Personal privileges are subdivided into individually (*singulariter*) personal, commonly (*communiter*) personal, and corporally (*corporaliter*) personal privileges. An individually personal privilege is one which is granted to a physical person, entirely because of his own merit, a commonly personal privilege is one which is granted to a physical person inasmuch as he belongs to a certain state, or possesses a certain dignity; and a corporally personal privilege is one which is conceded to a moral person, of which all the members usually enjoy the privilege, but only by reason of their association with the moral person. *Real* privileges are likewise subdivided: *real* privileges are called *local* (*privilegia localia*), if they are granted to a place; *muneral* (*privilegia muneralia*), if they are granted to a dignity, or to an office; and *properly real* (*privilegia stricte realia*), if granted to a movable corporal thing such as an altar, chalice, etc.[114]

With reference to the criteria for determining whether privileges are *real* or *personal*, there are several rules. First, the wording of the grant itself will very frequently decide the issue. The object of the privilege may also aid in dispelling a doubt. Similarly, the character of the person who receives the grant may offer help for the solving of a doubt. But if after the use of these criteria a doubt still remains, the principle in the *Liber Sextus* of Boniface VIII, which state: *"Odia restringi et favores convenit ampliari,"* can be applied. This means that favorable privileges can be considered *real*, and odious privileges *personal*.[115]

As seen above, Habitual Faculties are considered privileges outside the law, i.e., fundamentally favorable privileges, and consequently they should be classified among *real* privileges. Further, the wording of canon 66, § 2, itself sufficiently shows that the Habitual Faculties of which canon 66 treats are *muneral*.

[114] Roelker, *Principles of Privilege*, pp. 31-32. Cf. Michiels, *Normae Generales*, II, 512-514; Van Hove, *De Privilegiis*, nn. 245-248, pp. 236-237; canon 72.

[115] Roelker, *Principles of Privilege*, pp. 32-33.

The juridical consequences of their being *real* and *muneral* privileges are several:

1) The grantee of the Habitual Faculties (the Quinquennial Faculties for Ordinaries in Dioceses and the Decennial Faculties for Ordinaries in Quasi-Dioceses) is the *ordinarius qua ordinarius,* and not the individual person who *de facto et actualiter* possessed the office of the bishop when the faculties were granted, even though the faculties might have been granted by proper name to a given bishop, unless they contain a direct statement to the contrary, or were given to the bishop on account of some personal qualifications.

2) According to the norm of canon 72, § 3, Habitual Faculties cannot be renounced by the bishop who is ruling over the diocese or mission.

3) According to the provision of canon 73 and canon 207, § 1, these faculties are normally not affected in consequence of a vacancy of the Apostolic See.

4) These faculties likewise do not lapse with the vacancy of the see of the ordinary to whom they were granted, even though he had begun to make use of the faculties, but continue for the succeeding ordinary in the government of the same see. For, since the Habitual Faculties were granted to the *ordinarius qua ordinarius,* whose office does not come to an end with the death of the physical ordinary, the faculties are neither transmitted, nor changed, but remain the same and accordingly can be exercised by the one who becomes vested with the same juridical activity. Even though the ordinary had begun to make use of them, the faculties continue for the succeeding ordinary in the goverment of the see, so that the latter need not reiterate the executory acts begun by his predecessor.[116]

5) Since the Habitual Faculties are granted to the *ordinarius qua ordinarius,* the faculties which are granted to

[116] Cf. canon 66, § 2; *Fontes,* nn. 1193 and 1232. Also of Michiels, *Normae Generales,* II, 655-666; Van Hove, *De Privilegiis,* nn. 167-168, pp. 158-159.

the bishop are granted also to the vicar general, who constitutes one and the same juridical person with the bishop, by and for whom he was appointed as an ordinary in the same bishop's diocese.[117]

[117] Canons 66, § 2; 198, § 1; 368, § 2.

CHAPTER II

CONCESSION OF QUINQUENNIAL AND DECENNIAL FACULTIES FOR ORDINARIES IN DIOCESES AND QUASI-DIOCESES

INTRODUCTION

Since their approval, the Ordinary Formulas of the Apostolic Faculties were issued by the Sacred Congregation of the Holy Office; even when missionaries applied for them to the Sacred Congregation for the Propagation of the Faith, whose jurisdiction extended over them, theye were referred to the Holy Office. This practice of granting Apostolic Faculties had started even before the formulation of the *Quinque Typicae Facultatum Formulae,* and continued until the year 1765. The practice seems to have originated on the basis of the facts that Apostolic Faculties concerned matters of faith and morals, for which the Holy Office had been in charge from its creation, and that the Holy Office enjoyed seniority in years and more extensive jurisdiction than the other cited Sacred Congregation, at the time when there was no explicit competency assigned to any of the Sacred Congregations as to the issuance of the formulas of Apostolic Faculties.[1]

Since the year 1765, however, a new practice in the issuance of the formulas of Apostolic Faculties was introduced, i.e., they were issued by the pope, when in audience with the Secretary of the Sacred Congregation for the Propagation of the Faith, for all ordinaries and missionaries whether or not these were subject to the jurisdiction of the said Congregation.[2] For the prorogation of the

[1] Van Hove, *De Privilegiis,* n. 162, pp. 154-155; Michiels, *Normae Generales,* II, 658; Sartori, *Iuris Missionarii Elementa,* p. 72, n. 6.

[2] Regarding the *Stylus Curiae* in the issuing of the formulas, the form "Facultates concessae a SS. D.N. div. prov. PP.... referente infrascripto S.C. de P.F. Secretario ..., in audientia diei ... Romae...." was used for the issuance of an Ordinary Formula of Apostolic Faculties, while the statement: "Ex audientia SS. habita die ..., SS. N.D.

Apostolic Faculties contained in the formulas, ordinaries and missionaries were asked by the pope through the Holy Office, on August 7, 1789, to submit documents containing full mention of the earlier concessions of faculties to them.[3]

When Pope St. Pius X reorganized the Roman Curia through his Constitution *"Sapienti consilio"* of June 29, 1908,[4] each of the Sacred Congregations, Offices, and Tribunals was newly arranged with respect to competency and jurisdiction. As a consequence, the entire world was divided into two great regions for the purpose of its government, so that one great region was placed under the jurisdiction of the Sacred Consistorial Congregation and the other under the Sacred Congregation for the Propagation of the Faith. The pertinent parts of the Constitution *"Sapienti consilio"* read as follows:

> 6° *S. Congregatio de Propaganda Fide*
>
> 1. *Sacrae huius Congregationis iurisdictio iis est circumscripta regionibus, ubi, sacra Hierarchia nondum constituta, status missionis perseverat. Verum, quia regiones nonnullae, etsi Hierarchia constituta, adhuc incohatum aliquid praeseferunt, eas Congregationi de Propaganda Fide subiectas esse volumus.*
>
> 2. *Itaque a iurisdictione Congregationis de Propaganda Fide exemptas et ad ius commune deductas decernimus—in* EUROPA—*ecclesiasticas provincias Anglicae, Scotiae, Hiberniae, et Hollandiae, ac dioecesim Luxemburgensem; in* AMERICA—*pro-*

Divina Providentia PP...., referente infrascripto S.C. de P.F., R.P.D. sequentes facultates extraordinarias benigne concesit...." was employed for the issuance of an Extraordinary Formula of Apostolic Faculties. Cf. Konings-Putzer, *Commentarium*, pp. 144, 305, 376, 406, 426, etc.; Vermeersch, "De Formulis Facultatum," *Periodica* XI (1922), pp. (70)-(71); Michiels, *loc. cit.*

[3] *Collectanea*, n. 372, p. 213.

[4] *AAS*, 1 (1909), 7-19; *Sylloge Praecipuorum Documentorum Recentium Summorum Pontificum et S. Congregationis de Propaganda Fide necnon Aliarum SS. Congregationum Romanarum ad Usum Missionariorum* (Typis Polyglottis Vaticanis, 1939), pp. 14-15 (hereafter cited as *Sylloge*).

vincias ecclesiasticas dominii Canadensis, Terrae Novae et Foederatarum Civitatum seu STATUUM UNITORUM.[5] *Negotia proinde quae ad haec referuntur, tractanda in posterum non erunt penes Congregationem de Propaganda Fide, sed pro varia earumdem natura, penes Congregationes ceteras.*

3. *Reliquae ecclesiasticae provinciae ac dioeceses, iurisdictioni Congregationis de Propaganda Fide hactenus subiectae, in eius iure ac potestate maneant. Pariter ad eam pertinere decernimus Vicariatus omnes Apostolicos, Praefecturas seu missiones quaslibet, eas quoque quae Congregationi a Negotiis ecclesiasticis extraordinariis modo subsunt.*

4. *Nihilominus, ut unitati regiminis consulatur, volumus ut Congregatio de Propaganda Fide ad peculiares alias Congregationes deferat quaecumque aut fidem attingunt, aut matrimonium aut sacrorum rituum disciplinam.*

5. *Quod vero spectat ad sodales religiosos, eadem Congregatio sibi vindicet quidquid religiosos qua missionarios, sive uti singulos, sive simul sumptos tangit. Quidquid vero religiosos qua tales, sive uti singulos, sive simul sumptos attingit, ad Congregationem religiosorum Negotiis praepositam remittat aut relinquat.*[6]

2° *S. Congregatio Consistorialis*

1. *Duas haec sacra Congregatio, easque distinctas partes complectitur.*

2. *Ad primam spectat non modo parare agenda in Consistoriis, sed praeterea in locis Congregationi de Propaganda Fide non obnoxiis novas dioeceses et* CAPITULA *tum* CATHEDRALIA *tum* COLLEGIATA *constituere, . . .*

3. *Altera pars ea omnia comprehendit, quae ad singularum dioecesium regimen, modo Congrega-*

[5] Ecclesiastical provinces in the United States of America were thenceforth exempt from the jurisdiction of the S. Congregation for the Propagation of the Faith, and became subject to the common law, whereby they were placed under the jurisdiction of the S. Consistorial Congregation.

[6] *AAS*, 1 (1909), 12-13; *Sylloge*, pp. 14-15.

> *tioni de Propaganda Fide subiectae non sint, universim referuntur, quaeque ad Congregationes Episcoporum et Concilii hactenus pertinebant, et modo Consistoriali tribuuntur. . . .*[7]

However, none of the Sacred Congregations, Offices, and Tribunals was explicitly entrusted with the issuance of the formulas of Apostolic Faculties. And thus it followed that, although after the Constitution *"Sapienti consilio"* they were placed under the jurisdiction of the Sacred Consistorial Congregation, many of the ordinaries were still applying for the formulas of Apostolic Faculties to the Sacred Congregation for the Propagation of the Faith, and that on September 29, 1908, the *"Ordo Servandus in Romana Curia, Normae Peculiares"* was published.[8]

In the *"Normae Peculiares"* the competence of the Sacred Congregation for the Propagation of the Faith to issue the formulas of Apostolic Faculties was stated as follows: *"Indulta, quae hactenus haec Sacra Congregatio* [*de Propaganda Fide*] *concedere solebat iis etiam qui suae iurisdictioni non essent obnoxii, in posterum suis subditis tantum tribuet."*[9] Further, on November 12, 1908, the Sacred Consistorial Congregation clarified some duobts regarding the issuance of the formulas of Apostolic Faculties. As a general principle, the Apostolic Faculties were to be composed by the respective Roman Congregations and Offices in accord with the matters over which they enjoyed competence, and the faculties thus composed were to be conceded in the form of formulas through the Sacred Consistorial Congre-

[7] *AAS*, I (1909), 9. On the reorganization of the Roman Curia through the Constitution *"Sapienti consilio,"* and the respective competencies of the Sacred Congregations, Offices, and Tribunals, see Arthur Monin, *De Curia Romana* (Lovanii: Universitatis Catholicae Typographus, 1912), pp. 155-370. Monin (1881-1954) treated of the Sacred Congregation for the Propagation of the Faith prior to the Constitution *"Sapienti consilio,"* on pp. 64-70, and subsequent to this Constitution on pp. 274-280.

[8] *AAS*, I (1909), 59 ff.

[9] Art. VI, n. 3—*AAS*, I (1909), 97.

gation and the Sacred Congregation for the Propagation of the Faith to their respective ordinaries.[10]

Article I. Formulas of Apostolic Faculties Which Are Conceded Through the Sacred Consistorial Congregation: The Quinquennial Faculties for Ordinaries in Dioceses

The Sacred Consistorial Congregation sent to all local ordinaries under its jurisdiction the Decree *"Proxima sacra,"* on April 20, 1918,[11] with reference to the ruling on the general Apostolic Faculties which for these ordinaries was to become effective on May 19, 1918.

The Decree declared that, since many canons of the new Code provided bishops with ample powers, those faculties and indults which had previously been granted at the request of bishops either through briefs for a 25-year use, or through the printed general formulas of Apostolic Faculties for a 10, a 5, or a 3-year use, would be no longer needed,[12] and thus all special faculties earlier granted to bishops for the external forum and contained in the aforesaid briefs or formulas were to cease on May 19, 1918, for all bishops throughout the world,[13] with the exception of places subject to the Sacred Congregation for the Propagation of the Faith. The Decree made a provision for bishops who were in distant regions, and for those who for any reason would not receive notice of this Decree in time. In such conditions, the dispensations and ordinations which might have been conferred by these ordinaries in virtue of the old faculties were confirmed valid and lawful by the pope, with the condition that, from the date of receiving notice of the Decree, *si res adhuc sit integra,* the ordinaries were to conform themselves to it for the future.

[10] *AAS,* I (1909), 148-150; *Sylloge,* p. 22.

[11] *AAS,* X (1918), 190-192.

[12] Canons, 349, 239, 386, 468, 914, 534, 806, 822, 1006, 1043, 1045, 1245, 1125, 1304, 1532, etc., contain former faculties, indults, and privileges.

[13] Cf. Michiels, *Normae Generales,* II, 659; *AAS,* X (1918), 325.

The Decree *"Proxima sacra"* declared that Apostolic Faculties which had been conceded for the internal forum from the Sacred Penitentiary and those which had been granted because of the War, or which had been obtained by ordinaries for peculiar reasons, were not included in the Decree, so that they remained in full force and effect. As to the Apostolic Faculties for dispensations from matrimonial impediments, although by virtue of cc. 1043-1045 ordinaries were to have power to grant suitable dispensations in danger of death, and as often as the impediment was discovered when everything was ready for the marriage and the marriage could not be postponed without probable danger of grave harm, the Decree contained the following faculties:

> a. . . . *Ut locorum Ordinarii in America, in Insulis Philippinis, in Indiis Orientalibus, in Africa extra Mediterranei maris oras, et in Russia, per quinquennium a die 18 maii huius anni, dispensare valeant ab impedimentis minoris gradus quae recensentur in can. 1042, servatis regulis in eo Codicis capite statutis: itemque ut matrimonia nulliter contracta, ob aliquod eiusdem minoris gradus impedimentum, in radice sanare queant, iuxta regulas in capite XI, tit. VII, lib. III, Codicis* DE CONVALIDATIONE MATRIMONII *positas, monita parte impedimenti conscia de sanationis effectu;*
>
> b. *ut iidem locorum Ordinarii dispenare pariter per quinquennium valeant ab impedimentis maioris gradus, sive publicis sive occultis, etiam multiplicibus, iuris tamen ecclesiastici (exceptis impedimentis provenientibus ex sacro presbyteratus ordine et ex affinitatis in liena recta consummato matrimonio), nec non ab impedimento impediente mixtae religionis, si petitio dispensationis ad Sanctam Sedem missa sit et urgens necessitas dispensandi supervenerit, pendente recursu. . . .*
>
> c. *ut Ordinarii Galliae, trium regnorum Magnae Britanniae, Germaniae, Austriae et Poloniae, durante bello, quoties aditus ad S. Sedem difficilis aut impossibilis saltem per mensem praevideatur, iisdem facultatibus uti possint, quae supra sub titulo a et b recensentur.*[14]

[14] *AAS*, X (1918), 191-192. Cf. Lincoln Bouscaren, *Canon Law*

On May 19, 1918, the Code of Canon Law came into force, and thus the general faculties, except the faculties for the granting of dispensations from matrimonial impediments, were abrogated for all local ordinaries under the jurisdiction of the Sacred Consistorial Congregation. However, the necessity of new formulas of general faculties for ordinaries subject to the same Congregation was felt more and more as the days went by, both by the Roman Curia and by the ordinaries. At last the Sacred Congregation sent out a circular letter, dated March 17, 1922, to the said ordinaries, in which letter it listed the newly composed formulas of general Apostolic Facutlies, and declared that these formulas were to be available for their use.[15]

The "*Elenchus Facultatum Quinquennalium*"[16] which was attached to the said circular letter contained three formulas of Apostolic Faculties for local ordinaries subject to the Sacred Consistorial Congregation. These formulas were *Formula I,* for the local ordinaries in Italy;[17] *Formula II,* for the local ordinaries in Europe except those in Italy and in Russia;[18] *Formula III,* for the local Ordinaries in Russia and in other parts of the world than Europe. Accordingly this last formula was to be obtained by the local ordinaries of the United States.[19]

These formulas of the Apostolic Faculties were obtained from various Offices of the Roman Curia, i.e., the Sacred Congregation of the Holy Office, the Sacred Congregation

Digest, (4 vols., Milwaukee: The Bruce Publishing Co., 1934-1958), I, 74-75.

[15] This circular letter has not been published in the *Acta Apostolica Sedis,* nor was it reproduced for the sake of public reference. Cf. *AAS.* XV (1923), 193-194; Bouscaren, *Canon Law Digest,* I, 76-77.

[16] Michiels, *Normae Generales,* II, 659-660.

[17] *Il Monitore Ecclesiastico,* XXXVII (1925), 130-135; XLV (1933), 124.

[18] Cf. Vermeersch-Greusen, *Epitome,* I, n. 874, pp. 672; 675-680.

[19] Cf. Vermeersch, "Facultates Quinquennales, Formula II, Quae Ordinariis Europae anno 1932 Conceduntur," *Periodica,* XXI (1932), 220-223; Hilling, "Die neuen Quinquennalfakultäten vom Jahre 1923," *Archiv für katholisches Kirchenrecht,* CIV (1924), 287-297.

of the Sacraments, the Sacred Congregation for Religious, the Congregation of Sacred Rites, and the Sacred Penitentiary, at the time when the local ordinaries were complying with their duty of submitting the Quniquennial Report according to the norm prescribed in canon 340, § 2. Often, however, the petition for the formulas and the making of the Quinquennial Report were taken in hand by procurators in Rome who represented the respective local ordinaries before the various Offices of the Holy See.

Thus, in consequence of the above-mentioned circular letter, the grant of the general faculties in the form of formulas was restored for all ordinaries subject to the Sacred Consistorial Congregation. However, the process of obtaining the faculties of the formulas resulted in considerable inconvenience and expense on the part of the local ordinaries, as well as on the part of the Roman Curia. Accordingly Pope Pius XI issued the *Motu proprio "Post datam,"* on April 20, 1923,[20] to all local ordinaries under the jurisdiction of the Sacred Consistorial Congregation, decreeing that in future the quinquennial faculties, within the limits assigned, and according to the formulas in the *"Elenchus Facultatum Quinquennalium"* attached to the circular letter of March 17, 1922, should be granted by one Sacred Congregation, to which all bishops who were not subject to the jurisdiction of the Sacred Congregation for the Propagation of the Faith, or of the Sacred Oriental Congregation, were obliged to make their report, that is, by the Sacred Consistorial Congregation. According to the instruction given in the *Motu proprio,* the officers of the Sacred Consistorial Congregation were at the beginning of every five-year period to inquire of each of the Offices of the Holy See whether any change was to be made in the quinquennial faculties; and, if so, they were to introduce these changes in the formulas which were thereafter to be distributed. Thus the old-established practice, according to which general Apostolic Faculties had been obtained in a single

[20] *AAS,* XV (1923), 193-194.

printed formula and distributed by one office, was revived through the *Motu proprio "Post datam."*

As seen above, the formulas of the general faculties were not given through its own ordinary power by the Sacred Consistorial Congregation. For this reason, a formula of the Quinquennial Faculties from the said Congregation is known also as the *"Index Facultatum Quinquennalium."*[21]

For the local ordinaries under the jurisdiction of the Sacred Consistorial Congregation there are four formulas of the Quinquennial Faculties, i.e., *Formula I,* for the ordinaries in Italy, *Formula II,* for the ordinaries in Belgium, France, Spain, and Portugal; *Formula III,* for the ordinaries in other parts of Europe, and *Formula IV,* for the ordinaries in North and South America and the Philippine Islands.[22] The faculties contained in the formulas, as a whole, are changeable in their nature, and as a matter of fact they revealed slight changes when they were issued in 1933, 1938, 1944, 1948, and 1949.[23]

Since the circular letter of March 17, 1922, on the general Apostolic Faculties, the ordinaries of the United States of America received *Formula III,* but, as Bouscaren shows, they received *Formula IV* for the period between 1939-1944,[24] which formula remains as a whole the same up to the present time, although each one was supplanted after five years by Formula IV for the subsequent five-year period.[25] The latest *Formula IV,* which has been granted to the local ordinaries of the United States of America for the period between 1954-1959, consists of (I) four faculties

[21] *Archiv für katholisches Kirchenrecht,* CIV (1924), p. 287; *Le Canoniste Contemporain,* XLVI (1924), 302.

[22] Michiels, *Normae Generales,* II, 660; Van Hove, *De Privilegiis,* n. 164, pp. 156-157; Vermeersch-Creusen, *Epitome,* I, n. 874, p. 672.

[23] Cf. Stephanus Sipos, *Enchiridion Iuris Canonici* (6. ed., ed. L. Galos, Romae: Orbis Catholicus-Herder, 1954), pp. 207 ff.; Bouscaren, *Canon Law Digest,* I, 61-72; II, 30-42; III, 40-45; IV, 69-82.

[24] Bouscaren, *Canon Law Digest,* II, 30-42. Van Hove reported the same in his work *De Privilegiis, De Dispensationibus,* which was published in 1939.

[25] Cf. Bouscaren, *Canon Law Digest,* II, 42.

from the Holy Office; (II) a faculty to permit to all concerned, according to the norms of canon 534, § 1, and 1532, § 1, 2°, the alienation of ecclesiastical property or of pious causes as granted by the Sacred Consistorial Congregation; (III) four faculties from the Sacred Congregation of the Sacraments; (IV) seven faculties from the Sacred Congregation of Religious; (V) three faculties from the Sacred Congregation of the Council; (VI) twelve faculties from the Congregation of Sacred Rites; (VII) ten faculties from the Sacred Penitentiary, and finally (VIII) eight Rules regarding Fees. To these faculties the Holy Office, the Sacred Congregation of the Sacraments, and the Sacred Penitentiary respectively have added Official Notes in regard to the use of their faculties.[26]

Article II. Formulas of Apostolic Faculties Which Are Conceded Through the Sacred Congregation for the Propagation of the Faith: The Decennial faculties for Ordinaries in Quasi-Dioceses

Though at the time of the binding enactment of the Code of Canon Law the Sacred Consistorial Congregation through its Decree "*Proxima sacra*" practically declared the abrogation of the formulas formerly granted to the ordinaries under its jurisdiction for use *in foro externo,* the Sacred Congregation for the Propagation of the Faith published new formulas of Apostolic Faculties for ordinaries under its jurisdiction. New formulas of Apostolic Faculties were composed through the efforts of the prefect and the principal officials of the said Congregation, and they were approved "*in audientia*" by Pope Benedict XV, on February 6, 1919. These new formulas were sent out to all ordinaries

[26] *Ibid.,* IV, 69-82. Four faculties from the Holy Office of the formula 1944-1949 were in their entirety revised by the Supreme Sacred Congregation of the Holy Office, and notification of this was given in the letters of May 19, 1946, and of June 29, 1946, of the Apostolic Delegate to the United States. These faculties become effective on July 1, 1946. They remain the same in the formula of 1954-1959. Cf. *ibid.,* III, 40-45.

under the jurisdiction of the same Congregation in the form of letter on July 1, 1919.[27] In the same letter the Sacred Congregation declared that all Apostolic Faculties previously granted for use *in foro externo* to ordinaries under its jurisdiction would be abrogated as of December 31, 1919, and the faculties contained in the new formulas would be in force as of January 1, 1920.

The new formulas of Apostolic Faculties consisted of three *Formulae,* i.e., *Formula I, Formula II,* and *Formula III,* and each of these three *Formulae* had two forms, i.e., *Formula I maior* and *Formula I minor,* etc.[28] *Formulae maiores* were composed for ordinaries who had the episcopal character, whereas *Formula minores* were written for ordinaries who lacked the said character. *Formula I maior* and *Formula I minor*[29] comprised less extensive faculties for local ordinaries who ruled over regions whose status and conditions approximated those of the ordinary hierarchial dioceses, and whose location was less distant from the Holy See, for instance, regions such as Sweden, Norway, Denmark, Smyrna, Constantinople, Jerusalem, Aleppo, Isfahan, Bagdad, Arabia, Egypt, Lybia, and Morocco; *Formula II maior* and *Formula II minor*[30] had more extensive faculties for local ordinaries in regions more distant from the Holy See, for instance, Tasmania, Wellington (N. Zealand), the dioceses of colonial French Africa, the dioceses of Central America, Martinique, and the British colonies in Africa; *Formula III maior* and *Formula III minor*[31] consisted of most extensive faculties for local ordinaries in regions of China, Japan, Ocean Island, the Mari-

[27] Vermeersch, "De Formulis Facultatum," *Periodica,* XI (1922), p. (70): "Litterae S.C. de Propaganda Fide, 1 Iulii, 1919, ad omnes Ordinarios missae." Cf. Van Hove, *De Privilegiis,* p. 155, note (3).

[28] Michiels, *Normae Generales,* II, 661.

[29] *Sylloge,* nn. 207 and 210, pp. 581-586 and 604-609 respectively.

[30] *Ibid.,* nn. 208 and 211, pp. 586-593 and 609-615 respectively.

[31] *Ibid.,* nn. 209 and 212, pp. 593-603 and 616 ff. respectively.

[32] Michiels, *Normae Generales,* II, 661; Vermeersch, "De Formulis Facultatum," *Periodica,* XI (1922), p. (71).

ana Islands, Indochina, Guam, Tahiti, Africa (except Lybia, Egypt, and the dioceses of colonial French and British Africa), India, the Malay Peninsula, and the vicariates and prefectures in America.[32] To all of the three *Formulae maiores* there was added a supplement of faculties, as given in 1932. All formulas seemed to have been granted for a fifteen year period of use. And these *Formulae* were granted by the Sacred Congregation for the Propagation of the Faith, vested with all needed power from the Supreme Pontiff.[33] Besides the foregoing six formulas there also existed a formula called *"formula extra ordinem,"* which was given to the dioceses of Sarajevo, Banja Luca, Mostar, Antivari, and Skoplje in Yugoslavia.[33a]

The latest major change in the formulas of Apostolic Faculties for ordinaries in quasi-dioceses was made in 1941, when *Formula I maior, Formula I minor, Formula II maior,* and *Formula II minor* were suppressed, and *Formula III maior* became applicable to all ordinaries with the episcopal character, and *Formula III minor* to all ordinaries lacking the episcopal character, under the jurisdiction of the Sacred Congregation for the Propagation of the Faith throughout the world. These *formulae* have simply been called the *Formula maior* and the *Formula minor,* and they were sent to the respective ordinaries with a notification, the *"Notificatio de Facultatibus Formulae Maioris et Minoris,"* dated as of January 1, 1941.[34] According to this notification, all the general faculties which were contained in the old formulas of the Apostolic Faculties, and which were issued to all ordinaries of the missions, were to be supplanted by the new faculties attached to the notification from the day on which the new faculties would be received by the said ordinaries;

[33] "Vigore potestatis sibi a SS. D.N.... Divina Providenta PP.... tributae, haec S. Congregatio Christiano Nomini Propagando Revmo. P. Domino Ordinario... sequentes facultates concedit ad...."—Vermeersch, "De Formulis Facultatum," *Periodica,* XI (1922), p. (71). Cf. also *Sylloge, loc. cit.*

[33a] Cf. *Sylloge,* n. 213, pp. 625-634.

[34] Prot. n. 478/41. Cf. Paventi, *Brevis Commentarius,* p. 15.

the new faculties were to be granted for a ten-year period of use, and were not to cease *sede vacante* with reference to both the Holy See and the dioceses, and likewise were not to cease with the lapse from office of the ordinary to whom these faculties had been granted; these faculties were also shared by the vicars general in dioceses and prelacies *nullius* as well as by the vicars delegate in the missions, with all stated exceptions duly respected (*exceptis excipiendis*).

The *Formula Maior* contained fifty-three faculties, of which (I) twenty-one (nn. 1-21) were concerned with the sacraments and sacred rites; (II) seven (nn. 22-28), with matrimonial dispensations, the *sanatio in radice,* and the nuptial blessing; (III) twenty-one (nn. 29-49), with absolutions, benedictions, indulgences, various indults, etc., and (IV) four (nn. 50-53), with privileges for the ordinaries themselves.[35] The *Formula Minor* also had fifty-three faculties, but they were not entirely the same as those of the *Formula Maior.* The *Formula Minor* lacked Faculty n. II of the *Formula Maior;* Faculty n. XLIII of the *Formula Maior* corresponded to Faculties nn. 42 and 43 of the *Formula Minor.* Faculties nn. 19, 40, 50, and 53 of the *Formula Minor* corresponded to Faculties nn. XX, XLI, L, and LIII of the *Fomula Maior,* but they contained different wordings or different faculties (in the case of Faculty n. L of the *Formula Maior* and Faculty n. 50 of the *Formula Minor*).[36]

Thus, as of January 1, 1941, the former six *formulae* were reduced to two formulas, i.e., the *Formula Maior* and the *Formula Minor,* for a ten-year period of use. Each faculty in the *formulae* was numbered with arabic figures and marked with an asterisk if the faculty could be subdelegated

[35] Prot. nn. 449/41; 4200/47; 2416/50: "Facultates Decennales Ordinariis Missionum S.C. de Propaganda Fide Concessae. Formula Maior," *Monitor Ecclesiasticus,* LXXV (1950), 353-361. See also the *Adnotationes* furnished by Paventi, *ibid.,* pp. 371-383.

[36] "Facultates Decennales Ordinariis Missionum S.C. de Propaganda Fide Concessae. Formula Minor," *Monitor Ecclesiasticus,* LXXV (1950), 362-370.

by the ordinaries to priests.[37] As to the nature of the faculties of which mention was contained in the *formulae,* they remained, as before, privileges outside the law, and in the same way as in 1920 the *formulae* were granted by the Sacred Congregation for the Propagation of the Faith in virtue of the power received from the Supreme Pontiff.

With only slight changes, the formulas for use between January 1, 1951, and December 31, 1960, were renewed, or rather were made available for all ordinaries both with and without the episcopal character under the jurisdiction of the same Congregation throughout the world.[38] This renewal of the Apostolic Faculties through the *Formula Maior* and the *Formula Minor* was made *ex officio* by the Sacred Congregation, and not in consequence of any petition from the local ordinaries. And, in the new *formulae,* the duration of the use of the faculties for the fixed ten-year period was inflexibly determined as falling between January 1, 1951, and December 31, 1960, so that, although a *Formula Maior* had been conceded to a bishop in 1949 (when, for instance, he happened to be the first bishop of a newly established vicariate apostolic), the new formula became effective as of January 1, 1951. Likewise, when a bishop received the new formula on December 5, 1958, the faculties mentioned in the formula became effective on that day, but they will expire on December 31, 1960, as stated in the formula, despite their being decennial faculties.[39]

A change was made in Faculty n. XXIV of the *Formula Maior* (Faculty n. 23 of the *Formula Minor*). In the *formulae* of 1941-1950, the Faculty read: "*. . . dummodo moraliter certum sit partem acatholicam universae prolis tam*

[37] The *Animadversiones* I and II of the *formulae* indicated the numbers of Faculties which could be subdelegated by the ordinaries to priests, and the rules of the use of the faculties in the *formulae.* Cf. Paventi, *Brevis Commentarius,* p. 69.

[38] Prot. n. 2416/50. Cf. *arts. cit., Monitor Ecclesiasticus* LXXV (1950), 353-361; 371-380.

[39] Cf. Paventi, *Breviarium Iuris Missionalis* (Romae: Officium Libri Catholici, 1952), pp. 34-36 (hereafter cited as *Breviarium*).

natae quam nasciturae catholicam educationem non esse impedituram," but in the *formulae* of 1951-1960, the words *"tam natae quam"* have been withdrawn from the text of the Faculty. Another change in the *Formula Minor* of 1941-1950 was made when Faculty n. 53 was entirely abolished, and thus there exists no Faculty n. 53 in the *Formula Minor* of 1951-1960.[40]

Besides the foregoing two *formulae* of the Apostolic Faculties, a special Formula of the Apostolic Faculties for the ordinaries in Latin America under the jurisdiction of the Sacred Congregation for the Propagation of the Faith was put in effect through the Brief *"Litteris Apostolicis"* of April 30, 1929.[41] A new supplanting formula of the same Apostolic Faculties was given on May 3, 1941,[42] and lastly this formula was renewed by the Sacred Congregation on September 15, 1950.[43]

[40] Prot. nn. 449/41 and 2416/50. As matter of fact, these changes were made when the *formulae* were reprinted in 1947, and were effective from then on. Cf. Prot. n. 4200/47. The change in Faculty n. XXIV of the *Formula Maior* was necessitated in consequence of the Decree of the Sacred Congregation of the Holy Office on January 16, 1942. Cf. Sartori, *Enchiridion Canonicum* (8. ed., Romae, 1947), p. 207.

[41] *AAS*, XXI (1929), 554-557; *Sylloge*, n. 145.

[42] Prot. n. 1054/41. Cf. Paventi, *Brevis Commentarius*, pp. 70-72.

[43] Prot. n. 3394/50. Cf. Paventi, "Addenda ad Commentarium," *Breviarium*, fol. v. between pp. 32-33; "Epistola Qua Renovantur Particulares Facultates Ordinariis Missionum Americae Latinae," *Monitor Ecclesiasticus*. LXXV (1950), 562-565. Cf. also *Monitor Ecclesiasticus*, LXXIV (1949), 62-69.

CHAPTER III

GRANTEES OF THE QUINQUENNIAL AND DECENNIAL FACULTIES

ARTICLE I. GRANTEES OF THE QUINQUENNIAL FACULTIES

The *Formulae* of the Quinquennial Faculties are granted to local ordinaries who are not subject to the jurisdiction of the Sacred Congregation for the Propagation of the Faith or to that of the Sacred Oriental Congregation, and who are obliged to make their Quinquennial Reports to the Sacred Consistorial Congregation. In short, they are granted to local ordinaries who are subject to the Sacred Consistorial Congregation.[1]

Under the names of local ordinaries under the jurisdiction of the Sacred Consistorial Congregation come residential bishops, abbots and prelates *nullius*, and their vicars general, administrators, and those who in the case of vacancy in the above offices succeed to the office during that vacany by the provisions of the law, or of approved constitutions.[2] From this it follows that there are ordinaries *sede plena* and ordinaries *sede vacante*. Under the name of local ordinaries *sede plena* come residential bishops, abbots and prelates *nullius*, their vicars general and apostolic administrators, while under name of local ordinaries *sede vacante* come the cathedral chapter, the chapter of the abbacy or prelacy *nullius*, and the body of the diocesan consultors in places where there is no diocesan chapter, before the legitimate election of the vicar capitular by the chapter, or of the administrator by the body of the diocesan consultors; thereafter the vicar capitular or the administrator.

[1] Cf. the Constitution "*Sapienti consilio*,"—*AAS*, I (1909), 7-19; Decr. "*Proxima sacra*,"—*AAS*, X (1918), 190 ff.; Pius XI, Motu prop. "*Post datam*,"—*AAS*, XV (1923), 193 ff.

[2] Canons 198 and 66, § 2.

SECTION 1. ORDINARIES *Sede Plena*

The residential bishops,[3] as also abbots and prelates *nullius*[4] are explicitly mentioned among the ordinaries in canon 198, § 1, and enjoy ordinary jurisdiction within the limits of their respective territories and over their respective subjects, and according to the norm of canon 66, § 2, they enjoy, *ex officio,* the Quinquennial Faculties when they take canonical possession of their respective sees, as prescribed in canon 334, §§ 1 and 2. The *Formulae* of the Quinquennial Faculties are addressed directly to these ordinaries from the Holy See.

Bishops appointed as coadjutors or auxiliaries are titular bishops, and are grouped in three general classifications: (1) the coadjutor bishop given to the person of a residential bishop with the right of succession; (2) the coadjutor bishop given to the person of a residential bishop without the right of succession—he is called an auxiliary bishop; (3) the coadjutor bishop given to the episcopal see.[5] As a general principle, the coadjutors of bishops do not enjoy the Quinquennial Faculties in virtue simply of their appointment to the office, for their status is that of titular bishops. But they may have the faculties, *in toto,* depending upon their letters of appointment from the Sacred Consistorial Congregation and upon their commission from the residential bishops to whom they are appointed,[6] or they may enjoy the Quinquennial Faculties *ex officio,* namely, when they are appointed as vicars general of the residential bishops. Those coadjutors who are given the right of suc-

[3] Canon 334, § 1.—Episcopi residentiales sunt ordinarii et immediati pastores in dioecesibus sibi commissis. Cf. canon 335.

[4] Canon 323, § 1.—Abbas vel Praelatus *nullius* easdem potestates ordinarias easdemque obligationes cum iisdem sanctionibus habet, quae competunt Episcipis residentialibus in propria dioecesi.

[5] Canon 350. Cf. George E. Lynch, *Coadjutors and Auxiliaries of Bishops,* The Catholic University of America Canon Law Studies, n. 238 (Washington, D.C.: The Catholic University of America Press, 1947), Wernz-Vidal, *De Personis* n. 613, pp. 770-772.

[6] Canon 315.

cession acquire all the powers contained in the Quinquennial Faculties *ipso facto* on the vacancy of the episcopal sees to which they have been appointed, provided they have taken legitimate possession of their office, as demanded in canon 353;[7] thenceforward they enjoy the Quinquennial Faculties *ex officio* as ordinaries of their dioceses.

The apostolic administrator is an ecclesiastical official who for grave and special reasons is appointed by the Holy See to administer a canonically erected diocese, either while the bishop is still alive and in possession of the diocese, or during the vacancy; the administrator may be appointed permanently, or for only a certain length of time.[8] The Holy See may appoint an apostolic administrator *sede plena* in case the ordinary is incapacitated through old age or other habitual infirmities, from governing the diocese, or in case of his expulsion, imprisonment, etc., by the civil power, or for any other reason that the Holy See thinks sufficient. The Holy See may appoint an apostolic administrator *sede vacante,* if the men who have the right to elect the diocesan administrator choose an unworthy or otherwise disqualified person.[9] If the letter of appointment does not state otherwise, the apostolic administrator whose appointment is perpetual enjoys the Quinquennial Faculties *ex officio.*[10] The jurisdiction of the apostolic administrator does not expire or cease at the death of the Roman Pontiff, or of the bishop of the diocese, but it ceases when the new bishop takes legitimate possession of the diocese in the manner prescribed in canon 334.[11]

Vicars general in dioceses are enumerated among the

[7] Cf. Wernz-Vidal, *De Personis,* n. 620, pp. 784-785. Cf. also canon 355.

[8] Canon 312.

[9] S. Woywod-C. Smith, *A Practical Commentary on the Code of Canon Law* (1st printing of combined Vols. I and II, New York: Joseph F. Wagner, Inc., 1952), n. 233, p. 130 [hereafter cited as *A Practical Commentary*].

[10] Canons 315-316; 66, § 2.

[11] Canon 318.

ordinaries mentioned in canon 198, §§ 1 and 2. Regarding their right to use the habitual faculties given to bishops, canon 66, § 2, states that the habitual faculties granted to the bishops are granted also to the vicars general. Hence vicars general enjoy, *ex officio,* all the habitual faculties, including the Quinquennial Faculties, which are addressed to their respective bishops, provided that the faculties are not granted to the person of the bishop,[12] and that the vicars general have the episcopal character if it be essential, as it is in some instances, for the use of certain faculties. Since the vicars general enjoy the use of the Quinquennial Faculties by reason of their office, and since the faculties are granted by the Holy See, the bishops have no power to restrict or limit the powers of the Quinquennial Faculties with regard to their use by the vicars general.[13]

In its nature, the jurisdiction which the vicar general exercises in his bishop's diocese is ordinary,[14] but it is termed a *"iurisdictio ordinaria vicaria,"* because of the fact that with the bishop, by and for whom he has been appointed, the vicar general is constituted a juridical person which cannot exist apart from the bishop. In contrast to the jurisdiction of the vicar general, that of the bishop is termed a *"iurisdictio ordinaria propria."* As a consequence, the jurisdiction of the vicar general expires upon the vacancy of his bishop's see, and thus his office, and consquently also the right of the habitual faculties, including the Quinquennial Faculties which the vicar general has enjoyed, expires at the moment of the vacancy of the episcopal see. The office of the vicar general expires also upon a resigna-

[12] The Sacred Penitentiary declared, on July 18, 1919, that the faculties of the bishop to bless the various religious objects, the Stations of the Cross, etc. (cf. canon 349, § 1, n. 1°), are given as personal privileges in recognition of the episcopal dignity, and cannot be delegated habitually, nor even *per modum actus.* Cf. *AAS,* XI (1919), 332. And the same Sacred Penitentiary declared, on November 10, 1926, that the faculties which are mentioned in canon 349, § 1, n. 1°, do not belong to the vicar general. Cf. *AAS,* XVIII (1926), 500.

[13] *Collectanea* (16 Martii, 1865), n. 1488.

[14] Canons 197-198.

tion made according to norms outlined in canons 183-191, or upon a revocation made known to him by his bishop, etc.[15] However, when the faculties are withdrawn for a personal reason from a particular bishop, his vicar general continues to enjoy the faculties, unless the revocation explicitly mentions that the vicar general also loses the faculties. Since the vicar general enjoys the faculties by virtue of his office, and not through the medium of the bishop, the vicar general will retain his habitual faculties as long as he continues in office.[16]

SECTION 2. ORDINARIES *Sede Vacante*

Canon 66, § 2, states that the habitual faculties granted by the Apostolic See to the bishops and to other ordinaries mentioned in canon 198 do not lapse with the vacancy of the sees of the ordinaries to whom they were given, even though the bishops had begun to make use of the faculties, but are transmitted to the succeeding ordinaries.[17]

In places where the cathedral chapter is erected, the immediate successor of the bishop will be the same cathedral chapter. The canons of the cathedral chapter enjoy the succession in office until they have elected a vicar capitular;[18] in places where no cathedral chapter exists, the power of the ordinary passes to the body of diocesan consultors, who, too, enjoy the succession in office until they have elected an administrator of the diocese.[19] The election of the administrator as well as of the vicar capitular must be executed within eight days after the body of diocesan consultors or the cathedral chapter had been informed of the vacancy of

[15] Canon 371.

[16] Cf. Eagleton, *The Diocesan Quinquennial Faculties, Formula IV*, p. 36.

[17] Cf. S.C.S. Off., litt. encycl., 20 Febr. 1888—*Collectanea*, n. 1685; S.C.S. Off., decisio, 24 Nov. 1897—*Collectanea*, n. 1985; S.C.S. Off., decisio, 3 Maii 1899—*Collectanea*, n. 2045.

[18] Canons 431, § 1, and 435, § 2.

[19] Canon 427.

the diocese.[20] In case the body of diocesan consultors (or the cathedral chapter) fails, for any reason, to elect an administrator (or a vicar capitular) or an econome within the allotted time, the appointment of them devolves upon the metropolitan; but if it is an archdiocese, or if the latter is vacant at the same time that one of its suffragan sees is vacant, the appointment devolves upon the senior suffragan bishop.[21] Beyond these general principles, however, the Code of Canan Law provides for two contingencies, i.e., when by special arrangement of the Holy see the metropolitan bishop or some other bishop may have the right to appoint the diocesan administrator,[22] and when the officials who have the right to elect the diocesan administrator choose an unworthy or otherwise disqualified person, so that the Holy See will appoint a diocesan administrator.[23]

At the vacancy of an abbacy *nullius,* or also of a prelacy *nullius* if the latter was held by a religious, the chapter of the religious succeeds in the government of the district until the appointment of a new ordinary has been made, unless the constitutions rule otherwise; if the prelacy *nullius* was of a secular character, the chapter of canons succeeds.[24] When the secular prelacy *nullius* has a body of consultors instead of the chapter, the body of consultors is the suceeding ordinary of that vacant prelacy *nullius.*[25] Either the chapter of canons or the body of consultors must elect a vicar capitular or an administrator according to the norms of canons 423-438 and canon 427. These, in turn, are the succeeding ordinaries in their respective district, until the election of the new abbot or prelate *nullius* has been completed; and thus these ordinaries *sede vacante* enjoy, in

[20] Canon 432, § 1.

[21] Canon 432, § 2. Cf. canon 432, § 3.

[22] Canon 431, § 2.

[23] Cf. canon 312. Cf. also Woywod-Smith, *A Practical Commentary,* n. 233, p. 130.

[24] Canon 327.

[25] Canon 326.

virtue of canon 66, § 2, the Quinquennial Faculties which were granted to their preceding ordinaries.

The use of the Quniquennial Faculties by the cathedral chapter, by the chapter of religious, by the body of diocesan consultors, and by the body of consultors of a secular prelacy *nullius,* raises the question whether the Quinquennial Faculties are enjoyed by these groups of persons in group fashion only, or by the individual constituent members of these groups, or by the representatives of these groups. The answer must be sought in the light of the principle of canon 431, § 1, which states: *"sede vacante, nisi adfuerit Administrator Apostolicus vel aliter a Sancta Sede provisum fuerit, ad Capitulum ecclesiae cathedralis regimen dioecesis devolvitur."* Since the Quinquennial Faculties are instruments to be employed in the government of the diocese, they are transmitted to the moral person, i.e., to the cathedral chapter as a whole, and thus they must be used in a unit action by the individuals who constitute that moral person, and not by any individual of the chapter, nor by any representative of the chapter as such.[26]

Article II. Grantees of the Decennial Faculties

Missions can be divided into two general divisions, i.e., missions *non de facto, sed de iure,* in which the hierarchy has been canonically established, but which are placed under the jurisdiction of the Sacred Congregation for the Propagation of the Faith, and missions *de facto et de iure,* in which the hierarchy has not been canonically established, and which are subject to the jurisdiction of the same Sacred Congregation.[27]

[26] Cf. canons 391, 100, 101, 427, and 423. See also Eagleton, *The Diocesan Quinquennial Faculties, Formula IV,* p. 37.

[27] Cf. canon 252; const. *"Sapienti consilio"*—*AAS,* I (1909), 12-13; Victorius Bartoccetti, *Jus Constitutionale Missionum* (Taurini: L.I.C.E., 1947), nn. 14, 15, 17, 22-24.

SECTION 1. ORDINARIES IN MISSIONS *Non De Facto, Sed De Iure*

The ordinaries in missions *non de facto, sed de iure,* are the bishops, the abbots and the prelates *nullius* and their vicars general, and the apostolic administrators, who are subject to the common norms of the law. By reason of their dependency on the Sacred Congregation for the Propagation of the Faith, these ordinaries are bound to negotiate with the Holy See, in certain matters, through the said Sacred Congregation. Thus, they have the obligation to submit annual reports of the status of their respective sees to the same Sacred Congregation from which they receive the *Formula Maior* of the Decennial Faculties.[28]

Insofar as they are subject to the common law of the Church, vicars general of the bishops, of the abbots and the prelates *nullius,* and also the apostolic administrators in missions *non de facto, sed de iure,* must follow the provisions as made for these offices subject to the Sacred Consistorial Congregation. In the same way all the provisions and procedures prescribed in the Code for the case of a *sedes impedita* or a *sedes vacans* in places which are subject to this Sacred Congregation are to be observed in the case of a *sedes impedita* and a *sedes vacans* in missions *non de facto, sed de iure.* The Sacred Congregation for the Propagation of the Faith was asked whether, in mission territories where the hierarchy has been recently established, canon 309 is in effect for the government of the diocese during the vacancy of the see, or whether canons 429-444 are in effect, so that the diocesan consultors elect a vicar capitular. The said Sacred Congregation replied that mission diocese which are canonically erected are governed, when the See is vacant or impeded, in the same way as other dioceses.[29]

[28] Cf. "Ordo Servandus in Romana Curia, Normae Peculiares," in *AAS,* I (1909), 97; Paventi, *Breviarium,* p. 36.

[29] Prot. n. 166/54—Rome, 26 Ian. 1954. Cf. Bouscaren, *Canon Law Digest,* IV, 128.

SECTION 2. ORDINARIES *Sede Plena* IN MISSIONS *De Facto Et De Iure*

The ordinaries *sede plena* in missions *de facto et de iure* are the vicars and prefects apostolic, who govern vicariates and prefectures apostolic, and the superior of missions *sui iuris*. Vicars and prefects apostolic are the ordinaries to whom the Sacred Congregation for the Propagation of the Faith addressed the *formulae* of the Decennial Faculties. In consequence of the decree which was issued in 1896 the superiors of missions *sui iuris* are considered as prefects apostolic as to their rights and obligations,[30] and enjoy the Decennial Faculties as granted by the Sacred Congregation for the Propagation of the Faith.

Although the vicars and prefects apostolic and the superiors of missions *sui iuris* enjoy ordinary jurisdiction, the nature of their power is vicarious in the sense that these ordinaries govern their respective territorial circumscriptions in the name and in place of the Supreme Pontiff,[31] but the power of these ordinaries of the missions *de facto et de iure* is different from that of the vicar general in the canonically erected diocese, in view of the fact that the vicar general and the bishop (by and for whom the vicar general was appointed) constitute one juridical person, so that a jurisdictional act of the vicar general becomes identified with that of his bishop,[32] while the said ordinaries of the missions *de facto et de iure* do not constitute one juridical person with the Supreme Pontiff, in whose name and in whose place they govern the ecclesiastical circumscriptions, and their jurisdictional acts cannot become identified with those of the Supreme Pontiff.[33]

[30] See *infra*, p. 72.

[31] Wernz-Vidal, *De Personis*, n. 545, pp. 689-690; Augustinus Pugliese, "De Missione Sui Iuris Eiusque Praelato," *CpRM*, XVIII (1937), 38.

[32] Canon 366. Cf. Wernz-Vidal, *De Personis*, n. 635, p. 805; Ludovicus Bender, *Potestas Ordinaria et Delegata* (Roma-Paris-New York-Tournai: Desclée & Ci, 1957), n. 24, p. 18.

[33] Pugliese, "art. cit.," *CpRM*, XVII (1937), 38.

A. *Vicars and prefects Apostolic*[34]

Since the creation of the Sacred Congregation for the Propagation of the Faith and as now accepted in the present Code, vicars and prefects apostolic are ecclesiastical prelates who enjoy ordinary jurisdiction and fulfill the apostolic duties in place of the Supreme Pontiff in regions where the ordinary ecclesiastical hierarchy has not been restored or has never existed.[35] According to the provisions made in canon 294, both vicars and prefects apostolic enjoy in their respective territories the same rights and faculties as the residential bishops, unless the Apostolic See has made some restriction in a particular case. Since prefects apostolic generally lack the episcopal character, the Code grants to them faculties to exercise some of the powers pertaining to the order and the dignity of a bishop, for within the limits of their territories and during the time of their office prefects apostolic may perform all the blessings, except the pontifical blessing, reserved to the bishops, even though they themselves are not consecrated as bishops; they can consecrate chalice, patens, and portable altars with the holy oils blessed by a bishop; they grant fifty days' indulgence, and confer confirmation, first tonsure, and minor orders.[36] Relative to the granting of indulgences, by concession of the Sacred Penitentiary, on July 20, 1942, prefects apostolic may now grant an indulgence of one hundred days.[37]

All the particular rights and obligations of vicars and prefects apostolic are defined in canons 295-311, and an

[34] For the history of the institutions of vicars and prefects apostolic see *Collectanea*, nn. 22, 109, 161, 165, 249, etc.; De Martinis, *Ius Pontificium de Propaganda Fide* (7 vols. in 8, Romae, 1888-1897), Pars, I, Vol. I, pp. 279, 313; Vol. II, p. 493; Wernz-Vidal, *De Personis*, n. 544, pp. 687-688; Vromant, *Ius Missionarium*, Tom. II*(De Personis)*; (Bruxelles: Dewit, 1929), nn. 53-57 pp. 50-57 [hereafter cited as *De Personis*]; Francis J. Winslow, *Vicars and Prefects Apostolic*, The Catholic University of America Canon Law Studies, n. 24 (Washington, D.C.: The Catholic University of America, 1924).

[35] Vromant, *De Personis*, n. 56, pp. 54-55.

[36] Canon 782, § 3, and canon 957, § 2.

[37] *AAS*, XXXIV (1942), 240.

accurate definition of the respective rights and duties of the vicars and prefects apostolic (and those of the superiors of the missions *sui iuris*) is contained in an Instruction published on December 8, 1929, by the Sacred Congregation for the Propagation of the Faith.[38]

With reference to the Apostolic Faculties granted for use *in foro externo* on the part of vicars and prefects apostolic, the vicars apostolic receive the *Formula Maior* of the Decennial Faculties, while the prefects apostolic, provided they are not bishops, are granted the *Formula Minor* of the Decennial Faculties. If prefects apostolic are bishops, they receive the *Formula Maior* which is given to vicars apostolic.

B. Superiors of Missions SUI IURIS

Historical Note.—In the course of the history of the missions, many missions had been promoted to prefectures apostolic or vicariates apostolic, and then became independent ecclesiastical circumscriptions, having been dismembered from their mother-diocese or mother-vicariate apostolic. In the middle of the nineteenth century, however, there was a considerable number of prefectures within the territories of dioceses and vicariates apostolic. These prefectures were headed by the prefects apostolic, i.e., by the prefects of the missions of religious, who were not completely independent of the jurisdiction of the bishops, or of the vicars apostolic of the territories within which they existed.[39]

During the celebration of the Vatican Council (1869-1870), a complete abolition of such prefectures was proposed by the consultors of the Council, but nothing was accomplished about the said proposal[40] until the Sacred Congregation for the Propagation of the Faith promulgated

[38] *AAS*, XXII (1930), 111.

[39] Pugliese, "art. cit.," *CpRM*, XVIII (1937), 40-41; 175-177.

[40] *Acta et Decreta Sacrorum Conciliorum Recentiorum, Collectio Lacensis* (7 toms., Friburgi Brisgoviae: Herder, 1870-1892), VII, coll. 682 ff.; Mansi, Tom. LIII, pp. 49 and 45-156, *passim*.

the Decree "*Excelsum,*" on September 12, 1896.[41] By force of the cited decree, prefectures of apostolic missions among the Orientals, if they existed within the territories of other missions or dioceses and possessed no separate territories, were abrogated. In those prefectures of the missions possessing separate territories, the prefects of the missions were supplanted by superiors of the missions, who upon presentation by the supreme moderators of the religious orders were appointed by the Sacred Congregation for the Propagation of the Faith, and came to be considered as real ecclesiastical superiors along with the vicars and prefects apostolic; the office of superior of the mission was not to be joined with the office of the religious superior without the permission of the said Sacred Congregation.[42]

Thus the institution of missions *sui iuris,* at least among the Orientals, existed before the promulgation of the Code of Canon Law. Moreover, the *Schema Codicis* of 1912, 1914, and 1916 treated missions *sui iuris* and their superiors under Chapter VIII, "*De Vicariis Apostolicis, Praefectis Apostolicis ac Superioribus Missionum.*"[43]

The Code does not include missions *sui iuris* and their superiors among the ecclesiastical circumscriptions and their ordinaries. By reason of this omission in the Code, A. Pugliese was of the opinion that, since these missions were unstable of their very nature, it was desired that they be soon erected as vicariates or prefectures apostolic.[44] Hence, according to Pugliese' opinion, the Code actually intended to abrogate the existence of the institution of missions *sui iuris*. Contrary to this opinion. Vromant contends that since the said institution was in a state of experiment as an ecclesiastical territorial circumscription at the time

[41] *Collectanea,* II, n. 1953. Cf. Pope Leo XIII's Motu proprio "*Auspicis rerum,*" March 19, 1896—*ASS,* XXVIII (1895-1896), 585 ff.

[42] Xaverius Paventi, "Quaestiones de Iure Missionali," *Ephemerides Iuris Canonici,* III (1947), 244.

[43] Cf. Pugliese, "art. cit.," *CpRM,* XVIII (1937), p. 175, note 27.

[44] *Loc. cit.*

of the promulgation of the Code, it was impossible to define such missions and their superiors in the Code.[45]

It was through the letter of the Cardinal Prefect of the Sacred Congregation for the Propagation of the Faith, on November 7, 1929, that the status of the mission *sui iuris* was defined for the first time after the promulgation of the Code. The Cardinal Prefect Van Rossum wrote in the letter that there was no definitions of, or provisions for, missions *sui iuris* and their superiors in practice, i.e., in the Code, but that all provisions made for the prefectures apostolic and prefects apostolic in the Code should be applied to the missions *sui iuris* and their superiors.[46] The status of missions *sui iuris,* however, became clearer from the letter of the Sacred Congregation for the Propagation of the Faith, on August 31, 1934, which was given to Bishop Leo Peter Kierkels, Apostolic Delegate to India. The letter read as follows:

> In your letter of the 2nd of this month (n. 4008/34), Your Excellency submitted to this Sacred Congregation the question proposed by the Superior of Bellary, whether the Ecclesiastical Superior of a Mission *sui iuris* is bound *in justice* to apply the Mass *pro populo* according to Canon 339.
>
> The reply of this Sacred Congregation is in the affirmative for the reason that the Ecclesiastical Superior of a Mission *sui iuris* must be considered an Ordinary. It is true that the Code, as Your Excellency correctly observes, does not mention the "Superiors of Missions" among the Ordinaries; but it must be noted that, although a Mission *sui iuris* cannot be said to be, as a juridical type, a creation posterior to the Code, nevertheless, whereas even before the Code there were in existence some Missions *sui iuris,* it was only after the promulgation of the Code that the practice developed and was adopted by the Sacred Congregation, of erecting such Missions with a determined

[45] Paventi, "art. cit.," *Ephemerides Iuris Canonici,* III (1947), 187.

[46] (Private) S.C. Prop. Fid., 7 Nov. 1929; *Sylloge,* n. 146; Bouscaren *Canon Law Digest,* III, 74.

territory and with their own Ecclesiastical Superior.[47]

The *Annuario Pontificio* of 1958 reports that there are three missions *sui iuris* in existence under the jurisdiction of the Sacred Congregation for the Propagation of the Faith.[48]

Rights and Obligations of the Superior of Missions SUI IURIS.—From the response of 1929 and the letter of 1934 the Sacred Congregation for the Propagation of the Faith it is clear that the superiors of missions *sui iuris* are, *ex praxi et stylo* of the said Sacred Congregation, real *"Ordinarii loci,"* as defined in canon 198, and they govern the territories of their missions as their own territories in spiritual and temporal matters, as prescribed in canon 335, § 1, with no degelated power, but with an ordinary power, i.e., *ex officio,* in the name and in the place of the Roman Pontiff. Hence, by analogy, canons 293-311, which are established for the prefects apostolic, are applied for the superiors of missions *sui iuris, exceptis excipiendis et servatis servandis.*[49] Thus, the superiors of missions *sui iuris* are enumerated among the grantees of the Decennial Faculties, *Formula Minor.*[50]

C. The Vicars Delegate

1. *Historical Note.*—Before the promulgation of the Code

[47] Bouscaren, *Canon Law Digest,* II, 74-75; *Sylloge,* n. 187.

[48] These three are missions *sui iuris:* Ulan Bator (Urga) in the Mongolian Peoples' Republic, Drysdale River in the Province of Western Australia, and Tarahumara in the State of Chihuahua, Mexico. Cf. *Annuario Pontificio* (Città del Vaticano: Typografia Poliglotta Vaticana, 1958), pp. 826-829, *passim.* Tarahumara was elevated from the status of a mission *sui iuris* to the status of a vicariate apostolic, on June 23, 1958, by Pope Pius XII in his Constitution "*Si qua inter gentes.*" See *AAS*, LI (1959), 261-262.

[49] Cf. Pugliese, "art. cit., *CpRM,* XVIII (1937), 178-183; Paventi, "art. cit.," *Ephemerides Iuris Canonici,* III (1947), 245-246; Paventi, *Breviarium,* p. 85.

[50] G. Vromant, *Facultates Apostolicae* (3. ed. emendata, Paris: Desclée de Brouwer, 1947), n. 6, p. 4; J. de Reeper, *A Missionary Companion* (Westminster, Md.: The Newman Press, 1952), p. 4.

of Canon Law, by force of the Constitutions of Pope Benedict XIV, "*Ex sublimi,*" of January 26, 1753,[51] and "*Quam ex sublimi,*" of August 8, 1755,[52] and of the declaration of the Sacred Congregation for the Propagation of the Faith of February 20, 1888, which included the vicar and the prefect apostolic among the ordinaries,[53] the institution of the vicar general in the missions was in existence.[54] Upon the promulgation of the Code, canon 254 provided that vicars and prefects apostolic enjoy in their respective territories the same rights and faculties as the residential bishops, unless the Apostolic See had made a restriction in a particular case. Moreover, according to the norm of canon 366, whenever the proper government of the diocese demands it, the bishop should appoint a vicar general, who shall enjoy ordinary jurisdiction in the entire diocese. Theoretically, if these general provisions were applied, with the past papal statutes taken into consideration, then vicars and prefects apostolic could also appoint vicars general for the government of their respective vicariates and prefectures apostolic. In practice, vicars general existed in the missions where the ordinary hierarchy was not established.[55]

Nevertheless, since canon 198, § 1, which enumerates the local ordinaries and refers explicitly to the vicars general of residential bishops, and of abbots and prelates *nullius*, but is silent regarding those of vicars and prefects apostolic, there arose a doubt whether the *unless* clause of canon 294, § 1, should be applied regarding the provisions for vicars general in canon 198, § 1, or not. The Sacred Congregation for the Propagation of the Faith sent out a letter to

[51] *Collectanea*, n. 387.

[52] *Collectanea*, n. 396. Cf. also S.C. Prop. Fid., resp. 22 Ian. 1759—*Collectanea*, n. 412.

[53] *Collectanea*, n. 1685.

[54] Cf. Leurenius, *De Episcoporum Vicariis Eorumdemque Coadiutoribus* (Venetiis, 1709); Bouix, *De Iudiciis Ecclesiasticis* (2 vols., Parisiis, 1855), Tom. I, pars II, cap. 3; Wernz, *Ius Decretalium*, II, n. 804.

[55] Cf. *AAS*, XII (1920), 120; Bouscaren, *Canon Law Digest*, I, 144.

all vicars and prefects apostolic on December 8, 1919. It reads as follows:

> According to c. 198, Vicars and Prefects Apostolic have not the right to elect Vicars General, as resident Bishops have; but they have the power to appoint a delegate, with powers to be fixed in each case, and this delegate may be some one other than the Pro-Vicar mentioned in c. 309.
>
> On the other hand, since it seems advisable that mission Superiors should have the power to appoint a vicar who should have the same jurisdiction as Vicars General of Bishops have under the Code, including the same special faculties which the Sacred Congregation of Propaganda communicates to Ordinaries of places, His Holiness, Benedict XV, on 6 Nov., 1919: (1) healed the nullity of all acts of jurisdiction which may have been done by those missionaries who have acted as real Vicars General; and (2) granted to Ordinaries of missions the power to appoint a Vicar Delegate if they need one, who shall have in practice all the jurisdiction in spiritual and temporal matters, which the Code gives to Vicars General in dioceses.
>
> By virtue of this grant, which is made to all Superiors of missions, each one may name a Vicar Delegate, who shall have all the faculties of a Vicar General according to canon 368, § 1, 2°.
>
> As regards the number and the office of Vicar Delegate in each mission, the same provision which the Code makes in regard to Vicars General (c. 366 *sq.*) shall be applicable.[56]

In consequence of the above cited letter, the appointment of a vicar general in the missions *de facto et de iure* was absolutely prohibited, and a new institution of the vicar delegate was introduced. The office and power of the vicar delegate were clearly defined in the same letter. In a letter of November 7, 1929, the Sacred Congregation for the Propagation of the Faith granted to superiors of the mis-

[56] Bouscaren, *Canon Law Digest,* I, 144; *AAS,* XII (1920), 120; *Sylloge,* b. 76. Cf. *Periodica,* X (1921), 199.

sions *sui iuris* the right to appoint the delegate (superior delegate), as it did for vicars and prefects apostolic.[57]

2. *Nature of the Power of the Vicar Delegate.*—There existed still the question whether the jurisdiction of the vicar delegate was delegated or ordinary. It was a matter of considerable importance and of practical consequence to ascertain whether the vicar delegate had ordinary or merely delegated jurisdiction, insofar as the principles of delegation and subdelegation were based upon the nature of the jurisdiction that one possessed. On this letter of the Sacred Congregation for the Propagation of the Faith, the first comment was offered by Vermeersch (1858-1936) in the *Periodica* of 1921. It stated: "*. . . non tantum ei [vicario delegato] tribuitur practice potestas Vicarii Generalis, sed regulae de delegatione generali ei sunt applicandae.*"[58] Since in virtue of canon 368, § 1, the vicar general has by the very fact of his office a jurisdiction over the entire diocese in spiritual and temporal matters to the extent of the bishop's own ordinary jurisdiction, except in those affairs which the bishop has reserved to himself, or which by law require a special mandate from the bishop, Vermeersch's annotation admitted that the power of the vicar general is ordinary, and correspondingly asserted that the power of the vicar delegate likewise was ordinary, since he held a power analogical to that of the vicar general. Contrary to this, Vromant asserted that the power of the vicar delegate was merely a delegated power, for the source of the power in question was not the office of the vicar delegate, though in practice he held the power of a vicar general. The vicar delegate was not to be considered an ecclesiastical prelate, since he lacked the "*privilegia honorifica et insignia Protonotarii Apostolici Titularis,*" which the vicar general enjoys in a diocese, and thus the vicar delegate could not in

[57] *Sylloge*, n. 146; Bouscaren, *Canon Law Digest*, II, 75-76; III, 73-74.

[58] "Adnotationes," *Periodica*, X (1921), p. 200, n. 4. Cf Vermeersch, "De Munere et Officiis Vicarii et Praefecti Apostolici secundum Praesens Ius," *Periodica*, IX (1920), pp. (24)-(25).

view of canon 110 be enumerated among those who had ordinary jurisdiction in the external forum.[59]

In 1937, however, Bishop John Aerts, Vicar Apostolic of Netherlands New Guinea, asked the Sacred Congregation for the Propagation of the Faith whether the jurisdiction in spiritual and temporal matters which according to the letter of the Sacred Congregation had in practice been granted to the vicar delegate was of its nature ordinary or delegated jurisdiction. The said Sacred Congregation replied: "The jurisdiction of the vicar delegate is ordinary," in a letter dated November 16, 1937.[60]

Since the vicar delegate, as does the vicar general in the diocese, enjoys ordinary jurisdiction, which the authors call a *"iurisdictio ordinaria subvicaria,"* or *"iurisdictio ordinaria provicaria,"*[61] his rights and obligations are to be considered parallel to those of the vicar general, which receive mention in canons 366-371 in the Code. First of all, the vicar delegate constitutes one juridical person or one administrative forum with the vicar apostolic, by and for whom he was appointed. The vicar delegate has, by virtue of his office, jurisdiction over the entire vicariate apostolic in spiritual and temporal matters to the extent of the ordinary jurisdiction of the vicar apostolic himself, except in those affairs which the vicar apostolic has reserved to himself, or which by law require a special mandate from the

[59] Vromant, "De Natura Potestatis Vicarii Delegati in Territorio Missionis," *Jus Pontificium,* IX (1930), 19-26; Vromant *Ius Missionarium. Facultates Apostolicae Quas S.C. de Propaganda Fide Delegare Solet Ordinariis Missionum, Supplementum ad Commentaria in Formulam Tertiam* (Louvain: Éditions du Museum Lessianum, 1930), n. 114, p. 17.

[60] Prot. n. 4226/37: (Private) S.C. Prop. Fid., 16 Nov. 1937. This letter was for the first time published in 1941 in *Rassegna de Morali e di Diritto,* VII (1941), 144. In its entirety the letter was translated by Paventi in "Quaestiones de Iure Missionali," *Ephemerides Iuris Canonici,* III (1947), 248; its English translation is found in Bouscaron, *Canon Law Digest,* III, 75.

[61] Paventi, "art. cit.," *loc. cit.* This author cited Jarre, *Antonianum,* IV (1929), 359. Cf. also Vromant, "art. cit.," *Jus Pontificium,* IX (1930), 24.

vicar apostolic, or which for their execution postulate the episcopal character on the part of the executor.[62]

3. *Right to the Decennial Faculties.*—The *Notificatio* attached to the *Formula Maior* (and the *Formula Minor*) of 1941 mentions explicitly the right of the vicar delegate to make use of the Decennial Faculties and states as follows:

> *Quae facultates generales ad decennium conceduntur. Eae autem non cessabunt per Apostolicae Sedis aut dioecesis vacationem (can. 61): neque evanescent resoluto iure Ordinarii cui concessae sunt, etiamsi ipse eas exsequi coepit, sed ad Ordinarios qui ipsi in regimine successerint transibunt; atque competent quoque Vicario Generali dioecesis et Praelaturae nullius (can. 66, §2) ac Vicario Delegato in Missionibus, exceptis excipiendis.*[63]

Thus the *Formula Maior* of the Decennial Faculties in its entirety, *exceptis excipiendis,* avails for the vicar delegate in missions *de facto et de iure,* as well as for the vicar general in missions *non de facto, sed de iure.*

The phrase *"exceptis excipiendis"* may have reference to the *"nisi"* clause of canon 66, § 2, which states: *"nisi in earum concessione electa fuerit industria personae aut aliud expresse cautum sit."* However, in the concession of the *Formulae* of the Decennial Faculties, the element of personal qualification is not taken into consideration; all the faculties contained in the *Formulae* of the Decennial Faculties are general, not personal, faculties; no express exception is found either in the texts of the faculties themselves, or in the *Notificatio,* or in the *Animadversiones* of the *Formulae.*

Since some Decennial Faculties as granted in the *Formulae* postulate the episcopal order or the office either of vicar apostolic or of prefect apostolic on the part of their executor, the said phrase *"exceptis excipiendis"* has reference to those faculties which postulate these conditions.

[62] Canon 368, § 1. Cf. Francis J. Winslow, *A Commentary on the Apostolic Faculties* (New York, Field Afar Press, 1946), pp. 9-10 [hereafter cited as *The Apostolic Faculties*].

[63] Cf. Paventi, *Brevis Commentarius,* p. 15.

For, since the vicar delegate does not hold the office of the vicar apostolic, he cannot make use of those faculties which postulate this condition; and, although he is an ordinary, the vicar delegate is competent only for the faculties which concern the exercise of the power of jurisdiction of the ordinary in the missions *de facto et de iure,* but is not competent for those faculties which concern the exercise of the power of the episcopal order.[64] Consequently, the phrase *"exceptis excipiendis"* is of application with reference to Faculties nn. II, XIX, XX, XXXIII, L, and LIII in the *Formula Maior,* and to Faculties nn. 18, 32, 50, and 53 in the *Formula Minor.*

In the *Formula Maior,* Faculty n. II deals with the power of consecrating the Holy Oils with a limited number of ministers, and Faculty n. XX with the conferring of the major orders on week days. These faculties involve an amplification of the powers called for in the *Pontificale Romanum,* and in canons 734 and 1006, §§ 2 and 3, and these powers belong exclusively to ordinaries possessing the episcopal order. Faculty n. XIX is concerned with the administration of the first tonsure and of the minor orders on the same day. The power of conferring the first tonsure and the minor orders, however, is acknowledged in the Code for all bishops, and is granted also to vicars and prefects apostolic by reason of their office, even when they lack the episcopal order.[65] But the vicar delegate possesses neither the episcopal order, nor the office of the vicar apostolic. And thus the vicar delegate has no competence for the use of Faculty n. XX. As to Faculty n. XXXIII, this is an amplification of the bishop's privilege *a iure* to grant the papal blessing mentioned in canon 914, in which the vicar general is not included as competent to make use of the said privilege, and thus this faculty also does not avail for the vicar delegate.

Faculties nn. L and LIII in the *Formula Maior* are placed

[64] Cf. Woywod-Smith, *A Pratical Commentary,* n. 163, pp. 94-95.
[65] Canons 294, § 2; 782, § 3, and 957, § 2.

under the classification of "*Facultates pro ipso Ordinario.*" Because of this fact, authors are inclined to see this classification as an express restriction mentioned in the "*nisi*" *clause* of canon 66, § 2; consequently they assert that all of the four Faculties under the classification are to be used only by the vicar apostolic himself, but not by the vicar delegate.[66] But the classification "*Facultates pro ipso Ordinario*" in the Formula does not determine the nature of the faculties included under it, namely, whether they are personal or real. It simply indicates the fact that the beneficiaries of these faculties are the ordinaries themselves. From the fact that it does not expressly exclude the vicar delegate from the use of them, these faculties may be used by both the vicar apostolic and the vicar delegate. In practice, then, when they are used by the vicar delegate, the principle that is implied in the "*exceptis excipienis*" clause should always be taken into consideration. Since Faculties nn. L and LIII are given in view of the dignity and the office of the vicar apostolic who possesses the episcopal order, these faculties are not available for the vicar delegate. On the other hnad, Faculties nn. LI and LII contain no elements for the application of the said principle, and thus they are available for the vicar delegate. As a matter of fact, Faculties nn. LI and LII state that the ordinary can gain for himself the indulgences which, by virtue of the Decennial Faculties, *Formula Maior,* he can grant to others, and that the ordinary can make use, not merely on one's own behalf but on behalf of others, the faculties and permissions whose use he can grant to others. These Faculties appear simply to be applications of canon 201, § 3.[67]

[66] Paventi, *Brevis Commentarius*, p. 66; Petrus Ly-Yuh-Wen, *Vicarius Delegatus in Territorio Missionis* (Romae: Tyografia Polyglotta 'Cor Mariae'), pp. 23-24; Antonius Iglesias, *Brevis Commentarius in Facultates Quas S.C. de Propaganda Fide Dare Solet Missionariis* (Taurini-Romae: Marietti, 1924), p. 131; Winslow, *The Apostolic Faculties*, p. 11.

[67] Canon 201, § 3: Nisi aliud ex rerum natura aut ex iure constet, potestatem iurisdictionis voluntariam seu non-iudicialem quis exercere

Since the vicar delegate is an ordinary, and thus has an ordinary jurisdiction, he is competent for the use of all Decennial Faculties, *exceptis excipiendis,* in the *Formula Maior,* to the extent that he can use them either by himself, or by way of delegation, *servatis servandis.*[68]

The prefect delegate in a prefecture apostolic and the superior delegate in a mission *sui iuris* enjoy the right to the Decennial Faculties listed in the *Formula Minor* in the same way in which the vicar delegate enjoys the right to those which are listed in the *Formula Maior.*

SECTION 3. ORDINARIES *Sede Vacante* AND *Sede Impedita* IN MISSIONS *De Facto Et De Iure*

A. Canonical Provisions

Canons 309, 310, and 311 govern the administration of quasi-dioceses in the circumstances of the *sedes vacans* and the *sedes impedita.*

According to the norm of canon 309, at the beginning of their term of office the vicar and the prefect apostolic should appoint a qualified pro-vicar and pro-prefect respectively, who *ipso facto* takes charge of the respective district in the case of a vacancy or of some operational hindrance. The vacancy may be occasioned by the death of the vicar or the prefect apostolic, or by his loss or forfeiture of jurisdiction for various reasons. The operational hindrance sets in after

potest etiam in proprium commodum, aut extra territorium existens aut in subditum a territorio absente. Cf. Vermeersch, "De Formulis Facultatum," *Periodica,* XI (1922), nn. 75 and 78, pp. (106)-(108); Marcel Gérin, *Le Gouvernement des Missions,* Les Thèses Canoniques de Laval, Thèse n. 1 (Quebec: Faculté de Droit Canonique, Université Laval, 1944), p. 192; Stanghetti, *Prassi della S.C. de Propaganda Fide* (Romae: Officium Libri Catholici, 1943), p. 75.

[68] *Animadeversiones in Formulam Maiorem,* nn. I and II: "I. Praedictae facultates ea lege conceduntur, ut non omnes indiscriminatim subdelegari possint, sed illae tantum quae asterisco* notantur, seu quae habentur sub n. 16, 18, 22, . . . II. Ordinarius insuper supradictis omnibus facultatibus sive per se sive per alios uti tantum valeat *intra fines suae iurisdictionis. . . .*"—*Monitor Ecclesiasticus,* LXXV (1950), 361.

the manner delineated in canon 429, § 1. Thus, *ipso facto* upon the occurrence of the vacancy (*sedes vacans*) or of some operational hindrance (*sedes impedita*) the pro-vicar or pro-perfect must assume the entire administration of the vicariate or prefecture apostolic, and retain it until the Apostolic See has made other provisions. The pro-vicar or pro-prefect who succeeds in office must immediately appoint an ecclesiastical who shall succeed him in the event of his death or loss of jurisdiction. According to the provisions of canon 310, the pro-vicar or pro-prefect apostolic who succeeds in the administration of the vicariate or prefecture by the virtue of the law of canon 309 must as soon as possible inform the Apostolic See of the vacancy or operational hindrance. These provisional administrators, i.e., the pro-vicar and the pro-prefect, are ordinaries in their respective districts.[69]

Although they have no power at all during the period of the *sedes plena,* except such as is committed to them by their superiors,[70] canon 310 provides that, while the pro-vicar and the pro-prefect are taking charge of their respective district, namely, during the period of the vacancy or of some operational hindrance, they can make use of all the faculties, both the ordinary ones mentioned in canon 294 and the delegated ones which the vicar and the prefect apostolic had, unless they were given to the latter for the reason of some personal qualification. And canon 310 should be understood in the light of canon 66, § 2, which states that, unless they contain a direct statement to the contrary, or unless they were given to the vicar or the prefect apostolic on account of some personal qualification, the habitual faculties granted by the Holy See to the ordinaries mentioned in canon 198 do not lapse with the vacancy of the ordinaries' sees.

If during the lifetime of the vicar or the prefecct apostolic the Holy See has appointed a coadjutor with the right

[69] Canon 198, § 1.
[70] Canon 309, § 1.

of future succession to the vicar or the prefect apostolic, the coadjutor will immediately succeed to the office as a proper ordinary, and thereupon appoint his own pro-vicar or pro-prefect in the event of a future vacancy, or he will take charge of the district with full responsibilities and appoint an ecclesiastic as the pro-vicar and pro-prefect should do, in the event of some future operational hindrance. Even in the latter case, the coadjutor enjoys all the faculties of the pro-vicar or the pro-prefect apostolic, as is indicated in canons 310 and 66, § 2; in either case the coadjutor is an ordinary in his district.[71]

The Apostolic See may appoint an apostolic administrator to a vacant or impeded vicariate or prefecture apostolic.[72] An apostolic administrator may be given either permanently or for only a certain length of time. In either case, while he is holding the office, he is the ordinary of the district to which he has been appointed, and enjoys the rights, faculties, offices, and privileges which are determined in the document of his appointment of the Apostolic See, and, unless the document prescribes otherwise, the apostolic administrator in the vicariate or the perfecture apostolic enjoys all the rights, faculties, and privileges listed in canons 293-311 and 66, § 2, *exceptis excipiendis,* until the new vicar or prefect apostolic has taken canonical possession of the district.[73]

The fourth paragraph of canon 309 points to another provisional administrator for a vacant or impeded vicariate or prefecture apostolic. It states that if perchance it should happen that nobody was appointed as administrator either by the vicar or by the prefect apostolic, or by the pro-vicar or the pro-prefect apostolic, then the senior missionary present in the vicariate or the prefecture is to be considered delegated by the Apostolic See to assume the administration

[71] Canons 198, 355, § 1, and 353.

[72] Cf. canons 312 ff. Cf. also Paventi, *Breviarium*, pp. 85-86.

[73] Paventi, *Breviarium*, pp. 85-86; Vermeersch-Creusen, *Epitome*, I, n. 433, p. 342.

of the vacant (or impeded) vicariate or prefecture; seniority is determined from the letter of appointment of a missionary to the district; if several were appointed on the same date, the senior in the priesthood is preferred. Thus, by virtue of canon 198 and canon 310, the senior missionary has competence for the use of the ordinary and delegated faculties which his superior had, according to the norm of canons 66, § 2, and 311.[74]

Since a mission *sui iuris* has a status comparable to that of a prefecture apostolic, and its superior has the same rights, faculties, and duties as the prefect apostolic, as was seen above, the pro-superior will succeed in line with the indications given in canons 309-311, and will have the faculties according to the norms of canons 310 and 66, § 2, in the event of the vacancy (*sedes vacans*) or of some operational hindrance (*sedes impedita*) of the mission *sui iuris*. Likewise, the senior missionary will assume the administration of the mission in case the superior did not appoint the pro-superior in his lifetime.

B. *The Vicar Delegate* SEDE VACANTE *and* SEDE IMPEDITA

As seen in the foregoing, the vicar delegate in the vicariate apostolic, the prefect delegate in the prefecture apostolic, and the superior delegate in the mission *sui iuris* have an analogical canonical status comparable to that of the vicar general in a canonically erected diocese, in whatever relates to the latter's rights, faculties, and duties. According to the provisions of canon 429, however, the vicar general is the one who should take charge of the administration in the event of a *sedes impedita* in the ordinary's diocese, while according to the norm of canon 309 the pro-vicar is the one who should take charge of the administration in the event of a *sedes impedita* and *sedes vacans* in the quasi-diocese, i.e., the vicariate apostolic, without yielding place to the vicar delegate. Accordingly there arises the question whether the vicar delegate completely and entirely sup-

[74] Cf. Gérin, *Le Gouvernement des Missions*, pp. 203-205.

plants the pro-vicar, or whether his office continues both *sede impedita* and *sede vacante*.

For a proper solution of this question, the following should be observed. First of all, the canonical institution of the vicar delegate is based on the Circular Letter of December 8, 1919, of the Sacred Congregation for the Propagation of the Faith.[75] In this letter it is stated that according to canon 198 vicars and prefects apostolic have not the right to elect vicars general, as residential bishops have, but they have the power to appoint a delegate with power to be fixed in each case, and this delegate may be someone other than the pro-vicar mentioned in canon 309. From this statement it is clear that canon 309 has not been abrogated; rather, it leaves room for the existence of two offices, i.e., that of the vicar delegate, and that of the pro-vicar. Consequently, if the offices of the vicar delegate and the pro-vicar are combined in one and the same person, this ecclesiastic will succeed in the event both of the *sedes impedita* and of the *sedes vacans*. And this could prove the most practicable course if the shortage of personnel in the mission is considered. However, as it is stated, there still can be two persons for the said two offices, of whom one is the vicar delegate, and the other the pro-vicar in a given quasi-diocese. In this case, the pro-vicar is the one who, *sede vacante*, should take charge of the administration of the quasi-diocese, since the office of the pro-vicar exists for this exclusive purpose, as is stated in canon 309. Accordingly, the office of the vicar delegate ceases when the quasi-diocese becomes vacant, as does that of the vicar general when a vacancy occurs in the diocese.

In the event of an operational hindrance (*sede impedita*), the second paragraph of canon 309 in the present Code provides that, when the see of the vicar or the prefect apostolic is impeded in the manner described in canon 429, the pro-vicar or pro-prefect must assume the entire government of

[75] *AAS*, XII (1920), 120; *Sylloge*, n. 76; Bouscaren, *Canon Law Digest*, I, 144.

the quasi-diocese. In fact, however, canon 429 is concerned with the right of the vicar general in the event of the *sedes impedita,* and since the institution of the vicar general for the quasi-diocese was not in existence when the Code was promulgated, the Code singled out the pro-vicar, who directly corresponds to the vicar capitular in the canonically erected diocese, in the event of some operational hindrance (*sede impedita*). But after the promulgation of the Code the Apostolic See declared in the Circular Letter of December 8, 1919, which was addressed to all ordinaries to appoint a delegate, who should have the same jurisdiction, including the habitual power of executing papal rescripts and of making use of the special faculties which the Sacred Congregation for the Propagation of the Faith communicates to local ordinaries, in the same manner as the vicar general of a bishop has under the Code. In short, the vicar delegate was in practice to have all the jurisdiction in spiritual and temporal matters which the Code gives to a vicar general in a diocese. From this it follows that the ordinary, *sede impedita,* in the vicariate apostolic is the vicar delegate, while the ordinary, *sede vacante,* is the pro-vicar.[76] The two respectively enjoy the Decennial Faculties granted to their preceding ordinaries, but because of the fact that they lack the episcopal character they should make use of them as they appear in the *Formula Minor.*

[76] Cf. Ly-Yuh-Wen, *op. cit.*, pp. 33-34; Vromant, *De Personis,* n. 172, p. 196; Vermeersch-Creusen, *Epitome,* I, n. 429, p. 340; Conte a Coronata, *Institutiones Iuris Canonici,* I, n. 376, p. 447; S. Sipos, *Enchiridion Juris Canonici* (4. ed., Pecs, 1940), p. 237; *contra:* Jarre, "De Iis Qui Vicariatum vel Praefecturam Ap. Sede Vacante vel Impedita Regunt," *Antonianum,* III (1928), 207 and 358; Romani, *Institutiones Juris Canonici,* Vol. I (Romae, 1941), § 441; Wernz-Vidal, *De Personis,* n. 554, c), p. 699; Chenn-Tao Che, "De Normis Juridicis Continuitatis Regiminis Missionum Tuendae," *CpRM,* XXXVI (1957), 61-70; Chelodi, *Ius Canonicum, De Personis* (3. ed., Vicenza, 1942), § 183, pp. 283-284.

PART TWO

A COMMENTARY ON THE DECENNIAL FACULTIES NN. I-XXVIII IN THE *FORMULA MAIOR*

SECTION ONE

Faculties Concerning Sacraments and Sacred Rites: The Decennial Faculties NN. I-XXI in the *Formula Maior*

CHAPTER I

FACULTIES CONCERNING SACRAMENTS AND SACRED RITES, THE ADMINISTRATION OF WHICH REQUIRES *POTESTAS ORDINIS EPISCOPALIS*

ARTICLE I

Facultas II: FACULTY TO BLESS HOLY OILS WITH A LIMITED NUMBER OF MINISTERS

> *Conficiendi olea sacra cum numero ministrorum quos haberi contigerit; et si necessitas urgeat, etiam extra diem Coenae Domini.*[1]

This is the Faculty by virtue of which the ordinary in the missions may bless the holy oils with the assistance of any number of ministers available; in a case of necessity, the holy oils may be blessed even on a day other than Holy Thursday. The present Decennial Faculty is not included in the *Formula Minor*, and cannot be subdelegated. Corresponding to the present Decennial Faculty, *Facultas n. 8* of the faculties from the Congregation of Sacred Rites in *The Quinquennial Faculties, Formula IV*, reads as follows:

> *Benedicendi sacra olea cum eo presbyterorum et sacrorum ministrorum numero, quo pro loci rerumque adiunctis reperiri poterit, Feria V in Coena Domini (pro Episcopo celebrante)*.[2]

[1] Throughout this dissertation texts of the Decennial Faculties in the *Formula Maior* are taken from "Facultates Decennales Ordinariis Missionum S.C. de Propaganda Fide Concessae. Formula Maior," *Monitor Ecclesiasticus*, LXXV (1950), 353-361.

[2] Throughout this dissertation Latin texts of the Quinquennial Faculties, *Formula IV*, are taken from Eagleton's *The Quinquennial Faculties, Formula IV* (ed. 1948), and English texts (based upon the Latin texts of latest *Formula IV*, 1954-1959) from Bouscaren's *Canon Law Digest*, IV, 69-82.

The present Quinquennial Faculty is granted for the blessing of the holy oils with such a number of priests and ministers as, in view of the place and the circumstances, can be had, on Holy Thursday (for the Bishop celebrating).

SECTION 1. *Ex Iure*

Canon 734 prescribes that the holy oils which are required in the administration of several sacraments must have been blessed by the Bishop on the immediately preceding Holy Thursday. And for the blessing of these holy oils on Holy Thursday, according to the rubrics, twelve priests, seven deacons and seven subdeacons are required for the ceremony.[3] The consecrator must be a bishop, i.e., an ecclesiastic who has the episcopal character.

In procuring the number of priests as prescribed in the rubrics, the bishop is not limited to the priest-members of the cathedral staff. The Congregation of the Sacred Rites has issued responses indicating that secular priests subject to the bishop are to be summoned from parishes other than the cathedral.[4] In a case of necessity even regulars from within the territory of the bishop are to be called.[5] However, the bishop need not summon the priest who are at unreasonable distances which would have to be travelled by them, or who are needed by the parishes in which they

[3] *Pontificale Romanum Summorum Pontificum Iussu Editum, a Benedicto XIV et Leone XIII Pont. Max. Recognitum et Castigatum* (Ratisbonae-Neo-Eboraci-Cincinnati: Pustet, 1891), tit. *De Officio in Feria V. in Coena Domini.* Cf. *Decreta Authentica Congregationis Sacrorum Rituum, ex Actis Eiusdem Collecta Eiusque Auctoritate Promulgata sub Auspiciis Ss. Domini Nostri Leonis Papae XIII* (7 vols., Vols. I-V, Romae, 1898-1901; Vol. VI, Appendix, sub auspiciis Pii Papae X, Romae, 1912; Vol. VII, Appendix, sub auspiciis Pii Papae XI, Romae, 1927), n. 1660 [hereafter cited as *Decreta Authentica*].

[4] S.R.C., 18 Mart. 1679. Cf. Aloysius Gardellini, *Decreta Authentica Congregationis Sacrorum Rituum* (3. ed., 4 vols., cum appendicibus, Romae, 1856-1887), n. 2878 [hereafter cited as Gardellini, *Decreta Authentica*].

[5] S.R.C., 11 Nov. 1641. Cf. Gardellini, *Decreta Authentica*, n. 1354.

are stationed, or in similar circumstances which would render their assistance difficult.

SECTION 2. *Ex Facultate*

A. *Ex Facultate Quinquennali.*—The Quinquennial Faculty grants to the consecrator of the holy oils on Holy Thursday a dispensation from the law prescribed in the rubrics with respect to the number of priests and other ministers. Thus, by virtue of the present Quinquennial Faculty, the bishop may bless the holy oils on Holy Thursday with the number of sacred ministers available according to the place and circumstances. This provision cannot be interpreted to mean that the blessing of the holy oils may take place without any assistant priests. Two priests are indicated as the minimum in a response given by the Holy Office.[6] Hence, by virtue of the present faculty, the bishop may perform the ceremonies of the blessing of the holy oils with as many priests as are available—at least two, and with or without any number of deacons and subdeacons.[7]

The present Quinquennial Faculty needs a proportionate cause for its use, according to the norm of canon 84, § 1. Thus, if a sufficient number of sacred ministers be available, the said faculty cannot be used; however, it seems that if peculiar and unforeseen circumstances, such as extremely inclement weather or hindering accidents should arise, a bishop could use this faculty even though under ordinary circumstances a sufficient number of priests would have been available to him.[8]

The added phrase, *"pro Episcopo celebrante,"* indicates that this faculty is extended by the Congregation of Sacred Rites for use by the celebrating bishop. Thus, if another bishop, in a case of necessity, were asked to perform the

[6] S.C.S. Off., resp. 3 Aug. 1859. Cf. *Collectanea*, n. 1179.

[7] Cf. Reg. 40, R. J. in VI°: "Pluralis locutio duorum numero est contenta."

[8] Eagleton, *The Diocesan Quinquennial Faculties, Formula IV*, p. 139.

function of the blessing of the holy oils, he could make use of the present faculty, if all other provisions are fulfilled.[9] The same may be said of the vicar general, if he possesses the episcopal character, and performs the said function.

B. *Ex Facultate Decennali.*—The Decennial Faculty grants the bishop in the missions, who is the consecrator of the holy oils which are required in the administration of several sacraments, a twofold dispensation, i.e., one from the norm of canon 734 with respect to the date on which the holy oils are normally to be consecrated, and the other from the liturgical law in the *Pontifical Romanum* with respect to the number of ministers for the blessing of the holy oils on Holy Thursday, or on any day other than Holy Thursday.

As to the first dispensation, the bishop may bless the holy oils on any day other than Holy Thursday. By this is not meant that the bishop may do so as often as he needs the holy oils. Thus, inasmuch as Holy Thursday occurs once a year, he may do so only once on any day other than Holy Thursday, if there exists some urgent necessity for the oils. Consequently, there could be either an anticipated blessing or a postponed blessing of the holy oils. The anticipation of the blessing of the holy oils may take place in cases wherein the supply of the oils was destroyed in the damage caused by bombing, or fire, or flood, or from any other cause, and more oils are needed for confirmation, baptism, consecration, etc., and cannot be supplied by a nearby vicar apostolic, and the administration of the said sacraments and consecrations cannot be postponed until the next Holy Thursday. On the other hand, the postponement of the blessing of the holy oils may take place in case wherein for some good reasons, such as sickness, infirmity, absence, captivity, or exile, the bishop should be unable to celebrate Mass and to perform the sacred function in his quasi-diocese on Holy Thursday. A postponement may occur also when the bishop is unable to procure the minimum number of the ministers required for the consecration of the holy oils.

[9] S.R.C., 8 Iun. 1658. Cf. Gardellini, *op. cit.*, n. 1896.

Canon 734, § 2, provides that, if there is danger that the supply of the holy oils will give out, then more olive oil which has not been blessed may be added even repeatedly, but always in a quantity smaller than that of the holy oils. Thus, by the words, *"si necessitas urgeat,"* as they occur in the text of the Faculty, is meant that when the holy oils are needed for the administration of sacraments and for the consecration of sacred things, the blessing may take place when otherwise there are no holy oils on hand. If the holy oils are blessed on a day other than Holy Thursday, the ceremonies must be performed during the Mass of the current feast, but never outside or apart from the Mass.[10]

As to the second dispensation, the bishop may, by virtue of the present Decennial Faculty, bless the holy oils with a number of sacred ministers smaller than that which is prescribed in the rubrics of the *Pontificale Romanum,* if only such a smaller number of sacred ministers be available for the sacred function, on any day other than or on Holy Thursday. For the use of this faculty, however, a minimum number of two sacred ministers must be employed as is required also in the case of the Quinquennial Faculty; but they need not be priests, for the Decennial Faculty states: "... *cum numero ministrorum quos haberi contigerit,"* while the Quinquennial Faculty states: *"cum eo presbyterorum et sacrorum ministrorum numero. . . ."* Thus a deacon and a subdeacon, or two deacons, or also two subdeacons, may constitute the minimum number of sacred ministers required for the use of the present Decennial Faculty. Likewise this Decennial Faculty requires a proportionate cause less grave for its use than the Quniquennial Faculty does, since the phrase *"quos haberi contigerit"* is used in the former, while the phrase *"quo pro loci rerumque adiunctis*

[10] Cf. S.R. C., 19 Maii 1881—*Collectanea Constitutionum, Decretorum Indultorum ac Instructionum S. Sedis ad Usum Operariorum Apostolicorum Societatis Missionum ad Exteros,* selecta et ordine digesta cura Moderatorum Seminarii Parisiensis eiusdem Societatis (2. ed., Hongkong, 1905), n. 497 [hereafter cited as *Collectanea Sanctae Sedis,* Hongkong].

reperiri poterit" is used in the latter. The verb "*reperire*" implies a positive effort for the procurement of the prescribed number of priests and sacred ministers, while the verb "*contingere*" points simply to a readily available number.

ARTICLE II

Facultas III: FACULTY TO DELEGATE *Sacerdos Simplex* WITH POWER OF ADMINISTERING CONFIRMATION

> *Concedendi facultatem administrandi Confirmationis Sacramentum uni vel alteri ex suis sacerdotibus* (i.e., *omnino paucis et ita ut in eadem statione unus tantum sacerdos hanc facultatem habeat) in quacumque regione a sua residentia longe dissita, absente tamen quocumque Episcopo, servata Instructione "De Sacramento Confirmationis" in Appendice Ritualis Romani inserta.*

This concession authorizes for the ordinary in the missions the faculty of administering the sacrament of confirmation to one or two of his priests (at any rate to only a few, so that only one priest enjoys this faculty in the same station) in any district at a great distance from his own residence, when no bishop is available. The minister of the sacrament of confirmation should observe the *Instruction on the Sacrament of Confirmation,* inserted in the Appendix to the *Rituale Romanum.* This Decennial Faculty is *Facultas n. 2 in the Formula Minor,* and cannot be subdelegated in either the *Formula Maior* or the *Formula Minor. The Quinquennial Faculties, Formula IV,* do not include the present Decennial Faculty.

SECTION 1. *Ex Iure*

A. *In the Code of Canon Law.*—The ordinary ministers of valid confirmation are all bishops who have been formally consecrated,[11] and those of lawful confirmation are the local episcopal ordinaries for their own subjects and within their respective territories. Within their own territories

[11]Canon 782, § 1. Cf. Wernz-Vidal, *De Rebus,* Vol. I, n. 55, p. 59.

they can lawfully confirm even strangers, unless an explicit prohibition of their ordinaries forbids it.[12] In the diocese of another bishop, a bishop must have at least the reasonably presumed permission of the local ordinary, except when he confirms his subjects privately and without crozier and miter.[13]

The extraordinary minister of confirmation is a priest who either by the common law or by special indult of the Apostolic See has received the faculty of confirming. Those priests who by the common law have the faculty of confirming are the cardinals, the vicar and the prefect apostolic, and the abbot and the prelate *nullius*.[14] Now the superior of the mission *sui iuris* can, in view of a special declaration,[15] be said to have the same faculty of confirming. With the exception of the cardinals, these ecclesiastics can validly make use of the faculty only within the limits of their respective territory, and only during their term of office.[16]

Besides the above enumerated ecclesiastical prelates, a simple priest also can be an extraordinary minister of confirmation when he has obtained a special indult from the Apostolic See. Such an indult may come directly from the Apostolic See to an individual simple priest, or it may come through the local ordinary by way of an application of Special Faculties, such as were granted to the bishops and the priests of Latin America on April 30, 1929, by Pope Pius XI.[17] In principle, unless the indult explicitly provides otherwise, a priest of the Latin Rite, who has the special faculty to administer the sacrament of confirmation, can validly administer the sacrament of confirmation to Cath-

[12] Canon 783, § 1.

[13] Canon 783, § 2.

[14] Canons 232, § 1, and 782, § 2. These are all priests, i.e., ministers lacking the episcopal character; otherwise they are ordinary ministers of confirmation.

[15] Cf. *Sylloge*, nn. 146 and 187; *supra*, p. ?.

[16] Canon 782, § 3. Cf. S.C. de Sacr., instr., 20 Maii 1934—*AAS*, XXVII (1935), p. 11, n. 2; Bouscaren, *Canon Law Digest*, II, 185-186.

[17] Pius XI, Breve "*Litteris Apostolicis*," 30 Aprilis 1929—*AAS*, XXI (1929), 554-557; *Sylloge*, n. 145.

olics of his rite only; it is *nefas* for priests of the Oriental Rites, who have the faculty to administer the sacrament of confirmation together with baptism to infants of their own rites, to confirm infants in the Latin rite.[18]

B. *Ex Iure Universali Pontificali.*[19]—*Simple Priests as Extraordinary Ministers of Confirmation in Danger of Death.* Apart from the provision made in the Code, simple priests may, by virtue of a general indult of the Apostolic See, be extraordinary ministers of the sacrament of confirmation. The first decree containing such an indult was Pope Pius XII's Decree *"Spiritus Sancti munera"* of September 30, 1946. It was entitled *"Decretum de Confirmatione Administranda Iis, Qui ex Gravi Morbo in Mortis Periculo Sunt Constituti,"* and was issued by the Sacred Congregation for the Discipline of the Sacraments.[20] This decree contains a *Pontifical Universal Law,* which empowers all pastors and certain other priests of the Latin Rite, with no limitation of time or place, to confer confirmation[21] upon

[18] Canon 782, §§ 4 and 5.

[19] Cf. Henry J. Dziadosz, *The Provisions of the Decree* SPIRITUS SANCTI MUNERA: *The Law for the Extraordinary Minister of Confirmation,* The Catholic University of America Canon Law Studies, n. 397 (Washington, D.C.: The Catholic University of America Press, 1958), pp. 67-77 and 175.

[20] *AAS,* XXXVIII (1946), 349-354; Bouscaren, *Canon Law Digest,* III, 303-313. Cf. Dziadosz, *op. cit.,* pp. 178-187; John S. Quinn, *The Extraordinary Minister of Confirmation According to the Most Recent Decrees of the Sacred Congregations* (Romae: The Catholic Book Agency, 1951), pp. xiii-xvi.

[21] The indult contained in the Decree *"Spiritus Sancti munera"* is enjoyed by the following priests:

1. By general indult of the Holy See, the faculty to confer the Sacraments of Confirmation as extraordinary ministery (canon 782, § 2) [only in the case and under the conditions mentioned below] is given to the following priest and to them only:

a) To pastors who have a territory of their own, exclusive therefore of personal and family pastors unless these also have their own proper, even though cumulative territory;

b) To the vicars mentioned in canon 471 and to vicar administrators *(vicariis oeconomis)*;

c) To priests to whom the full care of souls *(plena animarum cura)*

the faithful who are staying in their territory, provided these faithful by reason of grave illness are in genuine danger of death from which it is foreseen that they will die.[22]

Since the general indult of the Decree *"Spiritus Sancti munera"* was not intended to be given to missionaries other than quasi-pastors in the missions,[23] the Sacred Congregation for the Propagation of the Faith issued the Decree *"Post latum,"* entitled *"De Confirmatione Administranda Iis, Qui ex Gravi Morbo in Periculo Mortis Sunt Constituti,"* on December 18, 1947.[24] Through the latter decree Pope Pius XII granted to all local ordinaries who depended on the Sacred Congregation for the Propagation of the Faith the power of an Apostolic Indult to give to all priests who are subject to them and have the care of souls the faculty validly to administer the sacrament of confirmation to the faithful who are within the territorial boundaries of the mission, and licitly to administer it in the place of residence of the bishop, provided there is no bishop present in that place who is not lawfully prevented from attending.

Both the Decree *"Spiritus Santic munera"* and the Decree *"Post latum"* were given *in forma specifica,*[25]but the for-

with all the rights and duties of pastors has been entrusted in an exclusive and stable manner in a definite territory with a determined church. (From Bouscaren, *Canon Law Digest,* II, p. 306. Cf. Dziadosz, *op. cit.,* pp. 81-101; Quinn, *op. cit.,* pp. 85-95.

[22] The Decree *"Spiritus Sancti munera,"* n. 2, states as follows: The aforesaid ministers can validly and licitly confer Confirmation themselves personally, only upon the faithful who are staying in their territory, including the persons who are staying in places which have been withdrawn from the parochial juristdiction; including, therefore, seminaries, guest-houses, sanitaria and other institutions of every sort, and religious Institutes howsoever exempt (c. 792); provided these faithful by reason of grave illness are in genuine danger of death from which it is foreseen that they will die.... (From Bouscaren, *Canon Law Digest,* III, 307). Cf. Dziadosz, *op. cit.,* pp. 116-142; Quinn, *op. cit.,* pp. 103-111.

[23] Cf. Dziadosz, *op. cit.,* p. 108.

[24] *AAS,* XL (1948), 41; Bouscaren, *Canon Law Digest,* III, 314.

[25] Cf. John R. Schmidt, *The Principles of Authentic Interpretation*

mer was given *in forma gratiosa,* while the latter was granted *in forma commissoria.*[26]

The recipients of the faculty to administer confirmation who are mentioned in the Decree *"Spiritus Sancti munera"* are pastors (including quasi-pastors), the vicars mentioned in canon 471, vicar administrators, and priests to whom the full care of souls (*plena animarum cura*) with all the rights and duties of pastors has been entrusted in an exclusive and stable manner in a definite territory with a determined church, while the faculty which was mentioned in the Decree *"Post latum"* may be given by the local ordinaries to all priests in the missions to whom the case of souls (*cura animarum*) has been entrusted, even if these are without the rights and duties of pastors or quasi-pastors, or without a definite territory with a determined church. The territorial boundary for the use of the faculty by the priest in the missions is the territorial extent of the diocese or quasi-diocese of the ordinary who grants him the said faculty by virtue of the Decree *"Post latum,"*[27] while the pastor mentioned in the Decree *"Spiritus Sancti munera"* may use the faculty to administer confirmation only within his parochial boundaries.

The Sacred Congregation for the Oriental Church, in turn, issued a decree, entitled *"De Sacramento Confirmationis Administrando etiam Fidelibus Orientalium Rituum a Presbyteris Latini Ritus, Qui Hoc Indulto Gaudeant, pro Fidelibus Sui Ritus,"* on May 1, 1948.[28] This Decree contained the Apostolic Faculty that whenever priests of the Latin rite in virtue of an indult can validly and lawfully administer the sacrament of confirmation to the faithful of

in Canon 17 of the Code of Canon Law, The Catholic University of America Canon Law Studies, n. 141 (Washington, D.C.: The Catholic University of America Press, 1941), p. 87.

[26] Michiels, *Normae Generales,* II, 287-289.

[27] Paventi, "Adnotationes," *Monitor Ecclesiasticus,* LXXV (1950), pp. 57-58.

[28] *AAS,* XL (1948), 422-423; Bouscaren, *Canon Law Digest,* III, 20-30.

their own rite, they can also administer it—provided it is clear that confirmation had not already been conferred after baptism, as is customary—to all the faithful of the Oriental rites whose spiritual care is committed to them according to the norm of the Apostolic Constitution *"Orientalium Dignitas"* of November 30, 1894.[29]

This Decree, which juridically is also to be considered as a *Pontifical Universal Law* because of its relation to the Decree *"Spiritus Sancti munera"* and its own specific approbation, extends to all Latin priests—provided these are empowered to confirm by an indult, either general or particular—the power to administer confirmation to certain members of the Oriental rites when certain conditions are verified.[30]

SECTION 2. *Ex Facultate*

The power given by virtue of *Facultas* III in the *Formula Maior* to the vicar and the prefect apostolic, and the superior of the mission *sui iuris,* is that of deputing one or two of his priests as extraordinary ministers of confirmation. However, the thus deputed extraordinary minister of confirmation differs from the extraordinary minister deputed by virtue of the Decree *"Spiritus Sancti munera"* or of the Decree *"Post latum"* for the former is deputed by means of a special faculty, but the latter, by way of a general indult; the former is deputed for the faithful under ordinary circumstances, i.e., for such as are in good health, but the latter is deputed for those who are in danger of death from a grave sickness; the former administers the ceremonies of confirmation in public and in a solemn manner, but the

[29] Article 9 of this Constitution provided that every Oriental who is living outside of the patriarchal territory shall be under the administration of the Latin clergy. Cf. *Fontes,* n. 627.

[30] Cf. Dziadosz, *op. cit.,* pp. 127-130; Quinn. *op. cit.,* pp. 117-121; Michael F. Diederichs, *The Jurisdiction of the Latin Ordinaries over Their Oriental Subjects,* The Catholic University of American Canon Law Studies, n. 229 (Washington, D.C.: The Catholic University of America Press, 1946), p. 86.

latter always in private in connection with the administration of the sacrament of extreme unction; the former faculty can be deputed to only one or two (or to a very few) priests in a mission, but the latter to as many priests as are set over quasi-parishes or residential stations.

The present Decennial Faculty to appoint an extraordinary minister of confirmation can be used by the ordinaries in the missions, *sede plena, sede impedita,* and *sede vacante,* respecetively.[31]

In general, the Decennial Faculties in the *Formula Maior* and the *Formula Minor* avail, *sede plena,* for vicars general in dioceses and in prelacies *nullius,* for vicars delegate in vicariates apostolic, for prefects delegate in prefectures apostolic, and for superiors delegate in missions *sui iuris,* but insofar as they may lack the episcopal character and do not receive mention in canon 782, and in the light of the norm of canon 210, they are not competent for the use of this particular Decennial Faculty.[32] But by virtue of this Decennial Faculty the vicar apostolic may depute the vicar delegate as an extraordinary minister of confirmation, if this is necessary.

Commentators are of the opinion that the phrase "*uni vel alteri* (i.e., *omnino paucis et ita ut in eadem statione unus tantum sacredos hanc facultatem habeat*)" has a relative meaning, so that "*uni vel alteri*" means "a few," the number of the extraordinary ministers depending upon the size of the ministers and the number of the faithful, and the phrase "*in eadem statione unus tantum*" implies a positive

[31] Canons 198 and 66, § 2. Cf. *supra,* pp. ?.

[32] Prot. N. 478/41. *Notificatio de Facultatibus Formulae Maioris et Minoris:* "... Quae facultates generales ad decennium conceduntur ... Ea ... atque competunt quoque Vicario Generali dioecesis et Prealaturae *nullius* (can. 66, § 2) ac Vicario Delegato in Missionibus, *exceptis excipientibus.*" See Paventi, *Brevis Commentarius,* p. 15. There is an answer from the Sacred Consistorial Congregation that the vicar general cannot depute an extraordinary minister for the administration of confirmation without a mandate from the episcopal ordinary, even in virtue of special faculties granted to ordinaries in Latin America. Cf. *AAS,* XXXI (1939), 224.

prohibition against deputing two extraordinary ministers for the mission if they have been appointed to one and the same station.[33]

As a papal provision for the deputing of simple priests as extraordinary ministers in Latin America, the Sacred Congregation of the Sacraments stated the following:

> *Ordinarii locorum deputare possunt, ad Sacramentum Confirmationis adminstrandum, sacerdotes quantum fieri potest in aliqua dignitate ecclesiastica constitutos vel munere Vicarii foranei fungentes; nunquam vero simplices sacerdotes commorantes illis in locis in quisbus praedictum Sacramentum administrandum erit. . . .*[34]

This could be also a practical direction for deputing extraordinary ministers of confirmation in quasi-dioceses, as well as in Latin America. The vicars apostolic can depute this extraordinary minister of confirmation only among his own priests (*ex suis sacredotibus*), but not among visiting priests nor among priests outside of his own mission. And he may depute the extraordinary minister habitually or *ad actum.*

As a condition for the deputing of the extraordinary minister of confirmation, the provision *"in quacumque regione a sua residentia longe dissita"* must be taken in the sense of referring not merely to the distance itself, but also to the difficulty of reaching a certain area because of the harsh climate, the laborious travel, the poor health of the vicar apstolic, and many other like reasons.[35] Another condition is that there be unavailable any bishop who is willing or able to administer confirmation as often as or as many times as the need demands. The condition mentioned in this

[33] Vermeersch, "De Formulis Facultatum," *Periodica,* XI (1922), p. (133); Iglesias, *Brevis Commentarius,* p. 33; Vromant, *Facultates Apostolicae,* p. 29; Winslow, *The Apostolic Faculties,* p. 36; Sartori, *Iuris Missionarii Elementa,* p. 87.

[34] *AAS,* XXI (1929), 555.

[35] Iglesias, *Brevis Commentarius,* pp. 33-34; Paventi, *Brevis Commentarius,* p. 18; Sartori, *Iuris Missionarii Elementa,* p. 87: "... In dubio lata interpretatio adhiberi potest."

paragraph are requisite simply for the lawfulness of the administration of confirmation.[36]

A thus deputed extraordinary minister must administer confirmation within the region committed to him according to the prescribed directives. These directives are contained to the Instruction of the Sacred Congregation of the Sacraments, which was issued on Pentecost Sunday, May 20, 1934.[37]

[36] Sartori, *loc. cit.;* Paventi, *loc cit.;* Vermeersch, "De Formulis Facultatum," *Periodica,* XI (1922), p. (114), d.

[37] "*Instructio pro Simplici Sacerdote Sacramentorum Confirmationis ex Sedis Apostolicae Delegatione Administrante*"—*AAS,* XXVII (1935), 11. Cf. *Appolinaris,* VIII (1935), 34-41; *Periodica,* XXVI (1935), 1829; Bouscaren, *Canon Law Digest,* II, 185-188; *Collectanea,* nn. 502, 940, 1539; Sartori, *Iuris Missionarii Elementa,* p. 88. The cited Instruction consists of three sections, of which the second section, entitled "The Discipline Introduced by the Code as Regards the Administration of Confirmation by a Simple Priest," consists of almost *verbatim* quotations of canons 732, 734, 766, 780, 781, 784-790, 793-800, and 1079. The only language of this section of the Instruction which is not already contained expressly in the canons themselves is the following: (1) The Instruction adds the following words to canon 781: "It is never lawful to administer Confirmation without chrism, or to receive the chrism from heretical or schismatical Bishops." (2) The Instruction adds the following explanation for the words *sufficienter instructus* of canon 786: "sufficiently instructed; that is, according to his capacity, upon the nature, dignity, effects, of the Sacrament, and the requisite dispositions for its worthy reception." The Instruction then adds: "According to an ancient practice in the Church, those who are to receive Confirmation should be fasting; and it would therefore be desirable that such a custom should be observed even now." (3) To canons 786 and 796 the following should be referred: Those who are to be confirmed must not present themselves for this Sacrament with dirty face or hair uncombed; but they should be dressed, as should the sponsors, simply and modestly. Women who are to receive the Sacrament or who are to act as sponsors must not come into the church decked in vain ornaments or with painted faces, but with all modesty and reverence. The third section of the same Instruction is entitled, "Rite to Be Observed by a Simple Priest Conferring the Sacrament of Confirmation." It consists of the rubrics and the texts of the rite, which may be read either in the official commentary, *Acta Apostolica Sedis,* Vol. XVII, page 19, or in new editions of the *Roman Ritual.* Cf. Bouscaren, *Canon Law Digest,* II, 187-188.

Article III

Facultas XIX: Faculty to confer Tonsure and Minor Orders on the Same Day

Conferendi, rationabili de causa, Ordines minores omnes simul, etiam cum prima tonsura.

This is the Faculty by virtue of which the ordinary in the missions may confer all the minor orders on one and the same day, or even all the minor orders together with the first tonsure on one and the same day, if there is any good reason to do so. It is *Facultas n. 18* in the *Formula Minor,* and cannot be subdelegated in virtue of either of the *Formulae.* The present Decennial Faculty is not included in *The Quinquennial Faculties, Formula IV.*

Section 1. *Ex Iure*

With respect to the interval for conferring the first tonsure and the minor orders, the first paragraph of canon 978 in the Code of Canon Law does not prescribe or even suggest intervals, but it is left to the prudent judgment of the bishop to determine what interval of time shall elapse between the first tonsure and the order of porter, as well as between the individual minor orders. However, in order to insure at least two intervals, the third paragraph of the cited canon declares that it is absolutely prohibited to confer the first tonsure and one of the minor orders, or all the minor orders collectively on a candidate on one and the same day, unless a special permission of the Roman Pontiff be obtained.[38] Three separate ordinations are thus contemplated by canon 978, since not only must the first tonsure be conferred separately, but also the minor orders themselves cannot be conferred conjointly.

The conferring of the first tonsure absolutely stands alone in law as a separate ceremony. There is no prohibitory clause in the law of the Code to forbid the conferring of two minor orders at each of two ordinations, or even of three at

[38] Wernz-Vidal, *De Rebus,* Vol. I, n. 222, pp. 286-289; Abbo-Hannan, *The Sacred Canons,* II, n. 978, pp. 108-110.

the first and of one at the second, or the reception of one minor order at the first ceremony and of the subsequent three minor orders at the second. It is entirely left to the decision of the bishop which plan he wishes to adopt. However, the custom of conferring the first tonsure first, then the orders of porter and lector, and finally those of exorcist and acolyte, appears as the most logical and balanced order, and this is widely adopted in the Latin Church.[39]

SECTION 2. *Ex Facultate*

The present Decennial Faculty gives to the mission ordinary the power to confer not only all the minor orders, but even the first tonsure together with the four minor orders on a candidate on one and the same day. It is clear from its context that the present faculty does not empower the mission ordinary to confer subdeaconship together with one or more of the minor orders, or two sacred orders upon a candidate on one and the same day.[40]

In order to make use of the present Decennial Faculty, the mission ordinary must have a reasonable cause, which need not be a *gravis causa* or any serious reason. Hence, interruption in the studies of the students, the necessity of a long journey for the ordination on the part of the ordinary or of the students, a busy schedule in missionary work on the part of the ordinary who confers the ordinations, etc., can serve as a reasonable cause.[41]

The present Decennial Faculty can be used by the mission ordinary, *sede plena, sede impedita,* and *sede vacante,*[42] for his own subjects and also for those who belong to other

[39] John M. Gannon, *The Interstices Required for the Promotion to Orders,* The Catholic University of America Canon Law Studies, n. 196 (Washington, D.C.: The Catholic University of America Press, 1944), pp. 26-29.

[40] Cf. canon 978, §§ 2 and 3.

[41] Cf. Sartori, *Iuris Missionarii Elementa,* p. 106; Vermeersch, "De Formulis Facultatum," *Periodica,* XII (922), p. (117); Vromant, *Facultates Apostolicae,* n. 53, p. 55.

[42] Cf. canon 66, §2; canon 957, § 2; *supra.*

ordinaries, if he has obtained dimissorial letters from the ordinaries who deputed him for the ordinations. Insofar as the power to confer the first tonsure and the minor orders is given, in the law, to the incumbent of the offices of the vicar apostolic and of the prefect apostolic (and the superior of a mission *sui iuris* through a special provision) when these prelates lack the episcopal character,[43] the vicar delegate, the prefect delegate, and the superior delegate cannot make use of it, *sede plena,* even if the latter are ordinaries in their respective missions. The same must be said for the vicar general in the mission *non de facto, sed de iure,* who lacks the episcopal character. The vicar general, the vicar delegate, the prefect delegate, or the superior delegate must have the special mandate of his superior before he may issue dimissorial letters to commit the ordinations of his subjects to the ordinary of another mission.[44]

ARTICLE IV

Facultas XX: FACULTY TO CONFER MAJOR ORDERS ON FERIAL DAYS EVEN CONTINUOUSLY

Conferendi, iusta de causa, omnes sacros Ordines, etiam Presbyteratum, diebus ferialibus etsi continuis.

This is the Faculty which dispenses the mission ordinary from the observance of the interstices and times prescribed for the conferring of sacred orders. According to the norm of canon 957, vicars and prefects apostolic, and also abbots and prelates *nullius,* if they have episcopal consecration, are regarded as equivalent to the bishops of dioceses in the matter of ordination; if they are not consecrated bishops, they may nevertheless confer the first tonsure and the minor orders in the territory of their jurisdiction, but only during their term of office; they may thus ordain not only their own secular subjects who are domiciled in their territory, but also others who have been presented to them by means

[43] Canon 957, § 2.
[44] Canon 958, § 1, 2°.

of the proper dimissorial letters from other local ordinaries. In the light of this canon, the vicar apostolic, the prefect apostolic, the abbot *nullius*, the prelate *nullius*, and the superior of the mission *sui iuris* who lack the episcopal character can confer only the first tonsure and the four minor orders, but they cannot confer the major orders. Nevertheless these enumerated ordinaries may issue dimissorial letters even for the major orders.[45] Thus, corresponding to the present Decennial Faculty in the *Formula Maior, Faculty n. 19* in the *Formula Minor* is given to those ordinaries who lack the episcopal character. The text reads as follows: *"Permittendi iusta de causa, ut suis subditis omnes sacri Ordines, etiam Presbyteratus, diebus ferialibus etsi continuis conferri possint."* Both Faculty XX in the *Formula Maior* and *Faculty n. 19* in the *Formula Minor* cannot be subdelegated, and are not included in the *Quinquennial Faculties, Formula IV.*

SECTION 1. *Ex Iure*

As to the interstices for conferring sacred orders, canon 978, § 2, states that, unless the necessity or the utility of the diocese in the bishop's judgment demands otherwise, there must be at least one year's interval between the last minor order, namely, the order of an acolyte, and subdeaconship; and at least three months between subdeaconship and deaconship as well as between deaconship and priesthood. The third paragraph of the cited canon states that, without special permission of the Roman Pontiff, minor orders and subdeaconship, or any two major orders, cannot be conferred on a candidate on one and the same day, all contrary custom being condemned.[46]

The calculation of one year or three months for the inter-

[45] Canon 958, § 1, 4°.

[46] A special Apostolic Indult, dispensing from the law of the interstices for the conferring of major orders was granted to all the archbishops and bishops of Ireland, on April 15, 1931, *ad quinquennium*, and it was renewed on May 13, 1936. Cf. Bouscaren, *Canon Law Digest*, II, 239.

vals between the major orders may be reckoned according to either the civil calendar (as well as the juridical calendar) or the liturgical calendar. Thus a candidate who was ordained an acolyte on Holy Saturday may receive subdeaconship on the following Holy Saturday, even though 365 days may not have elapsed; again, a period between the ember seasons may be taken as the equivalent of three months, even though it does not amount to ninety days.[47]

As to the time prescribed for the conferring of the major orders, canon 1006 rules that major orders are to be conferred during Mass on Ember Saturdays, on the Saturday before Passion Sunday, and on Holy Saturday, but for a grave reason the bishops may have these ordinations also on any Sunday or Holy Day of Obligation. The Code of Commission was asked whether the words, *festo de praecepto,* in canon 1006, § 3, include also feast days which have been suppressed in the Church by the Code, and the Commission replied in the negative.[48] On the other hand, there is an opinion that canon 1006, § 3, includes holy days which by the law of the Code are fundamentally binding everywhere (*quae ubique per se ex Codice vigent*), but are transferred by indult to the following Sunday, such as the Feast of Corpus Christi,[49] and thus major orders may be conferred on such holy days.[50]

An Apostolic Indult which permits the conferring of major orders outside the times fixed by law, i.e., on feasts of the double rite of the first or second class, though not of obligation, and on the last Saturday of May and the first two Saturdays of June, at the close of the scholastic year, has been granted since May 18, 1940, to the archbishops and bishops of the United States.[51]

[47] Cf. canon 1006. See Gannon, *op. cit.*, pp. 30-40.

[48] Pont. Comm., 15 Maii, 1936—*AAS*, XXVIII (1936), 120.

[49] Canon 1247, § 1.

[50] (Private) Apostolic Delegation, U.S., 13 May, 1938. Cf. Buscaren, *Canon Law Digest*, II, 248-249.

[51] (Private) S.C. de Sacr., 18 Maii, 1940. Cf. Bouscaren, *Canon Law Digest*, II, p. 249. This indult is to be renewed every three years;

SECTION 2. *Ex Facultate*

A. *Faculty XX in the* FORMULA MAIOR. By virtue of the present Decennial Faculty, the mission ordinary, if he has the episcopal character, may confer any of the major orders, i.e., subdeaconship, deaconship, or priesthood, even on any ferial day throughout the year, and furthermore the ordinary may confer two of the above enumerated major orders on two consecutive ferial days, or even three of the major orders, likewise on three consecutive ferial days.[52]

In order to make lawful use of the present Decennial Faculty, the ordinary must have a *"iusta causa,"* which cause is less weighty than a *"gravis causa."* The present Faculty is not barred from lawful use *"nisi necessitas aut utilitas Ecclesiae, iudicio Episcopi, aliud exposcat,"* for this condition as set in canon 978, § 2, is a more exacting condition than the simply requisite *"iusta causa."* Thus the inconveniences entailed by sending the candidates to the vicar apostolic, or any notable interruptions in the studies of the candidates, or the difficulties of travel for the vicar apostolic, etc., may be enumerated among the many just causes that warrant the use of the present faculty.[53] And this faculty can be used anywhere in favor of the ordinary's own subjects, and also in favor of the subjects of other ordinaries, provided the latter have sent to him the called for dimissorial letters for the particular ordination.[54]

the last renewal was made on March 10, 1958. Cf. Bouscaren, *Canon Law Digest,* IV, 316. In 1952, the archbishops and bishops of the United States enjoyed for that year an Apostolic Indult to confer major orders on each of the Saturdays of May and June. Cf. *op. cit., loc. cit.*

[52] Vermeersch, "De Formulis Facultatum," *Periodica,* XI (1922), p. (137); Sortori, *Iuris Missionarii Elementa,* p. 106. According to Vermeersch, the clause *"diebus ferialibus etsi continuis"* supplants the former *"diebus tamen non continuis."* Cf. *loc. cit.*

[53] Sortori, *Iuris Missionarii Elementa,* p. 106; Vromant, *Facultates Apostolicae,* n. 54, p. 56; Winslow, *The Apostolic Faculties,* p. 63.

[54] Cf. S.C. de Sacr., 15 Aug. 1909—*AAS,* I (1909), 656. Cf also Vromant, *loc. cit.*

B. *Faculty n. 19 in the* FORMULA MINOR. Since the prefect apostolic and the superior of a mission *sui iuris* who lack the eipscopal character are not empowered with the right to confer the major orders either by the general law or by apostolic indult, they cannot confer the major orders, but they may, by virtue of the present Decennial Faculty, permit their own subjects (whether these stay within or go outside the territory of the prefect apostolic or of the superior of a mission *sui iuris*) to be ordained to major orders, even on any ferial day throughout the year, or even on two or three consecutive ferial days, if necessary, whenever two or three different major orders are to be conferred.

Regarding the spiritual exercises which are to precede the reception of the major orders, the response of the Sared Congregation of the Sacraments with the *Animadversiones* of the Secretary, under date of May, 1928,[55] may be consulted with profit in connection with the use of the foregoing faculty.

ARTICLE V

Facultas XXI: FACULTY TO DISPENSE FROM THE LACK OF THE CANONICAL AGE FOR THE PRIESTHOOD

> *Dispensandi, gravi tamen de causa, cum suis utriusque cleri diaconis super defectu aetatis decem et octo mensium, ut ad S. Presbyteratus ordinem promoveri possint, dummodo idonei sint, et dimidiam partem quarti anni cursus theologici rite* (can. 976, § 3) *absolverint.*

This is a faculty by virtue of which the mission ordinary may dispense his subjects from the lack of canonical age for ordination to the priesthood. This is Faculty n. 20 in the *Formula Minor,* and cannot be subdelegated according to either of the two Formulae. The present Decennial Faculty is not included in *The Quinquennial Faculties, Formula IV*.

[55] *AAS*, XX (1928), 359; Bouscaren, *Canon Law Digest*, I, 489-592.

SECTION 1. *Ex Iure*

According to the present legislation in the Code of Canon Law, subdeaconship is not to be conferred before the completion of the twenty-first, and deaconship not before the completion of the twenty-second, and the priesthood not before the completion of the twenty-fourth year in the candidate's life.[56] Although the candidates for the major orders may possess the canonical age, neither seculars nor religious as candidates are to be promoted to subdeaconship until towards the end of the third year of theology, to deaconship until after the commencement of the fourth year, and to the priesthood until after the first semester of the fourth year.[57] And canon 2374 prescribes that a man who maliciously presents himself for ordinations before he has attained the canonical age is automatically suspended from the order unlawfully received.

After the promulgation of the Code of Canon Law, however, religious either by standing privilege or by temporary indult, have often obtained the faculty of ordaining their candidates to the priesthood after the third year of theology, the student completing his studies in the year after ordination. But on October 27, 1923, the Sacred Congregation for Religious warned superiors that in using such a faculty they have a grave moral obligation to comply with the following conditions: (1) to see that the *ordinandi* complete the fourth year of theology and (2) not to assign them to pastorates, preaching, the hearing of confessions, or work outside the community which would hamper their

[56] Canon 975, § 1. Regarding the requisite canonical ages before the promulgation of the Code of Canon Law, cf. c. 5, D. LXXVIII; c. 14, X, *de temporibus ordinationum et qualitate ordinandorum,* I, 11; c. 3, *de aetate et qualitate et ordine praeficiendorum,* I, 6, in Clem.; Conc. Trident., sess. XXIII, *de ref.*, c. 12; Benedictus XIV, const. "*Etsi pastoralis,*" 26 Maii 1742—*Fontes*, n. 328; instr. "*Eo quamvis tempore,*" 4 Maii 1745, § 19 ff.—*Fontes*, n. 357; S.C. Ep et Reg., *Alberna*, 5 Aprilis 1593—*Fontes*, n. 1480; S.C. C., *Fanen.*, 7 Sept. 1954 —*Fontes*, n. 2272.

[57] Cf. canon 976, §§ 2 and 3. Cf. Gannon, *op. cit.*, pp. 31-40.

studies.[58] In 1945 the same Sacred Congregation further limited the use of this faculty in favor of only those candidates who had completed their twenty-sixth year of life. This was applicable everywhere for religious who possessed a temporary indult in this matter.[59] On the other hand, an apostolic indult which allowed for a dispensation in all cases wherein the discrepancy did not exceed one year with reference to the requisite age was granted to all the archbishops and bishops in Ireland *ad quinquennium* for the first time on April 15, 1931,[60] and it was renewed *ad quinquennium* on May 13, 1936.[61]

SECTION 2. *Ex Facultate*

The present Decennial Faculty is concerned only with the possible dispensation of deacons from the lack of the canonical age required for their ordination to the priesthood. Therefore this faculty does not avail for dispensing the required studies for the priesthood, nor can it be used for candidates who are to be promoted to deaconship or to subdeaconship. Thus the ordinary in the missions, by virtue of the present Decennial Faculty, may dispense deacons who are to be promoted to the priesthood from the lack of the canonical age to the extent of eighteen months; in other words, the said ordinary may promote to the priesthood deacons under his own jurisdiction who in their lives have completed at least twenty-two years and six months.

[58] S.C. de Rel., declar., 27 Oct. 1923—*AAS*, XV (1923), 549; Bouscaren, *Canon Law Digest*, I, 486. Cf. Vermeersch, "De Formulis Facultatum," *Periodica*, XI (1922), p. (155).

[59] Woywod-Smith, *A Practical Commentary*, n. 918, p. 586.

[60] *Irish Ecclesiastical Record*, 5. series, XXXVII (1931), 642 [hereafter cited as *I.E.R.*].

[61] *I.E.R.*, 5. series, XLVII (1936), 657. A similar faculty had been granted to the archbishops and bishops of the United States on June 6, 1918. This was the faculty to ordain the candidates to the priesthood after the completion of the third year of theology, but it was granted for use only during World War I.—(Private) S.C. Stud., 6 Iunii 1918. Cf. *Ecclesiastical Review*, LIX (1918), 410; Bouscaren, *Canon Law Digest*, I, 483.

"Cum suis utriusque cleri diaconis." The mission ordinary may make use of the present Decennial Faculty in behalf of any deacons who have been incardinated or assigned to his vicariate or prefecture apostolic or mission *sui iuris*, whether they be secular or religious, and regardless of where they are pursuing their studies. The ordinary may use this faculty even in behalf of a deacon who is an exempt religious, provided that the latter has obtained a domicile or is attached to a house in the vicariate, in the prefecture apostolic, or in the mission *sui iuris* of the ordinary.[62]

"Gravi tamen de causa." The present Decennial Faculty can be used only when there exists a grave reason, such as the shortage of priests in the territory, or the urgent need for the employment of special aptitudes as possessed by a particular deacon, and thus it cannot be used for the mere convenience of either the ordinary or the candidate. Besides the extant necessity for such a dispensation, there must be present also the requisite fitness in the candidate for the priesthood, and furthermore the candidate must have completed the first semester of his fourth year of theology in the manner prescribed in canon 1364 and canon 1365, § 1, in a seminary or in some institution qualified as such.[63]

In order to judge properly regarding the fitness of the candidate for the priesthood, the ordinary will profitably consult the Instruction of the Sacred Congregation of the Sacraments, "On the Testing of Candidates before They Are Promoted to Orders," of December 27, 1930,[64] the Instruction of the Sacred Congregation for Religious, "On the Clerical and Religious Training of Members Who Are Called to the Priesthood, and on the Test to be Made before the

[62] Cf. Sartori, *Iuris Missionarii Elementa*, p. 107; Paventi, *Brevis Commentarius*, p. 30.

[63] Cf. canon 976, § 3.

[64] S.C. de Sacr., instr., 27 Dec. 1930—*AAS*, XXIII (1931), 120; Bouscaren, *Canon Law Digest*, I, 463-473. Cf. Vermeersch, "Annotationes [ad Instructionem de Scrutino Ordinandorum S. Congregationis de Sacramentis]," *Periodica*, XX (1931), 255.

Reception of Orders," of December 1, 1931,[65] and the circular letter of the Sacred Congregation of the Sacraments, entitled "Circular Letter to the Most Excellent Local Ordinaries in Which Is Emphasized the Examination of Candidate Which Is to be Made before They Are Promoted to Orders," of December 27, 1955.[66]

[65] S.C. de Rel., instr., 1 Dec. 1931—*AAS*, XXIV (1932), 74; Bouscaren, *Canon Law Digest*, I, 473-483. Cf. Vermeersch, "Annotationes [ad Instructionem de Formatione Clericali et Religiosa Alumnorum ad Sacerdotium Vocatorum, deque Scrutino ante Ordinum Susceptionem Peragendo]," *Periodica*, XXI (1932), 188.

[66] S.C. de Sacr., litt. circ., 27 Dec. 1925—Prot. n. 5374/55. Cf. Bouscaren, *Canon Law Digest*, IV, 303-315.

CHAPTER II

FACULTY CONCERNING THE BLESSING OF BAPTISMAL WATER

Facultas I: FACULTY TO GRANT THE USE OF THE PARTICULAR FORMULA FOR THE BLESSING OF BAPTISMAL WATER

> *Concedendi suis missionariis facultatem benedicendi aquam baptismalem ea breviori formula, quae in Appendice Ritualis Romani continetur.*

Through this faculty there is conceded to the mission ordinary the power to grant to his missionaries the option to bless the baptismal water in the shorter form, as it is found in the Appendix of the *Rituale Romanum.* The same faculty is conceded in the *Formula Minor* under Faculty n. 1. In both the *Formula Maior* and the *Formula Minor* this faculty cannot be subdelegated. This faculty is not contained in the *Quinquennial Faculties, Formula IV.*

SECTION 1. *Ex Iure*

Canons 755-758 regulate the rites and ceremonies of solemn baptism, and canon 2 enunciates the principles that all liturgical laws previously enacted for the celebration of the Holy Mass, for the recitation of the Divine Office, for the administration of the sacraments and sacramentals, and for the conduct of other sacred functions retain their force, except insofar as the Code explicitly corrects these laws.

According to the norm of canon 757, water blessed especially for this purpose shall be used in solemn baptism. And the time to bless this water is fixed in the liturgical laws, which prescribe that the baptismal water is to be blessed on the Vigil of Easter during the ceremonies of this Vigil according to the formula in the *Missale Romanum.*[1]

[1] Cf. S.C.C., decr., 10 Iunii 1922—*AAS*, XV (1923), 225. The Missale *Romanum* prescribes a simmilar blessing also on the Vigil of Pentecost. However, the recent Missal text for Holy Week states explicitly

A short formula for the blessing of the baptismal water is found in the *Rituale Romanum*[2] and it serves its use in case it becomes necessary to bless the baptismal water outside the Vigil of Easter.[3]

SECTION 2. *Ex Facultate*

The present Decennial Faculty, of its very nature, facilitates the rite of the blessing of the baptismal water in the circumstances recounted in the third paragraph of canon 757. The formula for the blessing of the baptismal water, with which the present Decennial Faculty is concerned, is not the above mentioned long and short formulas, but the "*brevior formula*" or the shorter formula, which can be found on the first page of the Appendix to the *Rituale Romanum.* The ordinary may grant this faculty habitually to his missionaries, who in turn may use the same whenever solemn baptisms are to be administered and the baptismal water is lacking for any reason, as well as for reasons described in the third paragraph of canon 757.[4]

"*Concedendi suis missionariis.*" The mission ordinary may grant the present Decennial Faculty habitually to all the missionaries, i.e., to priests and deacons, whether seculars or religious, who are engaged in the sacred ministry in his mission, even to such as are temporarily, but legitimately, engaged in the said work there, whether they be his subjects or not.[5] There is no reason for forbidding the

that on the Vigil of Pentecost the lessons and prophecies, the blessing of the baptismal water, and the litanies, are omitted. Cf. *Ordo Hebdomadae Sanctae Instauratus* (ed. typica, Romae: Typis Polyglottis Vaticanis, 1956), *Instructio,* n. 16.

[2] *Rituale Romanum Pauli V Pontificis Maximi Iussu Editum, Aliorumque Pontificum Cura Recognitum, atque Auctoritate Pii Papae XI ad Normam Codicis Iuris Canonici Accommodatum* (Neo-Eboraci: Benziger Brothers, 1945), Tit. II, cap. 8.

[3] Canon 757, § 3.

[4] Paventi states that this faculty may be used "*etiam nulla causa exigente.*" See his *Brevis Commentarius,* p. 16.

[5] Cf. Paventi, *loc. cit.;* Sartori, *Iuris Missionarii Elementa,* p. 84; Winslow, *The Apostolic Faculties,* p. 33.

mission ordinary to grant the faculty *per modum actus* to "*mere hospites seu peregrini,*" provided these are committed by the mission ordinary to administer solemn baptisms and the baptismal water must be blessed.[6]

As to the use of this faculty on the Vigil of Easter, if the sacred functions of the Vigil are performed and there is a baptismal font, the long formula for the blessing of the baptismal water in the *Missale Romanum* must be used; if the sacred functions are not performed, and yet baptismal water needs to be blessed, the shorter formula to which the present Decennial Faculty refers may be used.[7]

[6] Paventi, *loc. cit.; contra:* Vromant, *Facultates Apostolicae*, n. 32, p. 26; Sartori, *loc. cit.*

[7] Sortori, *loc. cit.*

CHAPTER III

FACULTIES CONCERNING THE CELEBRATION OF MASS

ARTICLE I

Facultas IV: FACULTY TO GRANT THE USE OF THE PORTABLE ALTAR, ETC.

Permittendi ut Missa celebrari possit, in casu necessitatis, super altari portatili; etiam sine ministro, et sub dio, et in navi, dummodo, debitis cautelis adhibitis, nullum adsit irreverentiae periculum, et locus decens sit; etiam si altare sit fractum vel sine Reliquiis Sanctorum; et praesentibus haeretics, schismaticis, infidelibus et excommunicatis, si aliter celebrari non possit; atque ut Missa inchoari queat una hora post mediam noctem.

This is the faculty whereby the mission ordinary may, in a case of necessity, allow priests to celebrate Mass on a portable altar; even without a server; outside of a church and on shipboard, if the proper precautions are employed against any danger of irreverence, and the place is decent; even on a broken altar stone or on an altar stone not containing the relics of Saints; in the presence of heretics, schismatics, infidels, and excommunicated persons, if otherwise Mass cannot be celebrated; and finally, to start celebrating Mass immediately upon one hour after midnight. This is Faculty n. 3 in the *Formula Minor,* and cannot be subdelegated. This faculty is not included in *The Quinquennial Faculties, Formula IV.*

PRELIMINARY NOTES

The present Decennial Faculty deals with dispensations from several canons and liturgical laws which have reference to the celebration of Holy Mass. The present faculty will be considered under several headings below. However, the following principles are applicable throughout the faculty:

(1) Since the exercise of this faculty does not require the episcopal character on the part of the one who uses it and is not reserved exclusively to the bishop, the present faculty is given to the vicar apostolic, the prefect apostolic and the superior of a mission *sui iuris* and is available also to the vicar delegate, the prefect apostolic, and the superior delegate of a mission *sui iuris*. Hence, these ordinaries in the missions can make use of the present Decennial Faculty for themselves or permit priests to do the same as they do by virtue of this faculty.

(2) Since this faculty does not explicitly envision a permission to be granted only to his missionaries (*suis missionariis*), the mission ordinary may grant this faculty to any or all of the missionaries laboring in his mission and to those of his subjects who are absent, and even to a newly assigned missionary destined for that mission, though he have not yet taken up residence in the place of his appointment.[1] Priests who have received this faculty from the ordinary in the mission can also use it outside his territory,[2] provided that the place of the celebration of the Mass is subject to the Sacred Congregation for the Propagation of the Faith.

(3) *"In causa necessitatis."* These words may be understood as meaning when otherwise one would be obliged to omit the celebration of Mass. Even if one wants to celebrate Mass merely *"devotionis causa,"* this constitutes a sufficient reason for the use of this faculty. The phrase, *"si aliter celebrari non possit,"* explains the condition that apart from the use of the faculty the priest would be deprived of Mass.

(4) This faculty can be granted habitually.

SECTION 1. FACULTY TO GRANT THE USE OF THE PORTABLE ALTAR

A. *Ex iure.*—In the Code of Canon Law, although the

[1] Paventi, *Brevis Commentarius*, p. 19; Vormant, *Facultates Apostolicae*, n. 36, p. 32; Winslow, *The Apostolic Faculties*, p. 94; Vermeersch, "De Formulis Facultatum," *Periodica*, XI (1922), p. (130).

[2] Cf. *Ephemerides Iuris Canonici*, III (1947), 243 ff.

privilege of the portable altar and that of a domestic (or private) oratory have much in common, they are not identical privileges.[3] The Code speaks of the privilege of the portable altar in canon 822. Its third paragragh determines the meaning of the said privilege as it imports the faculty of the celebrating of Mass anywhere, in a respectable and suitable place, but not at sea, and this necessarily implies the celebration of Mass on an altar stone. Its second paragraph states that this privilege is conceded either by law or by an indult obtainable only from the Holy See.

In law, the privilege of the portable altar—without taking into consideration the celebration of Mass at sea—is enjoyed only by the cardinals of the Holy Roman Church,[4] the residential bishops and titular bishops,[5] the abbots and prelates *nullius,*[6] the apostolic administrators,[7] and, finally, the vicars and prefects apostolic.[8] By virtue of Pope Pius X's *motu proprio* of February 21, 1905,[9] and of Pope Pius XI's Constitution *"Ad incrementum"* on August 15, 1934,[10] the same privilege is enjoyed by a very limited number of persons holding ecclesiastical dignities and charged with important duties in the Roman Curia, including the Most Reverend Protonotaries Apostolic *de numero participantium.* Vicars and prefects apostolic who are not consecrated as bishops have, by virtue of canon 308, the same privileges as the protonotaries *de numero participantium,* one of which privileges is the privilege of the portable altar. However, the privilege of vicars and prefects apostolic is restricted, so that it lasts only for the term of their office and is effective only within their territory.

[3] Thomas J. Welsh, *The Use of the Portable Altar,* The Catholic University of America Canon Law Studies, n. 305 (Washington, D.C.: The Catholic University of America Press, 1950), pp. 54-56.

[4] Canon 239, § 1, 7°.

[5] Canon 349, § 1, 1°.

[6] Canon 323, § 1.

[7] Canon 315.

[8] Canons 294, § 1, 308.

[9] *ASS,* XXXVII (1905), 491.

[10] *AAS,* XXVI (1934), 497.

As stated in canon 822, § 3, the privilege of the portable altar permits the celebrating of Mass in any decent and appropriate place, except at sea. The last phrase, *"non tamen in mari,"* of the cited canon, however, does not simply indicate the restriction of the use of the privilege of the portable altar. In fact, the privilege of the celebrating of Mass at sea and that of the portable altar are *per se* different privileges. This is clear from the text of canon 239, § 1, in which the privileges of cardinals of the Holy Roman Church are enumerated,[11] and from the practice of the Holy See.[12] In law, the privilege of saying Mass at sea is enjoyed by cardinals of the Holy Roman Church,[13] and residential bishops and titular bishops only.[14]

The Privilege of the Portable Altar for Priests. In virtue of canon 822, § 4, local ordinaries and major superiors of exempt religious can, for a just and reasonable cause, give to their priests permission for celebrating Mass outside of a church or oratory on a consecrated altar stone in a decent place, but never in a bedroom; the permission can be given only in an extraordinary case and *per modum actus,* i.e., in individual cases, not habitually.[15]

An apostolic indult to use the portable altar is available also for priests. The Instruction of the Sacred Congregation of the Sacraments on October 1, 1949, in Part II, "On Asking for the Privilege of a Portable Altar," pointed out that the said Congregation usually grants to priests the privilege of a portable altar for reasons of *real necessity* or *evident utility,* and exclusively or principally for the benefit of religious worship.[16] According to the Instruction, the

[11] Cf. canon 239, § 1, 7° and 8°.

[12] Cf. E. J. Mahoney-L. L. McReavy, *Priests' Problems* (New York-Chicago-Cincinnati-Boston-San Francisco: Benziger Brothers, Inc., 1957), pp. 86-87.

[13] Canon 239, § 1, 8°.

[14] Canon 349, § 1, 1°; canon 239, § 1, 8°.

[15] Welsh, *op. cit.*, pp. 60-90.

[16] S.C. de Sacr., instr. *"Quam plurimum"*—*AAS,* XLI (1949), 493-511.

principal cases, and those which most frequently occur, concern priests having the care of souls, either among the faithful living in remote localities which churches are either lacking or a great distance away, or in countries of heretics or schismatics, where the faithful are few and scattered, and are unable to assist at Mass unless it is said outside of sacred places or in the open air. Other reasons for a granting of the use of a portable altar are some great religious or even civil festivities which are to be celebrated by a great throng of people for whom there would not be room in the church, the celebration of a Eucharistic Congress, etc. For the personal and exclusive benefit of the priest, this privilege is granted only because of illness.

The same Instruction defines *"honestus ac decens locus"* of canon 822, § 3, by stating that an *appropriate* place demands security and roominess, so that the Mass may be offered safely and conveniently without any danger of profanation or of the spilling of the Precious Blood from the chalice, and that a *decent place* looks to the character of the location, that is, to the exclusion of someone's usual sleeping place, or any other place not befitting the dignity of so great a sacrifice. When applying for the indult of a portable altar, the ordinary must make a careful investigation according to the points delineated in the Instruction and describe all the circumstances with entire accuracy in the petition, which then is to be sent to the Sacred Congregation of the Sacraments. The ordinary must also furnish a recommendation for the petition, made personally by the bishop himself or by the prelate who is his successor in office.[17]

B. *Ex Facultate.*—The present Decennial Faculty, first of all, grants to the mission ordinary who is not a consecrated bishop the privilege to celebrate Mass at sea, and extends for him the privilege to use the portable altar even outside of his mission, and, secondly, it empowers the mission ordinary, whether he be a consecrated bishop or not, to permit *per mo-*

[17] *Ibid.*, n. 9, *e.*

dum habitus his missionaries to use the portable altar, i.e., to celebrate Mass, anywhere, even in the open air and at sea.

"Et sub dio, . . . dummodo, debitis cautelis adhibitis, nullum adsit irreventiae periculum. . . ." The use of the portable altar in the open air by the mission ordinary is granted in canon 822, § 3, because he can, by the privilege granted him by law, celebrate Mass anywhere in a respectable and suitable place, except at sea; and the mission ordinary may, by virtue of the privilege given to him in canon 822, § 4, permit his missionaries to celebrate Mass in the open air.[18] Thus the difference between the privilege granted in law and the present Decennial Faculty in regard to permitting the use of the portable altar in the open air lies in the fact that the mission ordinary can, by virtue of the former, permit it only *per modum actus,* while he can, by virtue of the latter, permit it *per modum habitus.*

When Mass is celebrated in the open air, the necessary safeguard must be taken for the preventing of any irreverence, or of any disturbance from the elements of nature; for that purpose, screens should be placed around the altar for the proper protection of the Sacred Species; if possible, a roof, by way of a canopy, should be constructed over the altar.

"Et in navi, dummodo, debitis cautelis adhibitis, nullum adsit irreverentiae periculum. . . ." The use of the portable altar at sea is permitted in law to cardinals of the Holy Roman Church, to residential bishops, and to titular bishops, but not to other prelates. Hence, it is forbidden in law for all priests and all mission ordinaries who are not consecrated bishops. But by virtue of the present Decennial Faculties all mission ordinaries may celebrate Mass at sea and may give this faculty to their missionaries, even *per modum habitus.* In case the Mass is offered on shipboard at sea, or on an inland waterway, river, or lake, etc., proper precautions must be employed against any danger of ir-

[18] Cf. canons 1249 and 66, § 3.

reverence to the Sacred Species. In the present *Formula Maior* (and in the *Formula Minor*) the clause *"dummodo mare sit tranquillum,"* which Formula III of 1920[19] had, is omitted. The sense is the same, however, and the use of the faculty on shipboard is to be determined according to the absence or the presence of the danger of irreverence to the Sacred Species. Prudence will forbid the celebration of Mass on shipboard during a severe storm or whenever the waves are so rough as to make likely the spilling of the contents of the chalice.

"Et locus decens sit." This condition as imposed in the faculty requires that the place be suitable and becoming for the Holy Sacrifice. A private cabin or stateroom on shipboard may be utilized in the absence of a more suitable place.[20] Since the clause which in canon 822, § 4, forbids the celebration of Mass in a bedroom is not included in the present faculty, and since the present faculty deserves a broad interpretation, a bedroom *per se* is not excluded in the use of the present Decennial Faculty. In fact, on various occasions the permission to celebrate Mass in a bedroom has been granted by the Sacred Congregation for the Propagation of the Faith;[21] and in many instances a bedroom would be the only place where Mass could be celebrated by the missionary. Canon 823, § 1, forbids the celebration of Mass in the churches of heretics and schismatics, even though such churches were at one time properly consecrated or blessed. However, the Holy Office permitted the saying of Mass in Malacca in a garrison chapel wherein Protestant services were habitually held,[22] and the use of churches in which both Catholics and Protestants held services at dif-

[19] Vermeersch, "De Formulis Facultatum," *Periodica*, XI (1922), p. (130).

[20] Cf. *Collectanea*, II, p. 421, fotnote. Cf. also Vermeersch, *ibid.*, pp. (82)-(83).

[21] Cf. *Collectanea*, nn. 746; 172; 411, ad 4. Cf. Mahoney-McReavy, *Priests' Problems*, p. 89.

[22] S.C.S. Off., 5 Iun. 1889—*Collectanea*, n. 1707.

ferent hours.[23] In short, a "*locus decens*" is a place "*ubi christiani convocantur vel convocari possunt ad orandum*"[24]

SECTION 2. THE CELEBRATION OF MASS ON AN ALTAR STONE WITH A FRACTURE OR NOT CONTAINING THE RELICS OF SAINTS

A. *Ex Iure.*—According to the norm of canon 1200, § 2, both the immovable altar and the movable altar, i.e., the portable altar stone, lose their consecration: (1) if they are considearbly broken, and (2) if the relics are removed, or if the cover of the sepulcher is broken or removed. The third paragraph of the same canon rules that a slight fracture of the cover does not induce a loss of the consecration and any priest can fill the crack with cement. If the stone slab was momentarily separated from its support, it can be reconsecrated by way of a very short formula, which was published by the Congregation of Sacred Rites, September 9, 1920.[25]

On the other hand, according to the prescription of canons 882 and 1199, to allow for the celebration of Mass the altar must be consecrated according to the laws of the liturgy. Conversely, Mass cannot be said on a non-consecrated altar or on a desecrated altar. And from ancient times permission to celebrate Mass on an altar stone not containing the relics of Saints, or on a considerably broken altar stone, was never given to anyone under any circumstance.[26]

B. *Ex Facultate.*—"*Et si altare sit fractum vel sine Reliquiis Sanctorum.*" By virtue of the present Decennial Faculty, missionaries can be permitted to celebrate Mass on an altar stone which is considerably broken, or from which the relics have been removed, so that it needs to be reconsecrated or replaced, in case the defect cannot be repaired in time and the repaired altar stone cannot before its use be reconse-

[23] S.C.S. Off., 13 Iun. 1634—*Collectanea*, n. 75.

[24] S.C. de Prop. Fid., 29 Febr. 1836—*Collectanea*, n. 846. It is there stated that Mass cannot be celebrated in a pagan temple. Cf. also Mahoney-McReavy, *Priests' Problems*, p. 89.

[25] *AAS*, XII (1920), 449.

[26] Sartori, *Iuris Missionarii Elementa*, p. 90.

crated[27] by means of the short formula, i.e., the "*Ritus seu Brevior Consecrationis Altaris,*" in the Appendix to the *Rituale Romanum,* or cannot before its use have another altar stone substituted for it (in case of considerable fracture).[28]

C. *The Use of the* ANTIMENSIUM LATINUM.—Besides the present Decennial Faculty, there exists a special indult applicable in favor of missionaries. On March 12, 1947, a decree was issued by the Congregation of Sacred Rites and was published in the *Ephemerides Iuris Canonici.* Through this decree missionaries were informed of the privilege of using in certain circumstances the so-called *Antimensium.*[29] This is described as a linen cloth, of the size of a corporal, blessed by the ordinary; the relics are enclosed in a small bag, sewn in the right top corner of the linen cloth, and certified as such by the ordinary. Missionaries are allowed to make use of the faculty only in cases in which they are satisfied in conscience that there is no church or public or private oratory available, and that it is very inconvenient to carry or procure an altar stone.[30]

For the use by missionaries application for this faculty must be made to the Sacred Congregation for the Propaga-

[27] Cf. *Facultas XXXII* in the *Formula Maior:* "Conferendi uni alterive i.e. paucis ex suis sacerdotisbus in casu necessitatis facultatem consecrandi, iuxta formam in Pontificali Romano praescriptam, calices, patenas et iuxta formulam breviorem altarium lapides, adhibitis tamen oleis ab Episcopo catholico benedictis [*Facultas n. 31* in the *Formula Minor:* this faculty cannot be subdelegated].

[28] Cf. I. Pauwels, "Annotationes [ad Ritum et Formulam Breviorem in Consecratione Altarium Quae Amiserunt Consecrationem]," *Periodica,* X (1921), 237.

[29] Xaverius Paventi, "Quaesitionis de Iure Missionali, n. 4. "De Antimensio Latino," *Ephemerides Iuris Canonici,* III (1947), 249-254. Cf. canons 822, § 1, and 823, § 2; Mahoney-McReavy, *Priests' Problems,* p. 90. According to Mahoney-McReavy, this faculty was first granted to ordinaries in Mexico, in 1929, and during World War II was enjoyed by army chaplains.

[30] Rescript permitting the *Antimensium Latinum* of S. C. Prop Fid., 8 March, 1950—Prot. n. 982/50. Cf. Bouscaren, *Canon Law Digest,* III, 361.

tion of the Faith by the mission ordinary for his own mission, and the faculty can only be *regularly* granted for those places which come under the jurisdiction of the Sacred Congregation for the Propagation of the Faith.[31] The same faculty is available also for those missionary priests who are subject to the Sacred Congregation of Religious in those places which do not come under the jurisdiction of the Sacred Congregation for the Propagation of the Faith, but where roads and vehicles are insufficient.[32] For the validity of the blessing of the *Antimensium Latinum,* the ordinary must use the prescribed formula,[33] and the local episcopal ordinary may lawfully bless it within and outside of their territories, and the vicar and the prefect apostolic, and also the superior of a mission *sui iuris* may bless it only within their respective territory and during the term of their office.[34]

SECTION 3. THE CELEBRATION OF MASS WITHOUT A SERVER

A. *Ex Iure.*—Canon 813, § 1, prescribes that the priest is not to say Mass unless he has a server who serves and answers him. The law requiring a server, commonly agreed to be a grave obligation in itself, is contained in the Decretal of Gregory IX,[35] and repeated in the rubrics of the *Missale Romanum.* All moralists and canonists are agreed that the obligation is grave in itself. The server at Mass must not be a woman, unless no male server can be had, and if she serves

[31] The Sacred Congregation for the Oriental Church grants the faculty of unsing the Greek *antimensium* in the territories over which it has jurisdiction.

[32] S.C. Rel., 8 Febr. 1955—Prot. n. 14703/54. Cf. Bouscaren, *Canon Law Digest,* IV, 266-267.

[33] This formula can now be found in *Ephemerides Iuris Canonici,* III (1947), 251-252; Bouscaren, *Canon Law Digest,* III, 362; IV, 267-268; Mahoney-McReavy, *Priests' Problems,* p. 90; *Monitor Ecclesiasticus,* LXXV (1950), 378-379.

[34] Eduardus F. Regatillo, *Interpretatio et Iurisprudentia Codicis Iuris Canonici* (3. ed., Santander: "Sal Terrae," 1953), pp. 334-335.

[35] C. 6, X, *de filiis presbyterorum ordinandis vel non,* I, 17.

she is to stay at a distance when answering the prayers and is not in any way to approach the altar. However, the Sacred Congregation of the Sacraments in the Instruction of October 1, 1949,[36] stated that according to the authorities there are only four cases in which, in the absence of an apostolic indult, Mass may be celebrated without a server, namely: (1) when it is necessary to consecrate in order to administer Viaticum to a sick person; (2) when it is necessary to celebrate in order to enable priest and people to satisfy the precept of hearing Mass; (3) in time of epidemics when otherwise the priest would have to refrain for a notable time from celebrating Mass, and, finally, (4) when after Mass has begun the server for any reason leaves, even before the Consecration or even before the Offertory, in which case the reverence due to the Holy Sacrifice requires that it be continued even in his absence.[37]

Outside of the above cited four cases, canon 813 is modified only by way of apostolic indult, which is given especially in mission lands. In the indults which have been granted by the Sacred Congregation of the Sacraments for the celebrating of Mass without a server, there is always added a clause requiring that care be taken *"ut ad mentem canonis 813, nedum pueri edoceantur de modo inserviendi S. Missae sed etiam fideles ipsaeque mulieres addiscant quomodo possint Missae inservire legendo responsiones sacerdoti celebranti reddendas,"*[38] along with the further proviso, *"dummodo aliquis fidelis Sacro assistat."* In the same Instruction it is pointed out that the latter clause cannot be modified, because of Pope Pius XII's order.[39] Thus, since the Instruction of 1949, the priest is not allowed to say Mass without a server *"devotionis causa,"* without a special indult from the Sacred Congregation of the Sacraments. Even if he

[36] *AAS*, XLI (1941), 506-508; Bouscaren, *Canon Law Digest*, III, 334-336.

[37] Bouscaren, *loc. cit.* For the qualifications of a server, see the cited Instruction, nn. 3-5.

[38] *AAS*, XLI (1949), 508.

[39] *Loc. cit.*

has the indult, he may use the indult only "*dummodo aliquis fidelis Sacro assistat.*"[40]

B. *Ex Facultate.—"Permittendi ut Missa celebrari posit, in casu necessitis . . . etiam sine ministro.*" This is an explicit exception to canon 813 and the above cited Instruction of 1949. When the Instruction stated that canon 813 and the rules contained in the same Instruction are modified only by way of apostolic indult, which is given especially in mission lands, it meant Faculty IV of the *Decennial Faculties, Formula Maior.*

As to the clause of the Instruction of 1949: "*nuper vero Sanctitas Sua aliam clausulam indulto litandi Missam sine ministro inserendam praecepit, nempe 'dummodo aliquis fidelis Sacro assistat,' cui nullimode derogari praestat,*" it is applicable only for future indults which may be given, and it does not, in its nature, have any retroactive juridical force. Moreover, the said clause is applicable only for the indult which the Sacred Congregation of the Sacraments may issue to permit the celebration of Mass without a server. However, the present faculty is one of the Decennial Faculties which are defined as *privileges outside the law* and this calls for a *broad interpretation,* according to the principles regulating the interpretation of privileges. Furthermore, the Sacred Congregation of the Sacraments does not enjoy direct jurisdiction over the matter of the general faculties for missionaries, such as the Decennial Faculties. Hence, until the Sacred Congregation for the Propagation of the Faith utilizes in any way this restriction, "*dummodo aliquis fidelis Sacro assistat,*" the Instruction does not affect the present Decennial Faculty.[41] Thus the words "*sine ministro*" can be interpreted in the liberal sense, i.e., "without anyone being present at all," or "with no one present at all." And the ordinary could not impose the restriction of the Instruction when he permits his mis-

[40] Cf. Mahoney-McReavy, *Priests' Problems,* pp. 82-84.

[41] Cf. Cappello, *Periodica,* XXXVIII (1949), 420; J. de Reeper, *A Missionary Companion* (Westminster, Md.: Newman Press, 1952), pp. 31-32; Paventi, *Breviarium,* p. 42.

sionaries to celebrate Mass without a server by virtue of the present Decennial Faculty.[42]

The present Decennial Faculty can be used also "*devotionis causa*" on ferial days,[43] if the conditions are verified. In which case the *Confiteor* is said only once,[44] the "*vobis fratres*" and "*vos fratres*" in the *Confiteor* may be omitted;[45] the priest should say the *Misereatur* and *Indulgentiam* only once, and "*nostri*" instead of "*vestri*" in the *Misereatur*. The celebrant himself makes all the responses usually made by the server; in the *Suscipiat*, however, he should say "*manibus meis*" instead of "*manibus tuis*."[46]

SECTION 4. THE CELEBRATION OF MASS IN THE PRESENCE OF HERETICS, SCHISMATICS, INFIDELS, AND THE EXCOMMUNICATED

A. *Ex Iure*.—The Code of Canon Law does not forbid the celebration of Holy Mass in the presence of heretics, schismatics, and infidels, but does so in case of the presence of an *excommunicatus*. Canon 2259 states that every excommunicated person is deprived of the right to assist at the divine offices, but not at the preaching of the word of God; if an *excommunicatus toleratus* assists passively, it is not necessary to expel him; an *excommunicatus vitandus* should be expelled, or if he cannot be expelled then the divine service must be stopped, provided it can be done without grave inconvenience; from active assistance, which entails some participation in the celebrating of the divine offices, not only an *excommunicatus vitandus* is to be barred, but also every excommunicated person after a declaratory or condemnatory sentence, or whose excommunication is otherwise notroious.[47]

[42] *Collectanea*, n. 1270.
[43] Sartori, *Iuris Missionarii Elementa*, p. 89.
[44] *Decreta Authentica*, n. 3368, ad 1.
[45] *Ecclesiastical Review*, XXXVII (1906), 657.
[46] Cf. *Ritus Servandus in Celebratione Missae*, VII, 7.
[47] Cf canon 2197.

B. *Ex Facultate.—"Permittendi ut Missa celebrari possit ... et praesentibus haereticis, schismaticis, infidelibus et excommunicatis, si aliter celebrari non possit."* The present Decennial Faculty allows the priest to say Mass even if an *excommunicatus vitandus* be among those present, on condition that otherwise he would not be able to celebrate Mass, and that all dangers, such as ridicule, indifference, disturbances, etc., are foreseen as excluded during the celebration of Mass, and the Faculty leaves further room for the *excommunicatus toleratus* to be allowed to be present at Mass, provided that his presence will not cause scandal for others.[48]

SECTION 5. FACULTY TO PERMIT THE CELEBRANT TO BEGIN MASS IMMEDIATELY ONE HOUR AFTER MIDNIGHT

A. *Ex Iure.*—According to the norm of canon 821, Mass shall not be begun earlier than one hour before dawn (*aurora*), or later than one hour after midday. On Christmas Day only the conventual or the parochial Mass may be begun at midnight, but no other Mass, apart from an apostolic indult. In all religious houses or pious houses having an oratory with the faculty of reserving the Blessed Sacrament there habitually, one priest may say at midnight on Christmas three Masses according to the liturgy of the day, or only one.

However, since the Decree of the Restoration of the Solemn Paschal Vigil as issued by the Congregation of Sacred Rites, on February 9, 1951,[49] the Mass for Easter Morning can be started at midnight between Holy Saturday and Easter Sunday for the same reason, and according to the

[48] *Collectanea,* nn. 447 and 1123. Cf. Sartori, *Iuris Missionarii Elementa,* p. 91; Winslow, *The Apostolic Faculties,* p. 44. Winslow suggests that regarding the presence of heretics, schismatics, infidels, and the excommunicated at divine services, the ordinary may lay down any regulations that he may deem fitting or opportune. Cf. *loc. cit.*

[49] *AAS,* XLIII (1951), 128. Cf. *AAS,* XLIV (1952), 48.

same manner, as the midnight on Christmas Day. Pope Pius XII in his Constitution *"Christus Dominus,"* on January 6, 1953,[50] granted the general faculty to local ordinaries to permit the celebration of Mass in the evening on Holy Days of obligation, on the first Friday of each month, on occasions of solemnity, etc. And such an evening Mass should not be begun before four o'clock in the afternoon. Thus the foregoing Decree and the Constitution of Pope Pius XII bring notable modifications.

As to the indults granted by the Holy See for beginning the celebration of Mass before the canonical hour, i.e., the celebration of Mass at any hour after midnight, they were granted often for various reasons and in various manners, i.e., *per modum actus* and *per modum habitus*, by the Congregation of Sacred Rites.[51]

B. *Ex Facultate.—"Permittendi . . . atque ut Missas inchoari queat una hora post mediam noctem."* The use of the present Decennial Faculty permits missionaries to anticipate the canonical time of the celebration of Mass for which canon 822 makes provisions, and allows the missionaries to begin one hour after midnight, the time to be computed according to the norm enacted in canon 33, § 1. The use of the faculty requires that there be some necessity for doing so,[52] e.g., to get an early start on a long journey, to make an early departure to insure arrival at one's destination before the intense heat of midday, to facilitate train or boat connections, or to serve the convenience of the local fatihful who want to begin their work in the early morning, or for any other sufficient reason.[53]

[50] *AAS*, XLV (1953), 15. Cf. Bouscaren, *Canon Law Digest*, IV, 269-277.

[51] Woywod-Smith, *A Practical Commentary*, n. 720, pp. 439-441.

[52] Cf. Vromant, *Facultates Apostolicae*, n. 37, 7), p. 36.

[53] Paventi, *Brevis Commentarius*, p. 19; Vromant, *loc. cit.*, footnote n. 2; Winslow, *The Apostolic Faculties*, p. 44.

ARTICLE II

Facultas V: FACULTY TO ALLOW THE CELEBRATION OF MASS WITH ONE LIGHT OR WITHOUT ANY LIGHTS

Permittendi ut Missa celebrari possit cum uno lumine cuiusvis generis, dummodo cera apum desit; nec non permittendi ut absque luminibus celebrari possit, in casu tamen verae necessitatis, et graviter onerata conscientia ipsius Ordinarii.

This is the Faculty by virtue of which the mission ordinary can permit the celebration of Mass with simply one light of any kind, if no beeswax is obtainable; he can also permit the celebrating of Mass even without any lights in a case of real necessity, and with a grave responsibility resting on the conscience of the ordinary. This faculty is *Facultas n. 4* in the *Formula Minor,* and cannot be subdelegated. *The Quinquennial Faculties, Formula IV,* do not include this Decennial Faculty.

SECTION 1. *Ex..Iure*

This faculty concedes the power of granting various dispensations from liturgical laws in regard to the candles, both as to their number and their quality, prescribed for the celebration of Mass. According to the *Rubricae Generales Missalis,* at least two candles must be burning on the altar during the celebration of Mass,[54] and according to the decrees of the Congregation of Sacred Rites these candles must be of pure beeswax.[55] Candles of stearine, paraffin, or tallow are not allowed on or immediately around the altar, either as substitutes for the beeswax candles[56] or in addition to the number of beeswax candles prescribed, either for Mass or for Benediction.[57] Two lighted candles are required

[54] *Rubricae Generales Missalis,* XX, *De Praeparatione Altaris, et Ornamentorum eius.* Cf. canon 2.

[55] *Decreta Authentica* (16 Sept. 1843), n, 2865; (4 Sept. 1875), n. 3376, ad III; (30 Iun. 1910), n. 4257, ad 5.

[56] *Decreta Authentica,* n. 3063.

[57] *Ibid.,* n. 4257, ad 5.

for a Low Mass which is strictly private and which is celebrated by any priest of lesser rank than a bishop.[58] Although electric, oil, or gas lights have been permitted for use in the sanctuary, the above mentioned general laws for the celebration of a Low Mass have not been modified. The latest decree on the matter, "*Urbis et Orbis,*" of August 18, 1949,[59] retains the same general laws.

The words "candles made of pure beeswax," however, must be understood as meaning "candles made of pure beeswax '*saltem in maxima parte*' or at least for the greater portion."[60] And the ordinary is to determine what exact proportion of pure wax is to constitute this "*in maxima parte*" beeswax.[61] In most places it appears that "*maxima pars*" is taken to be 60-75 per cent beeswax, and "*maior vel notabilis quantitas*" to be at least 51 per cent beeswax.

Regarding the violation of these norms, moralists generally agree with Cappello that it is a grave sin to celebrate Mass without any light; it would be a venial sin to celebrate Mass with one candle made of pure beeswax and another made of other material; and, finally, if there is no danger of scandal, it would be a venial sin to celebrate Mass with two oil lights.[62]

[58] *Ibid.*, nn. 1131, ad 21; 2583, ad 6; and 3262, ad 18.

[59] *AAS*, XLI (1949), 476; Bouscaren, *Canon Law Digest,* III, 518-518.

[60] S.R.C., decr. "*Plurium dioecesium,*" 4 Dec. 1904—*Decreta Authentica* n. 4147.

[61] *Loc. cit.* Cf. Harold E. Collins, *The Church Edifice and Its appointments* (Philadelphia: The Dolphin Press, 1936), p. 123; Adrian Fortescue, *The Ceremonies of the Roman Rites Described* (7. ed., revised by O'Connell, London: Burns, Oates and Washbourne, 1947), p. 7; Van der Stappen, *Sacra Liturgia* (3. ed., 5 vols., Mechliniae: H. Dessain, 1911-1915), Vol. III, p. 90. q. 59; J. B. O'Connell, *The Celebration of Mass* (new ed. revised, 3 vols. in one, Milwaukee: The Bruce Publishing Co., 1956), pp. 218-219; Erwin L. Sadlowski, *The Sacred Furnishings of Church,* The Catholic University of America Canon Law Studies, n. 315 (Washington, D.C.: The Catholic University of America Press, 1951), pp. 94-97.

[62] Cf. Felix M. Cappello, *Tractatus Canonico-Moralis de Sacramentis,* Vol. I, *De Sacrementis in Genere, de Baptismo, Confirmatione*

SECTION 2. *Ex Facultate*

"Cum uno lumine cuiusvis generis." By virtue of the present Decennial Faculty, the mission ordinary can permit his missionaries to celebrate Mass with one light of any type whatever. Thus, oil (vegetable and mineral as well as fat), gas, and electric lights, etc., are *per se* permissible in compliance with the requirement of a light for the celebration of Mass. In order to permit this, the ordinary must have a reasonable cause, i.e., "although neither beeswax nor oil is entirely lacking, yet, in view of their high cost"[63] it is not conveniently obtainable. Thus, the moral impossibility of obtaining pure beeswax suffices for the permission to be made operative.[64]

"Ut Missa absque luminibus celebrari possit." When olive oil, stearine candles, or any other substance, liquid or solid, suitable for lighting purposes, is not available, the ordinary can permit his missionaries to celebrate Mass without any light whatsoever burning on the altar. But, this becomes permissible only in case of a *"vera necessitas,"* e.g., when there is need to administer Holy Viaticum, to celebrate Mass on a holy day, or to enable the faithful to fulfill the paschal precept, or to renew the Blessed Sacrament in the tabernacle, or on a weekday when the priest is visiting his faithful in stations, or even when the faithful have been deprived of Holy Mass for many weeks or months because of the lack of materials for the light prescribed for the celebration of Mass.[65] A grave responsibility rests on the conscience of the mission ordinary to see that Mass is

et Eucharistia (6. ed., Taurini; Marietti, 1953), n. 728, pp. 689-690 [hereatfer cited as *De Sacramentis*, I].

[63] Cf. *AAS*, XLI (1949), 476; Bouscaren, *Canon Law Digest*, III, 518.

[64] Sartori, *Iuris Missionarii Elementa*, p. 93; Vromant, *Facultates Apostolicae*, n. 38, p. 37; Vermeersch "De Formulis Facultatum," *Periodica*, XI (1922), p. (132).

[65] Vromant, *Facultates Apostolicae*, n. 38, p. 37; Winslow, *The Apostolic Faculties*, pp. 45-46; Paventi, *Brevis Commentarius*, p. 19; Sartori, *loc. cit.*

never celebraed without any light—except in cases of genuine necessity, and then only when no substance suitable for lighting purposes is available.

The mission ordinary can use this faculty, as well as permit his missionaries to use this faculty, *per modum habitus.*[66]

Article III

Facultas VI: Faculty to Allow Purifying the Chalice with Water Alone

> *Permittendi ut in utraque purificatione calicis aqua tantum adhiberi possit, dummodo tamen extrema sit vini penuria.*

This is the Faculty by virtue of which the mission ordinary can permit his missionaries to use water for both ablutions of the chalice, if the supply of altar wine be extremely low. This is *Facultas n. 5* in the *Formula Minor*, and it is not included in *The Quinquennial Faculties, Formula IV.* This faculty cannot be subdelegated.

Section 1. *Ex Iure*

According to the *Ritus Servandus* in the *Missale Romanum,* the celebrant of Mass must take only wine for the first ablution of the chalice, and wine and water for the second ablution.[67] Moralists agree that in general a priest would be guilty of no more than venial sin if he used water only for both ablutions of the chalice.[68]

There was, however, an indult, issued by the Congregation of Sacred Rites, which relaxed this liturgical precept, i.e., the Roman Congregation, in view of the peculiar circumstances of the time, published on May 12, 1944, the following Decree:

[66] Cf. *Animadversiones* attached to the *Formula Maior.*

[67] *Ritus Servandus in Celebratione Missae,* X, *De Oratione Dominica et Aliis usque ad Factam Communionem,* ad 5.

[68] St. Alphonsus Liguori, *Theologia Moralis,* Lib. VI, n. 408; Cappello, *De Sacramentis,* I, n. 766, 3°, p. 719.

> ... For as long as these circumstances continue, [His Holiness] graciously permits that the purifications and ablutions of the chalice, which are to be made in the Mass according to the rubrics, first with wine and afterward with wine and water, may be made with water only, in those places where, according to the judgment of the ordinary, a scarcity of wine is already felt or is foreseen in the future, all things to the contrary notwithstanding.[69]

This general indult is no longer in effect.

SECTION 2. *Ex Facultate*

In virtue of the present Decennial Faculty, the mission ordinary can permit his missionaries to use water for both ablutions of the chalice, on condition that "a scarcity of wine is already felt or is foreseen in the future." Such a scarcity could arise because of the difficulty of supply or the high cost of wine in the missions,[70] and it ordinarily exists in the missions. The scarcity of wine can be habitual, e.g., during a war, a long interruption in the import, etc., and actual, e.g., when the priest is outside of his residential station or quasi-parish.[71]

The present Decennial Faculty can be used by the mission ordinary as well as by his missionaries, even when they celebrate Mass only *"devotionis causa."*[72] Thus, for the use of this faculty, no necessity of the celebration of the Mass is required on the part either of the celebrant or of the faithful.

ARTICLE IV

Facultas VII: FACULTY TO ALLOW THE USE OF INCENSE IN A SIMPLE HIGH MASS

> *Permittendi thurificationem in Missis cantatis a solo celebrante absque ministris, dummodo duo*

[69] This English translation of the Decree is taken from Bouscaren, *Canon Law Digest*, III, 357; *AAS*, XXXVI (1944), 154.

[70] Vromant, *Facultates Apostolicae*, n. 39, p. 38.

[71] Sartori, *Iuris Missionarii Elementa*, p. 93.

[72] Sartori, *loc. cit.;* Paventi, *Brevis Commentarius*, p. 20.

> *saltem clerici superpelliceo induti Missae inserviant.*

This is the Faculty by virtue of which the mission ordinary can permit his missionaries to use incense in the *Missa cantata,* celebrated by the celebrant without ministers, if at least two clerics vested in surplice are serving the Mass. This is *Facultas n. 6* in the *Formula Minor,* and in both Formulae it cannot be subdelegated. Corresponding to this, Faculty n. 9 from the Congregation of Sacred Rites in The Quenquennial Faculties, Formula IV, reads as follows:

> *Permittendi thurificationem in Missa cantata absque sacris ministris, in Festis tamen duplicibus primae et secundae classis, Dominicis et quando Missa cum cantu celebratur coram Ssmo Eucharistae Sacramento solemniter exposito.*

By virtue of the latter faculty, the ordinary can permit the use of incense in a sung Mass without the assistance of deacon and subdeacon, but only on feasts that are doubles of the first and second class, on Sundays, and when the high Mass is celebrated before the Most Blessed Sacrament of the Eucharist solemnly exposed.

SECTION 1. *Ex Iure*

As recognized by the sacred liturgy, a *Missa cantata* or a sung Mass is a Mass in which no deacon and subdeacon assist, and in which incense is not normally used, but it differs from a low Mass in that it is sung, and inasmuch as more than one server may take part in it in the sanctuary.[73] The rubrics of the *Missale Romanum* state that, if at any time the celebrant sings Mass without a deacon and subdeacon, a lector, in surplice, is to sing the Epistle in the usual place; he does not kiss the celebrant's hand; the celebrant himself, however, sings the Gospel at the Gospel corner, and at the end of the Mass he is to sing *Ite, Missa est,* or *Benedicamus Domino,* or *Requiescant in pace,* as the

[73] Cf. *Decreta Authentica,* n. 3059, ad 7 and 8; O'Connell, *The Celebration of Mass,* pp. 652-653.

occasion may demand.[74] And according to the decisions made by the Congregation of Sacred Rites, unless an indult has been granted, the use of incense is forbidden at a sung Mass.[75]

As to the number of ministers for a sung Mass, there is no explicit limitation, or direction, to follow as far as the rubrics and decisions of the Roman Congregation are concerned. Most liturgists, however, agree that at a sung Mass the use of more than one server is permitted, so that on the more solemn occasions there may be two acolytes, a thurifer when the use of incense is permitted, and two, or even four, torchbearers. In addition, the celebrant is allowed to have one special assistant who, if he is a layman, usually acts simply as a master of ceremonies, but, if he is a cleric, may perform other functions also, i.e., some of the duties that are assigned to the deacon and subdeacon at a solemn high Mass.[76] The ministers of a sung Mass, regardless of the number employed, are not necessarily clerics.

SECTION 2. *Ex Facultate*

A. *Ex Facultate Quinquennali.*—The Quinquennial Faculty extends to the ordinary the power of permitting the use of the incensations, as they are indicated in the rubrics of the *Missale Romanum.*[77] Since no specific number of ministers or servers is prescribed in the Faculty, fundamentally the said sung Mass can be celebrated with one server in attendance, whether he be a cleric, a layman, or just a boy, or also two or more; but the present Quinquen-

[74] *Ritus Servandus in Celebratione Missae,* VI, *De Epistola, Graduali,* etc., ad 8.

[75] *Decreta Authentica,* nn. 937, ad 3; 2515, ad 8; 3328, ad 1; 3611, ad 6; 3697, ad 3; etc. No priest may presume that such an indult exists.

[76] Cf. O'Connell, *The Celebration of Mass,* p. 652; *Decreta Authentica,* nn. 3377, ad 1; 4181.

[77] *Ritus Servandus in Celebratione Missae,* IV, ad 4; VI, ad 9; VIII, ad 9; VIII, ad 8; XIII, ad 2, etc.; O'Connell, *The Celebration of Mass,* pp. 662-671.

nial Faculty restricts the days on which the incensation is allowed at a sung Mass: those days are the doubles of both the first and second class,[78] all Sundays, and, in addition, the days when a sung Mass is celebrated before the Blessed Sacrament solemnly exposed.[79]

Since the faculty permits the said sung Mass with incensations only on doubles of both the first and second class, on Sundays, and on those days when a sung Mass is celebrated before the Most Blessed Sacrament solemnly exposed, it is the Mass of the feast or of the mystery that must be celebrated. Consequently, by virtue of the present Quinquennial Faculty, incensations are not permitted at a sung Mass *de Requie.*

B. *Ex Facultate Decennali.*—The mission ordinary, in virtue of the present Decennial Faculty, can permit missionaries within the territory of his jurisdiction to use the incensations at all sung Masses, which can be celebrated on any day without any qualification of the feasts as to their classes, even *"in die obitus seu depositionis,"* throughout the year, and for any intention, i.e., even for Masses *de Requie,* or for the Mass *pro Sponsis,* or for any votive Mass.[80]

"Dummodo duo saltem clerici, superpelliceo induti Missae inserviant." The faculty sets as a condition the presence at the altar of at least two clerics. May clerics alone act as servers? As was seen above, in the general liturgical precepts two cleric-servers are not a necessary requirement for the celebration of a sung Mass. Moreover, it is almost impossible to find two clerics available for the said Mass in rural residential stations in the missions, and, furthermore,

[78] Cf. *Duae Tabellae ex Rubrics Generalibus Breviarii iuxta Constitutionem "Divino Afflatu" Reformatis Excerptae* in the *Breviarium Romanum* (Pars verna, Neo-Eboraci: Benziger Brothers, Inc., 1942), pp. xxiii-xxvii; the quality of the feast is always indicated in the *Ordo Divini Officii Recitandi Sacrique Peragendi* of the place.

[79] Such days occur during the period that marks the erstwhile octave of Corpus Christi (cf. canon 1274, § 1), and also for the Mass of Reposition at the Forty Hours' Devotion (cf. canon 1275).

[80] Sartori, *Iuris Missionarii Elementa,* p. 94.

the Quinquennial Faculty does not require these to be necessarily clerics. Hence, *"duo saltem clerici"* should be understood as meaning "at least two servers," who should be vested in surplice and, what is obviously taken for granted, in casscok. For the use of this faculty no necessity is postulated, and thus, although a missionary have many servers at hand for a sung Mass, he still may celebrate the sung Mass with only two servers, or more; moreover, there is no law that imposes upon a missionary the duty to celebrate a sung Mass on certain feasts.

In the Decennial Faculty as well as in the Quniquennial Faculty, no limitation is placed in regard to the places in which a priest celebrating a sung Mass may use the privilege of performing the incensations. Hence the permission may be bestowed for use in any place where, either according to the canons of the Code, or in virtue of a privilege which the priest enjoys, Mass may be celebrated, but this place must be within the territory of the ordinary who has granted the permission to use the incensations at a sung Mass. Since neither of these faculties can be subdelegated, the missionary or the priest who enjoys this privilege cannot extend it to the visiting priest; furthermore, in case this privilege has been granted to the pastor (quasi-pastor and senior missionary) only, he cannot extend it even to his assistant priest when the latter is celebrating a sung Mass in the parish.[81] The ordinary may, however, give this privilege to all priests, including visiting priests, within the territory of his jurisdiction.

Article V

Facultas VIII: Faculty to Allow the Celebration of Mass in Vestments of Any Liturgical Color

Concedendi suis missionariis iter facientibus ut in celebrando S. Sacrificio uti possint paramentis cuiusvis coloris liturgici.

[81] Eagleton, *The Diocesan Quinquennial Faculties, Formula IV*, p. 141.

This is the Faculty by virtue of which the mission ordinary can concede to his missionaries who are on their missionary journeys the right to celebrate Mass in any one of the liturgical colors. This is *Facultas n. 7* in the *Formula Minor,* and cannot be subdelegated. The present Decennial Faculty is not included in *The Quinquennial Faculties, Formula IV.*

SECTION 1. *Ex Iure*

The *Rubricae Generales Missalis* indicate five colors, i.e., white, red, green, violet, and black,[82] for the sacred vestments used for Mass. Each of these colors has its liturgical meaning, and accordingly is assigned for certain Masses, feasts, and seasons.[83]

The rubrics governing the color of the sacred vestments are liturgically of strict obligation.[84] But the non-observance of the rubrics in regard to the liturgical colors inherently (*per se*) is no more than a venial sin, although on occasion (*per accidens*) it might be a mortal sin by reason of scandal or contempt, as, for instance, if a priest should celebrate Mass in a vestment of black color on Easter Sunday or on the Feast of the Nativity of Our Lord. Any reasonable cause would excuse from the obligation imposed by the rubrics in respect to the liturgical colors, for instance, when in a small rural parish there is only one set of white vestments which is the color of the day, but for some reason two priests must celebrate Mass at the same hour. The one

[82] XVIII, *De Coloribus Paramentis,* ad 1.

[83] *Rubricae Generales,* XVIII, *De Coloribus Paramentorum,* ad 2, 3, 4, 5, and 6. "A mixture of colours—so that no one colour predominates —is not admissible (*Decreta Authentica,* nn. 2675; 2682, ad 50, and 2769, ad 5). Vestments of real 'cloth of silver' are allowed to replace white; and those of real 'cloth of gold' can replace white, red, or green (*Decreta Authentica,* nn. 3145; 3191, ad 4; 3646, ad 2 and 3). These rules about colour apply only to the fabric out of which the vestment is made; the ornamentation may be of any suitable colour." —O'Connell, *The Celebration of Mass,* p. 228; Sadlowski, *The Sacred Furnishings of Churches,* pp. 141-142.

[84] *Decreta Authentica,* nn. 2675 and 2682, ad 50.

of them may celebrate Mass in the vestment of any other color. And it would be better to celebrate in any color than to omit the celebration of Mass for the reason simply that there is no vestment of the proper color of the day.[85] On the other hand, to celebrate Mass without the chasuble or without the vestments at all is, according to the common opinion of moralists, a mortal sin. In case the chasuble is missing, the cope or the dalmatic could be substituted.[86]

SECTION 2. *Ex Facultate*

The Mission ordinary is granted the faculty of permitting his missionaries on their missionary journey to celebrate Mass in any one of the liturgical colors. By virtue of this privilege, missionaries who otherwise are obliged to carry the requisites for Holy Mass along with them on their mission visitations can meet all needs with simply one set of vestments.

"Iter facientibus." The only condition set for the use of this privilege is that missionaries be travelling, i.e., either within their mission-stations, or anywhere either to or from their mission-stations outside their or other priests' residential stations (or quasi-parishes). This privilege can be used also anywhere on the way to or from other priests' residential stations or the town where the ordinary resides. Furthermore, the same privilege can be used when a priest celebrates Mass at a private house outside of residential stations for the consecration of the Holy Viaticum, and then the next morning has to celebrate Mass there for the deceased. Conversely, this privilege cannot be used in any residential station, whether it be his or another priest's.[87]

The Sacred Congregation for the Propagation of the Faith granted the missionaries in China the permission to use bicolored vestments, black on one side and yellow on the

[85] Cappello, *De Sacramentis*, I, n. 759, p. 711.

[86] *Loc. cit.*

[87] Sartori, *Iuris Missionarii Elementa*, p. 95; Winslow, *The Apostolic Faculties*, p. 48; Vromant, *Facultates Apostolicae*, n. 41, p. 39.

other, the faculty being given for ten years and with its use restricted to the missionary journeys, i.e., to visitations of the mission-stations, or Christian settlements.[88] However, this particular faculty is not necessary for those missionaries who enjoy the present Decennial Faculty, since the latter is broader than the former from the point of view of the scope of its use, and of the choice of the liturgical color. Again, since the faculty to use bicolored vestments differs from the present Decennial Faculty, those who enjoy the latter do not automatically have the former, and vice versa.

ARTICLE VI

Facultas IX: FACULTY TO ALLOW THE CELEBRATION OF THREE MASSES AT MIDNIGHT ON CHRISTMAS

Permittendi ut in ecclesiis et oratoriis publicis, quae privilegio iuris communis (can. 821, 2-3) haud guadent, tres Missae statim post mediam noctem Nativitatis Domini celebrari possit, cauto tamen ut omnia debita reverentia fiant.

This is the Faculty for permitting missionaries to celebrate three Masses immediately after midnight on Christmas Day in churches and oratories which do not enjoy the privilege stated in the common law (canon 821, §§ 2 and 3). This privilege is to be given under the caution that all due reverence be observed. This is *Facultas n. 8* in the *Formula Minor*, and it cannot be subdelegated. The presnet Decennial Faculty is not included in *The Quinquennial Faculties, Formula IV*.

SCTION 1. *Ex Iure*

Canon 821, § 2, states that on Christmas Day only the

[88] "Missionariis dum sunt in via ad visitandas christianitates facultas fit ad decennium utendi casulis bicoloribus, nigri scl. et flavi."—*Primum Concilium Sinense Anno 1924 Celebratum, Acta-Decreta et Normae-Vota, etc.* (Zi-Ka-Wei: Typographia Missionis Catholicae (T'ou-Se-We, 1929), p. 271 [hereafter cited as *Primum Concilium Sinense*].

conventual[89] or parochial Mass[90] may be begun at midnight; without an apostolic indult no other priest can say Mass earlier than one hour before the dawn of day, nor can the priest who said the Midnight Mass say a second or third Mass.[91] In the Code, however, there are two exceptions to this law: cardinals and residential and titular bishops have the privilege to celebrate anywhere, or to allow another to celebrate anywhere in their presence three Masses on Christmas night;[92] and in all religious and pious houses which have an oratory with the faculty of habitually reserving the Blessed Sacrament therein one priest may say at midnight on Christmas Day three Masses according to the liturgy of the day, or only one.[93] The latter provision cannot be applied to the churches of religious which serve as places of worship for the faithful generally.[94]

As to Holy Communion for the faithful at Midnight Mass on Christmas Day, since in the former law it was forbidden to give Holy Communion at midnight Mass in those churches and oratories which by the common law had the right to have midnight Mass, and the second paragraph of canon 821 is silent about Holy Communion of the faithful at the midnight Mass on Christmas Day, a doubt existed in the minds of some as to whether Holy Communion should be given at this midnight Mass. But the Code Commission declared that Holy Communion may be given at the midnight Mass on Christmas Day, when celebrated at that hour by law or by indult, unless the local ordinary forbids it in a

[89] *Rubricae Generales Missalis*, IV, ad 2 and 3; canons 413, 610, and 319. Cf. O'Connell, *The Celebration of Mass*, pp. 111 ff.

[90] *Additiones*, III, ad 12; *Decreta Authentica*, nn. 3059, ad 7 and 8; 3065. Cf. O'Connell, *ibid.*, pp. 109-110.

[91] "Quaelibet causa iusta excusat, ut Missae tres celebrentur."—Cappello, *De Sacramentis*, I, n. 742, b), p. 700.

[92] Canons 239, § 1, 4°; 349, § 1, 1°. Cf. Vermeersch-Creusen, *Epitome*, II, n. 97, p. 62.

[93] Canon 821, § 3; S.C.S. Off., decr., 1 Aug. 1907—*Fontes*, n. 1284.

[94] S.C.S. Off., 26 Nov. 1908—*Fontes*, n. 1285. Cf. Woywod-Smith, *A Practical Commentary*, n. 720, pp. 439-441; Cappello, *De Sacramentis*, I, n. 743, p. 701.

particular case for just reasons, according to the canon 869, and that local ordinaries have the right and duty to guard against anything unbecoming.[95]

SECTION 2. *Ex Facultate*

By virtue of the present Decennial Faculty, the mission ordinary can permit sacred edifices dedicated to divine worship either by way of a consecration or a blessing to have three Masses beginning at midnight on Christmas Day. The present Decennial Faculty is a local privilege, not a personal one.[96] Since it is a local privilege, it is in other words not a privilege granted on behalf of the priest, but on behalf of the place, i.e., the church and public oratory. The three Masses can be celebrated either by one priest, or by three different priests, or two Masses by one priest and the third by another priest, successively.[97] But not each of the priests at a church or public oratory can, in virtue of the present Decennial Faculty, celebrate three Masses simultaneously or successively, beginning at midnight on Christmas Day.

"In ecclesiis et oratoriis publicis." The privilege for the celebration of three Masses at midnight on Christmas Day can be given, by virtue of the Present Decennial Faculty, to all churches[98] and public oratories,[99] even to those having no canonical parochial Masses or conventual Masses because of the fact that they have not been established as canonical parishes, quasi-parishes, collegiate or conventual churches, etc., provided they have been legitimately recognized and solemnly consecrated or blessed as prescribed in law.[100]

[95] Code Comm., 16 Mart. 1936—*AAS*, XXVIII (1936), 178.

[96] Sartori, *Iuris Missionarii Elementa*, p. 95.

[97] Vromant, *Facultates Apostolicae*, n. 42, p. 40; De Reeper, *A Missionary Companion*, p. 39.

[98] Canon 1161.

[99] Canons 1188-1191.

[100] Canon 1165. Cf. Thaddeus S. Ziolkowski, *The Consecration and Blessing of Churches*, The Catholic University of America Canon Law Studies, n. 187 (Washington, D.C.: The Catholic University of America Press, 1943), pp. 36-101.

Hence, *"ecclesiae et oratoria publica"* include all parish churches, quasi-parish churches, residential station-churches, and public oratories in the missions,[101] and exclude all semipublic oratories[102] and private oratories.[103]

According to the response given by the Sacred Congregation for the Propagation of the Faith to the Superior General of the Scheut Fathers, on January 30, 1930, the word *"ecclesia"* in *Facultates IX, X, XI* in the *Formula Maior* is to be understood in the strict canonical sense of canon 1161, § 1.[104] From this it follows that all buildings which have not been dedicated by way of consecration or blessing, such as schools and catechumenates temporarily used as churches by the visiting missionary, are excluded from this privilege.

"Cauto tamen ut omnia cum debita reverentia fiant." When the mission ordinary permits to the above said churches and public oratories the celebration of three Masses at midnight on Christmas Day, he must employ caution that the faithful who want to receive Holy Communion at midnight Mass will pay due reverence to the Holy Eucharist, especially in the observance of the Eucharistic fast.[105] To this end the mission ordinary is free to impose any salutary precepts he may deem necessary.[106]

[101] Vromant, *Facultates Apostolicae*, n. 42, p. 40; Paventi, *Brevis Commentarius*, p. 21; *contra*: according to Sartori and Winslow, because of the clause, "... *quae privilegio iuris communis* (can. 821, 2-3) *haud gaudent*," the *ecclesiae et oratoria publica* do not include churches and public oratories which enjoy the right granted in canon 821, §§ 2 and 3.—Sartori, *Iuris Missionarii Elementa*, p. 96; Winslow, *The Apostolic Faculties*, p. 50.

[102] Canon 1188, § 2, 2°.

[103] Canon 1188, § 2, 3°.

[104] S.C. Prop. Fid., Prot. n. 239/30. Cf. Vromant, *Facultates Apostolicae*, p. 41, footnote n. 1.

[105] Cf. Pope Pius XII's motu propr., 19 Mart. 1957, *"Sacram Communionem,"* nn. 2 and 3—*AAS*, XLIX (1957), 177; Bouscaren, *Canon Law Digest*, IV, 287.

[106] *AAS*, XXVIII (1936), 178. Cf. Sartori, *Iuris Missionarii Elementa*, p. 96.

Article VII

Facultas X: Faculty to Allow the Celebration of the Holy Week Ceremonies in the Short Form

Permittendi ut in ecclesiis dissitis functiones Maioris Hebdonadae celebrari queant iuxta peculiarem Rituum a s. m. Benedicto Pp. XIII concessum pro ecclesiis minoribus paroecialibus, in quibus ministrorum numerus vel copia cantorum ad praedictas sacras functiones solemniter peragendas haberi nequeat: dummodo tamen constet ibidem satis esse consultum reverentiae sacris mysteriis debitae, nullamque exinde abusui patere occasionem; et quatenus neque praedictus Ritus servari possit, permittendi ut iisdem ecclesiis unica Missa lecta, loco solemnis, celebrari possit Feria V in Coena Domini.

SECTION 1. A BRIEF COMMENTARY ON THE FACULTY

This is *Facultas n. 9* in the *Formula Minor* and in both Formulae it cannot be subdelegated. By *"peculiaris Ritus a s.m. Benedicto Pp. XIII concessus"* in the faculty is meant the *"Memoriale Rituum."*[107] Thus, in short, the Decennial Faculty deals with a dispensation from the observance of the Rubrics and the order of the Functions in Holy Week, and grants the use of the *Memoriale Rituum* instead in the churches and the public oratories in the missions, under the two conditions that no ministers and singers be available to perform the ceremonies according to the Rubrics of the *Missale Romanum,* and that with at least three altar boys in attendance all the ceremonies be carried out with the proper decorum, so that there will be no opportunity for abuses to rise.[108]

[107] Paventi, *Brevis Commentarius*, p. 23, footnote n. 12; Vromant, *Facultates Apostolicae*, n. 43, p. 42; Sartori, *Iuris Missionarii Elementa*, p. 97.

[108] Cf. Bartholomew Eustace, *Ritual for Small Churches* (A Translation of the *Memoriale Rituum,* Issued by Pope Benedict XIII, and Revised by Authority of Pope Benedict XV) (New York: Joseph F. Wagner, Inc., Publishers, 1935); Odoricus Schell, *Compendium Sacrae*

Faculty n. 10 from the Congregation of Sacred Rites in *The Quinquennial Faculties, Formula IV,* however, reads as follows:

> *Permittendi usum* MEMORIALIS RITUUM *Benedicti PP. XIII in Ecclesiis seu Oratoriis publicis et semipublicis (non-parochialibus vel quasi-parochialibus) in functionibus Tridui Maioris Hebdomadae et in Benedictione Cinerum, Candelarum et Palmarum; dummodo tamen certo constet decori ac reverentiae sacrorum Mysteriorum satis esse consultum.*

The present Quinquennial Faculty also concerns itself with the use of the *Memoriale Rituum* in oratories either public or semipublic, which are neither parochial nor quasi-parochial churches.[109]

Both the Decennial Faculty and the Quinquennial Faculty are by their nature given to the above recounted places, rather than to persons. However, the present faculties to use the *Memoriale Rituum* have become entirely unnecessary because of the recent liturgical legislative directives.

SECTION 2. DECREES AND INSTRUCTIONS FOR THE RESTORING OF THE CELEBRATION OF THE SOLEMN PASCHAL VIGIL

On February 9, 1951, the Congregation of Sacred Rites edited the Decree *"Dominicae Resurrectionis Vigiliam,"* accompanied with new directive norms for the nocturnal celebration of the Paschal Vigil, for the restoring of the Solemn Paschal Vigil.[110] In the decree, local ordinaries were granted an optional faculty to celebrate the Solemn Paschal Vigil according to the new Rubrics, in 1951. The same optional celebration of the Solemn Paschal Vigil was extended for the next three years through the means of the Decree *"Instaurata Vigilia Paschalis"* of the Congregation of Sacred

Liturgicae (4. ed., Yen-Chow-Fu, Shantung: Typographia Missionis Catholicae, 1936), pp. 203 ff.

[109] Cf. Eagleton, *The Diocesan Quinquennial Faculties, Formula IV,* pp. 141-142.

[110] *AAS,* XLIII (1951), 128; Bouscaren, *Canon Law Digest,* III, 34-35.

Rites, on January 11, 1952.[111] This decree was accompanied with new ordinances and changes in the Rubrics, i.e., with respect to the preparation for, the proper hour for, and rite of, the Solemn Paschal Vigil; annotations on some Rubrics of Mass; on Holy Communion and the Eucharistic Fast; etc. On January 15, 1955, again the optional celebration of the Solemn Paschal Vigil was granted through the Decree "*Instauratae Vibiliae Paschalis*" for that year only.[112]

On November 16, 1955, however, the Congregation of Sacred Rites declared the definite restoration of the Order of Holy Week through the General Decree "*Maxima redemptionis nostrae mysteria,*"[113] which included new provisions concerning the new Order, and on the same day the Sacred Congregation published the *Instructio (de ordine hebdomadae sanctae peragendo) "Cum propositum instaurati Ordinis hebdomadae sanctae."*[114] The Decree declared the juridical forces of the restored Order of the Holy Week as follows:

> *Qui rituum romanum sequuntur, in posterum servare tenentur Ordinem hebdomadae sanctae instauratum, in editione typica Vaticana descriptum. Qui alios ritus latinos sequuntur, tenentur tantummodo servare tempus celebrationum liturgicarum in novo Ordine statutum.*
>
> *Novus hic Ordo servari debet a die 25 Martii, dominica II Passionis seu in Palmis, anni 1956.*[115]

And the new Order was published with the imprint *Typis Polyglottis Vaticanis,* to which the Decree "*Decreto Generali S. Rituum Congregationis*" of November 30, 1955, was attached. This decree declared that ". . . *in locum Ordinis hebdomadae maioris, hucusque in Missali et in Breviario*

[111] *AAS*, XLIV (1952), 48-52; Bouscaren, *Canon Law Digest,* III, 35-36.

[112] *AAS*, XLVII (1955), 48; Bouscaren, *Canon Law Digest,* IV, 25.

[113] *AAS*, XLVII (1955), 838-841; Bouscaren, *Canon Law Digest,* IV, 49-54.

[114] *AAS*, XLVII (1955), 842-847; Bouscaren, *Canon Law Digest,* IV, 54-61.

[115] The Decree "*Maxima redemptionis nostrae mysteria,*" I, nn. 1 and 2—*AAS*, XLVII (1955), 840.

inserti, Ordo hebdomadae sanctae instauratus substituitur."[116]

To the new Order thus restored there were added a newly arranged Gregorian chant[117] and a new declaration (*declaratio circa functiones 'tridui sacri' secundum ordinem hebdomadae sanctae instauratum) "In ordine hebdomadae sanctae instaurato*" of March 15, 1956,[118] which was perfected with further Ordinances and Declarations of February 1, 1957.[119]

SECTION 3. THE SIMPLE RITE OF THE RESTORED ORDER OF HOLY WEEK

As to the Simple Rite of the Restored Order of Holy Week, although the General Decree "*Maxima redemptionis nostrae mysteria*" contained no provisions modifying the rubrics for churches which could not secure the prescribed sacred ministers for the functions of Holy Week, the rubrics allowed lay ministers in the functions and the simple celebration of the functions of Holy Week.[120]

The general directive norms for the use of the Simple Rite of the Restored Order of Holy Week are laid down in the Declaration "*In Ordine Hebdomadae Sanctae Instaura-*

[116] *Ordo Hebdomadae Sanctae Instauratus* (editio typica, Typis Polyglottis Vaticanis, 1956), v.

[117] S.R.C., decr. (de cantibus gregorianis ad 'Ordinem hebdomadae sanctae instauratum' pertinentibus) "*Liturgico hebdomadae sanctae ordine instaurato*," 11 Febr. 1956—Hermanus A. P. Schmidt, *Hobdomada Sancta* (2 vols., Vol. I, *Contemporanei Textus Liturgici, Documenta Piana et Bibliographia;* Vol. II, sects. I-II, *Commentarius Historicus*, Romae-Friburgi Brisg.-Barcinone: Herder, 1956-1957), Vol. I, p. 233.

[118] *AAS*, XLVIII (1956), 153-154.

[119] S.R.C., ordinationes et declarationes "*Liturgica hebdomadae sanctae instauratio*"—*AAS*, XLIX (1957), 91-95.

[120] (Rubrics) "Omnia quae in sequentibus rubricis litteris inclinatis edita sunt, referuntur ad clebrationem simplicem, quando scilicet sacrae coeremoniae peraguntur a sacerdote, absque ministris sacris, Dominica II Passionis seu in Palmis, De Solemni Palmarum Processione."—*Ordo Hebdomadae Sanctae Instauratus*, p. 3. Throughout the Order the modes of the simple celebration of the functions of Holy Week are indicated by way of the Rubrics.

to,"[121] and their detailed applications in the functions of each day of Holy Week are shown in the Ordinances and Declarations entitled *"Liturgica Hebdomadae Sanctae Instauratio."*[122] In conformity with the above mentioned General Decree, Declarations, and Ordinances, the *Ritus Simplex Ordinis Hebdomadae Sanctae Instaurati* was composed and approved by the Congregation of Sacred Rites on February 5, 1957.[123] Authorizing the Simple Rite of the Restored Order of Holy Week, the Decree declared as follows:

DECREE

> After the publication of the *Ordo Hedomadae Sanctae Instauratus* it seemed appropriate to set forth by itself the simple rite to be performed without deacon and subdeacon, which is described together with the solemn rite in the *Ordo,* and to publish it in a manner similar to the well-known book entitled *Memoriale Rituum,* so that it might be readily available to all interested persons.
>
> Wherefore, Chapters III-VI of the *Memoriale Rituum* are suppressed, and the *Ritus Simplex Ordinis Hebdomadae Sanctae Instaurati* is substituted for them. The present Vatican edition is to be considered the typical edition and is to be followed accurately by publishers who have the required privilege.
>
> Everything to the contrary notwithstanding.
>
> The fifth day of February, 1957.[124]

From the foregoing decree it is clear that the *Memoriale Rituum,* which was allowed to be used by the Quinquennial Faculty and the Decennial Faculty, has been replaced for the functions of Holy Week by the *Ritus Simplex Ordinis Hebdomadae Sanctae Instaturati,* and the latter's general directive norms for its use are, according to the Ordinances and

[121] *AAS,* XLVIII (1956), 153-154.

[122] *AAS,* XLIX (1957), 91-95.

[123] Its English translation: *The Simple Rite of te Restored Order of Holy Week* (trans. Gerald Ellard-F. P. Prucha, and published by authorization of the Congregation of Sacred Rites, Milwaukee: Bruce Publishing Co., 1958).

[124] *The Simple Rite of the Restored Order of Holy Week,* p. ix.

Declarations contained in the *"Liturgica Hebdomadae Sanctae Instauratio,"* as follows:

THE USE OF THE SOLEMN OR OF THE SIMPLE RITE IN CELEBRATING THE LITURGY OF HOLY WEEK

1. In all churches and public and semipublic oratories where there is a sufficient number of sacred ministers, the sacred rites of the Second Sunday of the Passion, or Palm Sunday, of Holy Thursday *in Coena Domini,* of Good Friday on the Passion and Death of our Lord, and of the Paschal Vigil, can be celebrated in the solemn form (*Declaration* of 15 March, 1956, n. 1, and *Instruction* of 16 Nov., 1955, n. 4).

2. In churches and public and semipublic oratories where sacred ministers are not available, the simple rite may be used. But for performing this simple rite there must be a sufficient number of "servers," either clerics or at least boys, namely, at least three for the Second Sunday of the Passion, or Palm Sunday, and for the Mass *in Coena Domini,* and at least four for the celebration of the liturgical Action of Good Friday on the Passion and Death of our Lord, and of the Paschal Vigil. These "servers" must be carefully instructed as to what they have to do (*Instruction* of 16 Nov., 1955, n. 3). These two conditions, namely, a sufficient number of "servers" and their adequate preparation, are strictly required for performing the simple rite. Local Ordinaries should see that these two conditions for the simple rite are exactly observed (*Declaration* of 15 March, 1956, n. 2).

3. Where the liturgical actions of Holy Week are performed in the simple rite, if another priest or at least a deacon is available, there is no objection to having him, in the vestments of a deacon, sing the Gospel when it occurs, or the history of the Passion (but reserving the part of *Christus* to the celebrant), or the *praeconium paschale,* also lessons and invitations such as *Flectamus genua* and *Levate,* or *Benedicamus Domino,* or *Ite, Missa est;* in short, let him take the part of the deacon.[125]

[125] Bouscaren, *Canon Law Digest,* IV, 63-64; *AAS,* XLIX (1957), 91-92.

Formerly the use of the *Memoriale Rituum* was a privilege given to churches and public oratories in the missions and to public and semipublic oratories in canonically erected dioceses and archdioceses, but now the use of the Simple Rite of the Restored Order of Holy Week, which replaces the *Memoriale Rituum,* has been given to all churches and public and semipublic oratories in the entire Church, on condition that these should not be able to secure the sacred ministers prescribed for the Solemn Rite of the Restored Order of Holy Week, but should be able to secure the number of ministers, i.e., clerics or lay servers, prescribed for the performance of the Simple Rite, and that the servers be instructed to show due reverence to the sacred ceremonies and sacred vessels, and to perform correctly their services at the functions of Holy Week. The last two conditions, i.e., the securing of the minimum number of servers and their proper training, are absolute. Although this use of the Simple Rite does not belong to the local ordinaries' faculty, they have the duty to diligently see that the two conditions above prescribed for the Simple Rite be exactly observed, and the right to prevent the celebration of the Simple Rite, if they see that the prescribed conditions are not met for the celebration.

As to the functions of Ash Wednesday and Candlemas Day, by virtue of the Quinquennial Faculty, the *Memoriale Rituum* may be used, but, as a matter of fact, there exists no difference between the directions in the *Memoriale Rituum* and the Rubrics in the *Missale Romanum* for the days involving the use of the faculty. For the rubrics themselves show the celebrant how to perform the service without a deacon and a subdeacon. For this reason, there was no mention of Ash Wednesday and Candlemas Day in the Decennial Faculty. However, it can be stated that, if the celebrant is not assisted by sacred ministers at the functions of Ash Wednesday and Candlemas Day, he should have at least three servers,[126] who are sufficiently instructed in the proper performance of the functions of the days.

[126] *Decreta Authentica,* n. 2616; Eustace, *op. cit.,* p. iii.

Article VIII

Facultas XI: Faculty to Allow the Celebration of the *Missa Quotidiana de Requie* Three Times a Week

> *Permittendi ut in ecclesiis ter in hebdomada extra Quadragesimam, Missa privata de Requie celebrari possit, etiam diebus ritus duplicis maioris et minoris, exceptis dominicis, nec non feriis, vigiliis atque octavis privilegiatis, diebus tamen, quibus eadem Missa a Rubricis permittitur, computatis.*

This is *Facultas n. 10* in the *Formula Minor,* and in both Formulae cannot be subdelegated. Corresponding to this Decennial Faculty, Faculty n. 12 from the Congregation of Sacred Rites in *The Quinquennial Faculties, Formula IV,* reads as follows:

> *Celebrandi Missam* de Requie *lectam semel in heddomada ab Ordinario in proprio oratorio; dummodo ne occurrat Festum ritus duplicis primae aut secundae classis, Dominica aut Festum de praecepto etiam suppresso, nec non Octava privilegiata, Feria Quadragesimae, Quatuor Temporum, II Rogationum, Vigilia aut Feria in qua anticipanda vel primo reponenda est Missa Dominicae: servatis de cetero Rubricis.*

These faculties concern the privilege to celebrate private Masses *de Requie,* by way of exception from the general Rubrics of the *Missale Romanum,* in addition to those days on which the Rubrics permit the celebration of private masses *de Requie.*

Section 1. *Ex Iure*

"*Missa privata de Requie*" in the Decennial Faculty and "*Missa de Requie lecta*" in the Quinquennial Faculty are to be identified in their meaning. Both phrases refer to the low Mass, designated in the *Missale Romanum* as *Missa Quotidiana Defunctorum.* The private Mass *de Requie* is to be identified as apart from all sung Masses, even a sung *Missa Quotidiana Defunctorum,* and likewise as apart from all low Masses such as a funeral Mass, the Mass after the

Announcement of a Death, or the *Requiem* Mass on the Third, Seventh, Thirtieth, and Anniversary Day. Formerly the days on which the private Mass *de Requie* could be celebrated were set and were governed by the rules *De Missis Votivis* and *De Missis Defunctorum* in *Additiones et Variationes in Rubricis Missalis* of the Roman Missal. But those rules have been considerably modified by the General Decree *"Cum nostra hac aetate"* of the Congregation of Sacred Rites, March 23, 1955.[127]

In the light of these documents, the celebration of the private Mass *de Requie* is forbidden on the following days: (1) on any day on which there is an office of double rite (major or minor); (2) on any Sunday; (3) on any privileged ferial day,[128] and privileged vigil,[129] and any day within the privileged octaves;[130] (4) on any days of Lent (except the first free day of each week, i.e., a day on which a feast of simple rite or a non-privileged ferial day occurs and an Ember Day does not occur, in the calendar of the Church in which the Mass is celebrated);[131] (5) on any Ember Day and on Rogation Monday;[132] (6) on the ferials of the "Greater Antiphons," i.e., from December 17 to December 23, from January 2 to January 5, and from January 7 to January 12 (all days are inclusive), and the days between the Ascension and the Vigil of Pentecost (exclu-

[127] *AAS*, XLVII (1955), 218; Bouscaren, *Canon Law Digest*, IV, 25-32. Cf. J. B. O'Connell, *Simplifying the Rubrics of the Roman Breviary and Missal* (Milwaukee: The Bruce Publishing Co., 1956).

[128] Privileged ferial days are: Ash Wednesday, Monday, Tuesday, and Wednesday of Holy Week—the last three days are ranked as doubles of the first class. Cf. The *Duae Tabelle ex Rubricis Generalibus Breviarii* in the *Breviarium Romanum*, p. xxiv.

[129] Privileged Vigils of the first class are the Vigils of Christmas and Pentecost. Cf. *loc. cit.*

[130] The General Decree *"Cum nostra hac aetate,"* n. 11: "Celebrantur tantum octavae Nativitatis Domini, Paschatis et Pentecostes, suppressis omnibus aliis sive in calendario universali, sive in calendariis particularibus occurrentibus."—*AAS*, XLVII (1955), 220.

[131] *Additiones et Variationes in Rubrics Missalis*, III, ad 9.

[132] *Loc. cit.*

sive);[133] and, finally, (7) on any common (or non-privileged) vigil.[134]

SECTION 2. *Ex Facultate*

A. *Ex Facultate Decennali.*—By virtue of the present Decennial Faculty, the mission ordinary can permit churches and public oratories within the territory under his jurisdiction to have three private Masses *de Requie* each week, even on those days which, according to the calendar of the Church, are of greater (*maior*) or lesser (*minor*) double rite, throughout the year. However, the private Masses *de Requie* cannot be celebrated even by virtue of the present Decennial Faculty on the following days: (1) on Sundays throughout the year; (2) on doubles of the first and second class; (3) on ferials during the season of Lent, except the first free day of the week during the same season;[135] (4) on privileged ferials, privileged vigils, and the days within the privileged octaves.[136]

According to commentators of the Decennial Faculties, the clause *"exceptis dominicis nec non feriis,* etc. . . ." is to be interpreted as an all-inclusive enumeration of the exceptions.[137] Hence, from such an interpretation it follows that, in the present Decennial Faculty, the days of (5), (6), and (7), as enumerated above in the section of *Ex Iure,* are not days on which the celebration of the private Masses *de Requie* is prohibited.

[133] The General Decree *"Cum nostra hac aetate,"* nn. 14, 15, 17—*AAS,* XLVII (1955), 220-221; *Aditiones et Variationes in Rubricis Missalis, loc. cit.*

[134] The General Decree *"Cum nostra hac aetate,"* n. 9: "Vigiliae Communes sunt vigilia festorum Ascensionis Domini, Assumptionis B.M.V., S. Ioannis Baptistae, SS. Petri et Pauli, S. Laurentii. Omnes aliae vigiliae etiam quae calendariis particularibus sunt inscriptae, supprimuntur."—*AAS,* XLVII (1955), 220.

[135] See *supra,* division (4) and its footnote.

[136] Days of (2) and (3) are determined from the context of the present faculty and days of (1) and (4) from the very text of the faculty.

[137] Paventi, *Brevis Commentarius,* p. 24; Vromant, *Facultates Apostolicae,* n. 44, p. 44; Sartori, *Iuris Missionarii Elementa,* p. 98-99; Winslow, *The Apostolic Faculties,* p. 53.

B. *Ex Facultate Quinquennali.*—By virtue of the present Quinquennial Faculty, the ordinary under the jurisdiction of the Sacred Consistorial Congregation can celebrate a private Mass *de Requie* once a week in his private oratory on those days which are not: (1) doubles of the first and second class; (2) Sundays; (3) feasts of precept, even though suppressed; (4) days within the privileged octaves; (5) ferials during the season of Lent, except the first free day of the week during the same season; (6) Ember days and Rogation Monday; (7) the vigils, and, finally, (8) ferials on which a Sunday Mass is to be anticipated or to which it is to be transferred. These exceptions point to an all-inclusive enumeration. The privileged ferials which consist of Ash Wednesday, and of the Monday, Tuesday, and Wednesday of Holy Week are included in the ferials during Lent; since the vigils are stated without qualification, they include common vigils as well as privileged vigils.

The present Decennial Faculty as well as the present Quinquennial Faculty is operative on the days between January 2nd and 5th, and January 7th and 12th (all inclusive), and on the days from the Feast of the Ascension to the Vigil of Pentecost (both exclusive). For these days are not enumerated among the days on which the celebration of a private Mass *de Requie* is prohibited in the present faculties.

The use of the present Decennial Faculty and Quniquennial Faculty concerns the celebration of the private Mass *de Requie* on those days on which its celebration is forbidden by the Rubrics of the *Missale Romanum,* but they are different in that the Decennial Faculty is given to churches and public oratories in the missions and used by the mission ordinary or any priest, even by a visitor, while the Quinquennial Faculty is given to the ordinary and to his private oratory, so that it can be used only by the ordinary *sede plena, sede impedita,* and *sede vacante,* and only in the private oratory of the ordinary.

In both faculties, if during the week there occur three days on which, according to the rubrics, a low Mass *de*

Requie may be celebrated, the faculty cannot be used cumulatively, i.e., together with, or in addition thereto, to celebrate three more private low Masses *de Requie* (in the case of the Decennial Faculty) on the remaining three days of the week. If during the week the rubrics of the *Missale Romanum* permit only one private Mass *de Requie,* then the Decennial Faculty may be used for the celebration of a second and even a third private Mass *de Requie* on days which are not excluded from the use of the faculty.

"Servatis de certero Rubricis." This phrase refers to the Rubrics of the Mass *de Requie,* which govern the celebration of the private Mass *de Requie,* and are found in the *Additiones et Variationes in Rubricis Missalis* and in the General Decree *"Cum nostra hac aetate."*[138]

Article IX

Facultas XII: Faculty to Allow the Daily Celebration of the *Missa B.M.V.*

> *Permittendi etiam in omnibus diebus festis et dominicis Missam votivam de B.M.V., diebus autem ferialibus etiam Missam defunctorum, iis qui, ob defectum oculorum aliamve infirmitatem, legere nequeant Missas singulis diebus occurrentes iuxta Missalis Romani rubricas.*

The Faculty is *Facultas n. 11* in the *Formula Minor;* in both Formulae the present Decennial Faculty cannot be subdelegated; it is not included in *The Quinquennial Faculties, Formula IV.*

Section 1. *Ex Iure*

The present Decennial Faculty deals with the dispensation from the basic principle of all the Rubrics in the *Missale Romanum* that states: *"Missa cotidie dicitur secundum Ordinem Officii: de Festo duplici vel semiduplici, vel Dominica, vel Feria, vel Vigilia, vel Octava: et extra Ordinem*

[138] The General Decree, Tit. III, *De Commemorationibus.—AAS,* XLVII (1955), 222; *Additiones et Variationes in Rubricis Missalis,* III, *De Missis Defunctorum,* nn. 2, 10-11.

Officii, votiva, vel pro Defuncto."[139] In the Code of Canon Law, no rules nor any indults for the dispensation deriving through the present Decennial Faculty are mentioned, but the Congregation of Sacred Rites on January 12, 1921, issued an Instruction regarding the celebration of Masses which may be permitted by way of an apostolic indult to a priest who is losing his sight.[140] An Instruction issued on September 3, 1942, and substantially the same as the foregoing is reported in Bouscaren's *Canon Law Digest.*[141]

According to the Instruction of 1921, the dispensation with which the present Decennial Faculty deals may be obtained from the Supreme Pontiff or from the Congregation of Sacred Rites, if the ordinary does not enjoy the apostolic faculty therefor.[142] In case the thus obtained apostolic indult does not contain the clause "*dummodo orator non sit omnino caecus,*" and in the meantime the petitioner has become quite blind, he must abstain from celebrating Mass until he has obtained a new indult; and after he has obtained it he is bound by a grave obligation to make use of the assistance of another priest, even though this obligation be not expressly mentioned in the indult.[143]

SECTION 2. *Ex Facultate*

By virtue of the present Decennial Faculty, the mission ordinary can permit priests within the territory under his jurisdiction who are losing their sight, or whose sight is so weak either accidentally or habitually that they can read only very coarse type, or who are suffering from some infirmity such as nervousness, or from some defect such as stammering, and therefore are unable to read the Masses

[139] This is the opening paragraph of "*Rubricae Generales Missalis*" of the *Missale Romanum.*

[140] *AAS*, XIII (1921), 154.

[141] Vol. III, pp. 352-355. Bouscaren noted that, although this Instruction was given to a private person, he translated it from the official text published by the Congregation of Sacred Rites.

[142] Bouscaren, *Canon Law Digest,* I, 370.

[143] *Ibid.*, p. 371.

occurring each day in the *Missale Romanum,* to celebrate the votive Mass of the Blessed Virgin on all feasts and Sundays, and the *Missa quotidiana defunctorum,* on ferial days.

According to the Instruction given on September 3, 1942, the rules regarding the votive Masses of the Blessed Virgin and *de Requie* are as follows:

2. Rules Regarding the Votive Mass of the Blessed Virgin

I. *Which One of the Votive Masses of the Blessed Virgin Is to Be Said?*

1. A priest who has this dispensation should say the *fifth* of the votive Masses of the Blessed Virgin at all times of the year, always in white vestments.

2. If he still has enough eyesight to read also the other four votive Masses of the Blessed Virgin according to the different times of the year, he may say those Masses.

II. *When the Votive Mass of the Blessed Virgin Is to Be Said?*

1. The votive Mass of the Blessed Virgin *may* be said at any time of the year; it *must* be said on all days when, according to the calendar of the church where such a priest is celebrating, daily votive Masses for the deceased are not permitted; without prejudice, however, to the further privileges regarding Masses for the deceased, which are explained below in section 3 of this Instruction.

2. During the sacred triduum of Holy Week the priest must abstain entirely from celebrating Mass.

3. On the Feast of the Nativity he can say three Masses.

III. *The Rite of the Mass*

1. If a votive Mass of the Blessed Virgin is celebrated both for a grave reason and for a public cause, the priest with failing sight always says: one Oration, the *Gloria,* the *Credo,* the Preface in the solemn tone, the *Ite, Missa est* and the Last Gospel of Saint John, *In principio,* even though priests who have not this privilege should on that day make some commemoration, or say an *Im-*

perata ordered by the Ordinary, or say at the end the Gospel of a commemorated feast, according to the Rubrics.

2. In all cases:

a) The *Gloria in excelsis* is said:

I. Whenever it is to be said in the Mass of the day, according to the calendar of the church where the Mass is celebrated;

II. In the jubilee of the priest's own priestly ordination;

III. Within octaves, even simple ones, of the Blessed Virgin Mary, according to the calendar of the church where the Mass is celebrated;

IV. On Sundays.

b) As to Orations, the following rules are to be observed:

I. A second and third oration are not added when these are excluded by the rite of the Mass of the day, according to the calendar of the church in which the Mass is celebrated;

II. Otherwise three Orations are said, namely the second of the Holy Spirit and the third *contra persecutores Ecclesiae* or *pro Papa*.

c) The *Credo* is said:

I. Whenever it is to be said in the Mass of the day, according to the calendar of the church where the Mass is celebrated;

II. On the jubilee of the priest's own priestly ordination.

d) In the Preface, *et te in veneratione* is said, except on feasts and during octaves, even simple ones, of the Blessed Virgin Mary, in which cases the Preface is said just as if the Mass of the feast or of the octave were being celebrated.

e) The Last Gospel is always that of Saint John, *In principio*.

f) In private oratories the priest celebrating follows his own calendar.

3. Rubrics for the Mass of the Deceased

1. On days when the daily Mass for the de-

ceased is allowed according to calendar of the church in which the Mass is celebrated, or according to the priest's own calendar in a private oratory, the priest with failing sight can celebrate this Mass, either singing or reading it.

2. He celebrates this same Mass (and three times if he wishes) also on the day of the Commemoration of all the Faithful Departed, in which however he shall say only one Oration, namely, *Fidelium.* If he celebrates two or three Masses on this day, he shall observe the Constitution of Benedict XV, *Incruentum Altaris Sacrificium,* in virtue of which he can apply only one Mass for anyone he chooses, and can receive a stipend for that, but must apply the other Masses, without stipend, for all the faithful departed and according to the intention of the Supreme Pontiff, just as other priests.

3. In this Mass one single Oration is said, whenever this daily Mass takes the place of one in which, according to the Rubrics, only one Oration should be said. Otherwise at least three Orations should be said, but the first and second may vary according to the special intention and application of the Mass, according to the Rubrics.

4. The priest with failing sight is never bound to say the Sequence, *Dies irae.* However, in case he sings the Mass, even though he does not read the Sequence, the choir should not fail to sing it.[144]

On the observance of the foregoing rules, the same Instruction stated: "The conditions of this privilege must be exactly observed."[145] However, these rules must be modified in line with the General Decree *"Cum nostra hac aetate"* of the Congregation of Sacred Rites, March 23, 1955;[146] a priest's enjoyment of this privilege does not in the least prevent his saying the Mass of the day when he so desires and is able to do so, or another one of the Masses *de Requie,*

[144] Bouscaren, *Canon Law Digest,* III, 353-355.

[145] *Ibid.,* p. 353.

[146] *AAS,* XLVI (1955), 218; Bouscaren, *Canon Law Digest,* IV, 25-32. Cf O'Connell, *Simplifying the Rubrics of the Roman Breviary and Missal.*

instead of the *Missa quotidiana defunctorum,* when the rubrics permit it and the priest is able to do so. If the church or public oratory enjoys the Decennial Faculty XI in the *Formula Maior,* then by virtue of it the priest may say three Masses *de Requie* a week there, *servatis servandis.*[147]

Since the faculty is to be given to priests whose sight is failing, etc., it is a personal privilege, and thus, once this faculty is obtained by a priest under the prescribed conditions, he may make use of the faculty even outside of the territory of the ordinary who granted it. In case the priest's blindness should become total, he could still continue to make use of this Decennial Faculty without applying for a new apostolic indult, with which the Instruction of 1921 and of 1942 are concerned in the section of the *Praenotanda.*[148] For the present privilege, in that it is one of the Decennial Faculties in the *Formula Maior,* should receive a broad interpretation according to the norms of canons 66, § 1, and 50, inasmuch as the present Decennial Faculty does not contain any restrictive clause (such as "*dummodo orator non sit omnino caecus*") in its text. Nevertheless, the totally blind priest would "be bound by a grave obligation to make use of the assistance of another priest, even though this obligation be not expressly mentioned in the indult."[149]

As stated above, the present Decennial Faculty is not contained among *The Quinquennial Faculties, Formula IV.* However, the same faculty can be obtained from the Apostolic Delegate, the Internuncio and the Nuncio.[150] In the Index of Faculties for Apostolic Legates, however, two sepa-

[147] See the preceding Article, pp. 156-160.

[148] Bouscaren, *Canon Law Digest,* I, 371; III, 253.

[149] *Loc. cit.*

[150] Cf. Facultas. 34, f) and g) in the "*Formula Facultatum Quas S.C. Consistorialis Legatis Apostolicis, in Ditione Sua, Procurat,*" Vermeersch-Creusen, *Epitome,* I, 658 ff.; Woywod-Smith, *A Practical Commentary,* Appendix IV, pp. 679-689.

rate faculties are formulated, i.e., one for the clergy who suffer from weak sight, etc.,[151] and the other for the clergy who are totally blind.[152] As a consequence, each of them has its limited application according to the circumstances vary.

[151] *Faccultas n. 34, f).*
[152] *Facultas n. 34, g).*

CHAPTER IV

FACULTIES CONCERNING THE BLESSED SACRAMENT

ARTICLE I

Facultas XIII: FACULTY TO ALLOW THE EXPOSITION OF THE BLESSED SACRAMENT WITH TWO LIGHTS

Permittendi ut, iusta de causa, Ssmum Sacramentum cum duobus luminibus cuiusvis generis exponi possit, exclusa tamen expositione perpetua et XL horarum.

This is the Faculty by virtue of which the mission ordinary can permit his missionaries the public or private Exposition of the Blessed Sacrament, with two lights of any type whatsoever, if there is a just cause to do so, except in the cases of perpetual exposition or of the Forty Hours' Devotion. Thus, this faculty is concerned with a dispensation from the liturgical precept regarding the number and quality of candles prescribed for the Exposition of the Blessed Sacrament. This is *Facultas n. 12* in the *Formula Minor,* and is not included in *The Quinquennial Faculties, Formula IV.* The present Decennial Faculty as delineated in both the *Formula Maior* and the *Formula Minor* cannot be subdelegated.

SECTION 1. *Ex Iure*

According to the norm of canon 1274, in churches and oratories which have the right to reserve the Blessed Sacrament by law or by special concessions, private exposition, i.e., with the *ciborium,* can be held for any good reason without permission of the ordinary; public exposition, i.e., with the *ostensorium,* can be had in all churches during Mass and at Vespers on the Feast of Corpus Christi and on the seven days following, but not at other times except for a just and grave cause, especially a public one, and with the permission of the ordinary of the place, even though the church belong to an exempt religious institute.[1] There are two types of public exposition of the Blessed Sacrament. The first is the solemn public exposition, and it is so called when the Blessed Sacrament is exposed perpetually, or for several hours or days, e.g., throughout a Forty Hours' Devotion; the second is the less solemn public exposition, and it is so called when the Blesseed Sacrament is exposed at a church service described by Latin ceremonialists as *Laudes vespertinae,* or *Laudes Sanctissimi Sacramenti,* or a Benediction service.[2]

As to the number of candles prescribed for exposition of the Blessed Sacrament, according to the decree given by the Congregation of Sacred Rites, at private exposition at least six candles must be lighted on the altar,[3] and at solemn exposition at least twelve must be lighted on the altar.[4]

In 1910, the Congregation of Sacred Rites granted permission for the public exposition to be held with only six candles lighted on the altar in poor parishes where a special permission from the ordinary has been obtained.[5] Further, the same Sacred Congregation in its Decree *"Urbis et Orbis,"* under date of August 18, 1949, directed that the ordinary could permit for the solemn exposition of the Blessed Sacrament four beeswax candles, supplying with other lights for any larger number which might be required.[6]

[1] Canon 1274, § 1. Cf. O'Connell, *The Celebration of Mass,* pp. 404 ff.; L. J. O'Connell-W. J. Schmitz, *The Book of Ceremonies* (rev., Milwaukee: The Bruce Publishing Co., 1956), pp. 370-371; Regatillo, *Interpretatio et Iurisprudentia,* pp. 536-537; Cappello, *De Sacramentis,* I, nn. 346-356, pp. 317-322.

[2] O'Connell-Schmitz, *op. cit.,* p. 367; Regatillo, *loc. cit.*

[3] S.R.C., *Marnien.,* 15 Mart. 1698—*Decreta Authentica,* n. 1992.

[4] S.R.C., Aturen. et Aquen., 8 Febr. 1879—*Decreta Authentica,* n. 3480. Other numbers have been prescribed on different occasions: *ten* by the Decree *"Pro Regularibus Dioeceseos Mechliniensis"* of Pope Innocent XI, May 20, 1682; *twenty* in the *Instructio Clementina* (original by Clement XI in 1705; reformed version by Clement XII in 1731), nn. 6 ff. Cf. O'Connell, *The Celebration of Mass,* p. 90, footnote 39.

[5] S.R.C., *Tunquen.,* 30 Iul. 1910, ad 4—*Decreta Authentica,* n. 4257.

[6] *AAS,* XLI (1949), 476; Bouscaren, *Canon Law Digest,* III, 518.

This decree was intended to meet the emergency which arose after World War II, when the cost of wax candles became a burden on poor churches.[7]

SECTION 2. *Ex Facultate*

Exposition of the Most Blessed Sacrament in the present Decennial Faculty contemplates all kinds of exposition of the Most Blessed Sacrament, i.e., the solemn public exposition, the less solemn public exposition, and the private exposition—"*Cum duobus luminibus*." By virtue of the present Decennial Faculty, the mission ordinary may permit his missionaries to have Exposition of the Most Blessed Sacrament, whether it be the solemn public, the less solemn public, or the private exposition, with two light—"*Cuiusvis generis*." As to the quality or the nature of the lights, any substance whatever may be used, e.g., beeswax, mineral oils such as petroleum, or their extracts such as paraffin, vegetable oils, gas, electricity, etc.[8] Other supplying lights are not necessary when the present Decennial Faculty is applied.[9]

"*Iusta de causa*." The present Decennial Faculty can be used if there exists a "*iusta causa*," which could arise from the prohibitive cost of wax candles, or the inability or great inconvenience in obtaining them, of the difficulty experienced in keeping wax candles lighted during the exposition of the Most Blessed Sacrament.[10] The "*iusta causa*" need not be "*gravis*."[11]

[7]For the quality of candle prescribed for exposition of the Blessed Sacrament, see *supra*, pp. 135-136.

[8] Vromant, *Brevis Commentarius*, p. 25; Sartori, *Iuris Missionarii Elementa*, p. 100; Winslow, *The Apostolic Faculties*, p. 56. Cf. The Decree "*Urbis et Orbis*"—*AAS*, XLI (1949), 476; Bouscaren, *Canon Law Digest*, III, 518.

[9] Cf. The Decree "*Urbis et Orbis*"—*loc. cit.*

[10] Sartori, *Iuris Missionarii Elementa*, p. 100; De Reeper, *A Missionary Companion*, p. 44; Winslow, *The Apostolic Faculties*, p. 56.

[11] Vromant, *Facultates Apostolicae*, n. 46, p. 47; Paventi, *Brevis Commentarius*, p. 25; Sartori, *loc cit.* Cf. Conte a Coronata, *Institutiones Iuris Canonici*, I (4. ed., 1950), n. 114, p. 125.

In view of the clause "*exclusa tamen expositione perpetua et XL horarum,*" the present Decennial Faculty does not apply to Perpetual Exposition or to a Forty Hours' Devotion, either of which requires twenty beeswax candles on the altar,[12] and at least four beeswax candles with supplying lights of other substances, as given in the Decree "*Urbis et Orbis.*"[13]

ARTICLE II

Facultas XIV: FACULTY TO PERMIT THE RESERVATION OF THE BLESSED SACRAMENT WITHOUT ANY LIGHT

> *Permittendi ut, in locis ubi nulla materia ad lampades nutriendas haberi potest, Ssm̃um Sacramentum etiam sine lumine asservari possit, in casu tamen verae necessitatis et graviter onerata conscientia ipsius Ordinarii.*

This Faculty permits the mission ordinary to grant to missionaries in the territory under his jurisdiction a dispensation from the prescription contained in canon 1271, under specific postulated conditions. This is *Facultas n. 13* in the *Formula Minor,* and is not included in *The Quinquennial faculties, Formula IV.* In both the *Formula Maior* and the *Formula Minor,* the present Decennial Faculty cannot be subdelegated.

SECTION 1. *Ex Iure*

According to the norm of canon 1271, at least one lamp, fed either with olive oil or beeswax, must burn day and night, before the tabernacle in which the Blessed Sacrament is kept. When olive oil is not easily obtainable, the local ordinary may according to his prudent judgment allow the use of other oils, which should, insofar as it is possible,

[12] The *Instructio Clementina,* n. 6. Cf. Sartori, *Iuris Missionarii Elementa,* p. 100: "Pro Expositione autem XL Hor. ad minus 20 sint iuxta Instructionem Clementinam, quae tamen extra Urbem non obligat; at laudabiliter observatur." Cf. also O'Connell-Schmitz, *The Book of Ceremonies,* p. 406.

[13] *AAS,* XLI (1949), 476; Bouscaren, *Canon Law Digest,* III, 518.

be vegetable oils.[14] According to the moralists, a grave sin is committed by the person responsible for the failure of the lamp to burn if that condition has lasted for twenty-four hours.[15]

For the duration of the extraordinary circumstances created by World War II, the Congregation of Sacred Rites granted an execptional faculty to bishops to permit that "the lamp before the Blessed Sacrament be maintained with other oils, vegetable if possible, and in the last resort to permit even electric lights to be used," in case olive oil or beeswax be "either entirely lacking or cannot be obtained without grave inconvenience and expense."[16] In the Decree *"Urbis et Orbis"* of 1949, the same indult was declared to remain in effect in the following statement:

> Now, although neither beeswax nor oil is entirely lacking, yet in view of their high cost, this Sacred Congregation intends to modify the indult so that, whereas the indult remains in effect as regards the lamp before the Blessed Sacrament, for the celebration of private Mass, two wax candles are to be used. . . .[17]

SECTION 2. *Ex Facultate*

"Permittendi ut, in locis ubi nulla materia ad lampades nutriendas haberi potest, Ssm̃um Sacramentum etiam sine lumine asservari possit." By virtue of the Decree *"Urbis et Orbis,"* the mission ordinary, too, can permit missionaries in his territory to burn even an electric light for the lamp

[14] Cf. *Rituale Romanum,* Tit. IV, Cap. 1, *De Sacratissimo Eucharistiae Sacramento,* n. 6; S.R.C., decr., 23 Febr. 1916—*Decreta Authentica,* n. 4334.

[15] Conte a Coronata, *Institutiones Iuris Cononici,* Vol. II (4. ed., 1951), n. 850, p. 178. The author cites St. Alphonsus, Gasparri, Blat, Augustine, etc. Cf. also Cappello, *De Sacramentis,* Vol. I (6. ed., 1953), n. 339, p. 310.

[16] S.R.C., decr., 13 Mart. 1942—*AAS,* XXXIV(1942), 112; Bouscaren, *Canon Law Digest,* II, 389-390; *The Jurist,* II (1942), 393.

[17] S.R.C., decr., 18 Aug. 1949—*AAS,* XLI (1949), 476; Bouscaren, *Canon Law Digest,* III, 518.

before the Blessed Sacrament. In the absence of all the above mentioned, in virtue of the present Decennial Faculty, the mission ordinary can permit the Blessed Sacrament to be reserved without any light whatsoever. The absence of materials for a light is postulated to be such that, if the local ordinary did not permit the reservation of the Blessed Sacrament without any light whatsoever, a gievn church could not reserve the Blessed Sacrament despite the necessity of the Sacrament for the faithful.

"In casu tamen necessitatis." In addition to the foregoing condition, i.e., the absence of all materials for supplying the lamp before the Blessed Sacrament, there must be a genuine necessity for reserving the Blessed Sacrament. Such a necessity would arise from the obligation of administering Viaticum, which, as theologians hold, the faithful in danger of death are obliged to receive in consequence of a divine precept, or from the need of spiritual comfort and help through a visit to the Blessed Sacrament, which otherwise the faithful, or members of a religious community, would be deprived of. Thus parish churches, quasi-parish churches, and others which serve as such in the missions where quasi-parishes have not yet been canonically erected, also the chapels of religious communities may sense such a necssity and need.[18]

"Garviter onerata conscientia." It is not the missionary, but the mission ordinary who must judge about the sufficiency of the reasons to use the present Decennial Faculty. If there exists only a minor necessity for reserving the Blessed Sacrament in the chapels of religious communities, the local ordinary may give the permission to use a light of a substance other than those which are prescribed in canon 1271, as mentioned in the decrees of 1942 and 1949.[19]

In and of itself (*per se*), the present Decennial Faculty can be given habitually to missionaries; in practice, how-

[18] Cf. Sartori, *Iuris Missionarii Elementa*, p. 101; Vromant, *Facultates Apostolicae*, n. 48, p. 48; Paventi, *Brevis Commentarius*, p. 26; Winslow, *The Apostolic Faculties*, pp. 58-59.

[19] Cf. *AAS*, XXXIV (1942), 112; *AAS*, XLI (1949), 476.

ever, it should be given *per modum actus,* according as the above delineated condittons are verified by the mission ordinary.

ARTICLE III

Facultas XV: FACULTY TO PERMIT THE RESERVATION OF THE BLESSED SACRAMENT WITHOUT ANY LIGHT AS COMMUNION FOR THE SICK

> *Permittendi, si sit periculum sacrilegii, ut SSm̃um Sacramentum pro infirmis sine lumine in loco tamen decenti retineri possit.*

By virtue of the present Decennial Faculty the mission ordinary can under certain circumstances permit missionaries in the territory under his jurisdiction to reserve the Blessed Sacrament in a decent place and without the tabernacle lamp. Thus the present Decennial Faculty is concerned with dispensations from the norms prescribed in paragraphs 1, 2, and 3 of canon 1269. This is *Facultas n. 14* in the *Formula Minor,* and in both Formulae it cannot be subdelegated. The present Decennial Faculty is not included in *The Quinquennial Faculties, Formula IV.*

SECTION 1. *Ex Iure*

According to the norm of canon 1269, the Blessed Sacrament must be kept in an immovable tabernacle, placed in the middle of the altar;[20] the tabernacle must be well constructed, securely closed on all sides, properly ornamented according to the liturgical laws, free from all other things, and guarded so well that there is no danger of profanation.[21] For a grave reason and with the approval of the local ordinary it is allowed that the Blessed Sacrament be removed from the tabernacle overnight, and reserved in a safer but decent place on a corporal, and with a light burning before it, as canon 1271 demands.[22]

The Sacred Congregation of the Sacraments in an im-

[20] Canon 1269, § 1.
[21] Canon 1269, § 2.
[22] Canon 1269, § 3.

portant Instruction entitled *"De Sanctissima Eucharistia sedulo custodienda"* of May 26, 1938, reviewed the existing legislation of the Code on the custody of the Blessed Sacrament.[23] The Instruction enlarged upon each of the salient points of the legislation. It declared the obligation of having an immovable tabernacle, solidly enclosed on all sides, to be in and of itself (*per se*), a grave one, and required that the tabernacle be built of solid and strong material.[24] The same Instruction declared that the tabernacle must be carefully guarded so that all danger of sacrilegious profanation is obviated;[25] it imposed upon the local ordinary the obligation to investigate, at the time of visitation, about the observance of these rules, and whenever he found that not all the provisions of the law in regard to the structure and custody of the tabernacle were being observed, he was to order them to be put into execution within a certain period of time, under penalty of a heavy fine and even suspension *a divinis* in the case of the priest, or suspension *ab officio* in the case of others, according to the gravity of their offense.[26] The Instruction prescribed that in every case of sacrilegious theft and of violation of the Blessed Sacrament the local ordinary was always in person, or through a specially delegated official of his curia, to institute administrative proceedings against the pastor or other priest, whether secular or regular, responsible for the custody of the Blessed Sacrament.[27]

The Sacred Congregation of the Sacraments again issued a brief exhortation on February 10, 1941,[28] urging the local ordinaries to repeat their admonitions to all pastors

[23] S.C. de Sacr., instr., 26 Maii 1938—*AAS*, XXX (1938), 198; Bouscaren, *Canon Law Digest*, II, 377-389.

[24] The Instruction *"De Sanctissima Eucharistia sedulo custodienda,"* n. 4.

[25] *Ibid.*, n. 5.

[26] *Ibid.*, n. 10, a).

[27] *Ibid.*, n. 10, b), c), and d).

[28] S.C. de Sacr., exhortatio, 10 Febr. 1941—*AAS*, XXXIII (1941), 57; Bouscaren, *Canon Law Digest*, II, 389.

and rectors of churches to increase their diligence in carrying out in full all the prescriptions of the Institution *"De Sanctissima Eucharistia sedulo custodienda"* of May 26, 1938.

The Instruction *"De Sanctissima Eucharistia sedulo custodienda"* of May 26, 1938, also extended its directives to the third paragraph of canon 1269. According to the directives it is allowed, for some grave cause approved by the local ordinary, to keep the Blessed Sacrament during the night outside the altar in a safe and decent place; such a place is usually the sacristy, provided that it is really a safe and suitable place, or, if it prove preferable, a strong and well-locked safe set in the wall of the church. If neither the church nor the sacristy affords the necessary security, the Blessed Sacrament may be kept in some other safe place, even though it be private, in which case the pastor must take care that the Blessed Sacrament be guarded with due reverence and honor, and that the belief of the faithful in the Real Presence be not impaired.[29]

During World War II, on September 15, 1943, because of the then existing war conditions, the Sacred Congregation of the Sacraments issued an Instruction with respect to the "Protection of the Most Blessed Sacrament from the Incursion of War."[30] Referring to the third paragraph of canon 1269, this Instruction stated:

> . . . We have already explained this provision of law in the Instruction, *De Sanctissima Eucharistia sedulo custodienda,* of 26 May, 1938, n.5, where it was stated that this way of keeping the Most Blessed Sacrament provides greater security especially against thieves; but obviously the same holds good for attacks of war, and even in the daytime if necessary.
>
> The 'secure place' here referred to may also be

[30] *AAS,* XXXV (1943), 282; Bouscaren, *Canon Law Digest,* III, 515 ff.

[29] The Instruction *"De Sacratissima Eucharistia sedulo custodienda,"* n. 5. Cf. S.R.C., decr., 17 Febr., 1881—*Decrenta Authentica,* n. 3527.

> some special recess under the church or sacristy or in the parish rectory, especially if the sacred Species be enclosed in some sort of iron box constructed by skillful craftsmen so as to protect them from fire, dampness, and any other unwelcome environment—the box to be inserted in the lower walls of the church or inside the marble base of a pillar, observing as far as possible the liturgical laws and the above cited Instruction.
>
> ... It will be well to consecrate each day only as many hosts as will be sufficient for the Communion of the faithful, consuming those which may be left over, except some which may be kept for giving Viaticum or Communion to the sick; and these it would be advisable to put, not in an ordinary ciborium, but in some sort of box made of solid metal and entirely enclosed, suited to the purpose, which can easily be put away and moved from place to place.[31]

SECTION 2. *Ex Facultate*

By virtue of the present Decennial Faculty the mission ordinary can permit missionaries in the territory under his jurisdiction to reserve the Blessed Sacrament, which may be needed for the sick, in a decent place without the tabernacle lamp. if there exist any danger of sacrilege against the Blessed Sacrament.

"Si sit periculum sacrilegii." Since the faculty does not include any restrictive clause in regard to the source of the danger of sacrilege, the while the danger of sacrilege exists, whatever might be its source, the present faculty can be used. The danger of sacrilege could arise from heretics and infidels, from thieves, from incendiarism, from social disturbances such as riots, rebellions, etc., from war, from persecutions against Catholics, etc. If the danger of sacrilege exists only at night, the Blessed Sacrament should during the day be restored to the regular tabernacle; if the danger exists both at day and at night, the Blessed Sacra-

[31] Bouscaren, *Canon Law Digest*, III, 516-517; S.C. de Sacr., instr., 15 Sept. 1943, nn. 5 and 6—*AAS*, XXXV (1943), 282.

ment should be kept in a safe place after the sacred functions have been performed in the church.

"Pro infirmis." Even though the foregoing danger of sacrilege exists, if there is no need of the Blessed Sacrament for the sick, the present Decennial Faculty cannot be used. It is not necessary, however, that there should actually be a sick person in the place.[32] Thus, churches which under the common law must reserve the Blessed Sacrament can use this faculty, even though no person is actually known to be sick at the time; but sacred places where the Blessed Sacrament can be reserved only by way of a special indult may not use the present faculty.[33]

"Loco tamen decenti." The place where, by virtue of the present Decennial Faculty, the Blessed Sacrament can be kept must be a fitting place, i.e., an empty room in the priest's house, but not the priest's bedroom.[34] Priests in the missions also should follow as far as possible the rules and prescriptions given by the Sacred Congregation of the Sacraments in the Instructions of May 26, 1938,[35] and of September 15, 1943.[36]

"Sine lumine." In case the danger of sacrilege or profanation exists because of the light placed before the Blessed Sacrament, even if the reservation is undertaken in a supposedly safe place, the light should be removed. And, conversely, if the danger of sancrilege is sufficiently excluded by removing the Blessed Sacrament to the safe place, the sancturay lamp must be kept burning before It in that place. Even in the latter case, if it is necessary, the preceding Decennial Faculty can be applied.[37]

[32] Vromant, *Facultates Apostolicae*, n. 48, p. 49; Sartori, *Iuris Missionarii Elementa*, p. 102.

[33] Sartori, *loc. cit.* Cf. S.R.C., 4 Febr. 1871—*Collecanea*, n. 1365, ad 1.

[34] Vromant, *loc. cit.;* De Reeper, *A Missionary Companion*, p. 40.

[35] *"De Santissima Eucharistia sedulo custodienda,"* n. 5—*AAS*, XXX (1938), 198. See *supra*, p. 209[b].

[36] *AAS*, XXXV (1943), 282. See *supra*, p. 210.

[37] See *Facultas XIV* in the *Formula Maior*, *supra*, pp. 204-207.

This faculty is different from the preceding faculty (*Facultas XIV* in the *Formula Maior*) in that the present faculty is to be given because of the fear of the danger of sacrilege or profanation of the Blessed Sacrament, while the preceding faculty is to be given because of the lack of materials for supplying the sanctuary lamp. The present faculty can be used as long as the cause lasts. The use of this faculty implies a dispensation only from the liturgical precepts in regard to the place for reserving the Blessed Sacrament and the obligation of burning a sanctuary lamp before the Blessed Sacrament which is reserved in a safe and decent place outside the altar, but not from other liturgical laws such as the use of the corporal, and the observance of the rites and the ceremonies in removing the Blessed Sacrament from, and in restoring It to, the tabernacle. The two dispensations deriving from the present faculty are not always necessarily used together as a pair, for they can be used separately, simply as necessity demands.

Article IV

Facultas XVII: Faculty to Permit His Missionaries to Carry the Blessed Sacrament Without External Solemnities to the Sick and the Dying

> *Permittendi suis missionariis ut deferre et administrare valeant christianis aegrotantibus Ssm̃am Eucharistiam sine superpelliceo et stola, ac sine comite, dummodo constet de periculo cui exponerentur si induerent superpelliceum et stolam.*

This is the Faculty by virtue of which the mission ordinary can under certain circumstances permit a non-observance of the liturgical law of canon 847 and of the liturgical precepts in regard to the carrying of the Holy Eucharist to the sick. This is *Facultas n. 16* in the *Formula Minor,* and it cannot be subdelegated in either of the two Formulae. The present Decennial Faculty is not included in *The Quinquennial Faculties, Formulae IV.*

SECTION 1. *Ex Iure*

Canon 847 prescribes that Holy Communion should be brought to the sick publicly, unless some just and reasonable cause suggest a different procedure. The Sacred Congregation of the Sacraments has declared that the judgment as to whether there is a just and reasonable cause for bringing Holy Communion privately to the sick rests, not with the priest, but with the local ordinary; however, when the priest knows from common experience and opinion that in his diocese or in certain localities of it priests and people do not consider such a private carrying of Holy Communion of the sick improper, the local ordinary should not lay down general regulations to enforce a public bringing of It or reserve to himself the permission in each case for a private bringing of It, so as to hinder the frequest or even daily Communion for the sick.[38] According to the provision of canon 848, the right and the duty to carry Holy Communion publicly to the sick within a parish, even to non-parishioners, are vested in the local pastor. Other priests may do so only in a case of necessity, or with at least the presumed authorization of the pastor of the parish or of the local ordinary.

As to the manner of privately bringing Holy Communion to the sick,[39] Pope Benedict XIV (1740-1758) laid down in his Encyclical Letter *"Inter omnigenas,"* on February 2, 1744, the following regulations: The priest was to carry the Sacred Host in a pyx; the pyx was to be enclosed in a burse, which in turn was by means of a cord to be suspended from the neck, and carried under cover of the outer garments; the priest was not to go alone, but in the company either of another cleric or of a layman.[40] But the Encyclical

[38] S.C. de Sacr., resp., 5 Ian. 1928—*AAS*, XX (1929), 81; Bouscaren, *Canon Law Digest*, I, 404-407.

[39] As to the manner of publicly bringing Holy Communion to the sick, the priest must follow the liturgical rules set down in the *Rituale Romanum*, Tit. IV, Caput IV, *de Communione Infirmorum*, nn. 10-13.

[40] *Fontes*, n. 339; *Collectanea*, n. 345.

Letter *"Inter omnigenas"* prescribed that the priest was to wear the surplice when he was taking the Blessed Sacrament from the tabernacle, and while he was administering It to the sick.[41]

The foregoing regulations were also insisted upon in a response of the Sacred Congregation of the Sacraments, on December 23, 1912.[42] Thus, when administering Holy Communion, the priest must observe the liturgical rules prescribed in the *Rituale Romanum,*[43] i.e., upon entering the sick room the priest puts on the surplice if he has not already done so (the stole now must be visible), lights a candle and administers the Blessed Sacrament, in the usual manner.[44]

SECTION 2. *Ex Facultate*

"Sine superpelliceo et stola ac sine comite." By virtue of the present Decennial Faculty the mission ordinary may permit his missionaries within his own territory to carry and administer Holy Communion to the sick without wearing surplice and stole, and apart from anyone accompanying him with a lighted candle, *"dummodo constet de periculo cui exponerentur si induerent supercelliceum et stolam."*[45]

"Dummodo constet de periculo. . . ." This clause lays down a requisite for the proper and lawful use of the present Decennial Faculty. It is postulated that with moral cer-

[41] Cf. *Acta et Decreta Concilii Plenarii Baltimorensis* II, n. 264; Winslow, *The Apostolic Faculties*, p. 63.

[42] *AAS*, IV (1912), 725.

[43] Tit. IV, cap. IV, n. 29.

[44] Sartori, *Iuris Missionarii Elementa,* p. 103; Winslow, *The Apostolic Faculties, loc cit.;* James J. Hannon, *Holy Viaticum,* The Catholic University of American Canon Law Studies, n. 314 (Washington, D.C.: The Catholic University of America Press, 1951), pp. 60-62; 150 ff.

[45] In a similar manner, the Sacred Congregation of the Holy Office, in 1854, granted missionaries in Korea permission for the bringing of Holy Communion privately to prisons and to houses of infidels in which a member of the faithful happened to be, provided there was no danger of irreverence or contempt. Cf. S.C.S. Off., 5 Iul. 1854—*Fontes*, n. 926. Cf also *Collectanea,* nn. 778 and 1171.

tainty there is foreseen some danger of irreverence to the Blessed Sacrament, or some danger of harm to the administering priest, to his companion, or to the sick, and his relatives, if the priest observes the liturgical regulations prescribed for the carrying and the administering of Holy Communion to the sick, even in a private manner.[46]

"Christianis aegrotantibus." The use of the present faculty is not confined to the administration of Holy Viaticum, and thus it applies equally to the giving of Communion to the sick *devotionis causa,* for neither the term *"christianis aegrotantibus"* nor the term *"Ssmam Eucharistiam"* requires that the sick be grievously ill and that Holy Communion be administered in the manner of Holy Viaticum. Furthermore, the places where the sick stay are not envisioned simply as the homes of pagans, but they could be the homes of the faithful, non-Catholic hospitals, prisons, etc.

On the assumption that no danger of irreverence to the Blessed Sacrament, or of harm to the priest, to the sick and his relatives, or to the companion of the priest exists or threatens, the rubrics of the *Rituale Romanum* for the private administration of Holy Communion should as far as possible be faithfully observed.

ARTICLE V

Facultas XVIII: FACULTY TO ALLOW THE SICK TO RECEIVE HOLY COMMUNION THOUGH THEY HAVE NOT OBSERVED THE EUCHARISTIC FAST

> *Concedendi infirmis, de quibus certa spes non adsit ut cito convalescant, ut S. Communionem sumere possint bis vel ter in hebdomada (et si agatur de sacerdotibus vel religiosis, etiam quotidie) etsi aliquam medicinam vel aliquid per modum potus antea sumpserint.*

The present Decennial Faculty is concerned with the Eucharistic fast of the sick. It is *Facultas n. 17* in the *Formula*

[46] Sartori, *Iuris Missionarii Elementa,* p. 103.

Minor, and in both Formulae allows for subdelegation. The Decennial Faculty is not included in *The Quinquennial Faculties, Formula IV.*

SECTION 1. IN THE CODE OF CANON LAW

Canon 858, § 1, states that those who have not kept the natural fast from midnight are not allowed to receive Communion, except when they are in danger of death or unless it should become necessary to consume the Blessed Sacrament to safeguard It against irreverence. And the second paragraph of the same canon provides that the sick who have been confined to bed for a month without the certain hope of a speedy recovery may, with the advice of the confessor, receive Holy Communion once or twice a week, though they have taken medicine or liquid food.[47] However, canon 858 in its entirety was supplanted by the Constitution *"Christus Dominus"* of Pope Pius XII, on January 6, 1953,[48] and the Motu proprio *"Sacram Communionem"* of the same Pope, on March 19, 1957.[49]

SECTION 2. THE NEW LEGISLATION AND THE DECENNIAL FACULTY N. XVIII

The new legislation concerning the Eucharistic fast of the sick, both the faithful and the priests, as stated in the Instruction which was attached to the Constitution *"Christus Dominus"* by the Holy Office,[50] is as follows:

[47] Cf. Woywod-Smith, *A Practical Commentary,* nn. 757-758, pp. 469-472.

[48] *AAS,* XLV (1953), 15 ff.; Bouscaren, *Canon Law Digest,* IV, 269-277.

[49] *AAS,* XLIX (1957), 177 ff.; Bouscaren, *Canon Law Digest,* IV, 286-288. Cf. James Ruddy, *The Apostolic Constitution* Christus Dominus: *Text, Translation, with Short Annotations on the Motu Proprio* SACRAM COMMUNIONEM, The Catholic University of America Canon Law Studies, n. 390 (Washington, D.C.: The Catholic University of America Press, 1957).

[50] S.C.S. Off., instr. (de Disciplina circa Ieiunium Eucharisticum Servanda), 6 Ian. 1953—*AAS,* XLV (1953), 47 ff.; Bouscaren, *Canon Law Digest,* IV, 277-282.

Concerning the Sick, Both Faithful and Priests (Const. n. II)

1. The faithful who are sick, even though not confined to bed, can take something by way of drink, except alcoholic drink, if, by reason of their sickness, they are unable to observe the complete fast until the reception of Holy Communion without grave inconvenience; they can also take something by way of true medicine, either liquid (exclusive of alcohol), or solid, as long as there is question of true medicine, prescribed by a physician, or commonly accepted as such. It is to be noted, however, that not every solid taken as nourishment can be considered medicine.

2. The conditions under which one can enjoy the dispensation from the law of fasting, with no time limit prescribed before Communion, must be prudently weighed by a confessor, nor can anyone use the dispensation without his advice. A confessor, however, can give his advice either in the sacramental internal forum, or in the extra-sacramental internal forum. He can also give it once for all as long as the conditions of the same sickness last.

3. Sick priests, even though not confined to bed, can use the dispensation in like manner, whether they are going to say Mass, or receive the Most Holy Eucharist.[51]

In consequence of the present Decennial Faculty the sick can be allowed to receive Holy Communion twice or three times a week upon the prudent advice of their confessor, though medicine or liquid food has been taken by them; and the medicine was to be restrictively understood as something taken *"per modum potus,"* exclusive of medicine which was in the form of solid food. But, according to the new discipline stated in the above cited Instruction, the sick may, upon prudent advice from the confessor, receive Holy

[51] Translation of the Latin text under the heading "*Quoad Infirmos sive Fideles sive Sacerdotes*" (Const., n. II) in the cited Instruction of the Sacred Congregation of the Holy Office, taken from Ruddy, *op. cit.*, pp. 21-23; for Latin text, cf. *AAS*, XLV (1953), 47; for commentary on the cited passages, cf. Ruddy, *op. cit.*, pp. 72-81.

Communion as many times as they wish, though they have taken something by way of medicine, either in liquid or solid form, prescribed by a physician, or commonly recognized as such. Thus, in view of the greater number of times Holy Communion may be received by the sick, and in view of the added (solid) form in which the medicine may be taken, the new discipline is broader than the present Decennial Faculty.

Nevertheless, this new discipline was even further broadened in its scope for use by the sick in Pope Pius XII's Motu proprio *"Sacram Communionem,"* of March 19, 1957,[52] in which the legislation on the Eucharistic fast of the sick is stated as follows:

> The sick, even though not confined to bed, can take non-alcoholic drink and true and proper medicines, either liquid or solid, without limitation of time, before celebrating Mass or receiving Holy Communion.[53]

According to the foregoing newest discipline, the advice of a confessor is no longer required, and thus the sick may avail themselves of the privilege whenever they can be classified as such. Furthermore, *"infirmi"* with the descriptive clause *"quamvis non decumbant"* in the Motu proprio *"Sacram Communionem"* and *"etiamsi non decumbant"* in the Constitution *"Christus Dominus"* manifestly carry a more extensive connotation than *"infirmi"* with the descriptive clause *"de quibus certa spes non adsit ut cito convalescant"* in the preesnt Decennial Faculty.

The new general discipline on the Eucharistic fast of the sick is much broader than the present Decennial Faculty. Consequently, since the present Decennial Faculty can no

[52] *AAS*, XLIX (1957), 177; Bouscaren, *Canon Law Digest*, IV, 286-288.

[53] From Bouscaren, *ibid.*, p. 287. Latin text: "4. Infirmi, quamvis non decumbant, potum non alcoholicum et veras ac proprias medicinas, sive liquidas sive solidas, ante Missae celebrationem vel Eucharistiae receptionem sine temporis limite sumere possunt."—*AAS*, XLIX (1957), 177-178. For an annotation to the cited passage, cf. Ruddy, *op. cit.*, pp. 128-132.

longer be a favor granted for the faithful or the priest in the missions, it can no longer stand as a faculty.

ARTICLE VI

Facultas XVI: FACULTY TO PERMIT SISTERS RELIGIOUS TO WASH PALLS, PURIFICATORS, AND CORPORALS

Permittendi religiosis sororibus ut pallas, corporalia et purificatoria primo abluere valeant.

The power is conceded to the mission ordinary to permit the palls, corporals, and purificators in their first washing to be washed by sisters religious. This is *Facultas n. 15* in the *Formula Minor,* and in both Formulae it allows for subdelegation. The present Decennial Faculty is not included in *The Quinquennial Faculties, Formula IV.*

SECTION 1. *Ex Iure*

The second paragraph of canon 1306 prescribes that the purifications, palls, and corporals used in Holy Mass shall not be given to lay persons (even though they are religious) to be washed until they have first been washed by a cleric in major orders, i.e., by a priest, a deacon, or a subdeacon. The Congregation of Sacred Rites declared that the bishop is not allowed to authorize nuns, sisters religious, or lay brothers to do the first washing of the sacred linens.[54] From the foregoing provisions it follows that if the corporals, palls, and purificators have been first washed by a cleric in major orders, their second and third washings can be done by any person, whether he be a cleric or not, or whether he be a sacristan religious or not, and that a person who is not in major order may do the first washing of the sacred linens only in virtue of an apostolic indult.[55]

SECTION 2. *Ex Facultate*

The present Decennial Faculty makes an exception to the

[54] S.R.C., *Molinen.*, 12 Sept. 1857—*Decreta Authentica,* n. 3059, ad 26.

[55] Sadlowski, *The Sacred Furnishings of Churches,* pp. 77-79.

canonical prescription of canon 1306, § 2, "... *ne tradantur lavanda laicis etiam religiosis, nisi prius abluta fuerint a clerico in maioribus ordinibus constituto,*" and the mission ordinary can give this privilege to sisters religious.

Through the wording, "*sorores religiosae,*" in the faculty, brothers religious are excluded, so that sisters religious exclusively are contemplated as defined in canons 488 and 673. Under the terminology are included women religious with simple vows,[56] or also such women who without vows live[57] in societies approved by the legitimate ecclesiastical authority, and who as members strive after evangelical perfection in community life without taking public vows, either perpetual or temporal.[58] These societies may have either a pontifical approval, or simply a diocesan approval.[59] *A fortiori, moniales* or nuns are included under the expression "sisters religious" but other pious women who are not leading a community life after the manner prescribed in canons 673-681 are excluded from the use of the present privilege.

As clerics in major orders must do, so the sisters religious should pour the water of the first washing of the used corporals, palls, and purificators into the sacrarium, or, if there be none, into the fire, as is prescribed in canon 1306, § 2.

The present Decennial Faculty does not restrict the use of this privilege simply to sisters religious who at the same time are sacristans. In this point, accordingly, the present faculty is different from the privilege enjoyed by sacristans according to canon 1306, § 1.[60]

[56] Canon 488, 7°

[57] Canons 673-681. Cf. Vromant, *Facultates Apostolicae*, n. 49, p. 50; Sartori, *Iuris Missionarii Elementa*, p. 102; Paventi, *Brevis Commentarius*, p. 27.

[58] Canon 488, 1°, and 673.

[59] Canon 488, 3°.

[60] Canon 1306, § 1: "Curandum ne calix cum patena et ante lotionem purificatoria, pallae et corporalia, quae adhibita fuere in sacrificio Missae tangantur, nisi a clericis vel *ab iis qui eorum custodiam habent.*"

Since the present Decennial Faculty can be subdelegated, the mission ordinary can subdelegate this faculty to his missionaries in his territory in order to let them permit sisters religious to wash the purificators, palls, and corporals, beginning with their first washing.

SECTION TWO

Faculties Concerning the Sacrament of Matrimony: The Decennial Faculties NN. XXII-XXVIII In the *Formula Maior*

CHAPTER V

FACULTAS XXII: FACULTY TO DISPENSE FROM MATRIMONIAL IMPEDIMENTS OF ECCLESIASTICAL LAW

Facultas XXII in the *Formula Maior* contains a Decennial Faculty to dispense from Matrimonial Impediments of Ecclesiastical Law, and this same Faculty appears as *Facultas n. 21* in the *Formula Minor*. In both Formulae the present Decennial Faculty can be subdelegated; it corresponds to *Faculties nn. 2* and *3* from the Holy Office and to *Faculties nn. 1* and *2* from the Sacred Congregation of the Sacraments in *The Quinquennial Faculties, Formula IV*.

The present chapter, however, will first deal with the following headings: (1) Various Divisions of Matrimonial Impediments, and (2) Faculties to Dispense from Matrimonial Impediments Granted by the Common Law; then, (3) The *Decennial Faculty XXII* in the *Formula Maior*, and, finally, (4) the *Quinquennial Faculties* to Dispense from Matrimonial Impediments as Granted through Formula IV.

ARTICLE I. VARIOUS DIVISIONS OF MATRIMONIAL IMPEDIMENTS

Since the present Decennial Faculty deals with the matrimonial impediments of ecclesiastical law, and since it contains the phrase, "*super impediments matrimonialibus sive minoris sive maioris gradus* (can. 1042), *tam publicis quam ocultis, etiam multiplicibus. . . ,*" it is necessary to consider at least the classifications of the matrimonial impediments mentioned in this Decennial Faculty.

According to the norm of canon 1036, the matrimonial impediments are said to be diriment or prohibitive, depending on whether they render the matrimoniay invalid, or only illicit.[1] It is an applicable principle with reference to matri-

[1] Canon 1036, §§ 1 and 2.

monial impediments that the marriage is either illicit or invalid, even if only one of the parties concerning the marriage is affected directly by the prohibitive or the diriment impediment.[2]

The diriment impediments are: (1) nonage;[3] (2) impotence;[4] (3) previous bond;[5] (4) disparity of cult;[6] (5) sacred orders;[7] (6) vows;[8] (7) abduction;[9] (8) marital criminality;[10] (9) consanguinity;[11] (10) affinity;[12] (11)

[2] Canon 1036, § 3.

[3] Canon 1067. Males under sixteen years completed and females under fourteen years completed, computed according to the norm of canon 34, § 3, 3°.

[4] Canon 1068. Impotence is the inability to perform sexual intercourse; to invalidate marriage it must be antecedent and perpetual, absolute or relative, in either party, whether known or not.

[5] Canon 1069. A valid bond of previous marriage, even unconsummated. Exceptions are: (a) the Pauline privilege; b) dispensation from a purely legitimate marriage "*in favorem fidei*," and c) dissolution of a ratified non-consummated marriage through solemn religious profession or by way of a papal dispensation.

[6] Canon 1070. One party baptized in the Catholic Church, or converted to it from heresy or schism, and the other party unbaptized. The impediment remains if the baptized party afterwards falls away from the faith.

[7] Canon 1072. Subdeaconship, deaconship, and priesthood.

[8] Canon 1073. Solemn vows; also simple vows when fortified with an invalidating effect.

[9] Canon 1074. It arises between the abductor and the woman abducted with a view to marriage, or also between the forceful detainer and the woman forcefully detained with a view to marriage. The impediment remains as long as the woman is in the power of the abductor or detainer.

[10] Canon 1075. a) Adultery along with the murder of the spouse by one of the parties guilty of the adultery; b) the murder of the spouse by means of a mutual cooperation, whether moral or physical; c) adultery along with the mutually given and accepted promise of marriage, and d) adultery along with an attempted marriage.

[11] Canon 1076. This impediment arises from the blood relationship of the parties whether legitimate or natural, and it affects a) all the degrees in the direct line, ascending and decending, and b) three degrees in the collatral line, down to and including scond cousins.

[12] Canon 1077. This impediment arises from a valid marriage, whether ratified only, or whether ratified and consummated, and it

public propriety;[13] (12) spiritual relationship,[14] and (13) legal relationship.[15] The prohibitive impediments are: (1) vow;[16] (2) legal relationship,[17] and (3) mixed religion.[18]

affects a) all the degrees in the direct line and b) two degrees in the collateral line: the husband and the sister, the first cousin, the aunt, and the niece of the wife; the wife and the brother, the first cousin, the uncle, and the nephew of the husband.

[13] Canon 1078. This impediment arises: a) from an invalid marriage, whether consummated or non-comsummated, but not from a merely civil marriage apart from public concubinage, and b) from public or notorious concubinage. It affects the first and second degrees in the direct line: the man, and the mother, the grandmother, the daughter, and granddaughter of the woman; the woman, and the father, the grandfather, the son, and grandson of the man.

[14] Canon 1079. This impediment arises from a valid baptism, whether solemn or private, and exists only between the person baptized on the one hand and the minister or the sponsor on the other.

[15] Canon 1080. Persons who according to the civil law are regarded as incapable of marrying each other because of a legal relationship arising from adoption cannot validly contract marriage together according to canon law. In the United States of America, this diriment impediment of civil law exists in the Territory of Puerto Rico, and in some States (Mass., Conn., and R.I.). Cf. Lincoln Bouscaren-Adam C. Ellis, *Canon Law* (3rd rev. ed., Millwaukee: The Bruce Publishing Co., 1957), pp. 474-475, note 58; Carberry, "Legal Relationship as an Impediment to Marriage," *Ecclesiastical Review*, XC (1934), 394-401. Legal relationship is a diriment impediment in Italy, Spain, Poland, Greece, Bolivia, Brazil, Peru, etc. Cf. F. M. Cappello, *Tractatus Canonico-Moralis de Sacramentis*, Vol. V *(De Matrimonio)* (6. ed., Taurini-Romae: Marietti, 1950, n. 570, pp. 536-537 [hereafter cited as *De Matrimonio*]. "*Cognatio legalis.* Adoptio, qualis fit in Corea, impedimento non dat locum. Quum enim, ex lege civili, illicitae non sint nuptiae inter adoptantem et adoptatam, *nec ex iure canonico illicitae sunt* (can. 1059)."—*Directorium Commune Missionum Coreae Jussu Concilii Regionalis 1931 Editum* (Hongkong: Imprimarie de Nazareth, 1932), n. 340, p. 152 [hereafter cited as *Directorium Commune Missionum Coreae*].

[16] Canon 1058. A marriage is regarded illicit in the face of the following vows (made in or out of religion): the vow of virginity, the vow of perfect chastity, the vow not to marry, the vow to receive sacred orders, and the vow to embrace the religious state.

[17] Canon 1059. In those regions in which legal relationship arising from adoption is a prohibitive impediment by civil law it is also a prohibitive impediment by canon law. In France, Germany, Hungary,

The *diriment impediments* are divided into two groups, i.e., a) the diriment impediments of minor degree, and b) the diriment impediments of major degree. The following are of minor degree: (1) consanguinity in the third degree of the collateral line; (2) affinity in the second degree of the collateral line; (3) public propriety in the second degree; (4) spiritual relationship, and (5) marital criminality when it derives from adultery with a promise of or attempt at marriage, even by means of a merely civil contract.[19] All other diriment impediments are of major degree.[20]

Matrimonial impediments are considered *public,* if they are such that they can be proved in the external forum; otherwise they are *occult.*[21] Among the principal means of proof in the external forum are two trustworthy witnesses testifying to facts within their personal knowledge,[22] or one unexceptionably qualified witness regarding his official acts,[23] or an authentic public document.[24] The Committee for the Authentic Interpretation of the Code declared on

Switzerland, Belgium, Venezuela, Luxemburg, and Romania, legal relationship is a prohibitive impediment. Cf. Cappello, *De Matrimonio,* n. 324, pp. 331-333.

[18] Canon 1060. This impediment exists between two validly baptized persons of whom one is a Catholic whereas the other is a member of a heretical or a schismatical sect, even though the latter has abjured the sect without embracing the Catholic faith. If the baptism of the non-Catholic party is doubtful, there certainly exists either the impediment of mixed religion or that of disparity of cult; the presumption is in favor of the validity of the baptism and of the marriage until the contrary is proved (canons 1014 and 1070). On the validity of non-Catholic baptism, see William J. Doheny, *Canonical Procedure in Matrimonial Cases,* Vol. II *(Informal Procedure)* (2nd print., Milwaukee: The Bruce Publishing., 1948), pp. 42-54 [hereafter cited as *Informal Procedure*].

[19] Canon 1042, §§ 1 and 2.

[20] Canon 1042, § 3. Cf. Pius XII, Motu proprio "*Crebrae allatae,*" canon 31, § 2.—*AAS,* XLI (1949), 89.

[21] Canon 1037.

[22] Canon 1791, § 2. Cf. canons 1757-1975.

[23] Canon 1791, § 1.

[24] Canons 1812-1824.

June 25, 1932, that to make an impediment of marriage public in the sense of canon 1037 it is sufficient that the fact from which the impediment arises be public.[25]

Before the promulgation of the Code of Canon Law, canonists distinguished impediments into *impedimenta natura sua publica* and *impedimenta de facto occulta,* and again, into *impedimenta de facto publica* and *impedimenta natura sua occulta.* When the existence of the impediments could be proved by one of the above enumerated means of proof in the external forum, they were called *impedimenta natura sua publica;* otherwise they were called *impedimenta natura sua occulta.* Thus, the impediment of sacred orders, of solemn religious profession, of disparity of cult, of consanguinity, of affinity, of public propriety, of spiritual relationship, and of legal relationship are usually such as can be proved from public records, and hence they are called *impedimenta natura sua publica.* Yet these impediments may be, in fact, occult, i.e., *impedimenta de facto occulta,* and will be so classed according to canon 1037, if the record which normally should furnish the proof in the external forum happens to be wanting. Impediments are said to be only materially public, i.e., *impedimenta materialiter publica,* if the fact from which they arise is known, but the fact that it constitutes an impediment is not known. For example, a crime could be committed publicly by a person who is publicly known, the while it is not publicly known that the crime gave rise to an impediment. But, if the fact from which an impediment arises is publicly known and the fact is also publicly known to give rise to an impediment, then the impediment is called formally public, i.e., *impedimentum formaliter publicum.*

Some impediments are neither matters of public record, nor observed by witnesses, nor capable of proof in any legal manner in the external forum, and hence they are impediments occult by nature, i.e., *impedimenta natura sua occulta.*

[25] *AAS,* XXIV (1932), 284. Cf. Cappello, *Periodica,* XXI (1932), 285; Bouscaren, *Canon Law Digest,* I, 501.

Yet they may be public in fact, inasmuch as they may yield to proof in consequence of exceptional circumstances, and thus they are called impediments public in fact, i.e., *impedimenta de facto publica.* These impediments formally were termed simply occult impediments, i.e., *impedimenta simpliciter occulta* or *impedimenta quasi-occulta,* in contrast to entirely occult impediments, i.e., *impedimenta omnino occulta,* which are known to no one,[26] but can be called as public impediments under the Code, if they are capable of proof in the external forum.[27]

Thus, under the name of public impediments come all impediments both materially and formally public by nature, all impediments which are public by nature though occult in fact, and all impediments which are occult by nature but public in fact.

Impediments are said to be multiple when various impediments of different kinds occur in reference to one and the same marriage, for example, if a married person at any time during the continuance of the bond of his marriage commits adultery and exchanges a mutual promise of marriage with a person who is related by reason of consanguinity or affinity in a degree which constitutes the impediment of consanguinity or affinity. In this case there exist the impediment of consanguinity or affinity and also the impediment of marital criminality arising from the adultery along with the mutual promise of marriage. If the married

[26] Conte a Coronata, *Institutiones Iuris Canonici, De Sacramentis,* Vol. III (3. ed., aucta et emendata, Romae: Marietti, 1957), n. 119, pp. 138-139 [hereafter cited as *De Sacramentis,* III]; Petrus Gasparri, *Tractatus Canonicus de Matrimonio* (nova ed., 2 vols., Vaticanis: Typis Polyglottis, 1932), I, n. 209, pp. 126-127 [hereafter cited as *De Matrimonio*]; Wernz-Vidal, *Ius Canonicum,* Tom. V *(Ius Matrimoniale)* (3. ed., Romae: Apud Aedes Universitatis Gregorianae, 1946), n. 147, pp. 178-181 [hereafter cited as *Ius Matrimoniale*].

[27] Bouscaren-Ellis, *Canon Law,* pp. 478-479: "Yet for one purpose this old classification remains practical; namely, these so-called "simply occult" impediments may still be handled through the Sacred Penitentiary instead of having to be treated as public impediments, in the external forum."

person in the above-cited case kills his (or her) own partner in legitimate wedlock with the purpose of marrying the accomplice in the adultery who is his (or her) relative, then there exist the impediment of marital criminality which arises from adultery along with the mutual promise of marriage, of marital criminality which arises from adultery in connection with the murder of the spouse, and of consanguinity or affinity in line with the relationship that exists between the guilty parties. Thus, with reference to one and the same marriage there can exist multiple impediments.[28]

By reason of the greater or lesser degree of knowledge regarding their existence, impediments are said to be *certain* or *doubtful*. Doubt may arise when there is uncertainty about the existence or the extent of the legislation in regard to a certain impediment, or when there is uncertainty about the existence of the circumstances that give rise to diriment or prohibitive impediments of marriage in the Code of Canon Law. Thus the impediments may be doubtful *in law*, doubtful *in fact*, or doubtful *both in law and in fact.*[29]

ARTICLE II. FACULTIES CONCEDED *A Iure*

Regarding the authority to establish or to modify the law concerning matrimonial impediments in the Code of Canon Law, the principles are set up in canons 1038-1041. The Supreme Pontiff has the exclusive right to constitute prohibitive and diriment impediments for baptized persons by way either of a universal or of a particular law;[30] the Su-

[28] Canon 1075. Cf. Woywod-Smith, *A Practical Commentary*, nn. 1062-1064, pp. 723-726; Gasparri, *De Matrimonio*, I, n. 680, pp. 412-414. It should be noted that, since the impediment of marital criminality is an ecclesiastical impediment, it does not bind unbaptized persons. Wherefore, the Sacred Congregation for the Propagation of the Faith declared that, if both adulterers were unbaptized at the time of the commission of the crime, they did not contract the impediment of marital criminality arising from adultery in connection with the murder of the spouse. Cf. *Collectanea* (23 Aug. 1852), n. 1079, ad 5.

[29] Canon 1031. Cf. Bouscaren-Ellis, *Canon Law*, pp. 466-468; 475-477.

[30] Canon 1038.

preme Pontiff alone can abolish or modify the ecclesiastical impediments of marriage, both prohibitive and diriment; and likewise no other than the Supreme Pontiff can dispense from the laws concerning these matrimonial impediments, prohibitive and diriment alike of ecclesiastical law, except insofar as this power is conceded to him in the law of the Code or by special indult from the Holy See.[31]

In the present Code, the extensive powers conferred on local ordinaries in the matter of dispensing from matrimonial impediments are indicated in canons 15, 81, 1043, and 1045; pastors, confessors, and other priests have the faculties mentioned in canons 1044 and 1045. Canons 15 and 81 confer dispensing powers on local ordinaries by way of application of the general rules of ecclesiastical law, while canons 1043 and 1045 concede the powers to them specifically for use in marriage cases.

SECTION 1. FACULTIES CONCEDED TO ORDINARIES IN CANONS 15 AND 81 TO DISPENSE FROM MATRIMONIAL IMPEDIMENTS

Canons 15 rules that in a positive doubt of fact (*dubium facti*) the canon grants to ordinaries[32] the power of dispensing, provided that the law is one from which the Holy See usually dispenses. From this rule of law it follows that ordinaries can dispense if there exists any positive doubt regarding the existence of circumstances which constitute a matrimonial impediment (prohibitive or diriment), and the impediment in question is one from which the Holy See customarily dispenses. The same canon also rules that in a positive doubt of law (*dubium iuris*) ecclesiastical laws are not binding in accord with the principle: *"lex dubia non obligat,"* even if they are invalidating and incapacitating laws. Hence, by virtue of the power granted in canon 15, if the meaning or extent of the law in regard to a certain matrimonial impediment is positively doubtful, ordinaries

[31] Canon 1040.

[32] Cf. canon 198; canon 66, § 2.

or priests may validly marry the parties without previously obtaining a dispensation.[33]

Canon 81 empowers ordinaries with the needed authority for dispensing from the Church's universal law in cases where three conditions occur together, to wit: (1) recourse to the Holy See to obtain the faculty is difficult; (2) the delay occasioned by such recourse will probably result in grave danger; (3) the dispensation is one which the Holy See not only can but usually does grant. On this canon in relation to martimonial impediments, the Sacred Roman Rota decided the following points: the power given to ordinaries by canon 81 extends to matrimonial impediments of ecclesiastical law; canon 81 is broader than canon 1043 and 1045, and is certainly not limited by them; the powers granted in canon 81 can be used by ordinaries, not only in favor of their subjects, but also in favor of others within their territory; as long as these conclusions enjoy a positive probability, they are safe in practice by virtue of canon 209.[34] The Code Commission was asked whether by virtue of canon 81, as compared with canon 1045, an ordinary can dispense from matrimonial impediments within the limits of the said canon 81, even though not everything is ready for the wedding (*"etsi nondum parata sint omnia ad nuptias"*), and it replied in the affirmative.[35]

As to the first condition for the use of canon 81, it is difficulty of recourse to the Holy See that is considered. This difficulty may exist even though it might be easy to have recourse to the Apostolic Delegate or to someone else who has the faculty. But, if the Apostolic Delegate in a

[33] Doheny cities a few matrimonial cases involving a *"dubium iuris."* See his *Informal Procedure*, pp. 719-723. On the doctrine regarding the *"dubium iuris"* and *dubium facti,"* cf. A. G. Cicognani-O'Hara-Brennan, *Canon Law* (Philadelphia: The Dolphin Press, 1935), pp. 836-840.

[34] S.R. Rota, 10 Aug. 1926—*Sacrae Romanae Rotae Decisiones* (Romae, 1912-), XVIII (1926), 318 [hereafter cited as *Rotae Decisiones*]; Bouscaren, *Canon Law Digest*, II, 43-44.

[35] Code Comm., 27 Iul. 1942—*AAS*, XXXIV (1942), 241. Cf *The Jurist*, III (1943), 155.

certain country is in communication with the Holy See, so that recourse to the Holy See through the Apostolic Delegate is not difficult, then this condition for the application of canon 81 is not verified.[36] The ordinary means of recourse to the Holy See is mail; recourse by telephone, by telegraph, or by air travel need not be taken into consideration for the application of canon 81.

The difficulty need not amount to a moral impossibility. It may depend upon the distance, the time required for an answer,[37] the lack of opportunity for communication by mail, etc. Danger of grave harm in delay exists when, everything considered, a probable danger of grave harm is prudently feared. It may be private or public, physical or moral, or economic and financial.

Whether dispensations are usually granted by the Holy See can be known from the law itself and also from the practice of the Roman Curia. By virtue of canon 81, ordinaries may dispense from the matrimonial impediments of ecclesiastical law. But, they cannot dispense from the impediment of sacred orders, from the impediment of consanguinity when there is factual doubt whether it is of the first degree in the collateral line, or from the impediment of marital criminality when it involves the murder of the spouse. The expression, *"a generalibus Ecclesiae legibus,"* in canon 81 does not make room for the possible granting of a dispensation from vows reserved to the Holy See.[38]

[36] Letter of Apostolic Delegate to the United States of America, January 1, 1942—Bouscaren, *Canon Law Digest,* II, 44; Code Comm., 26 Iun. 1947—*AAS,* XXXIX (1947), 374; Bouscaren, *ibid.,* III, 56: "The Code Commission was asked: Whether the clause of canon 81, 'unless recourse to the Holy See is difficult,' applies when Ordinaries can easily have recourse to the Legate of the Roman Pontiff in the country, who is in communication with the Holy See. Reply: in the negative."

[37] Cf. Bouscaren, *Canon Law Digest,* IV, 83; *Monitor Ecclesiasticus,* LXXX (1955), 49.

[38] Code Comm., 26 Ian. 1949—*AAS,* XLI (1949), 158; *AAS,* XXIII (1931), 413; *Rotae Decisiones,* XVIII (1926), 318. Cf. Conte a

SECTION 2. FACULTIES TO DISPENSE FROM MATRIMONIAL IMPEDIMENTS CONCEDED IN CANONS 1043 AND 1044

Canon 1043 concedes to the local ordinaries a special power for dispensing from matrimonial impediments in cases involving danger of death, while canon 1044 grants the same power to the parish priest, to the priest mentioned in canon 1098, n. 2, and to the confessor, under the same circumstances and under certain specified conditions. For the sake of convenience, canon 1043 and canon 1044 can be rearranged as follows:

CANON 1043	CANON 1044
Urgente mortis periculo, locorum Ordinarii,	*Urgente mortis periculo tum parochus, tum sacredos qui matrimonio, ad normam can. 1098, n. 2, assistit, tum confessarius, sed hic pro foro interno in actu sacramentalis confessionis tantum,*
ad consulendum conscientiae et, si, casus ferat, legitimationi prolis,	*in eisdem rerum adiunctis de quibus in can. 1043,*
possunt	*potest*

tum super forma in matrimonii celebratione servanda, tum super omnibus et singulis impedimentis iuris ecclesiasticis, sive publicis sive occultis, etiam multiplicibus, exceptis impedimentis provenientibus ex sacro presbyteratus ordine et affinitate in linea recta consummato matrimonio, dispensare

proprios subditos ubique commorantes et omnes in proprio territorio degentes,	*[proprios subditos ubique commorantes et omnes in proprio territorio degentes,]*

remoto scandalo, et, si dispensatio concedatur super cultus disparitate aut mixta religione, praestitis consuetis cautionibus.

Coronata, *De Sacramentis,* III, nn. 121, 137, 139-142, pp. 142, 167, 169-175; Bouscaren-Ellis, *Canon Law,* pp. 67-68.

A. *The Circumstances in Which the Power Granted in Canons 1043 and 1044 Is to be Used*

"Urgente mortis periculo," or only in the case of an extant danger of death" of one of the parties who have been invalidly or unlawfully married is there present the circumstance in which the power granted in canons 1043 and 1044 is to be used.[39] As to how pressing the danger of death must be before it warrants the use of the said power, there is no statement in the text of the canons, nor is it possible to determine that danger more closely, for it is, by its nature, a matter which varies in every case. However, it is obvious that the phrase, *"urgente mortis periculo,"* permits a broader use of the said power than did the phrase, *"in gravissimo mortis periculo,"* as found in the Leonine Decree of February 20, 1888,[40] or in the phrase, *"imminente mortis periculo,"* as found in the Instruction of May 14, 1909, issued by the Sacred Congregation of the Sacraments.[41] Moreover, the *"urgens mortis periculum"* is not as serious as the *"articulus mortis."*[42] The *"urgens mortis periculum"* is to be estimated morally; a reasonably prudent judgment that there exists a proximate danger of death is all that is requisite under the circumstances. The classical definition of *"urgens mortis periculum"* seems to be Cappello's: *"Periculum motis significat illud rerum discrimen, in quo cum quis constitutus est, ipsum et superesse et occumbere posse, utrumque est vere graviterque probabile,"*[43] or Wernz-Vidal's short definition: *"Periculum—non articulus—mortis moraliter aestimandum est,* i.e., *agi debet de vera et gravi probabilitate secuturae mortis."*[44] As to the subject who can make an estimation or a judgment on such a danger of death, the ordinary may rely on the consciousness of the parties them-

[39] For other circumstances, cf. canons 15, 81, and 1045.

[40] S.C.S. Off., Decretum—*Fontes*, n. 1109.

[41] *Fontes*, n. 2097.

[42] Cf. Cappello, *De Matrimonio*, n. 231, p. 227; Wernz-Vidal, *Ius Matrimoniale*, n. 413, p. 533.

[43] Cappello, *loc. cit.*

[44] Wernz-Vidal, *loc. cit.*

selves, or on the judgment of those present, or on the verdict of the physicians, or on his own prudent judgment.[45] Their judgment may be mistaken, but it can be safely stated that the mistake will not affect the validity of the dispensation, provided that at the time of the dispensation it was prudently judged that death would probably follow, for the Code requires no more than an ordinary reasonable fear that such danger actually exists.

The danger of death in question may be indeed by intrinsic causes[46] or also by extrinsic causes.[47] Canon 1043 does not specify any particular cause from which the danger must result in order that the faculty may become operative, whereas the Leonine Decree of 1888 demanded that the danger of death arise from sickness—"*aegrotos in gravissimo mortis periculo constitutos.*"[48] Nor does canon 1043 restate the condition postulated in the Leonine Decree for the validity of the dispensation, namely, that there be question of a person who lived in concubinage, or who was joined only in a civil union. Hence this condition is not required in the present canon, neither for the validity nor for the lawfulness of the dispensation that is to be granted.

[45] Gerald M. O'Keefe, *Matrimonial Dispensations: Power of Bishops, Priests, and Confessors*, The Catholic University of America Canon Law Studies n. 45 (Washington, D.C.: The Catholic University of America Press, 1927), p. 56 [hereafter cited as *Matrimonial Dispensations*].

[46] Intrinsic causes are such as a bodily illness, a difficult childbirth, surgical operations, etc., from which death will probably follow or is prudently feared to follow as a consequence of the bodily indisposition.

[47] Extrinsic causes are such as the special or unusual circumstances which ordinarily cause an unnatural death to determined or undetermined persons. These circumstances can derive from nature or from human society. The former are exemplified in earthquakes, floods or inundations, widespread epidemics, very dangerous journeys, etc., and the latter are illustrated in mobilizations of troops, in impending air raids—even when it is the civilian population that is threatened—in condemnations to capital punishment, etc. Cf. *AAS*, XXXI (1939), 710-713; *Fontes*, n. IV, n. 1139; S. Poenit., resp., 10 Dec. 1940—*AAS*, XXXII (1940), 571. Cf. also Conte a Coronata, *De Sacramentis*, III, n. 136; Cappello n. 231, p. 227.

[48] *Fontes*, n. 1109.

The power conceded in canon 1043 can be used not only for the party on whose side alone the impediment lies, but also for the other party on whose side there is no impediment, even if the latter is in danger of death, and the other remains in good health;[49] It can also be used in case wherein separate impediments affect the two parties, e.g., the vow of chastity on the part of the woman, and the order of deaconship or subdeaconship on the part of the man, one of whom is in danger of death.[50]

B. The Canonical Conditions for the Use of the Power Granted in Canons 1043 and 1044

"Ad consuledum conscientiae, et, si casus ferat, legitimationi prolis," or "for the sake of relieving a person's conscience or for the sake of rendering the offspring legitimate, if there by any," is the phrase which determine the canonical conditions for the use of the power granted in canons 1043-1044. This cited phrase contains mention of two canonical conditions, and between the two mentioned conditions the conjunction *"et"* is used. These two are alternately stated, and thus at least one or the other is necessary for the validity of the dispensation granted by virtue of canons 1043-1044.[51]

"Ad consulendum conscientiae." The conscience of one party, at least, may be sufficiently relieved when, as the result of the marriage celebrated through such a dispensation, the sin itself, or at least the grave danger of sin, is removed. Such cases are verified in the convalidation of a marriage, civil or ecclesiastical, which was canonically invalid; or when the proximate occasion of sin, or some strong temptation, or scandal, when it has arisen from illicit relations, can be removed as a result of the marriage of the parties concerned, etc. The required relieving of a person's conscience,

[49] Wernz-Vidal, *op. cit.*, n. 413, p. 533; Gasparri, *De Matrimonio*, I, n. 393; Conte a Coronata, *op. cit.*, III, n. 136, p. 163.

[50] S.C.S. Off., 1 Iul. 1891—*Collectanea*, n. 1758, and *Fontes*, n. 1139.

[51] Cf. canon 84.

which is one of the set conditions for the use of the present power, may be motivated by the desire of the person who is in danger of death to restore the good name of another, or to repair, by means of the *"ius viduae acquisitum,"* some material damage done to the intended spouse, or by means of the marriage to bring an end to standing enmities, or disagreements, etc., between families, or for any other serious reasons. In short, the condition *"ad consulendum conscientiae'* is adequately met when there is necessity to relieve the conscience of one or both of the parties, no matter from what cause the necessity may arise.[52]

For the valid use of the power, the subject who needs the relieving may be either of the two parties, i.e., the person who is in danger of death, or the other party who is in good health, or both of them. Thus the power can be used either when the conscience of the person who is in danger of death needs the relieving, or when only the healthy party seeks for an adjustment of matters in his or her conscience, while that of the person who is in danger of death is quite at ease and undisturbed. It is also operative for the sake of relieving the conscience of the Catholic party, though the one who is in danger of death is a non-Catholic, and suffers no remorse of conscience.[53]

"Si casus ferat, ad consulendum legitimationi prolis." In the mention of this condition, the clause *"si casus ferat"* qualifies the next phrase in such a way that the contemplated *"proles"* is the offspring of the unlawful wedlock (according to the marriage laws of the Church) of the two parties, and thus is an illegitimate child of the two persons whose union is to be rectified by virtue of the power granted in canons 1043-1044. For the sake of the legitimation of

[52] Cf. S.C. de Sacr., resp., 16 Aug. 1909—*AAS,* I (1909), 656. Cf. Cappello, *De Matrimonio,* n. 231, n. 228; O'Keefe, *Matrimonial Dispensations,* p. 60; Wernz-Vidal, *Ius Matrimoniale,* n. 413, 2°, a, p. 533: "Porro consulitur conscientiae dum peccatum vel peccandi occasio proxima aut magna tentatio per celebrationem matrimonii tollitur ex quacumque causa derivet, non ex sola luxuria."

[53] O'Keefe, *Matrimonial Dispensations,* p. 63.

such offspring, then, the power granted in canons 1043-1044 becomes operative.

The conjunction *"et."* In short, this conjunction should be taken *disiunctive secundum quid.* For the two conditions, i.e., *ad consulendum conscientiae* and *ad consulendum legimationi prolis* need not co-exist at the same time, so that the power is operative even if no need for the legitimation of a child be present, or, in other words, the conception or the birth of a child is not a *conditio sine qua non* for the use of the dispensing power granted in canons 1043-1044;[54] on the other hand, the said power can be validly used in cases in which the two persons have an illegitimate child, when the person who is in danger of death, or also the party who is still in good health, seeks the dispensation simply for the sake of the legitimation of the child, without contemplating the relieving of the conscience of either of the two parties. However, the conjunction *"et"* is to be taken, not absolutely *disiunctive*, but *disiunctive secundum quid.* For it is morally impossible to see how the second condition, i.e., the legitimation of the offspring, could be verified apart from all relief of conscience to the parties concerned. If marriage is desired in some instance for the sake of the legitimation of the offspring, this latter reason would exist as the primary cause, but a secondary one, namely, the relieving of the conscience, would always seem implicitly included in the desire of the parties.

C. The Scope of the Power Granted in Canons 1043-1044

By virtue of the power granted in canons 1043-1044, a dispensation from the prescriptions made for the canonical

[54] Gasparri, *De Matrimonio,* I, n. 394, p. 232; Cappello, *De Matrimonio,* n. 231, p. 228; Vermeersch-Creusen, *Epitome,* II, n. 306, p. 216; Conte a Coronata, *De Sacramentis,* III, n. 136, p. 163; Wernz-Vidal, *Ius Matrimoniale,* n. 413, p. 532; DeSmet,*De Sponsalibus et Matrimonio* (4. ed., Brugis: Card. Beyaert, Editor Pontificius, 1927), p. 215, nota 2.

form of the marriage contract,[55] and from each and every non-excepted impediment of ecclesiastical law, public as well as occult,[56] and even if multiple,[57] is possible; but all possibility of a dispensation from impediments which derive from the divine law, or from the impediments arising from the sacred priesthood and from affinity in the direct line, if there has been a consummation of the union, is precluded.

In consequence of the phrase, "*impedimenta iuris ecclesiastici,*" the impediments which derive from the divine law, whether natural or positive, are excluded from the scope of the power granted in canons 1043-1044. The impediments arising from the divine law are (1) the extant bond of marriage (*ligamen*),[58] (2) consanguinity in all ascending and descending degrees of the direct line, and also in the first degree of the collateral line, even in case of doubt,[59] and (3) impotence.[60] As long as there is a solidly founded doubt whether the impediment is such as to derive from the divine law, either natural or positive, no dispensation can be granted within the scope of the dispensatory power conceded in canons 1043-1044.[61] From the impediments of the ecclesiastical law, two impediments, i.e., the *impedimentum proveniens ex sacro ordine presbyteratus* and the *impedimentum proveniens ex affinitate in liena recta, consummato matrimonio,* are excepted. The expression, "*im-*

[55] Canons 1094-1098.

[56] *Supra,* pp. 195-196.

[57] *Supra,* pp. 196-197.

[58] Canon 1069.

[59] Canon 1076. Cf. Cappello, *De Matrimonio,* n. 224, 1°, p. 222.

[60] Canon 1068.

[61] Conte a Coronata, *De Sacramentis,* III, n. 136, pp. 163-164: "Item, ut patet, excluduntur etiam impedimenta iuris divini et naturalis, et etiam quae solummodo probabiliter sunt iuris divini et naturalis." Cf. Vlaming, *Praelectiones Iuris Matrimonii ad Normam Codicis Iuris Canonici* (3. ed., 2 vols., Bossum in Hollandia, 1919-1921), II, n. 401, p. 24, nota 1 [hereafter cited as *Praelectiones Iuris Matrimonii*]; Gerardus Oesterle, *Consultationes de Iure Matrimonii* (Romae: Officium Libri Catholici, 1942), pp. 112-113.

pedimentum proveniens ex sacro ordine presbyteratus," does not contemplate the orders of deaconship and subdeaconship, and accordingly the impediment arising these sacred orders is subject to dispensation in virtue of the present canons. Likewise the appended clause, *"consummato matrimonio,"* leaves room for a dispensation from affinity in the direct line when the marriage from which the impediment arises has not been consummated.

"Super forma in matrimonii celebratione." In the present Code by the ordinary canonical form of marriage is meant the celebration of marriage in the presence of the pastor, of the local ordinary, or of a priest delegated by either of these, and simultaneously before at least two witnesses.[62] The presence of the pastor or of the local ordinary (or of a priest delegated by either of these) and of at least two witnesses is required for the validity of marriage. The extraordinary canonical form requires for the validity of the marriage the presence of two competent witnesses, and, in addition, for its licitness that of any priest, though he be without delegation (except an *excommunicatus vitandus,* or one who is under condemnatory or declaratory sentence of censure), if he can be easily had.[63] Thus a dispensation from the canonical form of marriage theoretically means a dispensation from the presence either of the pastor (or of the local ordinary, or of a priest delegated by either of these), or of two witnesses, or even from both combined. In practice, however, a dispensation from the form of marriage in the cases contemplated in canons 1043-1044 implies a dispensation from the presence of two witnesses at the celebration of the marriage.

From the context of canon 1043, there is nothing that restricts the use of the power on the part of its executor. In fact, the Holy Office declared that a dispensation could be granted from the observance of the form of marriage when it is morally impossible to have the witnesses. In ad-

[62] Canon 1094.
[63] Canon 1098.

dition, the Holy Office explained that there existed a moral impossibility to procure the witnesses when these could be had only at the expense of a serious inconvenience (*grave incommodum*) to the witnesses themselves, or to the parties concerned, or to the offspring to be legitimated.[64] Similarly, a dispensation from the observance of the form can be granted under the circumstances delineated in canon 1043, if there exists a physical impossibility to procure the two wintnesses. If one witness alone were to be available, there would be no obligation to summon him or her, since one witness would not satisfy the requirement of the canonical form of marriage.[65]

The power conceded in canons 1043-1044 is operative for the granting of dispensations from impediments to marriages yet to be contracted as well as to marriages which have been invalidly contracted. But this dispensatory power is not made available for the purpose of effecting a *sanatio in radice* in favor of an invalid marriage.[66]

D. The Precautions Requied in the Use of the Power Granted in Canons 1043 and 1044

"Remoto scandalo." (Pecaution n. 1).—Even though all other conditions are verified in a given case for the use of the power conceded in canon 1043, the executor of the power, before applying the dispensation, must see to the removal of scandal, if such there be. This precaution refers to all scandal, whether it is already current from the past, or whether it impends as a threat in the future. Past scandals must be repaired, and future scandal obviated.[67]

[64] S.C.S. Off., 20 Dec. 1899—*Collectanea*, n. 2072.

[65] N.B. "Si autem, in periculo mortis tales essent circumstantiae ut unus quidem testis (catechista vel simplex christianus), non autem duo, convocari et adstare possit, tunc detur dispensatio super forma servanda in celebratione matrimonii, quae dispensatio ab Ordinario regulariter dari debet (Can. 1043); sed, si adiri nequeat Ordinarius, etiam a simplici sacerdote dari potest. (Can. 1044)."—*Directorium Commune Missionum Coreae*, n. 386, p. 169.

[66] Cf. Wernz-Vidal, *Ius Matrimoniale*, n. 413, p. 534.

[67] Cf. O'Keefe, *Matrimonial Dispensations*, p. 81; Wernz-Vidal, *Ius*

Compliance with the precaution for the removal of scandal is necessary for the lawful use of the faculty of canon 1043. If the executor, therefore, should find the total removal of scandal a practical impossibility, its partial removal, joined with the parties' promise, or at least their willingness to do more, will give him enough ground for the granting of the dispensation. Furthermore, the executor may proceed, even if the scandal is irreparable, in a case wherein the parties have compunction of heart for the wrong done and the scandal created along with the readiness to embrace a little humiliation or inconvenience connected with the repairing of the scandal already spread.[68]

"Praestitis consuetis cautionibus, si dispensatio concedatur super cultus disparitate aut mixta religione." (Precaution n. 2).—In the case of a dispensation from the impediments of disparity of cult and of mixed religion, the prescribed *cautiones* or guarantees must be obtained. The *cautiones* for the dispensation from the impediment of mixed religion are prescribed in canon 1061, and according to the norm of canon 1071 the same *cautiones* are to be required for marriage when there is present the impediment of disparity of cult. The pertinent passage of canon 1061 reads as follows:

> Canon 1061, §1. *Ecclesia super impedimento mixtae religionis non dispensat, nisi:*
> 2°. *Cautionem praestiterit coniux acatholicus de amovendo a coniuge catholico perversionis periculo, et uterque coniux de universa prole catholice tantum baptizanda et educanda;*
> 3° *Moralis habeatur certitudo de cautionum implemento.*

Matrimoniale, n. 413, p. 534; Conte a Coronata, *De Sacramentis*, III, n. 136, p. 164. *Collectanea*, n. 1685.

[68] Cf. Ayrinhac-Lydon, *Marriage Legislation in the New Code of Canon Law* (3rd rev. ed., New York-Boston-Chicago: Benziger Brothers, Inc., 1957), p. 69 [hereafter cited as *Marriage Legislation*]; Payen, *De Matrimonio in Missionibus ac Potissimum in Sinis, Tractatus Practicus et Casus* (3 vols., Zi-Ka-Wei: Typographis, T'ou-Se We, 1935-1936), I, n. 646 [hereafter cited as *De Matrimonio in Missionibus*].

§ 2. *Cautiones regulariter in scriptis exigantur.*

This passage of canon 1061 is concerned with two promises (known as *cautiones* or guarantees), i.e., on the part of the non-Catholic party the promise to remove all danger of perversion from the Catholic party, and on the part of both the promise to baptize and educate all the children in the Catholic faith alone.[69] These promises are as a rule to be required in writing,[70] and are required for the validity of the dispensation. This is clear from the text of canon 1061 itself. For it declares that the Church does not dispense from the impediment of mixed religion unless the conditions therein specified are satisfied, among which conditions these promises are included. It is the constant practice of the Church to demand from both, i.e., the Catholic party and the non-Catholic party, that the promises be made formally and explicitly for the validity of the dispensation from the said impediment.[71]

Moral certainty that the promises will be kept by the parties must be duly established before a dispensation from the impediment of mixed religion or of disparity of cult can be granted. The establishing of this moral certainty derives in part from the promised compliance with the prescribed *cautiones,* and is required for the validity of the dispensation. In an Instruction of January 14, 1932, the Holy Office ruled that dispensation from the impediments of mixed religion and of disparity of cult must not be granted, unless the promises are so made that none can frustrate their fulfillment, even by recourse to the civil laws to which either

[69] Cf. S.C.S. Off., resp. 16 Ian. 1942—*AAS,* XXXIV (1942), 22. The promise to have all the children baptized and raised in the Catholic faith is concerned with only such children as will be born of the marriage contracted between the two parties upon the granting of the dispensation, although they should be admonished of their grave obligation from the divine law to provide for the Catholic rearing of the children already born.

[70] Cf. *infra,* pp. 239-242.

[71] Cf. *AAS,* IV (1912), 443; *AAS,* XXIV (1932), 25; *AAS,* XXXIII (1941), 294-295. Cf. Woywod-Smith, *A Practical Commentary,* n. 1055, p. 716; Vermeersch-Creusen, *Epitome,* II, n. 306, n. I, c.

party is subject and which are in force in their actual place of residence or the place where they intend to live; otherwise the dispensation will be null and void.[72] The said moral certainty must be obtained from the reliably made promises of the parties, and the judgment regarding the sincerity of the promises and the guarantees of their future fulfillment depends on the character of both the non-Catholic party and the Catholic party.[73]

E. The Grantees of the Power Made Available in Canons 1043-1044

The local ordinary[74] may use the power granted in canon 1043 on behalf of his subjects wherever they are. His subjects are those who have a diocesan domicile or quasi-domicile, or a parochial one in his diocese.[75] He may also use the same power in favor of all persons who are *hic et nunc* sojourning within the limits of his diocese, even though they do not possess a domicile or quasi-domicile in the diocese.

"Tum parochus, tum sacerdos qui matrimonio, ad normam can. 1098, 2, assistit." The same power belongs also to the pastor and to the priest who assists at marriage in line with the provisions made in canon 1098, 2°.[76]

By the pastor in canon 1044 is meant an individual priest upon whom a parish is conferred in his own right (*in titulum*), with the care of souls to be exercised under the authority of the ordinary of the place,[77] and any priest who

[72] *AAS*, XXIV (1932), 25.

[73] Cf. William F. Allen, "The Insincerity of the *Cautiones*—Disparity of Worship," *The Jurist*, XVI (1956), 59-86; Eduardus A. McCarthy, *De Certitudine Morali quae in Judicis Animo ad Sententiae Pronuntiationem Requiritur* (Romae: Officium Libri Catholici, 1948), pp. 56 ff.

[74] *Supra*, pp. 61-87.

[75] Canon 94, § 1.

[76] Cf. Edward A. Fus, *The Extraordinary Form of Marriage According to Canon 1098*, The Catholic University of America Canon Law Studies, n. 348 (Washington, D.C.: The Catholic University of America Press, 1954), pp. 144-147.

[77] Canon 451, § 1.

in the law is held equal in parochial rights to the pastor. In the diocese, the vicar for a moral person (such as an ecclesiastical corporation, a chapter, or a religious order) having the title of pastor,[78] the administrator (*vicarius oeconomus*) of a vacant parish,[79] and the substitute vicar (*vicarius substitutus*) of the pastor[80] are in law held equal to the pastor in parochial rights. All these are competent in law for the faculty conceded in canon 1044. The adjutant vicar (*vicarius adiutor*) may or may not have full parochial powers, depending upon his letter of appointment; if he takes the place of the pastor in everything, he has all the pastor's ordinary jurisdiction,[81] and accordingly is competent for the use of the faculty which in law is given to the pastor.

In the missions, the quasi-pastor who has charge of a quasi-parish in a mission is declared in law equivalent to the pastor in the diocese as to his rights and obligation (except that of the *Missa pro populo*).[82] In name and in fact, then, he has full parochial rights. Consequently, the quasi-pastor is competent in law for the use of the faculty delineated in canon 1044. From this it follows that the vicar for a moral person who has the title of quasi-pastor is equivalent to the vicar in canon 471; the administrator, the substitute vicar, and the adjutant vicar of the quasi-parish are equivalent to those of the parish respectively.

The assistant or curate (*vicarius cooperator*) of the parish or quasi-parish may receive general delegation for assistance at all marriages in the parish.[83] In some dioceses this general delegation is given along with the curate's

[78] Canon 471.

[79] Canon 472.

[80] He has full parochial powers unless the ordinary or the pastor has made some restriction. Cf. canons 465 and 474.

[81] Canon 475, §§ 1 and 2.

[82] Canons 451, § 2, 1°; 216, § 3; 466. C.C. de Prop. Fid., instr., 25 Iul. 1920—*AAS*, XII (1920), 331; Bouscaren, *Canon Law Digest*, II, 147-148. Cf. Vermeersch, *Periodica*, X (1921), 203.

[83] Canon 1096; Code Comm., 13 Sept. 1933. Cf. Bouscaren, *Canon Law Digest*, II, 333.

appointment.[84] And the Instruction of July 25, 1920, as given by the Sacred Congregation for the Propagation of the Faith, declared that where quasi-parishes are not yet constituted the missionaries are to be considered as assistants of the vicar or the prefect apostolic, and hence, with the general permission of the ordinary, they may validly and licitly assist at marriages.[85] However, such a general delegation or a general permission does not empower these curates and missionaries to use the faculty which in canon 1044 is conceded to the pastor, unless its delegation is specifically mentioned in the letter of the said general delegation by the ordinary of the place.[86]

The pastor may use the faculty granted in canon 1044, when there exists the impossibility of recourse to the ordinary of the place for the dispensation sought. Such an impossibility, however, should be understood as a moral one, which is present whenever one of the parties is in danger of death and it is prudently feared that death, or at least unconsciousness, may supervene before recourse to the ordinary of the place can be made and the dispensation obtained.[87]

As to the means for recourse to the ordinary of the place, for sending the petition for the dispensation, or for approaching the ordinary of the place, extraordinary means need not be employed. The use of a telegram, of telephone, or of an airplane for travel, etc., is rightly to be regarded as an extraordinary means for such a recourse.[88] If the pastor can get in contact with the local ordinary in person or by letter (even by special delivery, if necessary), in sufficient time through the employment of ordinary means to

[84] Bouscaren-Ellis, *Canon Law*, p. 221.

[85] *AAS*, XII (1920), 331; *Periodica*, X (1921), 203.

[86] For missionaries, the delegation of the faculty of canon 1044 is not necessary, if the ordinary of the place subdelegates to them the *Decennial Faculty, XXII* in the *Formula Maior*. For the latter is broader in its scope than the former. Cf. *infra*, pp. 223-244.

[87] O'Keefe, *Matrimonial Dispensations*, p. 104.

[88] Code Comm., resp., 12 Nov. 1922—*AAS*, XIV (1922), 662.

receive a dispensation, he is bound to do so. If, however, the use of even ordinary means for the recourse would cause a "*grave incommodum*" to the parties, arising especially out of the danger of the violation of a secret, the condition "*adiri non possit*" is verified, even if the pastor had enough time to make the recourse to the local ordinary.

As to the priest mentioned in canon 1098, 2°, canon 1098, 1°, provides for an extraordinary form of marriage, i.e., simply before two competent witnesses. For the valid use of this form of marriage, the canon defines the circumstances postulated for the celebration of the marriage. The first condition is the impossibility to have or to reach the ordinary or the pastor who should normally assist, or a delegate of either; the second is the danger of death of either party, or the fact that it is prudently foreseen that the first condition of affairs will last for a month. When these conditions are verified, the marriage can be celebrated simply before two competent witnesses. Canon 1098, 2°, then prescribes that, if any other priest (*alius sacerdos*) who can be present is available, he must be called and must assist at the marriage, together with the witnesses. Of course, *any other priest* in this paragraph is neither the pastor nor any priest delegated for the marriage by either the local ordinary or the pastor.

Canon 1044 grants its power to "any priest" as mentioned in canon 1098, 2°, so that, if he sees the need of granting a dispensation from matrimonial impediments as he assists at the marriage under the circumstances contemplated in canon 1098, he can dispense from them by virtue of canon 1044, provided that the limits and the conditions postulated in canon 1044 be observed.[89]

"*Confessarius, sed hic pro foro interno in actu sacramentalis confessionis tantum.*" The confessor is vested with the power which the pastor has by virtue of canon 1044, under the same circumstances and under the same conditions postulated for the valid use of the power by the pastor.

[89] Fus, *op. cit.*, pp. 104-183.

But the confessor may use the power only in the internal forum. According to the norm of canon 882, any priest may be the confessor of any person who is in danger of death. The Code does not mention the impossibility of approaching the parish priest or a delegated priest, if there be such. However, if it were possible to have recourse to the parish priest or to some other properly delegated priest apart from all danger to the sacramental seal and apart from serious inconvenience to the parties, the confessor would be bound to do so. The confessor can exercise in the internal forum the power conceded in canon 1044, but only in the act of sacramental confession, so that his dispensation from the matrimonial impediments is without force in the external forum as a means for establishing proof for the valid contracting of the marriage.

As to the nature of the matrimonial impediments from which the confessor in virtue of canon 1044 can grant a dispensation, some canonists assert that all impediments which are public by nature are excluded from the scope of power of the confessor. According to them, this is so because a dispensation from a public impediment given in the internal sacramental forum is something of an anomaly, and creates a conflict between the internal and the external forums. But there are also canonists who contend that the confessor can dispense from impediments which are public by nature, inasmuch as the case involves the danegr of death for at least one of the parties.[90]

SECTION 3. FACULTIES TO DISPENSE FROM MATRIMONIAL IMPEDIMENTS CONCEDED IN CANON 1045

While the faculties granted in canon 1043-1044 are to be used *"urgente mortis periculo,"* the faculties conceded in canon 1045 are to be operative for perplexing cases, i.e., *"quoties impedimentum detegatur, cum iam omnia parata sunt ad nuptias, nec matrimonium, sine probabili gravis*

[90] Cf. Bouscaren-Ellis, *Canon Law*, pp. 489-490; O'Keefe, *Matrimonial Dispensations*, pp. 119-124.

mali periculo, differri possit usque dum a Sancta Sede dispensatio obtineatur." For such a case, public or occult, the ordinary has full faculties; but only when these cases are occult does the pastor, the priest mentioned in canon 1098, 2°, or also the confessor enjoy these faculties.

As to the scope of the faculties granted in canon 1045, it is the same as in canon 1043-1044 in regard to the matrimonial impediments for which a dispensation may be granted, but no dispensation can be granted for non-compliance with the observance of the form of marriage, for there is no mention of this in the text itself; on the other hand, however, the same canon 1045 leaves room for the use of its granted faculties in favor of the convalidation of a marriage already contracted. The cautions prescribed in canons 1043-1044 are to employed in the public and occult perplexing cases, if the faculties conceded in canon 1045 are to be utilized licitly and validly alike.

Thus, from the context of canon 1045 and the foregoing statements the following rearrangement may be presented.

CANON 1045

CANON 1045, § 1	CANON 1045, § 3
Possunt Ordinarii locorum,	*Possunt, omnes de quibus in can. 1044* [i.e., *tum parochus, tum sacerdos qui matrimonio ad normam can. 1098, 2°, assistit, tum confessarius*]

quoties impedimentum detegatur, cum iam omnia sunt parata ad nuptias, nec matrimonium, sine probabili gravis mali periculo, differri possit

usque dum a Sancta Sede dispensatio obtineatur,	*solum pro casibus occultis in quibus ne loci quidem Ordinarius adiri possit, vel nonnisi cum periculo violationis secreti,*

dispensationem concedere super omnibus impedimentis de quibus in cit. can. 1043 [i.e., *super omnibus et signulis impediments iuris ecclesiastici, sive publicis sive occultis, etiam multiplicibus, exceptis impedimentis provenientibus ex sacro presbyteratus ordine et ex affinitate in linea recta, consummato matrimonio*], *sub clausulis in fine can. 1043 statutis* [i.e., *remoto scandalo, et, si dispensatio concedatur super cultus disparitate aut mixta religione, praestitis consuetis cautionibus*],

[*propriis subditis ubique commorantibus et omnibus in proprio territorio actu commorantibus*].	[*parochi propriis subditis ubique commorantibus et omnibus in proprio territorio actu commorantibus*].
Canon 1045, §2. Haec facultas valeat quoque pro convalidatione matrimonii iam contracti, si idem periculum sit in mora nec tempus suppetat recurrendi ad Sanctam Sedem.	[*Canon 1045, §2. Haec facultas valeat quoque pro convalidatione matrimonii iam contracti, si idem periculum sit in mora nec tempus suppetat recurrendi ad Ordinarium loci.*].

A. Perplexing Cases (for the Ordinary of the Place)

The faculties conceded to the local ordinary in canon 1045 can be validly used when a new impediment is detected only after everything has been prepared for a marriage, and at the same time the celebration of that marriage cannot without probable danger of grave evil be delayed until a dispensation of the thus detected impediment be obtained from the Holy See. Hence, there are three elements constituting a perplexing case: (1) the fact of detection of a new impediment after everything has been prepared for the marriage; (2) the moral impossibility to change the date set for the marriage, and (3) the insufficiency of time for obtaining from the Holy See a dispensation from that impediment.

As to the first element, namely, the fact of the detection of a new impediment, the impediment must be one of the impediments for which a dispensation can be granted in virtue of the faculty conceded in canon 1043; its detection can be made in the internal forum as well as in the external forum by the parties to the marriage themselves, or outside the sacramental confession by others, such as the parish priest, the priest mentioned in canon 1098, 2°, or any other third party.

When the Code Commission was asked whether the clause "*quoties impementum detegatur cum iam omnia sunt parata ad nuptias*" should be interpreted in the strict sense, i.e., in the sense that the impediment in question had been entirely unknown to the parties, and was discovered for the first time just before the celebration of the marriage, or whether, rather, it could be interpreted in the sense that, although the impediment was known before, it was only then that it was reported to the parties or to the ordinary, namely, after everything had been prepared for the celebration of the marriage, the Code Commission gave the following response: "*Negative ad 1am partem, affirmative ad 2am partem.*[91]

"*Cum iam omnia sunt parata ad nuptias, nec matrimonium, sine probabili gravis mali periculo, differri possit.*" Some authors restrict the meaning of this phrase in such manner as to let it become applicable only upon the completion of the canonical preparation which are prescribed in canons 1020-1033.[92] But others hold that, even though these canonical preparations have not been made or completed, if the invitations for the wedding have been sent out, if the date has been set for the wedding ceremony, and all other civil arrangements have been made, the condition "*cum iam omnia sunt parata ad nuptias*" is sufficiently verified in practice.[93]

[91] Code Comm., 1 Martii 1921—*AAS*, XIII (1921), 177.

[92] Cf. Cappello, *De Matrimonio*, nn. 232-234, pp. 229-234; O'Keefe, *Matrimonial Dispensations*, n. 133.

[93] O'Keefe, *loc. cit.;* J. Petrovits, *The New Church Law on Matrimony*, The Catholic University of America Canon Law Studies, n. 6 (Washington, D.C.: The Catholic University of America, 1919), n.

The second element, namely, the impossibility of delaying the celebration of the marriage must arise, not from an arbitrary source, but from a real probable danger of grave evil. It need not, however, be morally certain that some grave evil will result from the postponement, but there must be at least a prudent and well-founded fear that such an inconvenience will arise.[94] As to the nature of the impending evil, it is not defined in the Code. Hence, if it is grave, no matter what kind of harm is prudently feared—whether it be spiritual or corporal—the ordinary of the place can proceed with the dispensation.

The third element in a perplexing case is the insufficiency of time for obtaining from the Holy See a dispensation from the newly detected impediment. Thus, if such a dispensation can be obtained to the exclusion of any delay for the marriage, it must be done. The amount of time necessary for obtaining a dispensation will obviously differ according to the locality where the perplexing case arises, and according to the means which are employed. But the length of time needed for obtaining a dispensation under the circumstances of canon 1045, § 1, should be calculated according to the ordinary means of communication.

B. Occult Perplexing Cases (for the Parish Priest, the Priest Mentioned in Canon 1098, 2°, and the Confessor)

In the same circumstances as stated in the first paragraph of canon 1045, the pastor, the priest mentioned in canon 1098, 2°, and the confessor have the same faculty for dispensing from the matrimonial impediments which the ordinary enjoys by virtue of canon 1045, § 1, but the grantees

164; J. F. Connolly, "The Emergency Powers of Canons 1043, 1044, 1045,"—*The Jurist*, V (1945), 53-54.

[94] Wernz-Vidal, *Ius Matrimoniale*, n. 413, p. 535: "*Periculum gravis mali* sufficit *probabile* ex valde efficaci ratione timendum, nec necessarium est ut sit omnino certum."

mentioned in canon 1045, § 3, can make use of the faculty for occult cases only, and only if there is no time to recur to the local ordinary, or when recourse to him can be made only at the risk of violating the secret concerned.[95]

The clause *"solum pro casibus occultis"* does not limit the use of this power to impediments which are occult by nature, but includes impediments which, though they are public by nature, are in fact occult.[96]

C. Convalidation of an Invalid Marriage in Perplexing Cases

By virtue of canon 1045, the local ordinary, the pastor, the priest mentioned in canon 1098, 2°, and the confessor can convalidate invalid marriages already contracted. But, in the case of the ordinary, this faculty is operative when there exists danger in delaying the convalidation and there is no time for recourse to the Holy See, while in the case of the pastor, and of the priest mentioned in canon 1098, 2°, it is operative when there exists danger in delaying the convalidation, and then only for occult cases in which not even the ordinary of the place can be reached, or in which he cannot be reached without the risk of a violation of the secret involved in the case. In the case of the confessor, this faculty is operative in the same way as described in canon 1044, i.e., for the internal forum in the act of sacramental confession only, in addition to the presence of the conditions which are required when this faculty is used by the pastor and the priest mentioned in canon 1098, 2°.[97] Here, by the confessor is meant a priest who is neither the pastor nor the priest who is mentioned in canon 1098, 2°.

[95] Cf. Bouscaren-Ellis, *Canon Law*, pp. 491-493; Mahoney-McReavy, *Priests' Problems*, pp. 253-258.

[96] Code Comm., 28 Dec. 1927—*AAS*, XX (1928), Vermeersch, *Periodica*, XVII (1928), 42.

[97] Gasparri, *De Matrimonio*, I, n. 401, p. 236; Payen, *De Matrimonio in Missionibus*, I, n. 674; Vermeersch-Creusen, *Epitome*, II, n. 312, p. 222; Bouscaren-Ellis, *Canon Law*, p. 492.

In the convalidation of an invalid marriage already contracted, the probable danger of grave evil in delay would be present not only when ignorance of the invalidity of the marriage exists and it is impossible to maintain the brother and sister relationship for several days or even weeks, and the separation of the supposedly married couple cannot be effected without danger of scandal or loss of reputation, but such danger could also arise in the case of an invalid marriage publicly known as such, for it can easily happen that the parties refuse to separate for the time needed in making recourse to the Holy See, or that they could not do so without grave inconvenience.[98]

The faculty conceded in the first paragraph of canon 1045 does not include the power to dispense from the canonical form of marriage.[99] For it grants a faculty to dispense only from certain matrimonial impediments, and non-observance of the form of marriage is not a matrimonial impediment. And hence the renewal of consent must be given publicly in the prescribed form by both parties, if the impediment is public and the convalidation is made by virtue of the faculty conceded in canon 1045. If it is occult and known only to the interested parties, the consent likewise must be renewed by both of them, but a private renewal will suffice; when the impediment is occult and known only to one party, a private renewal by that party will suffice, provided it is certain that the consent of the other party continues.[100] But, if a lack of the observance of the form is the sole reason for the invalidity of the marriage, then the convalidation must take place in the form prescribed by law.[101]

[98] O'Keefe, *Matrimonial Dispensations*, p. 149; Conte a Coronata, *De Sacramentis*, III, n. 137, p. 167; Wernz-Vidal, *Ius Matrimoniale*, n. 413, p. 535.

[99] *Contra:* G. Arendt, "Dispensatio a Forma Matrimonii in Casu Perplexo," *Periodica*, XVI (1927), 1*-17*.

[100] Canon 1133-1135. Cf. O'Keefe, *Matrimonial Dispensations*, p. 151.

[101] Canon 1137.

ARTICLE III. *Ex Facultate,* I: *Facultas XXII*

SECTION 1. TEXT AND A BRIEF ANALYSIS OF THE FACULTY

ANALYSIS	TEXT
Power:	*Dispenandi,*
Canonical Causes for its Use:	*Canonicis existentibus causis,*
Scope of the Power:	*super impedimentis matrimonialibus sive minoris sive maioris gradus* (can. 1042), *tam publicis quam occultis, etiam multiplicibus, iuris tamen ecclesiastici,*
Exceptions:	*exceptis impedimentis provenientibus ex sacro Presbyteratus ordine, ex affinitate in linea recta, consummato matrimonio, et ex defectu praescriptae aetatis, quando sponsi ad aetatem ab antiquo iure praefixam nondum pervenerit (idest ad annum 14 completum pro viris et ad 12 completum pro mulieribus).*
Precautions for Its Use:	*Concedendo tamen has dispensationes, Ordinarius prae oculis habeat regulas statutas in Codice, a can. 1035 ad can. 1080, circa impedimenta in genere et in specie et,*
Particular Precautions in the Case of Marriage with the Impediment of Mixed Religion or of Disparity Cult:	*in impedimentis mixtae religionis et disparitatis cultus, servatis conditionibus ab Ecclesia praescriptis: videlicet de amovendo a catholico coniuge perversionis periculo, ac de universa prole utriusque sexus in catholicae religionis sanctitate tantum baptizanda et educanda, monita parte catholica de obligatione, qua tenetur, conversionem coniugis acatholici prudenter curandi; eaque lege ut, neque ante ne-*

que post matrimonium coram Ecclesia initum, partes adeant ministrum falsi cultus ad matrimonialem consensum praestandum vel renovandum.
Si agatur vero de matrimoniis cum hebraeis vel mahumetanis, peculiari ratione oportet ut: constet de status libertate partis infidelis, ad removendum priculum polygamiae; absit periculum circumcisionis prolis; et si civilis actus sit ineundus, sit tantum caeremonia civilis nullaque Mahumetis invocatio aut aliud superstitionis genus interveniat.

SECTION 2. CANONICAL CONDITIONS FOR THE USE OF DECENNIAL FACULTY N. XXII

As seen above, for its use canon 1043 (canon 1044) postulates the situation of an *"urgens mortis periculum,"* while canon 1045 presupposes some perplexing situation. In either case there must be present also a canonical cause for the granting of the dispensations. But the present Decennial Faculty simply requires *"canonicae existentes causae,"* patterned on the ordinary demand for canonical cases when dispensations are to be granted according to the norm of canon 84; it does not postulate the situation of an *"urgens mortis periculum,"* nor does it presuppose some perplexing situation for its licit and valid use.

A. Preliminary Notes on Canonical Causes for Matrimonial Dispensations

According to the norm of canon 84, no dispensation from an ecclesiastical law can be granted by an inferior without a *just* and *reasonable cause,* which must reflect a due proportion to the gravity of the law from which the dispensation is granted, for otherwise the dispensation granted by an inferior is both illicit and invalid; when it is doubtful whether the cause for a dispensation is sufficient, one may licitly ask for the dispensation, and the superior may validly and licitly grant the same.[102] Now, a cause is *just* when it sets up a proportionate reason between the law to be observed and the dispensation to be granted, and it is *reasonable,* if it is in accordance with prudence, equity, and practical conditions, taking into consideration the gravity of the law from which the dispensation is sought. A cause for a dispensation is said to be *sufficient* or *insufficient* according to the greater or lesser degrees of its *justness* and *reasonableness,* which characteristics are present only when there exists a due proportion between the claims for the law's observance on the one hand and the claims for its relaxation on the other. Such a *justness* and *reasonableness,* however, are to be estimated according to the rules which have been employed by the Roman Curia in such matters.[103]

Among the causes for dispensations there are *canonical* (or *ordinary*) *causes* and *non-canonical causes.* The former are those which are classified and held as sufficient by the Church's law, the Roman Curia, and canonical jurisprudence. They are considered *"causae motivae,"* which suffice of themselves, either individually or collectively, for matrimonial dispensations.[104] The latter are those which lack the approval or recognition of the Church's law or of the Roman Curia, and which do not suffice of their own nature, when they are considered singly and without an accompanying *"causa motiva"* for the granting of any dispensations from matrimonial impediments of major degree, although several of the same kind may amount to a *sufficient cause* for the dispensation. In the main, non-canonical causes serve as *"causae impulsivae,"* or as impelling causes for matrimonial dispensation.[105]

[102] Cf. Michiels, *Normae Generales,* II, 737-753.

[103] Carolus Holboeck, *Tractatus de Jurisprudentia Sacrae Romanae Rotae* (Graetiae-Vindobonae-Coloniae: In Officina Libraria "Styria," 1957), 46.

[104] Gasparri, *De Matrimonio,* n. 297; Holboeck, *loc. cit.*

[105] Holboeck, *loc. cit.*

Of canonical causes, not all have the same weight, and any given canonical cause may be made more or less grave according to the circumstances of the individual case and according to the individual matrimonial impediments. Furthermore, although they are held sufficient for matrimonial dispensations in general, some of them are not sufficient for sufficient for dispensations from certain matrimonial impediments of consanguinity, of mixed religion, of disparity of cult, etc.[106] For a dispensation from these impediments requires *just* and *grave causes,* as enunciated in canons 1061, § 1, and 1071.

In principle, "no bishop may validly dispense on the basis of causes which Rome has adjudged to be insufficient for the impediment to be dispensed";[107] and "bishops, acting by delegated powers, are bound to follow the *praxis* of Rome in their judgment of canonical causes, and this under pain of invalidity."[108] The Church does not grant dispensations from the impediments of disparity of cult and of mixed religion in favor of or for the benefit of non-Catholic parties.[109]

According to the norm of canon 1054, a dispensation from a matrimonial impediment of minor degree[110] is not invalidated in consequence of a petitioner's positive proposal of a lie or of his concealment of the truth in his petition, even though the only "*causa motiva*" as advanced in the dispensation rests on a falsified basis.[111] This norm supposes that in such a case there should be at least a non-canonical cause (or a *causa impulsiva*) ; and from this very norm it follows that a dispensation from an impediment of

[106] Cf. Eric F. MacKenzie, "Insufficient Canonical Causes for Matrimonial Impediments," *The Jurist,* V (1945), 55-58; Gasparri, *De Matrimonio,* I, n. 298, p. 182.

[107] MacKenzie, *ibid.,* p. 64.

[108] *Ibid.,* p. 63. Cf. *Collectanea,* instructio S.C. Prop. Fid., 9 Maii 1877, n. 1470.

[109] Cf. Doheny, *Informal Procedure,* pp. 734-735; MacKenzie, "art. cit.," *The Jurist,* V (1945), 64.

[110] Canon 1042, § 2.

[111] Cf. canon 40.

major degree is invalidated in consequence of the proposal of a positive lie by the petitioner in his request, if the only "*causa motiva*" advanced in the petition of the dispensation rests on a falsified basis.[112]

B. A List of Canonical Causes for Matrimonial Dispensations

There are two lists of causes that are recognized by the Roman Curia. The first was published on May 9, 1877, in the Instruction "*Cum dispensatio sit*" of the Sacred Congregation for the Propagation of the Faith.[113] This list enumerates sixteen canonical causes for matrimonial dispensations and these causes are the following:

> 1. *Angustia loci.* 2. *Aetas feminae super-adulta.* 3. *Deficientia aut incompent
entia dotis.* 4. *Lites super successione bonorum iam exorta, vel earumdem grave aut imminens periculum.* 5. *Paupertas viduae.* 6.*Bonum pacis.* 7. *Nimia, suspecta, periculosa familiaritas nec non cohabitatio sub eodem tecto, quae facile impediri non possit.* 8. *Copula cum consanguinea vel affini vel alia persona impedimento laborante praehabita, et praegnantia, ideoque legitimatio prolis.* 9. *Infamia mulieris, ex suspicione orta.* 10. *Revalidatio matrimonii, quod bona fide et publice, servata Tridentini forma, contractum est.* 11. *Periculum matrimonii mixti, vel coram acatholico ministro celebrandi.* 12. *Periculum incestuosi concubinatus.* 13. *Periculum matrimonii civilis.* 14. *Remotio gravium scandalorum.* 15. *Cessatio publici concubinatus.* 16. *Excellentia meritorum.*[114]

Of these canonical causes, causes nn. 4, 6, 8, and 10-15 are those which affect the public good, but are private in

[112] Cf. canons 40-42; Michiels, *Normae Generales*, II, 352-373; Cicognani-O'Hara-Brennan, *Canon Law*, pp. 710-718.

[113] *Collectanea*, n. 1470.

[114] For a commentary on each of these canonical causes cf. Gasparri, *De Matrimonio*, I, nn. 303-318, pp. 184-191; Cappello, *De Matrimonio*, nn. 257-267, pp. 256-264; Conte a Coronata, *De Sacramentis*, III, nn. 163-178, pp. 198-211; G. Vromant, *De Matrimonio* (3. ed., emendata et aucta, Paris: Desclée de Brouwer, 1952), nn. 143-158, pp. 141-149; Winslow, *The Apostolic Faculties*, pp. 86-93.

their nature; causes nn. 1-3, and 5 are private in their nature and affect the good of individuals, and accordingly suffice for dispensations from certain impediments;[115] and causes nn. 7, 9, and 16 are insufficient of themselves for the granting of a dispensation, although they will be sufficient when taken together with other individually insufficient causes.[116] And all of these sixteen canonical causes were declared in the Instruction *"Cum dispensatio sit"* as "COMMUNIORES POTIORESQUE *causae, quae ad matrimoniales dispensationes impetrandas adduci* SOLENT, *de quibus copiose agunt theologiae ac sacrorum canonum interpretes.*"[117]

The other list of canonical causes was published by the Apostolic Datary in 1901, and it contains twenty-eight causes under the heading of *"causae canonicae ordinariae matrimonialium dispensationum sufficientes sive coniunctae plures sive solae et aliarum normae."*[118] In spite of their

[115] All of the latter four cases prove insufficient for a dispensation from the impediments of disparity of cult and of mixed religion; causes nn. 2, 3, and 5 do not suffice for a dispensation from the impediment of consanguinity in the collateral line when the relationship is that of the first degree touching the second. Cf. *AAS*, XXIII (1931), 415; MacKenzie, "art. cit.," *The Jurist*, V (1945), 54-72; W. Conway, "Cause Required for a Matrimonial Dispensation," *I.E.R.*, ser. 5, LXIV (1944), 267-268.

[116] A. M. Quigley, *A Summary of the Canon Law on Matrimonial Impediments and Dispensations* (4th print., Lancaster, Pa.: The Dolphin Press, 1954), p. 12, footnote 14.

[117] *Loc. cit.*, i, f.—*Collectanea*, n. 1470.

[118] *ASS*, XXXIV (1901-1902), 34-35. "Causae honestae et famosae: 1. Propter angustiam loci. 2. Propter angustiam locorum. 3. Propter angustiam cum clausula, '*et si extra*,' dos non esset competens. 4. Propter incompetentiam dotis oratricis. 5. Propter dotem cum augmento. 6. Pro indotata. 7. Quando alius auget dotem. 8. Propter inimicitias. 9. Pro confirmatione pacis; et propter foedera inter Principes et Regna. 10. Propter lites super successionem bonorum. 11. Propter dotem litibus involutam. 12. Propter lites super rebus magni momenti. 13. Pro oratrice filiis gravata; vel parentibus orbata. 14. Pro oratrice excedente 24 annum aetatis. 15. Propter difficultatem virorum accedendi ad locum, ad contrahendum cum loci habitatoribus, e.g., quia expositi pyratarum invasionibus. Propter virorum paucum numerum, e.g., ratione belli. 16. Propter catholicam religionem con-

greater number, the canonical causes contained in this list were identical in their nature with those of the previous list. But the following causes are worthy of attention: *"Propter spem conversionis compartis ad catholicam religionem"* (n. 17), *"Ob familiarum honestatem conservandum"* (n. 20), *"Ex ceteris rationibilibus causis"* (n. 27, and *"Ex ceteris specialibus rationabilibus causis . . ."* (n. 28).

C. A List of Non-Canonicad Causes for Matrimonial Dispensations

From the long praxis of the Roman Curia, canonists list the following causes as *non-Canonical Causes* for Matrimonial Dispensations:

> 1. *Oratrix alterutro vel utroque parente orbata;* 2. *Ex natalibus illegitimis orta;* 3. *Infirmitate deformata aliove defectu detenta;* 4. *Iam ab alio deflorata;* 5. *Si orator sit infirmitate detentus;* 6. *Orator viduus prole oneratus seu bonum prolis oratoris vidui;* 7. *Si vir aut mulier adiutorio indigeat, e.g., ad rem domesticam administrandam;* 8. *Si omnia iam parata sunt ad nuptias;* 9. *Propositum contrahendi matrimonium propalatum seu plane divulgatum, aut propositi pertinacia;* 10. *Boni mores utriusque oratoris;* 11. *Convenientia matrimonii;* 12. *Munificentia oratorum erga bonum publicum;*

trahentis in tuto ponendam; et periculum matrimonii mixti. 17. Propter spem conversionis compartis ad catholicam religionem. 18. Ut bona conserventur in familia. 19. Pro illustris familiae conservatione regiae stirpis. 20. Ob excellentiam meritorum. 21. Ob familiarum honestatem conservandam—quod, si, qui ex honestis familiis sunt, ad eandem conservandam familiarum honestatem. 22. Ob infamiam; et scandalum. 23. Ob copulam; ob raptum. 24. Ob matrimonium civile. 25. Ob matrimonium coram ministro protestante. 26. Ob matrimonium nulliter contractum. 27. Ex ceteris rationabilibus causis—scilicet, ob copiosiorem compositionem in gradibus aliquantulum remotis; vel in gradbius remotioribus ob causam boni publici Pontificis animum moventem. 28. Ex ceteris specialibus rationabilibus causis, oratorum animos moventibus et Sanctitati vestrae expositis—scilicet ob copulam, vel actus inhonestos, quos ob honorem oratorum, attenta eorum qualitate, non expedit explicare." Cf. also *ASS*, XXXIV (1901-1902), 53-84.

13. *Bonum parentum, si nempe alterutrius vel utriusque pater vel mater indiget adiutorio;* 14. *mutuum auxilium in provecta aetate.*[119] 15. *Aetas adhuc iunior viduae;* 16. *scandalum ob tentatam fugam reparandum;* 17. *Si oratores sint reginae dignitatis;* 18. *Si matrimonium sit necessarium pro conservatione familiae illustris;* 19. *Si matrimonium conferat ad conservationem bonorum in familia illustri;* 20. *Si matrimonium avertat imminens periculum vitae oratoribus;* 21. *Si puella ceteroquin sufficienter dotata ex matrimonio, notabiliem fortunae meliorationem obtinere possit;* 22. *Si matrimonium evitare possit divisionem bonorum quae hucusque fuerunt communia inter sponsos.*[120]

D. A List of Canonical Causes for Dispensations from the Impediments of Disparity of Cult and Mixed Religion

The following causes are cited to be sufficient of themselves for the granting of dispensations from the matrimonial impediments of disparity of cult and mixed religion:

1. A grave scandal arising from defamation, pregnancy, or from some other source, that cannot be prevented except through a mixed or disparate marriage.[121]

[119] These fourteen causes are cited by Gasparri, *De Matrimonio*, I, n. 319, p. 191; Cappello, *De Matrimonio*, n. 268, p. 264; Vromant, *De Matrimonio*, n. 159, p. 149. Thirteen causes, excepting cause n. 5, are cited by Wernz-Vidal, *Ius Matrimoniale*, n. 433, p. 561; Paventi, *Brevis Commentarius*, p. 35.

[120] The last eight causes (i.e., nn. 15-22) are cited by Conte a Coronata, *De Sacramentis*, III, n. 179, pp. 211-213, and Vlaming, *Praelectiones Iuris Matrimonii*, II, n. 439. These are taken from the list published by the Apostolic Datary, in 1901, and are insufficient of themselves for the granting of a matrimonial dispensation.

[121] Francis J. Schenk, *The Matrimonial Impediments of Mixed Religion and Disparity of Cult*, The Catholic University of America Canon Law Studies, n. 51 (Washington, D.C.: The Catholic University of America Press, 1929), n. 290, Cappello, *De Matrimonio*, n. 314, f, p. 323; Vromant, *De Matrimonio*, n. 161, p. 151; Vlaming, *Praelectiones Iuris Canonici*, II, n. 216.

2. The predominance of heretics or schismatics (or infidels) in a given region, provided that Catholics are secure and free in professing their religion.[122]

3. If a mixed or disparate marriage is the only means whereby children born of another mixed or disparate marriage will be educated in the Catholic Faith.[123]

4. Danger of apostasy of the Catholic party if the dispensation is denied.[124]

5. Danger of a civil marriage, or of contracting the union before a non-Catholic minister.[125]

6. The cause of conversion: (a) a probable hope that a favorably disposed non-Catholic family will come into the Church together as the result of a mixed or disparate marriage;[126] (b) a written promise, or an oral promise before witnesses made by the non-Catholic party to embrace the Catholic Faith after the marriage;[127] (c) Hope of the conversion of the non-Catholic party.[128]

Vromant also lists the following causes: (1) *excellentia meritorum oratoris;* (2) *cessatio publici concubinatus;* (3) *suspecta familiaritas;* (4) *copula divulgata vel praegnantia;* (5) *socialis conditio familiae;* (6) *angustia loci;* (7) *aetas superadulta;* (8) *pauptertas viduae;* (9) *incompetentia dotis.*[129]

SECTION 3. THE SCOPE OF THE DECENNIAL FACULTY N. XXII

The scope of the present Decennial Faculty is the same as that of canon 1043 without the phrase: *"tum super forma*

[122] Cappello, *ibid.*, n. 314, b, p. 322; Vromant, *loc. cit.;* Schenk, *loc. cit.* Cf. *Collectanea*, n. 684.

[123] Schenk, *loc. cit.;* Capello, *ibid.*, n. 314, e, p. 322; Vromant, *loc. cit.*

[124] Schenk, *loc. cit.*

[125] *Loc. cit.*

[126] *Loc. cit.* Cappello, *ibid.*, n. 314, d, p. 322; Vromant, *loc cit.*.

[127] Schenk, *loc cit.;* Cappello, *ibid.*, n. 314, c, p. 322; Vromant, *loc. cit.;* Wernz-Vidal, *Ius Matrimoniale*, p. 207, footnote 30; Valming, *loc. cit.*

[128] *ASS*, XXXIV (1901-1902), 34-35.

[129] *Loc. cit.*

in matrimonii celebratione servanda, but with an additional clause among its exceptions, i.e., *ex defectu praescriptiae aetatis quando sponsi ad aetatem ab antiquo iure praefixam nondum pervenerint (idest ad annum 14 completum pro viris et ad 12 completum pro mulieribus).* Thus, by virtue of the present faculty a dispensation can be granted for each and every one of the matrimonial impediments of ecclesiastical law, diriment as well as prohibitive, of major degree as well as minor degree, even multiple, public as well as occult, to the exception of all the impediments deriving from the divine law,[130] and the three impediments of ecclesiastical law as stated in the text of the faculty itself, i.e., the impediments arising from the sacred priesthood, from affinity in any degree of the direct line if the marriage has become consummated, and from the lack of the requisite age when the male party to the marriage has not yet completed his fourteenth, or the female her twelfth, year.[131]

Hence the impediments from which a dispensation can be granted by virtue of the present Decennial Faculty are the following:

I. *Prohibitive Impediments*:

1. Simple vows (canon 1058, § 1);[132]
2. Legal relationship (canon 1059 and 1080);

[130] *Supra*, p. 207.

[131] Cf. canon 34, § 3, 3°. Since canon 1067, § 1, prescribes that a man cannot contract a valid marriage before completing his sixteenth year, or a woman before completing her fourteenth, the present Decennial Faculty empowers the ordinary in the missions to dispense from the lack of the requisite age as stated in canon 1067, provided that the parties have reached the age of fourteen and twelve respectively, as was prescribed before the Code. The parties' age is to be computed according to the norm of canon 34, § 3, 3°, but in a case of factual doubt regarding the completion of the requisite age the provision of canon 15 becomes operative.

[132] The simple vows of virginity, of perfect chastity (even though public and made in a religious institute, but not such as would fall under the provision of canon 1058, § 2), of not contracting marriage, of receiving sacred orders, and of embracing the religious state. The vows of poverty and obedience are not subject to possible dispensation by virtue of the present faculty.

3. Mixed religion (canon 1060-1064).[133]

II. *Diriment Impediments of Major Degree*:

1. Disparity of cult (canons 1070-1071);[134]
2. Nonage (canon 1067, § 1);[135]
3. Sacred orders of subdeaconship and deaconship (but not of priesthood (canon 1072);
4. Solemn vows and also simple vows when qualified with like juridical effect (canon 1073);
5. Abduction (canon 1074);
6. Marital criminality (canon 1075, 2° and 3°);
7. Consanguinity in the second degree of the collateral line (canon 1076), not excluding the second degree touching the first degree of the collateral line;[136]
8. Affinity in the direct line, if the marriage has remained unconsummated, and in the collateral line (canons 1077 and 97);
9. Public propriety, even in the first degree (canon 1078);
10. Legal relationship (canon 1080).

III. *Diriment Impediments of Minor Degree*:

1. Consanguinity in the third degree of the collateral line (canon 1076);
2. Affinity in the second degree of the collateral line (canon 1077 and 97);

[133] This faculty cannot be applied to a *neo-conversus* who makes use of the Pauline privilege, for according to the prescription of canons 1123-1124 such a person is bound to marry a Catholic. Cf. *Periodica*, XIX (1930), p. (77).

[134] From the context of the present faculty it is clear that a dispensation from the impediment of disparity of cult existing between a Catholic party and a Jewish party or a Mohammedan party can be given by virtue of the present faculty. However, this faculty cannot be applied in favor of a *neo-conversus* who makes use of the privilege of the Faith. For this case a special faculty from the Holy Office is necessary. Cf. Vromant, *Facultates Apostolicae*, p. 60, note 2; *Periodica*, XIV (1925), 114-115; Paventi, *CpRM*, XXIII (1942), 11; *Collectanea*, nn. 1114, 1297, and 1377.

[135] Supra, p. 232, note 131.

[136] Cf. S.C. de Sacr., instr., 1 Aug. 1931—*AAS*, XXIII (1931), 413.

3. Public propriety in the second degree (canon 1078);
4. Spiritual relationship (canon 1079);
5. Marital criminality resulting from adultery along with the mutual promise of marriage or the attempt of marriage, even by way of merely civil contract (canon 1075, 1°).

SECTION 4. RULES, GUARANTEES (*Cautiones*), AND CONDITIONS FOR THE USE OF DECENNIAL FACULTY XXII

A. *Requisite Rules*

Since the present Decennial Faculty is contemplated for use in ordinary circumstances, all the rules delineated in canons 1035-1080, the observance of which is postulated for dispensing from matrimonial impediments in ordinary circumstances, must be duly honored. The general rules for all matrimonial dispensations are treated in canons 1035-1057, and the special rules for individual prohibitive impediments and diriment impediments are delineated in canons 1058-1066 and 1067-1080 respectively.

Among the general rules, those of canon 1050 on the concurrenec of impediments, of canon 1051 on the legitimation of the children, and of canon 1047 regarding the notation of the granted dispensations in the Registry of Marriages or in the Secret Archives, etc., call for particular attention on the part of the missionary who makes use of the present faculty.

According to the rule given in canon 1050, if together with a *public* impediment from which the missionary can dispense by virtue of a faculty subdelegated to him by the ordinary there is also present in the case a *public* impediment from which he cannot dispense, he must have recourse to the ordinary for the dispensation from all the impediments in the case, even though only one of them is reserved to the ordinary; if after he has obtained the power to dispense from a reserved impediment, another impediment is discovered in the same case, but it is one (whether *public* or *occult*) from which he can dispense by virtue of his faculty, then the missionary can dispense from all the impediments in the case without having any recourse to the ordinary. However, if together with an *occult* impediment from which the missionary can dispense by virtue of his faculty there is also present a *public* or an *occult* impediment which is reserved to the ordinary himself, then the missionary must have recourse to the ordinary for the reserved impediment alone.[137]

According to the norm given in canon 1051, by reason of having the present Decennial Faculty, the missionary has also the power to legitimate the children in the event that any have already born or conceived by the parties who are being dispensed, with the execption of children whose existence is traceable to a sin of adultery or also of sacrilege. The reason of this effect is that the present Decennial Faculty is one of the general indults, i.e., The Decennial Faculties, *Formula Maior*.[138] The legitimation takes place *ipso facto*, that is, upon the granting of the dispensation itself, independently of the subsequent marriage of the parties, even though the failure to follow up the dispensation by actual marriage be due to the fault of the parties.[139] As a norm for the legitimation of an illegitimate child by way of the subsequent marriage of the parties, canon 1116 prescribes that the parties whose child is being legitimated must have been legally capable of contracting marriage together at the time of the conception, the gestation, or the birth of the child in question. Thus, in the event that the parents of the child were subject to any of the diriment impediments such as nonage, disparity of cult, consanguinity, affinity, etc., throughout the time of the conception, the

[137] Vromant, *De Matrimonio*, n. 138, pp. 136-137.

[138] Vromant, *De Matrimonio*, n. 139, pp. 137-138; S.C.S. Off., 11 Dec. 1906—*Collectanea*, II, p. 568 (addendum); Bouscaren-Ellis, *Canon Law*, p. 497.

[139] Bouscaren-Ellis, *Canon Law*, p. 496; Payen, *De Matrimonio*, n. 713; Cappello, *De Matrimonio*, n. 291, p. 296; *contra*, Gasparri, *De Matrimonio*, n. 358, p. 212.

gestation, and the birth of the child, then for the legitimation of such a child there is necessary some special faculty from the Holy See. But, when this occurs in the missions the missionary may legitimate the child by virtue of the present Decennial Faculty.[140]

When a dispensation from matrimonial impediments is granted by the missionary by virtue of the present Decennial Faculty, it is necessary to mention in the dispensation the fact that it was granted by virtue of the power subdelegated by the ordinary through his application of the Decennial Faculty,[141] and to record the granting of the dispensation in the Registry of Marriages, or in the Secret Archives, according to the norms prescribed in canons 1046, 1047, and 379.[142]

B. The Guarantees (CAUTIONES) *and Conditions Required for Dispensation from the Impediments of Mixed Religion and of Disparity of Cult*

1. *Guarantees.—"De amovendo a catholico coniuge perversionis periculo ac de universa prole utriusque sexus in catholicae religionis sanctitate tantum baptizanda et educanda."* The guarantees receive mention in canon 1061, § 1, 2°, and consist of two promises: (a) that the non-Catholic party give assurance that the danger of perversion for the Catholic party will be removed, and (b) that both parties give assurance that all the children will be baptized and brought up in the Catholic Faith only.

The danger of perversion for the Catholic party includes any danger which might weaken or destroy the religion of the said party throughout their whole married life, and the term "religion" comprehends not only the Catholic party's

[140] S.C. de Prop. Fid., resp., 27 Nov. 1930—*Prot.* n. 4757; *Periodica,* XIX (1930), pp. 26*-28*; Vromant, *De Matrimonio,* n. 139, pp. 137-138. Also cf. Code Comm., 6 Dec. 1930, ad II—*AAS,* XXIII (1930), 25.

[141] *Animadversiones,* II, for the Decennial Faculties, *Formula Maior.* Cf. Paventi, *Brevis Commentarius,* p. 69.

[142] Cf. Vromant, *De Matrimonio,* nn. 121 and 134, pp. 121 and 134 respectively.

religious belief but also his or her morals, religious practices, the standards and duties of a Catholic, and indeed of a married Catholic, as defined by the tradition and authoritative statements of the Church.

Both parties must give assurance that all the children will be baptized and brought up in the Catholic Faith only. Whether or not *"universa prolis utriusque sexus"* included also such of their children as had been born to these parties from a previous putative marriage or invalid union or to either of them from a former marriage or union with a different party, now deceased, was rather a long-disputed question,[143] but it is now settled by an authentic reply of the Holy office, on January 16, 1942. The question was asked:

> 1°. *Utrum cautiones quae ad normam can. 1061 praestari debent de universa prole catholice tantum baptizanda et educanda comprehendant solummodo prolem nascituram, an etiam prolem ante matrimonii celebrationem forte iam natam;*
> 2°. *Quid sentiendum de matrimoniis celebratis cum cautionibus de prole nascitura, neglecta prole forte iam nata.*

The reply was *"Ad 1um: Affirmative ad primam partem; negative ad secundam; ad 2um: Provisum in primo."*[144] In connection with this reply, the Sacred Congregation made known its intent with regard to the children already born before the celebration of the marriage, namely that, although *per se,* according to the canon cited, promises are not required with reference to the children born before the marriage, the parties are definitely to be warned of their grave obligation under the divine law to see also to the Catholic education of the children already born.[145]

In line with the demands made in canon 1061, § 1, 2° and 3°, canon 1063, § 2, and canon 1071, a dispensation from the impediments of mixed religion and of disparity of cult is

[143] Cf. Gasparri, *De Matrimonio,* I, n. 451, p. 266.

[144] S.C.S. Off., resp., 16 Ian. 1942—*AAS,* XXXIV (1942), 22. Cf. *Periodica,* XXXI (1942), 175-183; Bouscaren, *Canon Law Digest,* II, 286; Vromant, *De Matrimonio,* n. 165, pp. 153-154, and note 3 on p. 153.

[145] *AAS, loc. cit.; Periodica, loc. cit.*

never to be granted by virtue of the Decennial Faculty unless the proper guarantees have been obtained from the parties, and unless there is moral certainty of their fulfillment in the mind of the grantor of the dispensation. In other words, the guarantees on the part of both parties to the marriage and the moral certainty on the part of the grantor of the dispensation are required for the validity of the dispensation, and for the validity of the marriage, when the impediment of disparity of cult is present.[146]

The study of recent decisions on the question of whether the fact that the promises are *insincere* when given renders the dispensation invalid shows that, if the insincerity is fully proved, the dispensation is to be regarded invalid.[147] According to the Decree of the Holy Office, on January 14, 1932, a dispensation from the impediments of mixed religion and of disparity of cult must not be granted, unless the promises are so made that none can frustrate their fulfillment, even by recourse to the civil laws to which either party is subject and which are in force in their actual place of residence or the place where they intend to live.[148] But the same Sacred Congregation declared in September, 1934, that the said Decree did not concern the territories under the jurisdiction of the Sacred Congregation for the Propagation of the Faith.[149] Thus, the missionary who has the present Decennial Faculty may grant dispensations and execute rescripts for mixed marriages under due observance of the requirements of law and provided that the mis-

[146] N.B. These guarantees and the subsequent moral certainty are required for the same effect in the dispensation and the marriage, even in the case of an "*urgens mortis periculum.*" Cf. canon 1044; S.C.S. Off., decr., 14 Ian. 1932—*AAS*, XXIV (1932), 25; *Periodica*, XXI (1932), 100; Bouscaren, *Canon Law Digest*, I, 505.

[147] Cf. Bouscaren, *Canon Law Digest*, IV, 323-329; *Periodica*, XXXVIII (1949), 305; J. Norbert Kelly, "Insincere *Cautiones* in the Light of Recent Decisions," *The Jurist*, XIII (1953), 33-56.

[148] *AAS*, (1932), 25; Bouscaren, *Canon Law Digest*, I, 505-506.

[149] (Private); reply of Holy Office reported in Letter of S.C. de Prop. Fid., 9 Nov. 1934—*Sollyge*, n. 186. Cf. Bouscaren, *Canon Law Digest*, II, 280.

sionary judges that there exists in every case a moral certainty that the promises will be lived up to, although the civil laws do not recognize the binding power of the said promises made by the parties of mixed marriages.

According to the norms of canon 1061 and 1071, the guarantees which are required for the validity of the dispensation should be made in a *formal* and *explicit* form.[150] However, on May 10, 1941, the Holy Office in a general session expressed its mind in regard to the form of the guarantees, namely that the use of the faculty for dispensing, whether it be ordinary or delegated, cannot be called invalid if both parties at least *implicitly* gave the guarantees, that is, if they placed acts from which it must be concluded and can be proved in the external forum that they were conscious of their duty to fulfill the conditions and that they manifested a firm purpose to perform that duty.[151] Hence, now the guarantees may be accepted either in a *formal and explicit form* or in a *formal and implicit form.* It is clear from the text of the faculty that the guarantees in a *formal form* are required for the validity of the dispensation in the case of the use of the present Decennial Faculty.

The use of the *equivalent* guarantees (*cautiones aequipollentes*)[152] was first permitted to the missionaries in China

[150] "Cautiones *formales* seu ordinariae sunt contractus solemnis quo uterque contrahens promittit baptismum et educationem catholicam universae prolis; *acatholicus* seu pars acatholica promittit amotum esse a coniuge catholico perversionis periculum;" "*explicitae* cautiones sunt promissiones externae manifestatae per signum aptum, scripturam aut verba ore prolata, de adimplendis conditionibus."—Vromant, *De Matrimonio,* n. 164, pp. 152-153.

[151] *AAS,* XXXIII (1941), 294; Bouscaren, *Canon Law Digest,* II, 292-293. Cf. *The Jurist,* II (1942), 59.

[152] "Cautiones *aequipollentes* seu extraordinariae habentur, quando pars catholica sincere manifestat firmum propositum faciendi ex sua parte quod facere potest, ut universa proles in fide catholica baptizetur et educetur, et, consideratis singulorum casuum condicionibus, moraliter certo constat: manifestatam sinceram partis catholicae voluntatem de universa prole catholice baptizanda et educanda, etiam effectum habituram esse."—Vromant, *De Matrimonio,* n. 164, p. 153.

by a special provision of the Holy Office, on April 5, 1919.[153] The document reads in English as follows:

> If the guarantees cannot be obtained from the infidel woman in writing, let them be obtained at least orally. If even this cannot be obtained, it is left to the prudnet and conscientious judgment of the respective Vicars Apostolic to decide in each case whether the guarantees are contained equivalently, either in the serious promise of the woman to embrace the Catholic Faith, or in her enrollment among the catechumens, or finally in the laws and customs of the people, according to which the woman has no power over the religious education of the children, which depends exclusively on the will of the husband; in all these cases, however, the obligation remains to demand the guarantees of the Catholic party, and not to grant the dispensation unless there is moral certainty of their fulfillment.[154]

This decree contains the permission of the acceptance of the equivalent guarantees, which are valid for the cases wherein the impediment of disparity of cult is present, and for the cases wherein the non-Catholic party of the marriage is a woman, and which are judged to be such in three different ways according to the accompanying respective extraordinary circumstances.

On March 30, 1938, however, the Holy Office permitted to ordinaries of Japan the use of the equivalent guarantees for the cases wherein either the impediment of disparity of cult or the impediment of mixed religion is present, and the equivalent guarantees may be used by both the Catholic party and the non-Catholic party.[155] The peculiar circumstances contemplated in the use of the equivalent guarantees in Japan are that Catholics, catechumens, and non-Catholics in that country have lost all right of control over their minor

[153] *Primum Concilium Sinense*, n. 404, 2°, p. 139; Bouscaren, *Canon Law Digest*, III, 427-428.

[154] Bouscaren, *Canon Law Digest, loc. cit.*

[155] *Sylloge*, n. 206 bis, pp. 561-566; Bouscaren, *Canon Law Digest*, II, 281-285.

children, inasmuch as they are obliged to turn them over to their pagan or even Mohammedan parents, who prevent the children's Catholic education, and that on this account the parties are unable to promise to baptize and educate all the children to be born. The permission of the use of these equivalent guarantees was given under the condition that the Catholic party is sincerely prepared to do all he can to have the children baptized and educated as Catholic, and such guarantees can be used with a grave obligation in conscience upon the local ordinaries.[156] According to later documents, the use of the equivalent guarantees, which was permitted to the ordinaries of Japan, on March 30, 1938, was extended also to all ordinaries in China under communist rule, through a letter of the Papal Internuncio to China, on January 27, 1949.[157] In the said letter it was stated that the equivalent guarantees, according to a Reply of the Holy Office given for Japan, are had when the Catholic party sincerely manifests a firm resolve to do what he can to see that all the children are baptized and educated in the Catholic faith; if the non-Catholic party refuses to formulate and manifest the same resolve, the equivalent guarantees, according to the Reply cited, are not thereby destroyed. On February 21, 1949, by order of His Excellency the Assessor of the Holy Office, the following Supplement regarding the *cautiones* was sent out to all ordinaries of China under communist rules:

> Equivalent *cautiones* are to be considered sufficient for contracting marriage with a pagan party or with a baptized non Catholic party, only if, on consideration of the circumstances of the individual cases, it is morally certain that the sincere manifested will of the Catholic party to have all

[156] Cf. Vromant, *De Matrimonio,* n. 173, pp. 165-168.

[157] This letter contained the questions proposed by the Most Rev. Leopold Brellinger, Bishop of Kinghsien to the Holy Office, and the reply of the Holy Office to the questions. (Private); S.C.S. Off., 27 Ian. 1949. Cf. Bouscaren, *Canon Law Digest,* III, 407-408; *Periodica,* XXXVIII (1949), 187.

the children baptized and educated as Catholic will also *have effect.*[158]

2. *Precautions.*—(a) "*Monita parte catholica de obligatione, qua tenetur, conversionem coniugis acatholici prudenter curandi.*" This condition is a restatement of canon 1062, which prescribes that the Catholic party is obliged to strive prudently for the conversion of the non-Catholic party. The grantor of the dispensation must admonish the Catholic party of the marriage of this obligation. Before the Code, a formal promise was asked of the Catholic to labor for the conversion of the other. This is no longer required as part of the regular guarantees.[159] It is, however, a serious obligation of charity induced not only by the natural law itself,[160] but also by way of canonical prescript. It is the duty of the grantor of the dispensation by virtue of the present Decennial Faculty to admonish the Catholic party of this obligation.

(b) "*Eaque lege ut, neque ante neque post matrimonium coram Ecclesia initum, partes adeant ministrum falsi cultus ad matrimonialem consensum praestandum vel renovandum.*" This precaution derives from canon 1063, § 1, according to which, even though a dispensation from the impediment of mixed religion has been obtained from the Church, the parties may not, either before or after the celebration of their marriage according to the law of the Church, either in person or by proxy, approach also a non-Catholic minister. The third paragraph of canon 1063, however, states that it is not forbidden in case the civil law requires it that the parties must present themselves before a non-Catholic minister acting only as civil officer, merely for the purpose of performing the civil act of marriage for the sake of the civil effect. But if the civil law recognizes pastors as empowered to officiate at marriages, it is never necessary to approved a civil officer.[161]

[158] Bouscaren, *Canon Law Digest*, III, 410.
[159] Ayrinhac-Lydon, *Marriage Legislation*, p. 111.
[160] *Loc. cit.;* Bouscaren-Ellis, *Canon Law*, p. 509.
[161] Bouscaren-Ellis, *Canon Law*, p. 510.

The second paragraph of canon 1063 prescribes that, if the pastor definitely knows that the parties intend to violate, or that they have violated, the condition stated in the paragraph of the same canon, he must not assist at their marriage except for the gravest reasons, on condition that scandal be removed, and after consulting the ordinary. If, however, there exist very serious reasons which make it advisable to grant the dispensation, although the grantor knows certainly that the parties intend to violate, or that they have already violated, this law, the ordinary or the priest who enjoys the present Decennial Faculty can grant the dispensation validly and licitly on condition that the scandal be removed.[162]

3. *Special Precautions for Disparate Marriages between Catholic Parties and Jews or Mohammedans."*—By virtue of the paragraph: *"Si agatur vero de matrimonio cum hebraeis vel mahumetanis peculiari ratione oportet ut. . .,"* the present Decennial Faculty is operative also for a dispensation from the impediment of disparity of cult which exists between a Catholic and a Jew[163] or a Mohammedan in a marriage case. However, when a dispensation from such an impediment of disparity of cult is given by virtue of the present Decennial Faculty, special precautions, in addition to the above-mentioned guarantees and conditions which are required for an ordinary impediment of disparity of cult, must be taken as prescribed in the text of the faculty itself. Those special precautions are: (a) the grantor

[162] Vromant, *Facultates Apostolicae*, n. 71, p. 72; Vermeersch, "De Formulis Facultatum," *Periodica*, XI (1922), p. (122).

[163] In the present Decennial Faculty, by Jews are meant all persons who are of Jewish origin, even though they have abandoned or never followed the observance of their religion. Cf. S.C.S. Off., resp., 7 Iul. 1943—Bouscaren, *Canon Law Digest*, III, 420. Those who are descended from ancestors who were once Jewish, but who were converted to the Catholic faith for one or more generations and afterwards fell away, even though these descendants have never received baptism and profess no religion, are not to be regarded as Jewish. Cf. S.C.S. Off., resp., 11 Apr. 1945—Bouscaren, *Canon Law Digest*, III, 420-421.

must be absolutely sure of the free status (*status libertatis*) of the non-Catholic party; (b) there must be no danger that ritual circumcision will be performed on any and all of the children born to them, and (c) if a civil ceremony has to be performed with a view of obtaining the civil effects of the marriage, this must be limited to a merely civil ceremony, and no invocation of Mohammed or other superstitious practices may be tolerated.[164]

Article IV

Ex Facultate, II: Quinquennial Faculties in Formula IV

The Quinquennial Faculties in *Formula IV* for dispensing from matrimonial impediments are: Faculties nn. 2-3 of those which are granted by the Sacred Congregation of the Holy Office; Faculties nn. 1-3 of those which are granted by the Sacred Congregation for the Sacraments; and Faculty n. 8 of those which are granted by the Sacred Penitentiary.

Section 1. Faculties from the Holy Office

A. Texts of the Faculties nn. 2-3

Faculty n. 2	*Faculty n. 3*
To dispense, for just and grave reasons, their own subjects even outside their territory, and other persons within it,	
from the impediment of mixed religion, and if need be also from that of disparity of cult, *ad cautelam,* whenever there exists a prudent doubt of the reception of baptism by the non-Catholic party;	from the impediment of disparity of cult (except for a marriage with a Mohammedan),
when it has been found impossible before the	when this can be done without irreverence to

[164] Cf. canon 1063, § 3; Vromant, *Facultates Apostolicae,* n. 72, p. 73.

marriage either to bring the non-Catholic party to the true faith or to deter the Catholic party from the marriage;

the Creator, and when it has been found impossible before the marriage either to bring the non-Catholic party to the true faith or deter Catholic party from the marriage;

provided that the promises have been regularly made in advance according to can. 1061, § 2, guaranteeing the fulfillment of the conditions required by the Church, and *provided the Ordinary himself be morally certain of their fulfillment;* to wit: on the part of the non-Catholic party, the promise to remove the danger of perversion from the Catholic party, and on the part of both, the promise to baptize and educate all the children of both sexes in the holiness of the Catholic faith.

Moreover, the Catholic party must be informed of his or her obligation to use prudent measures to convert the other party to the Catholic faith.

The parties should be warned that according to canon 1063, § 1, they may not, either prior to or subsequent to their marriage before the Church, present themselves also before a non-Catholic minister in order to express or renew their matrimonial consent.

This is forbidden to the Catholic party under pain of *excommunication latae sententiae* reserved to the Ordinary according to canon 2319, § 1, 1°.

Moreover, the provisions of canon 1063, § 2, regarding the manner in which the pastor should act in such a case, are to be strictly observed.

As regards the legitimation of the children, let canon 1051 be attended to.

If the parties are actually living in concubinage, appropriate measures must be taken to remove any scandal that may exist, and the Catholic party must be prepared to receive the grace of God, first receiving absolution from the excommunication which has been contracted if there has been an attempt to marry before a non-Catholic minister; and in this case also appropriate salutary penances are to be imposed.

If a child has already been born of the illicit union, the parties must be warned of their grave obligation under the divine law to provide as well as they can for its conversion and baptism; an explicit promise should be required of the Catholic party to fulfill this obligation.

If the parties are actually living in concubinage, appropriate measures must be taken to remove any scandal that may exist, and the Catholic party must be prepared to receive the grace of God.

If a child has already been born of the illicit union, the warning must be given and the promise required as provided above in n. 2.

For the rest, whether the impediment be mixed religion or disparity of cult, let the provisions of canon 1026, 1102, and 1109 be observed as regards the publications, the questioning of the parties as to consent, and the sacred rites. After such a marriage has been celebrated, whether within or outside his own territory, let the Ordinary be watchful to see that the parties faithfully fulfill the promise they have made.

B. A Brief Commentary on the Faculties

With reference to the Quinquennial Faculties for dispensing from the impediments of mixed religion and of disparity of cult, the canonical reasons for their use, the circumstances in which they are to be used, the subjects for whom they are to be used, the canonical guarantees and conditions required for their use, the rules concerning the legitimation of the children, etc., are the same as those which obtain with reference to the Decennial Faculty (*Facultas XXII*, in the *Formula Maior*), except for the fact that from the impediment of disparity of cult existing between a Catholic and a Mohammedan a dispensation cannot be granted in virtue of the Quinquennial Faculty.

The clause, "when this can be done without irreverence to the Creator," is new in the Quinquennial Faculty for the dispensation that is to be granted with reference to the impediment of disparity of cult. But, if the non-Catholic party solemnly promises to remove the danger of perversion from the Catholic party and to secure the baptism and education of all the children to be born to them in the sanctity of the Catholic faith only, and if the grantor of this dispensation can be morally certain in regard to the fulfillment of these promises of the non-Catholic party, there exists no threat of irreverence to the Creator on the part of the non-Catholic party. Hence, this clause does not create a new condition or circumstance in addition to those already required in the Decennial Faculty.

On the other hand, the cause, "when it has been found impossible before the marriage either to bring the non-Catholic party to the true faith, or to deter the Catholic party from the marriage," is new in the Quinquennial Faculties, but these provisions should be applied also in the cases which call for the use of the Decennial Faculty. These provisions are naturally derived not only from canon 1060, through which the Church everywhere most severely forbids the contracting of marriage between two baptized persons of whom one is a Catholic and the other a member of some heretical or schismatical sect, but also from canon 1061, § 1, 1°, which prescribes that for the impediment of disparity of cult there is to be no dispensation unless there are just and grave reasons therefor. If the attempts as prescribed in the Quinquennial Faculty were not made, a cause could scarcely be warranted for the dispensation. Nevertheless, these provisions do not pertain to the validity of the dispensation granted by virtue of the present Quinquennial faculties.[165]

SECTION 2. FACULTIES FROM THE SACRED CONGREGATION FOR THE SACRAMENTS

A. Texts of the Faculties nn. 1-3

> *Faculty n. 1.* To dispense, *for a just and reasonable cause,* from the matrimonial impediments of minor degree which are mentioned in canon 1042,[166] and also from the impediments mentioned in canon 1058[167] with a view simply to marriages still to be contracted.
>
> *Faculty n. 2.* To dispense, *for a grave and urgent reason,* whenever there is danger in delay and the marriage cannot be postponed until a dispensation be obtained from the Holy See, from the following impediments of major degree:
>
> a) Consanguinity in the second or third degree touching the first, provided there be no scandal or sensation therefrom.

[165] Cf. Eagleton, *The Liocesan Quinquennial Faculties, Formula IV,* pp. 53-54.

[166] These are: (1) Consanguinity in the third degree of the collateral line; (2) Affinity in the second degree of the collateral line; (3) Public propriety in the second degree; (4) Spiritual relationship; (5) Marital criminality when it results from adultery along with a mutual promise of marriage, or also an attempt of marriage, even by way of a merely civil contract.

[167] They are the vows of virginity, of perfect chastity, of not contracting marriage, of receiving sacred orders, and of embracing the religious state. Simple vows which are endowed with the power of invalidating marriage by special provision of the Holy See are diriment impediments, and thus are not included among the above- mentioned simple vows. Cf. canons 1073, and 1058, § 2.

b) Consanguinity in the second degree of the collateral ine;

c) Affinity in the first degree of the collateral line, either simple or mixed with the second degree.

d) Public propriety in the first degree, provided there be no possibility that one of the parties is the offspring of the other.

Faculty n. 3. To dispense, only during the time and in the act of the pastoral visitation or of sacred missions, from all the above-mentioned impediments in the case of those who are found to be living in concubinage.

(OFFICIAL NOTE. *1. The Ordinary may use these faculties either personally or though other suitable ecclesiastical persons to be specially deputed for the purpose, for marriages that are to be contracted or that have been invalidly contracted, in the case of his own subjects wherever they may be, and of all other persons within his territory, making express mention in every case of this Apostolic delegation, according to c.1057*

2. In the use of these faculties let the provisions of canons 1048-1054 be kept in mind.

3. At the end of each year the Ordinary must report to the Sacred Congregation of the Sacraments, through the Sacred Consistorial Congregation the number and the kinds of dispensations which he has granted by virtue of this Indult.)

B. A Brief Commentary on the Faculties

With reference to the foregoing texts of the Quinquennial Faculties, the diriment impediments of minor degree and the prohibitive impediments as enumerated in canon 1058 allow for dispensation by virtue of the Quinquennial Faculty n. 1 in consideration of a *just and reasonable cause,* and with a view only to marriage to be contracted, while the diriment impediments of major degree which are mentioned in the Quniquennial Faculty n. 2, allow for dispensation for a grave and urgent reason (*ex gravi urgentique causa*), whenever there is danger in delay and the marriage cannot be postponed until a dispensation is obtained from the Holy See. Nevertheless, by force of the Official Note given by the Apostolic Delegation, all the above-mentioned impediments allow for dispensation both for marriages still to be contracted and for marriages already invalidly contracted, by virtue of the Quniquennial Faculties under consideration.

"A grave and urgent reason" is required for the valid use of the cited Quniquennial Faculty n. 2 in dispensing from the diriment impediments of major degree which are mentioned in the same faculty. The list given by the Sacred Congregation for the Propagation of the Faith[168] enumerates the causes which may be considered grave, and in any given case may be considered to furnish a sufficient reason for the granting of a dispensation by virtue of the Quinquennial Faculty under consideration. In addition to the fatcor of gravity, the note of urgency must also be present in the case. The clause, "whenever there is danger in delay and the marriage cannot be postponed until a dispensation be obtained from the Holy See" (*quoties periculum sit in mora et matrimonium nequeat differri usque dum dispensatio a Sancta Sede obtineatur*), explains the urgency postulated for the valid use of said faculty. The existence of these conditions, however, depends upon the circumstances surrounding the contemplated marriage, in the judgment of the ordinary, who in turn is dependent upon the facts presented by the pastor preparing the parties for the marriage. Whenever there is danger in delay and the marriage cannot be postponed until a dispensation is obtained from the Holy See, there exists the postulated urgency for the application of the faculty, but the urgency need not be of the same intensity as that which is postulated in canon 1045: *"cum iam omnia sunt parata ad nuptias, nec matrimonium, sine probabili gravis mali periculo, differri possit usque dum a Sancta Sede dispensatio obtineatur."*[169]

Faculty n. 3 of the Sacred Congregation for the Sacraments empowers the ordinary with the faculty to dispense from all the above-mentioned impediments, i.e., the diriment impediments of minor degree, the prohibitive impediments

[168] *Collectanea*, n. 1470; *supra*, pp. 227-228. [169] *Supra*, pp. 218-222.

enumerated in canon 1058, and the four diriment impediments of major degree enumerated in Faculty n. 2,[170] in the case of those who are found to be living in concubinage, but only during the time and in the act of the pastoral visitation or of sacred missions, but for marriages still to be contracted and also for the convalidation of those which have been invalidly contracted.

The pastoral visitation spoken of in Faculty n. 3 is that visitation which is required of the ordinary by canon 343, § 1.[171] If the task of the pastoral visitation is delegated, the Quinquennial Faculty can also be delegated to the same individual. In this case the subdelegation of the faculty must be made by means of an express act of subdelegation from the ordinary.[172] And the missions spoken of in the present faculty are the ones mentioned in canon 1349, § 1, during which missions the said faculty can be used, *servatis servandis*.

Dispensations can be granted by virtue of Faculty n. 3 only in those cases in which the parties are actually living in concubinage. This condition is postulated for the valid use of the prsent faculty.[173] In cases in which the concubinage is either public or concurrent with an invalid marriage whose status of invalidity was occasioned either by reason of the non-observance of the requisite canonical form or in consequence of the existence of publicly known impediments, care should be exercised to make certain that any penalties contracted by the parties are remitted before a dispensation is granted.[174]

[170] Eagleton excluded the impediments enumerated in Faculty n. 1. Cf. his *The Diocesan Quinquennial Faculties, Formula IV*, p. 82.

[171] Cf. Slafkosky, *The Canonical Episcopal Visitation of the Diocese*, The Catholic University of America Canon Law Studies, n. 142 (Washington, D.C.: The Catholic University of America Press, 1941).

[172] Eagleton, *op. cit.*, p. 83.

[173] Canon 39. Cf. Eagleton, *loc. cit.*

[174] Cf. canons 2319, 1°; 36, § 2. Also cf. John J. Heneghan, *The Marriages of Unworthy Catholics, Canons 1065 and 1066*, The Catholic University of America Canon Law Studies, n. 188 (Washington, D.C.: The Catholic University of America Press, 1944), pp. 113-114.

SECTION 3. THE QUINQUENNIAL FACULTY N. 8 OF THE SACRED PENITENTIARY

A. Text of the Faculty

Faculty n. 8. To dispense from the impediment of crime [marital criminality] when it is occult, provided there is no question of any plotting of death, and the marriage is already contracted. The putative spouses should be informed that it is necessary to make a secret renewal of consent, and a grave and long salutary penance should be imposed on them.

Also to dispense from the same occult impediment, without any plotting of death, even for marriages still to be contracted, with a grave and long salutary penance duly enjoined.

B. A Brief Commentary on the Faculty

Faculty n. 8 of the Sacred Penitentiary concedes to the ordinary the power to dispense from the impediment of occult marital criminality. The power of the faculty as it is expressed in the text can be used validity only when the impediment is occult in marriages which have been invalidly contracted or are to be contracted, and when the impediment was contracted without any plotting of the murder of the spouse of either party, by either or both of the parties to the marriage.

The diriment impediment of marital criminality is classified in canon 1075 as follows:

Canon 1075. *Valide contrahere nequeunt matrimonium:*

1°. *Qui, perdurante eodem legitimo matrimonio, adulterium inter se consummarunt et fidem sibi mutuo dederunt de matrimonio ineundo vel ipsum matrimonium, etiam per civilem tantum actum, attentarunt;*

2°. *Qui, perdurante pariter eodem legitimo matrimonio, adulterium inter se consummarunt eorumque alter coniugicidium patravit;*

3°. *Qui mutua opera physica vel morali, etiam sine adulterio, mortem coniugi intulerunt.*

Thus in view of the wording, "provided there is no question of any plotting of death" (*dummodo sit absque ulla machinatione*), the impediment as described in 2° and 3° of the above cited canon is excluded from the dispensing power granted through Faculty n. 3.

When the faculty is used for dispensing from the impediment of marital criminality for marriages which have been invalidly contracted, the parties are to be warned that they must renew their matrimonial consent, since the power of the faculty does not comprehend the sanation of the invalid marriage in which the parties are now living, so that unless the parties renew their matrimonial consent they will not be validly married. In addition to the request for the renewal of their matrimonial consent, a grave penance of long duration is to be imposed on all those who are granted a dispensation by virtue of the present Quniquennial Faculty.

CHAPTER VI

FACULTIES CONCERNING THE *SANATIO IN RADICE*

The Formulae of the Decennial Faculties for the missions include two faculties pertaining to the *sanatio in radice* of marriages. These faculties are *Facultas XXIII* and *Facultas XXIV* in the *Formula Maior,* and the same faculties are numbered in the *Formula Minor* as *Facultas n. 22* and *Facultas n. 23* respectively. They are faculties which can be subdelegated. Those faculties in the *Quniquennial Faculties, Formula IV,* by virtue of which the *sanatio in radice* is granted, are Faculty n. 3 of the Sacred Congregation for the Sacraments, and Faculty n. 4 of the Holy Office, and these two correspond to the Decennial Faculties, XXIII and XXIV respectively.

ARTICLE I. *Ex Iure*: CANONS 1138-1141

As canon 1138 states, the essential features of the *sanatio in radice* are: (1) it is a dispensation from the law requiring a renewal of consent,[1] the while it implies also a dispensation from or a cessation of the impediment;[2] and (2) by a fiction of law it operates retroactively, as regards the canonical effects, from the very start of the marriage.[3] Hence, the *sanatio in radice* is different from the simple convalidation of a marriage.[4] In the simple convalidation

[1] Canon 1138, § 1.

[2] Canon 1138, § 3. Cf. Thomas C. Rayan, *The Jurdical Effects of the Sanatio in Radice,* The Catholic University of America Canon Law Studies, n. 355 (Washington, D.C.: The Catholic University of America Press, 1955), pp. 77-93; Conte a Coronata, *De Sacramentis,* III, n. 683, pp. 946-949; Wernz-Vidal, *Ius Matrimoniale,* p. 859, footnote n. 12.

[3] Canon 1138, § 2.

[4] For the simple convalidation of marriage, cf. canons 1133-1137, and James H. Brennan, *Simple Convalidation of Marriage,* The Catholic University of America Canon Law Studies, n. 102 (Washington, D.C.: The Catholic University of America Press, 1937).

of marriage the Church merely cancels out the diriment impediment, and so renders the parties capable of contracting a valid marriage, while in the *sanatio in radice* the Church accepts the consent previously given (besides canceling out the impediment), and through it lets the matrimonial bond come into being. More precisely, in a simple convalidation the renewal of consent by the parties involved is absolutely necessary for the emergence of a valid marmarriage and no convalidation will be effected without it,[5] while in a *sanatio in radice* the convalidation carries with it a dispensation from the law requiring the renewal of consent; moreover, as regards its canonical effects, a simple convalidation looks only to the future, while a *sanatio in radice* extends some of its effects to the past.

Marriages can be invalid in three ways, i.e., first, because of the existence of a diriment impediment,[6] secondly, because of a lack of the needed consent,[7] and, lastly, because of a non-observance of the canonical form in which marriage is to be contracted.[8] According to the norm prescribed in canon 1139, the *sanatio in radice* can be granted for marriages which are invalid in consequence of a diriment impediments of ecclesiastical law, but the Church does not sanate marriages when their invalidity is traceable to a diriment impediment set up by the natural or positive divine law.[9] The second paragraph of canon 1139 rules that a marriage which was contracted with an impediment of the natural or positive divine law, even though the impediment has since ceased to exist, is not convalidated through a *sanatio in radice* by the Church, even from the time when the impediment ceased. These marriages which are invalid in consequence of a non-observance of the requisite juridical form can be convalidated through a *sanatio in radice.*[10] The above-listed mar-

[5] Canon 1133.
[6] Canon 1036, §§ 2-3.
[7] Canon 1081.
[8] Canon 1094-1103.
[9] Canon 1139, § 1.
[10] Loc. cit.

riages, whether they are invalid because of the existence of some diriment impediment of the ecclesiastical law, or be-because of the non-observance of the requisite form, but were contracted with a naturally adequate but juridically inadequate consent of the parties which still perseveres in their wills become valid when the *sanatio in radice* is granted.[11] If the consent is wanting in both parties or in either party, the marriage cannot be convalidated by means of a *sanatio in radice,* whether the consent was wanting from the beginning, or whether it was originally given and later revoked; if consent was wanting in the beginning but was afterward supplied, a *sanatio in radice* can be granted from the moment when the consent was supplied.[12] These are consequences derived from the principle of canon 1081, § 1: *"Matrimonium facit partium consensus inter personas iure habiles legitime manifestatus; qui nulla humana potestate suppleri valet."* To consider the marriage valid prior to any exchange of consent simply by means of a fiction of the law would be an absurdity. The existence of any act which for its validity depends inherently upon an exchange of consent exceeds all the limits of any fiction of the law. A fiction of the law is but a disposition of the law contrary to fact, and employed for just cause in a matter which allows of that possibility.[13] A valid marriage without consent is an impossibility. No fiction of the law, therefore, can be conjured up for a union which was not contracted with the consent of both patries; where such consent is not present the *sanatio in radice* cannot be granted.

A *sanatio in radice* is called *perfect* if there is a dispensation for both parties from the renewal of consent and also a retroactive efficiency which in all respects reaches back to the very start of the marriage; if any of these elements

[11] *Loc. cit.*

[12] Canon 1140.

[13] Vromant, *De Matrimonio,* p. 233, note 1: "Fictio iuris fundatur in voluntate legislatoris, et est legis adversus veritatem in re possibili ex iusta causa dispositio."

is lacking, the *sanatio in radice*, is called *imperfect.* An imperfect *sanatio in radice* would be applicable in cases in which only one party is dispensed from the renewal of consent, while the other party renews the consent; or the *snatio in radice* may be given after the death of one of the parties (in this case, although the bond of marriage cannot be brought into being, the other effects are produced by the fiction of the law); or the retroactive efficiency may not extend as far back as the union itself, for the reason that a mutual matrimonial consent did not exist at the time when the union was formed, but was supplied only at some later date.[14]

With reference to the authority granting the *sanatio in radice,* canon 1141 states that the *sanatio in radice* can be granted only by the Apostolic See. The competent agency in the Apostolic See for granting it is: (1) for the internal forum, the Sacred Penitentiary; (2) for the external forum, in marriages other than mixed and disparate marriages, the Sacred Congregation for the Sacraments, and (3) for the external forum in mixed and disparate marriages, the Holy Office. However, ordinaries in dioceses as well as in quasi-dioceses have Quinquennial Faculties and Decennial Faculties respectively for granting the *sanatio in radice, servatis servandis.*

ARTICLE II. *Ex Facultate,* I. FACULTIES FOR GRANTING THE *Sanation in Radice* FOR MARRIAGES OTHER THAN MIXED AND DISPARATE MARRIAGES

Faculties by virtue of which the *sanatio in radice* is granted for marriages other than mixed and disparate marriages are *Facultas XXIII* in the *Formula Maior* and Faculty n. 4 of the Sacred Congregation for the Sacraments in *Formula IV.*

[14] Bouscaren-Ellis, *Canon Law,* pp. 623-624; Vromant, *De Matrimonio,* nn. 249-250, pp. 233-234; Wernz-Vidal, *Ius Matrimoniale,* n. 659, pp. 860-862.

SECTION 1. TEXTS OF THE FACULTIES

A. FACULTAS XXIII *in the* FORMULA MAIOR

Sanandi in radice, iuxta regulas in Codice a can. 1138 ad can. 1141 statutas, matrimonia ob aliquod impedimentum, de quo supra (n. 22) *nulliter contracta. Quod vero attinet ad prolis legitimationem, Ordinarius prae oculis habeat canones 1051, 1138.*

Facultas sanandi in radice non extenditur ad casus in quibus supervenerit amentia unius vel utriusque partis. In singulis hisce casibus igitur ad S. Sedem recurrendum erit.

B. *The Quinquennial Faculty n. 4 of the Sacred Congregation for the Sacraments*

Sanandi in radice matrimonia nulliter contracta ob aliquod ex impedimentis iuris ecclesiastici maioris vel minoris gradus, exceptis iis provenientibus ex sacro presbyteratus ordine et affinitate in liena recta, matrimonio consummato, si magnum adsit incommodum requirendi a parte, ignara nullitatis matrimonii, renovationem consensus, dummodo tamen prior maritalis consensus perseveret et absit periculum divortii; monita tamen parte conscia impedimenti de effectu huius sanationis et debita facta adnotatione in libro baptizatorum et matrimoniorum.

SECTION 2. MARRIAGES FOR WHICH THE *Sanatio in Radice* CAN BE GRANTED

A. *The Decennial Faculty.* The present Decennial Faculty allows a *sanatio in radice* to be granted for a marriage null and void by reason of any of the impediments for which a dispensation is available by virtue of *Facultas XXII* in the *Formula Maior,* even though they are multiple in a case, public or occult, or of major or minor degree. Of the diriment impediments, those which arise from the sacred order of priesthood and from affinity in the direct line when the marriage has become consummated are excepted from the scope of the dispensing power of the Decennial Faculty XXII in the *Formula Maior;* by virtue of the same Faculty, the impediment of nonage can be dispensed, provided that a man has completed his fourteenth and a woman her twelfth year.[15]

Since *Facultas XXII* in the *Formula Maior* makes inclusive mention of only the diriment impediments of the ecclesiastical law within the scope of its dispensing power, all the diriment impediments of the natural and positive divine law are excluded therefrom, and canon 1139, § 2, states that a marriage which was contracted with an impediment of the natural or positive divine law is not convalidated by the Church through a *sanatio in radice.* Thus, by virtue of the present Decennial Faculty, the mission ordinary cannot grant a *sanatio in radice,* for marriages rendered null and void by reason of impotence, previous bond, or consanguinity in all degrees of the direct line and in the first degree of the collateral line, for all of these are set up as diriment impediments by the divine law itself.[16]

B. *The Quinquennial Faculty.* The present Quinquennial Faculty empowers the ordinary with the faculty to grant the *sanatio in radice* for marriages which has been invalidly contracted because of some impediment of ecclesiastical law of major or minor degree, except the impediments resulting from the sacred order of priesthood and from affinity in the direct line when the marriage has become consummated. By their very nature and implicitly also by the context of the faculty marriages which are null and void by reason of any of the natural and positive divine law are excluded from the scope of the present Quniquennial Faculty. In addition, the impediments of mixed religion and of disparity of cult likewise lie beyond the scope of the present Quinquennial Faculty, since the exclusive competency in regard to these impediments remains with the Holy Office, and a separate

[15] *Supra,* p. 232.
[16] Canon 1076, § 3.

Quinquennial Faculty for them is provided by this Sacred Congregation.[17]

It is manifest from the text of the Decennial Faculty under consideration that the *sanatio in radice* cannot be granted for marriages which have remained invalid solely for lack of the proper juridical form. Payen, however, has asserted that, if a marriage is invalid by reason of the presence of one (or more) of the impediments which as enumerated in *Facultas XXII* in the *Formula Maior* allow for a dispensation, and, in addition, by reason also of a lack of the juridical form, the mission ordinary may grant a *sanatio in radice* by virtue of the present Decennial Faculty.[18] But this claim was disputed by Vromat,[19] who cited the reply of the Sacred Congregation of the Sacraments, on March 10, 1937, which declared that the word *"impedimentum"* in the text of the faculty must be interpreted in the strictest sense as one of those impediments which are treated in canons 1067-1080.[20] The same is true for the Quinquennial Faculty under consideration.

SECTION 3. CONDITIONS FOR THE GRANTING OF THE *Sanatio in Radice*

By virtue of the present Decennial Faculty as well as the present Quinquennial Faculty, the *sanatio in radice* can be granted for those marriages which are invalid by reason of one or more diriment impediments of the ecclesiastical law, but these marriages must have been contracted with a naturally adequate, though judicially inadequate, consent of the parties, which still perseveres in their wills when the

[17] Faculty n. 4 from the Sacred Congregation of the Holy Office, in *Formula IV*. Cf. *infra*, pp. 267-268.

[18] *De Matrimonio in Missionibus*, II, n. 2619. Also cf. Robert J. Harrigan, *The Radical Sanation of Invalid Marriages*, The Catholic University of America Canon Law Studies, n. 116 (Washington D.C.: The Catholic University of America Press, 1938), pp. 161 ff.

[19] *De Matrimonio*, n. 256, pp. 238-239.

[20] (Private). *Periodica*, XXVI (1937), 347; Bouscaren, *Canon Law Digest*, II, 29-30; Vromant, *De Matrimonio*, p. 239, footnote n. 1.

sanatio in radice is granted,[21] or which consent, if wanting in the beginning of these marriages, was afterwards supplied.[22]

In connection with the question of the existence of matrimonial consent for the marriage, the Decennial Faculty carries a warning that the faculty does not extend to cases in which one or both parties to the marriage have become insane.[23] But, if the insanity was only temporary and the person had lucid intervals, then the *sanatio in radice* could be granted during the lucid intervals.[24] All cases involving the insanity of one or both parties should be sent to the Holy See, as stated in the text of the present Decennial Faculty.

"Dummodo tamen prior maritalis consensus persevert et absit periculum divortii." This clause of the present Quinquennial Faculty postulates two conditions for the validity of its use, i.e., that the previously exchanged matrimonial consent continue to exist,[25] and that there be absent the danger of divorce. The first condition is not particular requisite for the use of the present faculty, and it has been already explained. In connection with this condition, what has been stated in regard to the insanity of one or both

[21] Canon 1139, § 1.

[22] Canon 1140, § 2.

[23] "CJC loquitur simpliciter de amentia, quae incapacem reddat tum ad consensum matrimonialem (can. 1982) tum ad delictum, et debilitate mentis, quae minorem delicti imputabilitatem secum fert (can. 2201, §§ 1-4). Iuxta jurisprudentiam SSR amentes dicuntur insanientes quoad omnia, dementes vero, qui quoad unum alterumve punctum insaniunt; quoad rem, circa quam insaniunt, amentibus aequiparantur; amentes semper incapaces sunt ad matrimonium valide contrahendum, dementes vero dumtaxat, si eorum insania respicit rem matrimonialem."—Holboeck, *Tractatus de Jurisprudentia Sacrae Romanae Rotae*, p. 101.

[24] For the insanity cases and decisions, cf. *ibid.*, pp. 105-115; William J. Doheny, *Canonical Procedure in Matrimonial Cases*, Vol. I, *Formal Juridical Procedure* (2. ed., Milwaukee: The Bruce Publishing Co., 1948), pp. 787 ff.; Bouscaren, *Canon Law Digest*, I, 518; II, 299-300; III, 435.

[25] Cf. canons 1139, 1140, § 2, and 1093.

parties to the marriage in the use of the Decennial Faculty should be followed also in cases in which the present Quinquennial Faculty comes into question. As to the second condition, the term *"divortium"* is to be taken as simply indicative of the separation of the parties, whether this separation be effected by means of a civil divorce or even apart from the use of any legal process or court procedure. In cases where this danger is evident the present Quinquennail Faculty cannot be used validly.[26]

SECTION 4. CAUSES FOR GRANTING THE *Sanatio in Radice*

A. *The Decennial Faculty.*—According to the norm of canon 84, a *sanatio in radice* is unlawful and invalid if granted in virtue of the present Decennial Faculty but without a just and reasonable cause, in consideration particularly of the gravity of the law which concerns the *sanatio in radice.*[27] Thus a grave and urgent cause is required for the granting of the *sanatio in radice.*[28] Such a grave and urgent reason for a *sanatio in radice* exists whenever there is need of relieving one or both parties' conscience, or of rendering the offspring legitimate, if there be any,[29] under the following circumstances: (1) the refusal or reluctance of one of the parties of the marriage to renew the expression of the matrimonial consent in the proper form;[30] (2) the

[26] Eagleton, *The Diocesan Quinquennial Faculties, Formula IV*, p. 85.

[27] Canon 1141. Sanatio in radice concedi unice potest ab Apostolica Sede.

[28] Gasparri, *De Matrimonio,* II, n. 1229, p. 273; Wernz-Vidal, *Ius Matrimoniale*, n. 667, pp. 873-874; Cappello, *De Matrimonio,* n. 853, 4°, p. 863; Vromant, *Facultates Apostolicae*, n. 74, p. 75.

[29] Gasparri, *loc. cit.* Cf. the commentary on the phrase, "ad consulendum conscientiae et, si casus ferat, legitimationi prolis," *supra*, pp. 204-206.

[30] Gasparri, *loc. cit.*: "Eadem causa gravis et urgens habetur in casu quo una vel altera pars cum scientia impedimenti matrimonium inivit et postea alterutra peccatum lugens cupit conscientiae consulere, renuente altera consensum canonica forma renovare, priore tamen posito perseverante." Cf. Conte a Coronata, *De Sacramentis*, III, n.

danger of scandal, or of divorce, or of other consequent great loss, if the nullity of the marriage, known to one party only, is made known to the other;[31] etc. Although there be no need of relieving one or both parties' conscience, or of rendering the offspring legitimate, if there be any, there exists a grave and urgent reason for the *sanatio in radice*: (1) when there is danger of scandal in revealing the nullity of their marriage to the parties concerned inasmuch as the nullity was caused through some fault either of the ordinary or of the pastor;[32] (2) when there exists a moral impossibility or at least a serious difficulty of convalidating a large number of invalid marriages except by way of a *sanatio in radice*:[33] (3) when both parties are in good faith, but cannot be warned of the nullity of their marriage (which was caused through some fault either of the ordinary or of the pastor), e.g., when they have left the city or region,[34] etc. The mission ordinary may grant the *sanatio in radice* by virtue of the present Decennial Faculty in view of the existence of any of the above-enumerated grave and urgent reasons.[35]

B. *The Quinquennial Faculty.—"Si magnum adsit incommodum requirendi a parte, ignara nullitatis matrimonii, renovationem consensus."* The fact that there is great inconvenience in obtaining a renewal of consent from the party who is ignorant of the nullity of the matrimony is a prerequisite for the use of the present Quinquennial Faculty, and the presence of a *magnum incommodum*" is postulated for the validity of the application of the Quinquennial Fac-

691, p. 958; Winslow, *The Apostolic Faculties*, p. 136; Cappello, *loc. cit.*

[31] Winslow, *loc. cit.;* Cappello, *loc. cit.;* Conte a Coronata, *loc cit.;* Vromant, *loc. cit.;* Wernz-Vidal, *loc. cit.*

[32] Gasparri, *loc. cit.;* Cappello, *loc. cit.;* Winslow, *loc. cit.;* Conte a Coronata, *loc. cit.*

[33] Conte a Coronata, *loc. cit.;* Winslow, *loc. cit.*

[34] Winslow, *loc. cit.*

[35] Cf. Vromant, *loc. cit.;* Sartori, *Iuris Missionarii Elementa*, p. 112; Paventi, *Brevis Commentarius*, p. 38.

ulty.[36] And such a *"magnum incommodum"* exists when there is the danger of scandal, of divorce, of separation, or of some other consequent great loss, if the nullity of the marriage, known to one party only, is made known to the other. The presence of such a *"magnum incommodum"* can be determined by the judgment of the ordinary, which is dependent upon the facts and circumstances of each individual case.

It is apparent from the text of the present Quinquennial Faculty itself that this faculty can be used only in cases in which one of the parties does not know of the nullity of the marriage, although the party might know of the material existence of the impediment.[37] Thus, the present Quinquennial Faculty cannot be used, when both parties of the marriage are unaware of the nullity of their marriage, or when both know the nullity but one or both refuse to have their marriage convalidated by way of a *sanatio in radice.* But it may be used when the nullity was caused through some fault either of the ordinary or of the pastor, both parties being then unaware of the nullity, and this nullity has later become known to one party, but it is morally impossible without a *"magnum incommodum"* to make the nullity known to the other party.

SECTION 5. CONSEQUENCES OF THE *Sanatio in Radice*

A. *The Decennial Faculty.*—In the present Decennial Faculty it is stated that in consequence of the *sanatio in radice* as effected by virtue of the present Decennial Faculty, a legitimation of the offspring is obtained according to the provisions of canons 1051 and 1138, the latter of which implies a retroactive legitimation of the offspring, together with the canonical effects that accompany legitimacy, while the former simply effects a legitimation in connection with the granting of the dispensation for the marriage newly to be contracted.

[36] Canon 39.

[37] Cf. Eagleton, *The Diocesan Quinquennial Faculties, Formula IV,* p. 84; Harriagan, *The Radical Sanation of Invalid Marriages,* p. 157.

Canon 1051 provides that by a means of the dispensation from a diriment impediment, when granted either by virtue of ordinary power or in virtue of a power delegated though a general indult, there is *ipso facto* granted also a legitimation of the children, in case any have already been born or conceived by the parties who are being dispensed; children who are the fruit of adultery or of sacrilege are excepted from the benefit of this rule. Thus, according to the provision incorporated in the Decennial Faculty, children who are the fruit of sacrilege[38] or of adultery[39] are excepted from the effects of the retroactive legitimation which normally accompanies the use of the present Decennial Faculty.

B. *The Quinquennial Faculty.*—Whatever is stated as requisite for the legitimation of the offspring is to be observed when the present Quinquennial Faculty is being applied, for teh Faculty itself is set up within the framework of the general principles enunciated in canons 1051 and 1138.

In the text of the Quinquennial Faculty, it is stated that the party who knows of the nullity of the marriage is to be informed of the fact of the *sanatio in radice* and its effects. Further, it is stated that the proper entries are to be made in the matrimonial registers and also in the baptismal registers. However, if the *sanatio in radice* was granted in the internal sacramental forum, it is clear that no record of the *sanatio in radice* can be kept; if the *sanatio in radice* was granted in the internal non-sacramental forum, a secret record of the *sanatio in radice,* with expedient indications, is to be kept in the episcopal archives with a view to render-

[38] If solemn religious profession or the reception of a sacred order exists either as diriment impediment or as an obstacle to the licit use even of a valid marriage on the side of either one or both of the parents at the time of the children's conception, then such children are the fruit of sacrilege. Cf. canons 1114, 1072, 1073.

[39] If the impediment of a previous bond of marriage exists for either one or both of the parents at the time of the children's conception, then such children are adulterine. Cf. canons 1069, § 1, 1114, 1139, § 2. The impediment of a previous bond of marriage is an impediment set up by the divine law itself.

ing it available for the external forum; if the *sanatio in radice* was granted in the external forum: (1) a marginal entry should be made in the ordinary marriage register, when the previous marriage had been celebrated before the Church and had already been entered, and (2) a fresh entry of the convalidation should be made in the marriage register, and a notification of the marriage should be sent to the pastor of the place of baptism, i.e., of the place where the parties were baptized, for insertion in the baptismal register, when the earlier invalid union had not been celebrated before the Church.[40] A record of the *sanatio in radice,* when granted in the external forum, is also to be preserved in the diocesan archives.[41]

ARTICLE III. *Ex Facultate,* II: FACULTIES FOR GRANTING THE *Sanatio in Radice* FOR MIXED AND DISPARATE MARRIAGES

SECTION 1. TEXTS OF FACULTIES

A. FACULTAS XXIV *in the* FORMULA MAIOR

Sanadi pariter in radice matrimonia mixta attentata coram magistratu civili vel ministro acatholico, dummodo moraliter certum sit partem acatholicam universae prolis nasciturae catholicam educationem non esse impedituram.

This is *Facultas n. 23* in the *Formula Minor,* and in both Formulae it allows for subdelegation.

B. The Quinquennial Faculty n. 4 of the Holy Office

To grant a *sanatio in radice* for marriages that have been attempted before a civil officer or a non-Catholic minister, either in the case of their own subjects even outside their territory, or of other persons within it, where there was the impediment of mixed religion or disparity of cult; provided that matrimonial consent continues to exist in both

[40] Winslow, *The Apostolic Faculties,* pp. 147-148; Vromant, *Facultates Apostolicae,* n. 75, p. 76.

[41] Eagleton, *The Diocesan Quinquennial Faculties, Formula IV,* p. 85.

parties, and that the same cannot be legitimately renewed, either because the non-Catholic party cannot be informed of the validity of the marriage without danger of grave damage or inconvenience to the Catholic party, or because the non-Catholic party can by no means be induced to renew consent before the Church or to give the promise as required by canon 1061, §2; provided:

1° that it is morally certain that the non-Catholic party will not impede the baptism and Catholic education of all children who may thereafter be born;

2° that the Catholic party explicitly promise to provide, to the best of his or her ability, for the baptism and Catholic education of of all children who may thereafter be born, and (in a proper case) also for the conversion, baptism, and Catholic education of children already born;

3° that the parties did not, before their attempted marriage, bind themselves either privately or by a public act to educate the children as non-Catholics;

4° that neither party be actually insane;

5° that at least the Catholic party know of the sanation and ask for it;

6° that there be no other canonical diriment impediment for which the ordinary himself has not the faculty to dispense or to grant a sanation.

But the Most Reverend Bishop himself must seriously admonish the Catholic party of the grave crime he or she has committed, must impose salutary penances, and, if need be, absolve the party from the excommunication incurred under canon 2319, § 1. He must at the same time declare that, as a result of the favor of the sanation which has been received, the marriage has been rendered valid, lawful, and indissoluble by divine law, and that the children who may have been born or may thereafter be born are legitimate. Moreover, he must remind the Catholic party of his or her obligation to take prudent measures for the conversion of the other party to the Catholic faith.

Since there must be proof in the external forum of the validity of marriage and the legitimation of

> the children, the Most Reverend Bishop shall give orders that in each case the written document of sanation together with the attestation of its execution be carefully preserved in the local Curia. He must also see to it, unless in his prudent discretion he judge otherwise, that the notice of the validation of the marriage, with a notation of the day and year, be entered in the baptismal register of the parish where the Catholic party was baptized.
>
> It is the mind of the Holy Office that the Bishop exercise this faculty of sanating marriages *in radice* himself personally, that is, that he do not subdelegate it to anyone.
>
> (OFFICIAL NOTE. 1. In granting each of the above sanations or dispensations, the Bishop or Ordinary should mention expressly his delegation by the Holy See [c. 1057].
>
> 2. At the end of each year the ordinary shall report to the Sacred Congregation of the Holy Office the number and kind of dispensations which he has granted in virtue of this Indult).[42]

The difference between the Decennial Faculty and the Quinquennial Faculty treated in the previous Article and the ones treated in the present Article lies in the following facts: (1) The former faculties deal with those marriages which have been contracted before the Church and accordingly reflect the appearance of a true marriage (*species veri matrimonii*), while the latter concern those marriages which are only attempted ones, i.e., which were not contracted before the Church, and thus do not have the appearance of a true marriage; (2) by virtue of the former faculties, the *sanatio in radice* is granted for marriages which are invalid because of the presence of one or more diriment impediments, *exceptis excipiendis*, while by virtue of the latter faculties the *sanatio in radice* is granted for marriages which are invalid because of the fact that they were not celebrated before the Church, i.e., in view of the absence of the juridical form of marriage, in addition to the presence of the impediment of disparity of cult or that of

[42] Bouscaren, *Canon Law Digest*, IV, 72-73.

mixed religion. It is evident from the text of the present Decennial and Quinquennial Faculties that marriages which are invalid solely by reason of the non-observance of the canonical form are excluded from the scope of the present faculties.

SECTION 2. MARRIAGES FOR WHICH THE *Sanatio in Radice* CAN BE GRANTED BY VIRTUE OF THE PRESENT FACULTIES

A. *The Decennial Faculty.*—The words *"mixta matrimonia"* in the text of the Decennial Faculty are to be interpreted in the broad sense according to the norms of canons 66, § 1, and 68, to the extent that they include all marriages that can exist between Catholics and non-Catholics,[43] whether the latter be baptized non-Catholics, or Jews, or Mohammedans, or any other non-baptized persons. *"Matrimonia mixta attentata coram magistratu civili vel ministro acatholico"* are all marriages celebrated before a non-Catholic minister, whether heretical, schismatical, Jewish, or Mohammedan, or before a competent civil official, or in accord with the *mores* of the country, if no civil ceremony is required for a legitimate marriage.[44]

B. *The Quinquennial Faculty.*—The powers as recounted in the present Decennial Faculty are granted for use also in the present Quinquennial Faculty, except that by virtue of the latter faculty the *sanatio in radice* cannot be granted for marriages which were contracted between Catholics and Mohammedans before the non-Catholic minister. Condition n. 6 states that the bishop can grant the *sanatio in radice* on condition that there be no other canonical diriment impediment for which the bishop himself has not the faculty of dispensing or of granting a sanation. Now, the

[43] Code Comm., 10 Nov., 1925—*AAS*, XVII (1925), 583, ad IX; 10 Martii 1928—*AAS*, XX (1928), 120, ad II. Cf. Vromant, *De Matrimonio*, n. 264, p. 243; Sartori, *Iuris Missionarii Elementa*, p. 113.

[44] Cf. Holboeck, "De Matrionio Solo Ritu Civili Contracto," *Tractatus de Jurisprudentia Sacrae Romanae Rotae*, pp. 242-246; Payen, *De Matrimonio in Missionibus*, II, n. 2619; S.C.S. Off., resp., 22 Iun. 1938—*Sylloge*, n. 260.

diriment impediment of disparity of cult arising between a Catholic and a Mohammedan is excepted from the dispensatory power which the Holy Office grants through the Quinquennial Faculty n. 3 to the ordinary in the diocese.[45]

The mixed marriages here under consideration have been contracted with a naturally sufficient, though judicially insufficient, consent of the parties which still perseveres at the time of the granting the *sanatio in radice.* This is a general and basic principel for the granting of any *sanatio in radice,*[46] and is explicitly stated in the text of the Quinquennial Faculty. If the consent is wanting in either one or both of the parties, the *sanatio in radice* cannot be granted, regardless of whether the consent was wanting from the beginning, or, if originally given, was later revoked; if the consent was wanting in the beginning but was afterwards supplied, a *sanatio in radice* can be granted from the moment when the consent was supplied.[47]

SECTION 3. CONDITIONS FOR THE VALID USE OF THE PRESENT FACULTIES

In the text of the Decennial Faculty, no specific conditions are listed for the valid use of the faculty. However, in most cases they will be the same as the condition stated in the present Quinquennial Faculty. The conditions under which the Faculty can be used are the following, namely, the renewal of the matrimonial consent is not feasible: (1) because the non-Catholic party cannot be informed of the invalidity of the marriage in question apart from the simultaneous subjection of the Catholic party to either grave harm or serious inconvenience, or (2) because the non-Catholic party cannot in any manner be induced to renew the matrimonial consent according to the proper form of the Church, or to give the promises as required by

[45] Eagleton, *The Diocesan Quinquennial Faculties, Formula IV,* pp. 63-64.

[46] Canon 1139, § 1.

[47] Canon 1140.

canon 1061, § 2. The wording of the faculty does not permit its use in cases in which it is the Catholic party who is unaware of the invalidity of the marriage.

A. The Decennial Faculty.—In view of the use of the word *"pariter"* in the present Decennial Faculty, all the rules, considerations and conditions required for the use of the previous Decennial Faculty (i.e., *Facultas XXIII* in the *Formula Maior*), must be observed and verified here also.[48]

From the clause, *"dummodo moraliter certum sit partem acatholicam universae prolis nasciturae catholicam educationem non esse impedituram,"* it can be concluded that no formal *cautiones* (or guarantees) as prescribed in canons 1061 on the part of the non-Catholic party are essential for the valid use of this faculty,[49] provided that the grantor of the *sanatio in radice* have moral certainty of the fact that the non-Catholic party will not impede the Catholic education of any and all of the children to be born (*universae prolis nasciturae*).[50] However, the said clause by no means abstracts from the need of moral certainty on the part of the grantor regarding the fact that the Catholic party will keep his *cautio* (or guarantee) and the promises that he makes according to the norms of canons 1061, § 2, 1062, and 1071.[51] The Catholic party must make the *cautio* ex-

[48] *Supra*, pp. 260 ff.

[49] Vromant, *De Matrimonio*, n. 259, p. 240. Paventi, *Brevis Commentarius*, p. 40.

[50] The phrase, *"universae prolis tam natae quam nasciturae,"* as it appeared in the former Formulae of the Decennial Faculties, was changed to the present form *"universae prolis nasciturae,"* through a Notification of the Sacred Congregation for the Propagation of the Faith, on August 15, 1947. Cf. Paventi, "Addenda ad Commentarium in Facultates S.C. de Propaganda Fide," in *Brevis Commentarius*, inserted between pp. 32-33. The said change was occasioned by the Decree which the Holy Office issued on January 16, 1942—*AAS*, XXXIV (1942), 22.

[51] Cf. condition 2° in the Quinquennial Faculty, n. 4, of the Holy Office, Formula IV; *supra*, p. 267; Paventi, *Brevis Commentarius*, p. 40.

plicitly, or at least implicitly.[52]

Besides the above-mentioned conditions, the ones stated in the text of the present Quinquennial Faculty in Formula IV are also postulated for the use of the present Decennial Faculty. For the conditions and precautions stated in the Quinquennial Faculty derive from the general principles in respect of the dispensation from the impediments of mixed religion and disparity of cult as well as in respect of the *sanatio in radice,* and they call for a universal application.

B. *The Quinquennial Faculty.*—The conditions for the valid granting of the *sanatio in radice* by virtue of the present Quinquennial Faculty are clearly stated in the text of the faculty, so that there is no need of any detailed explanation.[53]

With respect to the moral certainty on the part of the grantor, for the valid use of the present Decennial Faculty a verification of the condition, *"dummodo moraliter certum sit partem acatholicam universae prolis nasciturae catholicam educationem non esse impedituram,"* is required, while for the valid use of the present Quinquennial Faculty there must be a fulfillment of the condition, *"dummodo moraliter certum sit partem acatholicam non esse impedituram baptismum et catholicam educationem universae prolis forte nasciturae."* These conditions are practically and fundamentally one and the same. Although the baptism of the children to be born is not mentioned in the condition for the use of the Decennial Faculty, the Catholic education presupposes a Catholic baptism, without which the Catholic education is purposeless. For the application of the present Quinquennial Faculty the Catholic party must make the *cautiones* explicitly.[54]

Condition 6°, as postulated for the valid use of the Quin-

[52] Cf. *supra,* p. 267; for the use of the equivalent *cautiones,* cf. *supra,* pp. 239-241.

[53] For a brief commentary on the present Quinquennial Faculty, cf. Eagleton, *The Diocesan Quinquennial Faculties, Formula IV,* pp. 65-67.

[54] Cf. condition 2° in the text of the faculty.

quennial Faculty, is that there be no other extant diriment impediment to the marriage, with reference to which the ordinary has not the power of granting of dispensation or the *sanatio in radice.* The excepted diriment impediments are recounted in Faculty n. 4 of the ones which are granted by the Sacred Congregation for the Sacraments. Since the scope of the power of the mission ordinary for dispensing from diriment impediments of marriage is larger than that of the ordinary who makes use of the Quinquennial Faculties, Formula IV, the power of the former for granting *sanatio in radice* is more extensive than that of the latter.

Article IV. Procedure in the Granting of the *Sanatio in Radice*

In the text of the Decennial Faculty, no specific procedure is mentioned. However, it may safely be said that the procedure in the granting of the *sanatio in radice* by virtue of the present Decennial Faculty should follow the manner outlined for its use by virtue of the present Quinquennial Faculty. Nevertheless, it should be noted that according to the notation attached to the text of the Quniquennial Faculty it is the mind of the Holy Office that the Quinquennial Faculty here under consideration be used only by the Most Reverend Bishop himself, that is to say, that the faculty be subdelegated to no one; on the other hand, the present Decennial Faculty can be subdelegated by the mission ordinary to any or all of his missionaries, so that there is no limitation for the subdelegation of the faculty. The mind of the Holy Office in the case of the present Quinquennial Faculty does not exclude the vicar general of the diocese from the use of the faculty, for he enjoys the use of the faculty equally with, and with the same obligations as, the bishop by virtue of canons 66, § 2, and 368, § 2.[55] Thus the grantor of the *sanatio in radice* by virtue of the present Quinquennial Faculty is either the bishop or his vicar general, while the grantor of the

[55] Eagleton, *The Diocesan Quinquennial Faculties, Formula IV*, p. 68.

same by virtue of the present Decennial Faculty is either the mission ordinary (including his vicar delegate, or prefect delegate, or superior delegate of the mission *sui iuris*) or any priest to whom he has subdelegated his faculty.

As the second paragraph of the text of the Quinquennial Faculty notes, the grantor of the *sanatio in radice* must seriously admonish the Catholic party of the grave crime he or she has committed, and he must impose a salutary penance, and, if need be, absolve the party from the excommunication incurred under canon 2319, § 1. He must at the same time declare that, as a result of the favor of the *sanatio in radice* received by the party, the marriage has been rendered valid, lawful, and indissoluble by the divine law, and that the children who may already have been born or may thereafter be born are legitimate. Moreover, the grantor must remind the Catholic party of his or her obligation to take prudent measures for the conversion of the other party to the Catholic faith. All these measures are postulated for the licit use of the faculty, which by way of commission can be executed by a third party, such as the pastor of the Catholic party.[56]

The grantor is also directed to procure the making of the proper entries in the matrimonial register and also in the baptismal register,[57] and to preserve in the episcopal court the document attesting the granted *sanatio in radice* in order that proof of the validity of the marriage and of the legitimation of the children may, if need arise, be proved at any future date.

[56] Canon 54, § 1, and canon 55. Cf. Eagleton, *op cit.*, pp. 68-69.

[57] *Supra* p. 266; Sartori, *Iuris Missionarii Elementa*, p. 114; Payen, *De Matrimonio in Missionibus*, II, n. 2623.

CHAPTER VII

FACULTIES TO DISPENSE FROM THE INTERPELLATIONS

The present chapter deals with the Decennial Faculties by virtue of which a dispensation may be granted from the observance of the law in regard to the interpellations. These faculties are *Facultates XXV, XXVI, and XXVII* in the *Formula Maior*, or Facultates nn. 24, 25, and 26 in the *Formula Minor*. They allow of subdelegation. In the Quinquennial Faculties, Formula IV, there is no faculty which corresponds to any of these Decennial Faculties.

The Code of Canon Law in its canons uses the phrase "*omissio interpellationum* EX DECLARATIONE. . . ."[1] Nevertheless, this chapter is entitled "Faculties to *Dispense* from the *Interpellations*," and the words "dispensation" (from the interpellations) and "to dispense" (from the interpellations) will be used throughout the present chapter, in view of the fact that their use is reflected in the traditional practice of the Holy See[2] as also in the texts of the Faculties here to be treated.

In the Code, canons 1121-1123 are concerned with the fundamental principles of the interpellations with respect to the use of the Pauline privilege, and canon 1125 deals with the dispensation from the interpellations. However, for the sake of convenience, this chapter will be divided into three Articles, i.e., Article I: *Preliminary Notes*, which looks to the general principles of the interpellations and an analysis of the Pauline privilege; Article II: *Dispensation from the Interpellations for the Dissolution of Marriages Contracted between non-Bapitized Monogamous Persons*,

[1] Cf. canon 1121, § 2, and 1123.

[2] Vromant, *De Matrimonio*, p. 301, note n .1; Arthur A. Sego, *Dispensation from the Interpellations*, The Catholic University of America Canon Law Studies, n. 316 (Washington, D.C.: The Catholic University of America Press, 1951), pp. 123-127.

and Article III: *Dispensation from the Interpellations for the Dissolution of Marriages Contracted between non-Baptized Polygamists.*

ARTICLE I. PRELIMINARY NOTES

SECTION 1. THE PAULINE PRIVILEGE

In the Code of Canon Law, canon 1120, § 1, states that a legitimate marriage between non-baptized persons, even though it has been consummated, is dissolved in favor of the faith by virtue of the Pauline privilege.[3] But, for the valid and lawful use of the Pauline privilege, the following three conditions must be verified: (1) *legitimum matrimonium inter duos infideles contractum;* (2) *conversio unius partis dum altera in infidelitate persistit,* and (3) *manifestus partis infidelis discessus physicus vel moralis.*

(1). *"Legitmum matrimonium inter duos infideles contractum." "Legitimum Matrimonium."* The marriage which allows of dissolution must be a legitimate marriage. Now, a marriage between non-baptized persons, when validly celebrated, is clearly called a legitimate marriage, according to canon 1015, § 3. As the Holy Office has declared, those marriages which are celebrated with the usual ceremonies of the country, when the mutual and present consent of the parties has been sufficiently expressed according to the common estimation of the locality,[4] and in which no diriment impediment either of the natural and positive divine law or of the civil law is found, must be considered as valid

[3] For detailed works on the Pauline privilege, cf. Donald J. Gregory, *The Pauline Privilege,* The Catholic University of America Canon Law Studies, n. 68 (Washington, D.C.: The Catholic University of America Press, 1931); Winslow, *The Pauline Privilege and the Constitutions of Canon 1125* (New York: The Field Afar Press, 1948) [hereafter cited as *The Pauline Privilege*]; George Joyce, *Christian Marriage: An Historical and Doctrinal Study* (2nd ed., London: Sheed and Ward Publishing Co., 1948), pp. 469, 506; Wernz-Vidal, *Ius Matrimoniale,* n. 631, pp. 810-821, and notes nn. 54-66 on the same pages.

[4] S.C.S. Off., 17 Aug. 1898—*Fontes,* n. 1205; *Collectanea,* n. 1188.

marriages.[5] If the union has been entered into invalidly, there is no place for the application of the Pauline privilege.[6]

"Matrimonium inter duos infideles contractum." The Pauline privilege cannot be applied in the case of a marriage contracted between two persons who have validly received the sacrament of baptism; the same privilege likewise cannot be applied in the case of a marriage contracted between a baptized person and a non-baptized person when it was entered into with a dispensation from the impediment of disparity of cult.[7] In case a marriage was validly contracted between a party who is certainly unbaptized and a party whose baptism is doubtful in its validity, the case must be referred to the Holy Office.[8]

(2) *"Conversio unius partis dum altera in infidelitate persistit."* The second condition which is postulated for the valid use of the Pauline privilege is a "valid baptism" on the side of one of the parties of the marriage, while the other party remains in infidelity. Sincerity in the conversion is required for the licit use of the Pauline privilege.[9] The Pauline privilege cannot be invoked if both parties have received baptism or intend to receive baptism.[10]

(3) *"Manifestus partis infidelis discessus physicus vel moralis."* The condition which is required for the licit use of the Pauline privilege is the fact that there is a physical

[5] *Fontes* nn. 1036, 1019, and 1050; Vromant, *De Matrimonio*, n. 280, p. 254; Gregory, *The Pauline Privilege*, pp. 53-54; *Collectanea*, n. 1392.

[6] In the case of doubt in regard to the validity of the marriage, cf. canon 1127.

[7] Canon 1120, § 2. Cf. *Fontes*, nn. 810, 918, 931, and 1061.

[8] S.C.S. Off., decr., 10 Iun. 1937—*AAS*, XXIX (1937), 305; Bouscaren, *Canon Law Digest*, II, 343. (Private) S.C. de Prop. Fid., 16 Iul. 1926—Prot. n. 2457/26; *Periodica*, XXI (1926), 177; Bouscaren, *op. cit.*, I, 552.

[9] Vromant points out four conditions for a sincere baptism as required for the licit use of the Pauline privilege: "1) mens recta; 2) animus redeundi ad compartem; 3) probitas; 4) separatio ab illegitimo coniuge."—*De Matrimonio*, nn. 285-292, pp. 258-262.

[10] S.C.S. Off., 11 Iul. 1866—*ASS*, XXVI (1893-1894), 184-187; *Fontes*, S.C.S. Off., (Natal), 11 Iul. 1866, n. 996; *Collectanea*, n. 1295.

or a moral departure on the part of the non-baptized party, and this departure must be proved either by means of the interpellations duly made, or under circumstances in which there has been a lawful dispensation from making them.[11] Physical departure exists when the non-baptized party cannot *de facto* cohabit with the newly converted and baptized party, or when the non-baptized party refuses to cohabit with the baptized party when the interpellations are made by the latter.[12] On the other hand, a moral departure exists when, despite an expressed intention to cohabit with the baptized party, the non-baptized party refuses peaceful cohabtiation with the latter.[13]

As canon 1123 prescribes, to satisfy the condition for the use of the Pauline privilege, the "departure" whether physical or moral must not be warranted for a cause furnished by the baptized party since baptism. If the baptized party has been guilty of some act sufficient in itself to provide the infidel with a just cause for the "departure," for example, by the commission of adultery after baptism, the former may not take advantage of the Pauline privilege.[14] But, if the adultery was committed by the baptized party before conversion, the infidel party is no longer furnished a legitimate excuse for the departure. If there exist any doubt whether a sufficient cause furnishes the unconverted

[11] Gregory, *The Pauline Privilege*, pp. 58-64; Vromant, *De Matrimonio*, nn. 295-307, pp. 263-273; Francis J. Burton, *A Commentary on Canon 1125*, The Catholic University of America Canon Law Studies, n. 121 (Washington, D.C.: The Catholic University of America Press, 1940), pp. 5-7.

[12] Vromant, *De Matrimonio*, n. 295, pp. 263-264; Winslow, *The Pauline Privilege*, p. 7. Doheny lists seven possible hypotheses of physical departure on the part of the infidel party in his *Informal Procedure*, p. 512.

[13] Canon 1121, § 1, 2°. Cf. Gregory, *The Pauline Privilege*, pp. 60-64; Winslow, *The Pauline Privilege*, pp. 8-10. Doheny also lists some possible hypotheses of a moral departure on the part of the non-baptized party: *op. cit.*, p. 513. Also cf. Vromant, *De Matrimonio*, nn. 303-306, pp. 268-272.

[14] *Collectanea*, nn. 634 and 690. Cf. *Periodica*, XIV (1925), pp. (72)-(73).

party a legitimate excuse for the departure, the decision is always to be rendered to the advantage of the faith.[15]

In the use of the Pauline privilege, however, the departure of the infidel party is a fundamental condition in the sense that, even if the other two conditions are verified, the Pauline privilege cannot be invoked without full verification of this condition. And this fundamental condition cannot be presumed; it must be demonstrated. Hence, it is clear from this that the essential condition for the use of the privilege, namely, the departure of the infidel party, must have been in some way or other definitely determined and proved. The normal way in which the demonstration will be made is through the formal declaration of the infidel party in answer to the interpellations, first whether he desires to be converted and receive baptism, and secondly, whether at least he desires to cohabit with the baptized party peacefully and without insult to the Creator. Hence, the purpose of the interpellations is to ascertain in the external forum, formally and officially, the presence of the third condition, namely, the departure of the infidel party.

Thus, if the infidel party has replied to the interpellations in the negative, expressly or tacitly, the baptized party has the right to contract a new marriage with a Catholic person, with a due observance of the form prescribed in the Code of Canon Law for the contracting of marriage.[16] The new marriage which is to be contracted by virtue of the Pauline privilege must be with a Catholic party,[17] unless a special apostolic indult allow a deviation from this set rule.[18]

[15] *Fontes*, nn. 1123 and 810; *Collectanea*, nn. 634 and 690. Cf canon 1127.

[16] Canon 1123.

[17] Canon 1123.

[18] The Holy Office has permitted the application of the Pauline privilege in connection with a dispensation from mixed religion, and *ad cautelam* from disparity of cult, for a new marriage with a doubtfully baptized non-Catholic. Cf. (Private) S.C.S. Off., Nov., 1949—Prot. n. 1907/49. See Bouscaren, *Canon Law Digest*, IV, 345-346; *The Jurist*, X (1950), 215. The same Sacred Congregation also granted a special faculty to ordinaries in Japan to dispense from disparity of

Although the effect of the interpellations brings about for the baptized party the right to contract a second marriage solely with a Catholic party, the bond of the former marriage which was contracted in infidelity is dissolved only at the time when the baptized party contracts a new marriage validly.[19]

SECTION 2. THE NECESSITY OF, AND NATURE OF DISPENSATION FROM, THE INTERPELLATIONS

The purpose of the interpellations is to ascertain, formally and officially, the two points, i.e., whether the non-baptized party wishes to be converted and to receive baptism, and whether the non-baptized party is at least willing to cohabit peacefully without contumely to the Creator.[20]

A. The Necessity of the Interpellations

The question whether the obligation to make the interpellations is of divine origin or simply of ecclesiastical origin, and also the question whether the making of the interpellations as required in the cited canons is necessary for the validity or for the licitness only of the application of the Pauline privilege are still not definitely answered.[21] In practice, however, if the departure of the infidel party is not proved from other sources, then the interpellations are required for the validity of the second marriage.[22] If the

cult and mixed religion for marriages which are to be contracted in virtue of the Pauline privilege. Cf. (Private) 9 Aug. 1954—Prot. n. 1349/54. See Bouscaren, *loc. cit.*

[19] Canon 1126.

[20] Canon 1121, § 1. Cf. Sego, *Dispensation fgrom the Interpellations*, pp. 88-93.

[21] Cf. E. M. Woeber, *The Interpellations*, The Catholic University of America Canon Law Studies, n. 172 (Washington, D.C.: The Catholic University of America Press, 1942), pp. 49-57; Sego, *op. cit.*, pp. 99-122.

[22] S.R. Rota, 5 Dec. 1925—*S.R.R. Decisiones*, XVIII (1925), 396; Bouscaren, *Canon Law Digest*, II. 341.

departure is certain from other sources, canon law still requires the interpellations for a lawful dispensation from them, even if it seems, or is actually certain, that the interpellations will be useless, or impossible of completion, or gravely dangerous.[23] Hence, if the interpellations were illegitimately omitted insofar as there was no official declaration that authorized their omission, the case must be referred to the Holy Office, which alone is competent to make any final decision in regard to the Pauline privilege,[24] although a thus contracted second marriage of the baptized party is to be presumed valid in virtue of canons 1014 and 1127.[25]

The interpellations must be made after the baptism of the converted party, before the baptism of the other party, and before the second marriage.[26] It would be illicit to make the interpellations before the baptism, unless a dispensation had been specifically granted for this.[27] And the interpellations should be made as soon as posisble after the baptism of the converted party, if the latter contemplates an early marriage with a Catholic party. However, if by the proper authorities there has been made a declaration authorizing the omission of the interpellations, the converted party could not licitly contract marriage after the expiration of one year without a renewal of the declaration, provided that

[23] Canons 1121 and 1123. Cf. Vromant, *De Matrimonio*, n. 313, p. 277; Sego, *op cit.*, p. 121; Wernz-Vidal, *Ius Matrimoniale*, n. 632, and nota n. 68 on pages 822-825; Payen, *De Matrimonio in Missionibus*, II, n. 2356; Winslow, *The Pauline Privilege*, p. 16; Bouscaren, "An Inquiry into the Practical Application of Canon 1125," *Miscellanea-Vermeersch* (2 vols., Romae: Pontificia Universitas Gregoriana Soc. Tipogr. A. Macioce & Pisani, 1935), Vol. I, pp. 279-302; Bouscaren-Ellis, *Canon Law*, p. 598; Gregory, *The Pauline Privilege*, pp. 66-71.

[24] Canon 247, § 3. Cf. Doheny, *Informal Procedure*, pp. 521-522.

[25] Bouscaren-Ellis, *op. cit.*, p. 598; Cappello, *De Matrimonio*, n. 777, p. 767; Woeber, *op. cit.*, p. 62; Vermeersch-Creusen, *Epitome*, II, n. 340, p. 298; Gregory, *op. cit.*, p. 70; Sego, *op. cit.*, p. 122.

[26] Canon 1121, § 1.

[27] Cappello, *De Matrimonio*, n. 775, p. 765.

the declaration had been granted in a general manner for any marriage whatsoever.[28]

B. The Nature of Dispensation from the Interpellations

Since it is the purpose of the interpellations to ascertain in the external forum, formally and officially, the presence of the fundamental condition for an application of the Pauline privilege, namely, the departure of the infidel party, the interpellations serve as a means of establishing whether or not such a departure has taken place. Logically, it may well be that this end can, at times, be attained through some other more effective means. Hence, if that departure is clearly known from some other means, then, according to the rule of law: *"Eum, qui certus est, certiorari ulterius non oportet,"*[29] the interpellations are not only unnecessary, but they become entirely useless. However, this uselessness, or even impossibility, with reference to the interpellations cannot be presumed by any individual, but must be officially and formally declared by the Church. And this declaration is reserved soley to the Holy See.[30] Thus, a dispensation from the interpellations is an official and formal declaration vouching by way of a moral certainty for the departure of the infidel party. Hence, even if it seems, or is actually certain, that the interpellations will be useless, or impossible of completion, or even certainly and gravely dangerous, the said official and formal declaration of the facts by way of a dispensation from the Holy See is necessary. Dispensation from the interpellations is an act which authorizes the omission of the interpellations, which otherwise should be made.

The act of the Church in authorizing the omission of the interpellations is a declaration and at the same time a dis-

[28] Cf. *Fontes*, n. 4717; Payen, *De Matrimonio in Missionibus*, II, n. 2342.

[29] Reg. 31, R. J., in VI°. Bartoccetti, *De Regulis Juris Canonici*, pp. 136-138.

[30] Canon 1121, § 2.

pensation, or sometime it reflects primarily a dispensation from the ecclesiastical law, or at other times it is under specific circumstances a comprehensive declaration of the licitness of the use of the Pauline privilege apart from all interpellations. For instance, when the interpellations are useless or impossible, then the act of authorizing their omission is a declaration and at the same time a dispensation; when the objective departure of the infidel party is not certain, then the act is simply a dispensation; and when the validity of the marriage is truly doubtful, or the bad will of the infidel party is certainly existing, then the interpellations would be in and of their nature superfluous, so that the act which authorizes the omission of the interpellations would be nothing more than a comprehensive declaration of the licitness of the use of the Pauline privilege. It is in all probability for this reason that the Code of Canon Law uses the words *"declarare"* and *"delaratio"* for the said act.[31]

SECTION 3. FORMS OF THE INTERPELLATIONS

According to the norm prescribed in canon 1122, the interpellations must normally be made in at least a *summary and extrajudicial form;* if the summary and extrajudicial form cannot be duly observed, a *private form* of the interpellations may be valid and licit.

A. The Summary and Extrajudicial Form

In the Code, there is no exact definition or description of the nature of the *summary and extrajudicial form,* except as reflected in the words of canon 1122, which prescribes that the ordinary of the converted party should preside over this procedure, and that the same ordinary should also grant to the infidel party, if he or she ask for it, an extension of the time in which to deliberate, with the warning however

[31] Canon 1121, § 2; canon 1123. Cf. Gregory, *The Pauline Privilege,* p. 77; Sego, *Dispensation from the Interpellations,* pp. 123-128.

that, in case the time so extended elapses without a reply, a negative reply will be presumed. Now, if one takes into consideration the nature of the interpellations with reference to the dissolution of the former marriage and the nature of the dispensation from the interpellations, the *summary and extrajudicial form* of the interpellations can be understood in such a way that the interpellations should be made after the manner of the *extrajudicial procedure* delineated in canons 2142-2146, and the dispensation from the interpellations could be granted upon a *summary procedure* similar to that which is mentioned in canon 1990, but there may be omitted certain formalities and the intervention of the *defensor vinculi,* which are otherwise prescribed for the latter procedures.[32] In fact, the expression of *"summarie et extrajudicialiter"* has its origin in the Constitution *"Populis"* of Pope Gregory XIII, under date of January 25, 1585.[33]

The following processes are recognized by authors as proper for this *summary and extrajudicial procedure*: the interpellations are made by authority of the ordinary or his delegated official,[34] with any means of dealing with the infidel party or of communicating with him being deemed sufficient. Accordingly the interpellations can be made either by the ordinary or by some priest subdelegated by him, whether personally or by means of the "epistolary judicial form."[35]

In case the interpellations are made by the bishop's deputy personally, the following procedure should be observed: whenever it proves convenient, at least one priest and a notary (either a priest or a laic) should conduct the inter-

[32] Cf. Woeber, *Tre Interpellations,* p. 78; Doheny, *Informal Procedure,* p. 526; Sego, *op. cit.* p. 180.

[33] *Documentum VIII, Codex Iuris Canonici.*

[34] Woeber, *op. cit.,* p. 78; Conte a Coronata, *De Sacramentis,* III, n. 634, p. 888; Doheny, *Informal Procedure,* p. 526; Sego, *op. cit.,* p. 180; Winslow, *The Pauline Privilege,* n. 41, p. 21; Vromant, *De Matrimonio,* n. 321, p. 285.

[35] Bouscaren-Ellis, *Canon Law,* p. 599.

pellations;[36] *testis qualificatus;*[37] if the circumstances are such that a priest cannot conduct the interpellations, two laics or even one laic may be duly appointed.[38]

The questions should not be proposed in a vague or indirect manner; in the interpellations it is not sufficient merely to exhort the infidel party to become a Christian without specifically explaining the full import of the departure from the converted and baptized party.[39] Thus, in case laics are duly delegated for the interpellations, it is highly advisable that the questions be written beforehand by the ordinary or the priest, and that the questions be submitted, as written, to the infidel party for his replies, either orally or in writing;[40] the laics should afterwards be questioned separately as to the facts of the case, and their testimony should be taken down by the notary; they should be under oath for the deposition; and then take the oaths *de veritate dictorum et de secreto servando.*[41]

If the infidel party replies to the interpellations in the affirmative or in the negative, he should be asked to make the response in a statement and to sign the document, which likewise must be subscribed by the one who made the interpellations; if the infidel party is reluctant to endorse the document, the substance of the interview must nevertheless be written and subscribed to by those who made the interpellations.[42]

The ordinary is authorized by the Code to grant the infidel party time for reflection and deliberation, if the latter requests it.[43] Since this is a right accorded to the infidel

[36] Doheny, *Informal Procedure,* p. 527.

[37] Canons 373, § 3; 1791, § 1; Conte a Coronata, *loc. cit.*

[38] Doheny, *loc. cit.;* Woeber, *op. cit.,* p. 78

[39] Vromant, *De Matrimonio,* n. 322, p. 285.

[40] Doheny, *loc. cit.*

[41] Canon 1623, § 3; 1767, § 1; 1769; 1780. Cf. Doheny, *loc. cit.;* Woeber, *loc. cit.;* Payen, *De Matrimonio in Missionibus,* II, n. 2362; Winslow, *The Pauline Privilege,* n. 41, 2), p. 21.

[42] Conte a Coronata, *De Sacramentis,* III, n. 634, p. 888; Woeber, *op. cit.,* p. 82.

[43] Canon 1122, § 1.

party by law, justice demands that the petition always be granted whenever it is sought, or whenever circumstances indicate the prudence or wisdom of a delay. The grant of an extension of time may be refused if it is foreseen that the delay would seriously endanger the faith or morals of the converted and baptized party.[44] The permission of a delay must be accompanied with the admonition that, should the infidel party neglect to declare his intentions before the expiration of the allotted time, his neglect will be considered as a tacit unwillingness to abide by even the minimum requirement, namely, to live peacefully with the converted and baptized party. If the warning were omitted, the presumption that such a neglect on the part of the infidel party is to be considered as a tacit unwillingness to live peacefully with the converted and baptized party cannot be held.[45]

When these processes of the interpellations have been completed and the infidel party has answered either in the negative or in the affirmative, or the extension of time for reflection and deliberation by the infidel party has lapsed without a reply,[46] then upon a careful analysis of the circumstances relating to the case and to the processes of the interpellations the ordinary (or the priest who in the latter's name conducted the interpellations) can make a judgment regarding the outcome of the investigation made by him. Then, if the ordinary judges the case in favor of the converted and baptized party, he issues a decree certifying that fact and authorizing the party to proceed to the second marriage.

All the facts known or gathered in connection with the interpellations together with the judgment of the ordinary (or of the priest) should be committed to writing, and there should be listed briefly all the reasons that warrant the use of the Pauline privilege by the converted and baptized

[44] Cappello, *De Matrimonio*, n. 779, p. 769; Woeber, *op. cit.*, p. 79.

[45] Conte a Coronata, *op. cit.*, III, n. 634, p. 889.

[46] Cf. S.C.S. Off., 29 Nov. 1882, ad 2—*Fontes*, n. 1075; Conte a Coronata, *op. cit.*, III, n. 634, p. 888.

party.[47] The complete and authentic records of the entire case, signed by the ordinary (or the priest) and the notary, are to be filled in the archives of the diocese, and the proper notation should be made in the baptismal and marriage registers.[48]

The *epistolary judicial form* of the interpellations can be employed by authority of the ordinary in the form of a letter. The interpellations are sent to the infidel party by registered mail, including notice that if no answer is received within a stated time the converted and baptized party intends to marry again, and that this second marriage will effect the dissolution of the former one.[49]

Upon receipt of a negative answer, or after a lapse of the predetermined time without a reply, the ordinary issues a decree certifying that fact and authorizing the converted and baptized party to proceed to the second marriage with a Catholic party. This *epistolary judicial form* is the usual method for the interpellations.

B. The Private Form

The private form of the interpellations is licit only when the *summary and extrajudicial form* cannot be employed.[50] The private interpellations are not made with the authority of the ordinary (or his delegate) of the converted and baptized party; they are made in the name of the converted and baptized party who is planning to contract a new marriage with a Catholic party. The private form of the interpellations may be made by the converted and baptized party personally in the presence of two witnesses, or by a

[47] Cf. Sego, *op. cit.*, p. 181; Doheny, *Informal Procedure*, p. 528; Winslow, *The Pauline Privilege*, n. 41, 3), pp. 21-22; Conte a Coronata, *op. cit.*, III, n. 634, p. 889.

[48] Doheny, *loc. cit.*

[49] Bouscaren-Ellis, *Canon Law*, p. 599; Conte a Coronata, *loc. cit.*

[50] Canon 1122, § 2; Bouscaren-Ellis, *Canon Law*, p. 599; Winslow, *The Pauline Privilege*, n. 42, p. 23.

third and disinterested party of known probity in the presence of a witness,[51] or in the form of a letter.[52]

The processes of the interrogation either of the two witnesses and the converted and baptized party or of the third and disinterested party and a witness are required in the same manner in which the laics are to interrogate in the case of the *summary and extrajudicial form.* The private interpellations in the form of a letter are to be made after the manner of the epistolary judicial form of the interpellations with reference to the contents of the letter and to the mailing of the letter. For the valid use of the private interpellations in the form of a letter, two witnesses must attest before the ordinary (or his delegate) the fact that they read the letter of the interpellations, that the interpellations were properly made in the letter, that they were present at the singing and mailing of the letter, and that they inspected the reply of the infidel party. These facts they should recount under oath.[53]

Article II

Facultas XXVII: Faculty to Dispense from the Interpellations for Dissolution of Marriages by Virtue of the Pauline Privilege

Section 1. Text of *Facultas XXVII* and Preliminary Notes

Permittendi ut, accedente gravi causa, interpellatio coniugis infidelis ante baptismum partis quae ad fidem convertitur fieri posit; nec non, gravi pariter de causa, ab eadem interpelatione, ante baptismum partis quae convertitur, dispensandi, dummodo hoc in casu ex processu saltem summario et extraiudiciali constet interpellationem fieri non posse, vel fore inutilem.

[51] Winslow, *loc. cit.* Cf. S.C.S. Off., 12 Ian. 1757, ad 4—*Fontes*, n. 807.

[52] Bouscaren-Ellis, *loc. cit.;* Winslow, *loc. cit.;* Conte a Coronata, *op. cit.*, III, n. 635, p. 890.

[53] Bouscaren-Ellis, *loc. cit.;* Gregory, *op. cit.*, pp. 94-95; Doheny, *Informal Procedure*, pp. 528-530; Weober, *op. cit.*, pp. 80-83.

The laws of the Code in which the present Decennial Faculty has its roots are canon 1121, § 1, and canon 1123. According to canon 1121, § 1, before the party who has been converted and baptized can by virtue of the Pauline privilege validly contract a new marriage with a Catholic party, he or she must interpellate the non-baptized party; and a dispensation from the obligation of the making of the interpellations can be granted by the Holy See in line with the provision contained in canon 1123, but this dispensation is regularly granted only after baptism and before the second marriage of the converted party. However, in virtue of the present Decennial Faculty, the mission ordinary can permit the converted party to make the interpellation even before his baptism, and further, the mission ordinary can under certain circumstances dispense from the obligation of the making of the interpellations even before the converted party's baptism, but the permission or the dispensation must always be given before the converted and baptized party's second marriage. Thus, the present Decennial Faculty deals with two powers, i.e., one that dispenses from the temporal requirement in the making of the interpellations, and the other that in addition dispenses from the obligation of the making the interpellations at all at any time.

Insofar as this faculty makes possible a relaxation of the prescriptions of canons 1121-1123, the cases with which the present Decennial Faculty deals are those which involve the Pauline privilege in the strict sense, and hence are concerned with the physical or the moral departure of the infidel party.

SECTION 2. THE FIRST POWER IN THE FACULTY: TO DISPENSE FROM THE OBSERVANCE OF THE TIME IN THE MAKING OF THE INTERPELLATIONS

The first paragraph of canon 1121 in unmistakable terms gives the rule by which the converted party is to be guided in selecting the time that is suited for the valid and licit use of interpellations. The law states that the period during which the interpellations are to be made starts after the baptism of the converted party and ends before he has entered a second valid marriage. This, then, is the general law, which has frequently been insisted upon by the Holy See.[54] Nevertheless, the holder of the present Decennial Faculty can permit the converted party to make the interpellations before his baptism, provided that there exists a sufficiently grave cause for such a dispensation. For the granting of this dispensation, no previous summary and extrajudicial procedure is postulated at all,[55] provided that the user of the present Decennial Faculty is morally certain of the existence of a sufficiently grave cause, as is required for the validity of the dispensation.

"Accedente gravi causa." A grave cause is postulated if the interpellations are to be made in anticipation of the converted party's baptism. The basic considerations for the use of the present Decennial Faculty are the infidel party's physical or moral departure prior to the time of the converted party's baptism,[56] and the urgency to make ready for a new marriage on the party of the converted party, in the event that a negative reply was given to the interpellations by the infidel party. In addition to these, the following considerations are cited as sufficiently grave ones for the application of the present faculty:

(1) If there should be good reason to presume that the infidel party would later give fictitious answers.[57]

[54] S.C.S. Off., (Cochinchin. Orient.), 6 Aug. 1956—*Fontes*, n. 939; (Pondichery), 20 Iun. 1858—*Fontes*, n. 947; (Tchely Orient.), 13 Apr. 1859—*Fontes*, n. 951; instr. (ad Vic. Ap Sutchuen. Orient.), 3 Iun. 1874—*Fontes*, n. 1030; S.C. de Prop. Fide (ad C.P. pro Sin.), 5 Mart. 1816—*Collectanea*, n. 704.

[55] Vromant, *De Matrimonio*, n. 364, p. 326; Paventi, *Brevis Commentarius*, p. 46; Sartori, *Iuris Missionarii Elementa*, p. 118; Vermeersch, "De Formulis Facultatum," *Periodica*, XI (1922), p. (141).

[56] The same departure is presumed still to persevere after the baptism of the converted party. S.C.S. Off., 3 Iun. 1874—*Collectanea*, n. 1415.

[57] De Reeper, *A Missionary Companion*, p. 107.

(2) If the anticipated interpellations will prove helpful to the converted party who is reluctant to resume conjugal life with the infidel party, even if the latter were to reply in the affirmative to the interpellations made after the convert's baptism, because the converted party thinks that he could only under severe stress and strain fulfill some obligation connected with baptism on the ground: (a) that there exists a well-founded serious fear of spiritual harm for the converted party, if he resumes conjugal life with the infidel party,[58] or (b) that the converted party cannot be certain that the infidel party would cohabit with him in peace and without contumely to God.[59]

(3) If the anticipated making of the interpellations is the only way to ensure the conversion and baptism of the catechumen and to secure the spiritual welfare of others.[60]

(4) If the anticipated making of the interpellations will aid conversion, by removing the serious inconveniences arising from a temporary separation of the parties were such a separation necessitated after the baptism of the converted party.[61] For instance, at times it may be difficult to obtain a temporary separation after the baptism of the converted party if the latter lives with another party in good faith, although in an invalid union. In such a case, if the infidel party's negative answer to the interpellations did not precede the baptism of the converted party, then a temporary separation would be necessary after the baptism until the

[58] Vromant, *De Matrimonio*, n. 364, p. 325; Paventi, *Brevis Commentarius*, p. 45; Sartori, *op. cit.*, p. 118; Winslow, *The Pauline Privilege*, n. 69, p. 41.

[59] S.C.S. Off., 21 Nov. 1883—*Collectanea*, n. 1607, ad 3. Cf Payen, *De Matrimonio in Missionibus*, II, n. 2415; Winslow, *loc. cit.*

[60] S.C.S. Off., 3 Iun. 1874—*Collectanea*, n. 1415. Cf. Vromant, *loc. cit.;* Paventi, *op. cit.*, pp. 45-46; Winslow, *The Apostolic Faculties*, p. 159.

[61] S.C.S., Off., 24 Sept. 1896—*Collectanea Sanctae Sedis, Hongkong*, n. 1409, ad 3. Cf. Vromant, *loc. cit.;* Vermeersch, "De Formulis Facultatum," *Periodica*, XI (1922), p. (141); Sartori, *loc. cit.;* Paventi, *loc. cit.;* Winslow, *loc. cit.;* De Reeper, *op. cit.*, p. 108.

receipt of the negative response that the former infidel spouse refuses cohabitation.

Although it is not necessary to utilize the summary and extraordinary procedure before granting permission to make the anticipated interpellations, the mission ordinary or the delegated priest should reach a judgment regarding the truthfulness of the petition and the sufficiency and the gravity of the cause after a careful analysis of the circumstances and the character of the persons involved in the case, regarding the marriage to be dissolved (there is postulated a valid contracting of it *in infidelitate*), regarding the sincerity of the conversion and the rightfulness of the converted party's admission to baptism in the case, etc.

Though the text of the present Decennial Faculty employs the word *"interpellatio,"* both questions as contained in canon 1121, § 1, are to be proposed to the infidel party. The method to be used in the making of the interpellations and all the factors incidental thereto are to be adjudged and executed according to the norms prescribed in canons 1122-1124.[62]

SECTION 3. THE SECOND POWER IN THE FACULTY: TO DISPENSE FROM THE OBLIGATION OF MAKING THE INTERPELLATIONS BEFORE AND AFTER THE BAPTISM OF THE CONVERTED PARTY

The second power in the present Decennial Faculty is the power by virtue of which the mission ordinary or his delegated priest can dispense the converted party from the observance of the obligation of making the interpellations, either before or after the baptism of the converted party, if certain conditions are verified.

The present power is applicable for the cases of the Pauline privilege.[63] In the law of the Code the period set for the

[62] Cf. Vromant, *De Matrimonio*, nn. 319-339, pp. 283-300, and Woeber, *The Interpellations*, pp. 84-105, on the juridical effect of the interpellations; cf. Gregory, *The Pauline Privilege*, pp. 73-74, on the response of the infidel.

[63] Canons 1120-1124.

making of the interpellations starts after the baptism of the convert and ends before he has entered a second valid marriage,[64] but with a special apostolic indult a dispensation from this law may be invoked,[65] though quite generally the dispensation looks simply to the period in which the converted party should normally make the interpellations. However, the grantee of the present Decennial Faculty can dispense from the said obligation even *before the baptism* of the converted party, even as he can also dispense from the same *after the baptism* of the converted party.[66]

The conditions required for the use of the present Decennial Faculty consist in the reasons underlying the dispensation and the *procedure* through which the element of impossibility or uselessness in the matter of the interpellations is to be determined. Two conditions are requisite: the condition common to the faculty of dispensing after baptism from the interpellations, and the condition proper to the use of this specific faculty.

The said common condition is the impossibility, whether physical or moral, and also the uselessness[67] attaching to the interpellations. The element of futility can be equated with that of uselessness.[68] These conditions are required for the validity of the dispensation,[69] whether it be granted before or after the converted party's baptism. The condition proper to the use of the present faculty is the presence of a specially grave cause, in addition to the aforementioned common condition. The specially grave cause is necessary for the licitness of the dispensation, and the presence of a cause sufficing for the use of the first power listed in the

[64] Canon 1121, § 1.

[65] Canon 1123.

[66] Reg. 35, R. J., in VI°: Plus semper in se continent quod est minus." Cf. Bartoccetti, *De Regulis Juris Canonici*, pp. 145-148. Cf. Vromant, *De Matrimonio*, n. 365, p. 326.

[67] See *infra*, pp. 308-309.

[68] See *infra*, pp. 309-310.

[69] Canon 84, § 1. Cf. Vromant, *loc. cit.*

present Decennial Faculty would satisfy this condition.[70] But, in the event that the existence of the *specially grave cause* cannot be proved, the dispensation can be given *only after the baptism* of the converted party.[71]

"Dummodo hoc in casu ex processu saltem summario et extraiudiciali constet. . . ." The mere fact of existence of a specially grave cause in addition to the common conditions does not absolutely warrant the use of the power listed in Decennial Faculty XXVII, since moral certainty must be established for the existence of the impossibility, whether physical or moral, and also the uselessness attaching to the interpellations, through a *summary and extrajudicial procedure,* which is required for the validity of the dispensation.[72]

The full scope of the dispensation is the total omission of the interpellations, and the dispensation may be given either orally or by means of a decree at the end of the summary and extrajudicial procedure. Thereupon the converted party obtains the right to contract a new marriage with a Catholic party in the *"forma canonica."* But he must have received baptism before he can enter the second marriage. And, if the new marriage is postponed for more than a year after the dispensation has been granted, a new dispensation becomes necessary.[73]

[70] Vromant, *loc. cit.;* Paventi, *Brevis Commentarius,* p. 46; Sartori, *op. cit.,* p. 118.

[71] Vromant, *op. cit.,* n. 365, pp. 326-327.

[72] Canon 39. According to Vromant, moral certainty of the impossibility or the uselessness of the interpellations is a requisite for the validity of the dispensation, but the summary procedure is postulated for the licitness of the same. Cf. Vromant, *De Matrimonio,* n. 365, p. 326.

[73] *Collectanea,* n. 743. Cf. Cappello, *De Matrimonio,* n. 781, ad 5, p. 771; Gregory, *The Pauline Privilege,* p. 80; Woeber, *The Interpellations,* p. 117; Vromant, *De Matrimonio,* n. 367, p. 328.

ARTICLE III. DISPENSATION FROM THE INTERPELLATIONS FOR THE DISSOLUTION OF LEGITIMATE MARRIAGES CONTRACTED BETWEEN NON-BAPTIZED MONOGAMISTS

SECTION 1. *Ex Iure*

In the Code of Canon Law special faculties are granted to local ordinaries, pastors, etc., for dispensing under certain circumstances from the interpellations in marriages contracted between non-baptized monogamous persons and in marriages contracted between non-baptized polygamous persons. This grant is made in canon 1125. As a matter of fact, canon 1125 incorporates the legislation contained in three different constitutions: Pope Paul III's Constitution *Altitudo* of June 1, 1537; Pope St. Pius V's Constitution *Romani Pontificis* of August 2, 1571; and Pope Gregory XIII's Constitution *Populis* of January 25, 1585. Of these the last mentioned constitution grants faculties for dispensing from the interpellations in marriages of monogamous converts, and the other two constitutions in marriages of polygamous converts.

The text of the Constitution *Populis* is found in the Code of Canon Law, *Documentum VIII*. The faculties mentioned in this Constitution were imparted to the local ordinaries, pastors, quasi-pastors, confessors of the Society of Jesus, etc., in Ethiopia, Angola, Brazil, and other parts of the West Indies, with special consideration for the particular circumstances and demands existing in these regions.[74] Now, in consequence of the clause incorporated in canon 1125, *"quaeque pro peculiaribus locis scripta sunt, ad alias quoque regiones in eisdem adiunctis extenduntur,"* the same Constitution becomes universally applicable for cases which are substantially the same as those originally contemplated in it, no matter wherever in the world they may occur.[75]

[74] Burton, *A Commentary on Canon 1125*, pp. 69-71; 172-176.

[75] Cf. Vermeersch, "De Canone 1125 eiusque vi extensiva," *Periodica*, XX (1931), pp. 1*-5*; F. Woods, *The Constitutions of Canon 1125 and Their Application in the United States* (Milwaukee: Bruce Publishing Co., 1935), pp. 73-82; Bouscaren, "An Inquiry into the Practical Application of Canon 1125, etc.," *Miscellanea-Vermeersch*, I,

A. The Marriage Which Is to be Dissolved by Virtue of the Constitution Populis

The first condition with reference to the marriage which yields to a possible dissolution by virtue of the Constitution *Populis* is that the marriage must have been contracted between two infidels according to non-Christian matrimonial ceremonies (... *infideles, post contracta gentili ritu matrimonia*). This condition is entirely the same that is set for the application of the Pauline privilege. Thus the marriage must have been lawfully and validly contracted between two persons who had never received the sacrament of baptism.

The second essential condition with reference to such a marriage looks to an extant physical separation of the two parties of the marriage to the extent that communication between them has ceased and that they are not physically or morally able to communicate with each other. In the text of the Constitution *Populis*, the original cause for such a separation is stated as follows:

> ... *Multos utriusque sed praecipue virilis sexus infideles, post contracta gentili ritu matrimonia, ex Angola, Aethiopia, Brasilia, et aliis Indicis regionibus, ab hostibus captos, a patriis finibus et propriis coniugibus in remotissimas regiones exterminari, adeo ut tam ipsi, captivique qui in patria remanent, si postea ad fidem convertantur, coniuges infideles tam longo locorum intervallo disiunctos....*

The occasion for the grant contained in the Constitution *Populis* was the inhumane treatment forced upon the victim of the flourishing slave trade of the later sixteenth century. An African husband might be captured and carried across the sea far from his wife, or both husband and wife might be captured and taken each to a different place. The difficulties arising from this separation of spouses was a *causa*

283-286; Payen, *De Matrimonio in Missionibus*, II, n. 2404; Vromant, *De Matrimonio*, n. 240, pp. 301 ff.; Burton, *op. cit.*, pp. 113-116; Sego, *Dispensation from the Interpellations*, pp. 51-87.

impulsiva for the grant incorporated in the said Constitution. Now, such a separation of husband and wife by force, in exactly the same framework of circumstances as described in the Constitution, may perhaps never happen again. However, if a similar physical separation befalls married infidel parties through equally far-reaching causes, such as iron curtain or bamboo curtain methods in the shifting of entire populations, traceless dispersions of prisoners of war, etc., then the faculty granted through the Constitution *Populis* is operative. It is apparent that this second essential condition, the physical separation of the two infidel parties of the marriage, is far different from the use of the Pauline privilege. For, if there be no separation of the two parties of the marriage previous to the time of the baptism of one of them, the faculty granted in the Constitution *Populis* cannot be operative; on the other hand, such a separation is not presupposed for the use of the Pauline privilege. The physical departure in the case of the Pauline privilege can by no means be identified with the physical separation in the case contemplated in the Constitution *Populis*. The former is based primarily on the hatred or non-acceptance of Christian doctrine or Christianity's way of life, and its starting point is the conversion and baptism of the one party during the marital life of two infidel persons, while the latter has no basis whatsoever in the same reason, nor does it have its starting point at the conversion and baptism of one of the parties of the marriage. As a matter of fact, even if the baptism of the one party be not known to the other party, the faculty granted in the Constitution *Populis* is not only operative, but this circumstance was the original *causa impulsiva* for the grant bestowed. Furthermore, the reason for the impossibility or the uselessness of the interpellations in the case of the Pauline privilege is basically found in the unwillingness to reply to them on the part of the non-baptized party only, while that in the case of the Constitution *Populis* is the incommunicability, whether physical or moral, between the parties of the marriage.

B. Conditions Required for the Use of the Faculty Granted in the Constitution Populis

For the valid use of the faculty granted through the Constitution *Populis* mentioned in canon 1125, the following three conditions must be verified, i.e., (1) one of the parties of the marriage must upon conversion have received baptism, the while nothing is known about the other party with reference to his possible baptism or to his willingness to cohabit with the baptized party; (2) from a summary and extrajudicial examination it must appear that there exists a physical or moral impossibility or uselessness to offer any intimation, or that, if the intimation was made by the baptized party to the other party, the latter has not answered within the specific time, and (3) the baptized party may marry only a Catholic with all due observance of the canonical form of marriage.

Of the foregoing three conditions, the first and third conditions need no explanation. The *"monitio"* or intimation which plays a part in the second condition has its origin in the text of the Constitution itself,[76] but it can be identified with the two interpellations which are mentioned in canon 1121, § 1. In the Constitution *Populis* it is the interpellations that are implied in the clause, *"monere an sine contumelia Creatoris secum cohabitare velint,* while canon 1121, § 1, states: *"An velit et ipsa converti ac baptismum suscipere; an saltem velit secum cohabitare pacifice sine contumelia Creatoris."*

In order to satisfy the second condition, *"absentem moneri legitime non posse"* or *"monitum intra tempus in eadem monitione praefixum suam voluntatem non significasse,"* i.e., the incommunicability between the two parties must be established after at least a summary and extrajudicial inquiry.

In order to verify the condition *"absentem moneri legi-*

[76] In the text of the Constitution *Populis,* the words *"interpellare"* and *"interpellationes"* are not used, but *"monere nequeant," "absentem moneri legitime non posse,"* and *"monitum intra tempus in eadem monitione praefixum suam voluntatem non significasse"* are used.

time non posse, it is not necessary that there exist the condition of slavery, or of capture, or of abduction. The said condition may be verified if, after an inquiry which is at least summary and extrajudicial in form, the impossibility of the making of the *"monitio"* is established through one of the following causes: (1) the impossibility of communication with a barbarous or belligerent country, where the other party resides; (2) ignorance of the whereabouts of the other party, after all effective means were conscientiously employed for the ascertainment of the actual residence of the missing party; (3) the great distances that bring well-nigh insuperable difficulties with them; (4) inconveniences or hardships which render the *"monitio,"* morally impossible or constitute it a portent of grave harm,[77] and (5) moral certainty of the absolute futility of the making of the *"monitio,"* etc.[78] But, these are not exhaustive enumerations. According to the common opinion of the authors, a moral impossibility suffices as a warrant for the use of the faculty contained in the Constitution *Populis.* Circumstances may be as various as the cases and the places. Judgment regarding the difficulty or danger which may be accounted as a moral impossibility must be left to the ordinary or the priest who uses the faculty after

[77] "... Saepe contingit multos ... ex Angola, Aethiopia, Brasilia, et aliis Indicis regionibus, ab hostibus captos, a patriis finibus et propriis conugibus in remotissimas regiones exterminari adeo ut tam ipsi, captivique qui in patria remanent, si postea ad fidem convertantur, coniuges infideles tam longo locorum intervallo disiunctos, an sine contumelia Creatoris secum cohabitare velint, ut par est, monere nequeant, vel quia interdum ad hostiles et barbaras provincias ne nuntiis quidem accessus pateat, vel quia itineris longitudo magna afferat difficultatem. ..."—From the text of the Constition *Populis.*

[78] Cf. S.C.S. Off. (Ind. Orient.), 13 Ian. 1757—*Fontes,* n. 807; (Mongoliae), 29 Nov. 1882—*Fontes,* n. 1075; *Collectanea,* n. 1581. Also cf. Doheny, *Informal Procedure,* p. 560; Payen,*De Matrimonio in Missionibus,* II, n. 2409; Sego, *Dispensation from the Interpellations,* pp. 156-171; Bouscaren, "art. cit.," *Miscellanea-Vermeersch,* I, 294; Vromant, "De Dispensatione ab Interpellationibus in Ordine ad Privilegium Fidei," *Periodica,* XX (1931), p. 116*.

the summary and extrajudicial investigation has been made.[79]

"Monitum intra tempus in eadem monitione prafixum suam voluntatem non significasse." On the other hand, if the baptized party was able to make the *"monitio,"* but the duly interpellated party fails to reply within a reasonably allotted time—ordinarily one month,[80] and if this is proved after an investigation which is of at least *summary and extrajudicial form,* the faculty granted in the Constitution *Populis* is sufficiently operative.[81] However, from the context of the Constitution it is quite clear that the failure of the reply to the interpellations on the part of the other party must be due to the impossibility, whether physical or moral, of communication by reason of the great distances, of extreme hardship, etc., on his part, i.e., on the part of the interpellated party. Thus, his failure to reply is not based upon his unwillingness to cohabit with the baptized party peacefully and without contumely to the Creator.[82] Consequently, this failure cannot be identified simply with the tacit negative answer of the infidel party to the interpellations.[83]

[79] S.C.S. Off., 29 Nov. 1882—*Fontes,* n. 1075. Cf. Woeber, *The Interpellations,* p. 125; Sego, *op. cit.,* pp. 171-183; Vromant, *De Matrimonio,* n. 348, p. 314.

[80] Doheny, *Informal Procedure,* p. 561; Gregory, *The Pauline Privilege,* p. 93; Burton, *A Commentary on Canon 1125,* p. 171. Computation of one month should be made according to the norm of canon 35, i.e., *tempus utile.*

[81] Cf. *Collectanea,* n. 1746, *in fine;* Doheny, *op. cit.,* pp. 560-561; Woeber, *loc. cit.;* Burton, *loc. cit.*

[82] "... Quae quidem matrimonia, etiamsi postea innotuerit coniuges priores infideles suam voluntatem iuste impeditos declarare non potuisse, et ad fidem etiam tempore transacti secundi matrimonii conversos fuisse, nihilominus rescrindi nunquam debere, sed valida et firma, prolemque suscipiendam legitimam fore decernimus." Also cf. the circumstances in which the use of the faculty of the Constitution was originally contemplated, in Section 1 of the present chapter.

[83] Canon 1123.

C. The Effects of the Dispensation from the Interpellations by Virtue of the Faculty Granted in the Constitution Populis

The effects of the dispensation granted by virtue of the faculty contained in the Constitution *Populis* are stated in the text as follows:

> ... *Concedimus facultatem dispensandi cum quibuscumque utriusque sexus Christifidelibus incolis dictarum regionum et serius ad fidem conversis qui ante baptismum susceptum matrimonium contraxerunt, ut eorum quilibet, superstite coniuge infideli,* ... *matrimonia cum quovis fideli alterius etiam ritus contrahere et in facie Ecclesiae solemnizare, et in eis postea carnali copula consummatis quoad vixerint remanere licite valeant* ... *quae quidem matrimonia, etiamsi postea innotuerit coniuges priores infideles suam voluntatem iuste impeditos declarae non potuisse, et ad fidem etiam tempore transacti secundi matrimonii conversos fuisse, nihilominus rescindi nunquam debere, sed valida et firma, prolemque inde suscipiendam legitimam fore decernimus.*

As stated in the foregoing passage of the text of the Constitution, the dispensation is to be granted by means of the faculty here under consideration in order that those who have in serious mind embraced the fatih when they had contracted marriage before their baptism may, despite the survival of the infidel party and without his or her consent or awaiting his or her reply, licitly contract a second marriage with a Catholic and solemnize it before the Church, and after its consummation remain in it as long as they live.

In addition, the dispensation from the interpellations has the specific effect that the second marriage with a Catholic will be valid, even if afterwards it appears that his or her spouse of the first marriage had, at the time of the second marriage, already embraced the faith and received baptism. In such a case the first marriage between the two converts remains in the nature of a ratified but non-consummated union, which however becomes dissolved through the contracting of the new Christian marriage entered into in virtue of the grant contained in the Constitution *Populis*. This effect "really transcends the limits of the Pauline privilege."[84] For it is definitely determined that the Pauline privilege ceases to be applicable upon the conversion of both parties in such manner that a second marriage contracted in consequence of a supposed use of the Pauline privilege is invalid if the other party of the marriage which had originally been contracted in infidelity had also actually received baptism.

D. The Nature of the Faculty Granted in the Constitution Populis

In line with the norm of canon 1123, the Constitution *Populis*, as mentioned in canon 1125, authorizes the ordinary, the pastor, the quasi-pastor, etc., to execute, under certain conditions, what canon 1123 implies, namely, that the grantees of the power contained in the Constitution *Populis* are empowered to authorize the baptized party to bypass the making of the interpellations and still licitly make use of the right (or privilege) granted in the same Constitution, or to proceed without awaiting a reply to the interpellations.

The Constitution *Populis* was originally issued for local ordinaries, for pastors (and quasi-pastors), and for the priests of the Society of Jesus approved by the Superiors of that Society for the hearing of confessions in the specific regions mentioned in the same Constitution. The priests of other religious orders, by staying in the same regions, acquired the same faculty that belonged to authorized priest-confessors of the Society of Jesus, namely, through the juridical institute of the interparticipation of privileges.[85]

[84] Bouscaren, "art. cit.," *Miscellanea-Vermeersch*, I, 301. Cf. Doheny, *Informal Procedure*, p. 561; Sego, *Dispensartion from the Interpellations*, pp. 135-144; Gasparri, *De Matrimonio*, II, n. 1159, p. 235; Conte a Coronata, *De Sacramentis*, III, n. 644, a., p. 900.

[85] Cf. Burton, *op. cit.*, pp. 172-176; Doheny, *Informal Procedure*, pp. 562-565.

Now the power of dispensing by virtue of the Constitution *Populis* as mentioned in canon 1125 is connected *ipso iure* with the office of local ordinaries, of pastors, and of quasi-pastors[86] in any part of world.[87] This power is therefore ordinary and may be delegated, and it may be used in both forums. Moreover, local ordinaries, pastors, and quasi-pastors may use the power for the benefit of their own subjects wherever the subjects may be, and also for all those who actually live in their territory. As to religious, under the present law, the jurisdiction for hearing the confessions of the faithful must be obtained, even by exempt religious, from the ordinary of the place. If they have this jurisdiction, they enjoy the faculty which is granted through the Constitution *Populis* as mentioned in canon 1125.[88] Simple confessors, *qua* confessors (i.e., other than religious confessors), do not enjoy this power.[89]

As to missionaries who are not canonically pastors or quasi-pastors, they do not enjoy this power *ipso iure,* but they have it by reason of enjoying the use of the Decennial Faculty XXV in the *Formula Maior.*[90]

SECTION 2. *Ex Facultate*: *Facultas XXV* AND *Fcultas XXVI*

A. *Texts of* FACULTASXXV *and* FACULTAS XXVI

FACULTAS XXV

Dispensandi super interpellatione coniugum in infidelitate relictorum pro omnibus casibus ordinariis, quando scilicet adhibitis antea omnibus diligentiis, eti-

FACULTAS XXVI

Itemque dispensandi super interpellatione coniugis in infidelitate relicti, siquidem certo constiterit ex processu saltem summario et extra-

[86] Code Comm., 3 Aug. 1919—*Sylloge,* n. 72, pp. 110-111.

[87] Burton, *loc. cit.;* Doheny, *loc. cit.;* Vromant, *De Matrimonio,* n. 351, p. 315; Winslow, *The Pauline Privilege,* n. 138, pp. 78-79.

[88] Code Comm., 30 Dec. 1937—*AAS,* XXX (1937), 73; Bouscaren, *Canon Law Digest,* II, 172-173.

[89] Vermeersch-Creusen, *Epitome,* II, n. 435, p. 266; Vromant, *De Matrimonio,* n. 351, p. 207, nota 2; Doheny, *op. cit.,* p. 564.

[90] See *infra,* pp. 317-318.

am per publicas ephemerides ad reperiendum locum ubi coniux infidelis habitat, iisque in irritum cessis, constet ex processu saltem summario et extraiudicialiter coniugem absentem moneri legitime non posse aut monitum intra tempus in monitione praefixum suam voluntatem non significasse.

Nota ad n. XXV. Pro dispensandis infidelibus plures uxores habentibus, ut post baptismum quam ex illis maluerit, si etiam ipsa fidelis fiat, retinere possint, nisi prima voluerit converti, cfr. can. 1125.

iudicialiter, interpellatione fieri non posse sine evidenti gravis damni aut coniugi iam ad fidem converso (etsi nondum baptizato), aut christianis inferendi periculo.

These two Decennial Faculties are treated together in the present Article, because they are intimately related to each other. More precisely, these Decennial Faculties concern, in fact, one and the same power of dispensing from the interpellations, but *Facultas XXV* permits its grantees the use of the power for *Ordinary Cases,* while *Facultas XXVI* permits them to make use of it for *Extraordinary Cases.*

The common law, to which the powers granted in these two Decennial Faculties are pertinent, is Pope Gregory XIII's Constitution *Populis* of January 25, 1585, of which mention is contained in canon 1125. In fact, the Decennial Faculty n. XXV and the Constitution *Populis* are granted for one and the same purpose, which is the dissolution of the marriages contracted between two non-baptized persons in their infidelity for the new marriage of the one who has been converted and baptized; in order to attain this purpose, these faculties empower ecclesiastical authorities to dispense *in favorem fidei,* from the interpellations which are regularly required for the new marriage. For a close examination of the Decennial Faculty n. XXV and the faculty granted in the Constitution *Papulis,* they are compared by juxtaposition of their texts as follows:

The Constitution POPULIS	FACULTAS XXV
... *Dispensandi cum quibuscumque ... ad fidem conversis qui ante baptismum susceptum matrimonium contraxerunt, ut eorum quilibet, superstite coniuge infideli, et eius consensu minime requisito, aut responso non expectato, matrimonia cum quovis fideli ... contrahere et in facie Ecclesiae solemnizare ...valeant:*	... *Dispensandi super interpellatione coniugum in infidelitate relictorum in omnibus casibus ordinariis,*
	quando scilicet adhibitis antea omnibus diligentiis, etiam per publicas ephemerides ad reperiendum locum ubi coniux infidelis habitat, iisque in irritum cessis,
dummodo constet etiam summarie et extraiudicialiter, coniugem, ut praefertur, absentem moneri legitime non posse, aut monitum intra tempus in eadem monitione praefixum suam voluntatem non significasse ...	*constet ex processu etiam summario et extraiudicialiter coniugem absentem moneri legitime non posse aut monitum intra tempus in monitione praefixum suam voluntatem non significasse.*

As it appears in the foregoing comparison, the only difference between the two faculties exists in the fact that the Decennial Faculty contains the phrase, "*in omnibus casibus ordinariis,*" which the faculty granted in the Constitution lacks. As to the clause: "*quando scilicet adhibitis antea omnibus diligentiis, etiam per publicas ephemerides ad reperiendum locum ubi coniux infidelis habitat"* (provided all diligence has been used, including published notices in the papers, in order to find the place where the infidel party resides), although it is not stated in the Constitution *Populis,* it is necessary, in modern times, to comply with the same in order to verify the actually stated condition: *"absentem moneri legitime non posse,"* in the *summary and extrajudicial form* of investigation.[91]

Insofar as the phrase: *"in omnibus casibus ordinariis"* may set only a circumstantial condition, it cannot be said that the presence of the said phrase may effect any essential change in the nature of the power granted in the Constitution *Populis.* And thus it seems safe to conclude that the power granted in the Decennial Faculty n. XXV in the Formula Maior is essentially the same power which is granted in the Constitution *Populis,*[92] although there can be a circumstantial difference with reference to the cases for which the powers are to be applied.

The distinction between *Ordinary Cases* and *Extraordinary Cases* (for granting dispensations from the interpellations) was made even before the promulgation of the Code of Canon Law.[93] The former are concerned with the

[91] Questionnaire for Application to the Apostolic Delegate for a Dispensation from the Interpellations contains the following questions:

If the Infidel Spouse Cannot be Found Please Answer the Following:

17. Has the impossiblility of finding the infidel been proved at least by a *summary and extrajudical process?*
18. Has all *diligence* been used in order to find that person?
19. Was that person *advertised for in the public press?*
20. To what *extent* was the advertising done?

See Bouscaren, *Canon Law Digest,* III, 477.

[92] This view is held by Vromant, *De Matrimonio,* p. 320; Vermeersch, "De Formulis Facultatum," *Periodica,* XI (1922), p. (139); Bouscaren "art. cit.," *Miscellanea-Vermeersch,* I, 279; Bouscaren-Ellis, *Canon Law,* pp. 604-605; Sego, *op. cit.,* p. 75; Payen, *De Matrimonio in Missionibus,* II, n. 2410; Louis Ch. de Léry, *Le Privilège de la Foi* (Montréal: Ex Typis Collegii Maximi Immaculatae Conceptionis, 1938), n. 94, p. 121.

[93] S.C.S. Off., 29 Nov. 1882—*Collectanea,* n. 1581; *Fontes,* n. 1075.

circumstances when the interpellations are either impossible or useless,[94] the latter, when the interpellations could indeed be made, but to do so would result in danger to the baptized party or to Christians generally.[95]

B. FACULTAS XXV *in the* FORMULA MAIOR

1. The Marriage Which Is to Be Dissolved by Virtue of *Facultas XXV*

Regarding the kind of marriage that is subject to dissolution by virtue of the present Decennial Faculty, it is identical with the one for which the Constitution *Populis* as mentioned in canon 1125 makes provision.[96] For its first condition, the mariage must have been contracted validly between two infidels according to non-Christian or pagan marriage ceremonies. For its second essential condition, there must have supervened the physical separation of the two infidel parties of the marriage, which is quite different from the physical departure or the moral departure postulated for the use of the Pauline privilege, for the present Decennial Faculty deals with the interpellations that are to be made to the *"coniux in infidelitate relictus,"* and not of the infidel party who has departed morally or physically from the baptized party.

2. The Object of the Dispensation in the Use of the *Facultas XXV*

In the text of the present Decennial Faculty, the object of the dispensation by virtue of the same faculty is designated as the *"interpellatio,"* just as in the text of the Constitution *Populis* it is referred to under the term *"monitio,"* in place of the word *"interpellationes"* of canon 1121. With the term *"interpellatio"* in Facultas XXV, as the word

[94] Benedictus XIV, *De Synodo*, lib. XIII, cap. 21; S.C.S. Off., 8 Iun. 1836; 18 Iun. 1884; 4 Febr. 1891—*Collectanea*, n. 848; 1620; 1746. Cf. Payen, *De Matrimonio in Missionibus*, II, n. 2413.

[95] S.C.S. Off., 29 Nov. 1882—*Fontes*, n. 1075. See also *Collectanea*, n. 1499; *Fontes*, n. 1057.

[96] *Supra*, pp. 296-297.

"monitio" in the Constitution *Populis,* there is made a direct reference to the interpellation *"an sine contumelia Creatoris secum cohabitare velint,"* but this direct reference carries with it also an implied reference to the earlier interpellation *"an velit et ipsa converti ac baptismum suscipere,"* of canon 1121, § 1, 1°. So the power of dispensing is the same regardless of the possible dual source. The faculty *"dispensandi super interpellatione coniugum in infidelitate relictorum"* envisions the power, by virtue of the Decennial Faculty XXV, to grant a dispensation from both of the interpellations when the postulated conditions are present.[97]

Thus, when the condition, *"coniugem absentem moneri legitime non posse,"* has been verified after the requisite procedural investigation, there becomes available the faculty to dispense the baptized party from making any interpellations, *"an velit et ipsa [pars non-baptizata] converti ac baptismum suscipere,"* and *"an sine contumelia Creatoris secum cohabitare velit,"* and at the same time to declare formally and officially that the baptized party may lawfully enter into a new marriage with a Catholic. On the other hand, when the condition, *"monitum intra tempus in monitione praefixum suam voluntatem non significasse,"* has been verified after the prescribed form of investigation, then the use of the faculty will involve simply the formal and official declaration to the baptized party of the right to lawfully contract a new marriage with a Catholic. In the latter case there is no dispensation from the interpellations in the proper sense, for the *"monitio,"* i.e., the *"interpellatio,"* has preceded, and the lack of a response remains to be interpreted as a negative reply.[98]

3. Conditions Requisite for the Use of *Facultas XXV*

Regarding the conditions for or the circumstances in which, a dispensation from the interpellations is granted

[97] Winslow, *The Apostolic Faculties,* p. 153; Burton, *A Commentary on Canon 1125,* pp. 167-172, *passim;* Sego, *Dispensation from the Interpellations,* p. 148.

[98] Cf. canon 1121, § 1.

by virtue of the present Decennial Faculty, *ordinary cases* arise from such circumstances in which the making of the interpellations is physically or morally impossible[99] or useless.[100]

The physical or moral impossibility of making the interpellations in consequence of the extant condition, *"coniugem absentem moneri legitime non posse,"* ordinarily exists: (1) when the exact whereabouts of the infidel party is entirely unknown; (2) when a long and difficult journey is necessary for the making of the interpellations, and great expense and serious inconvenience are both involved; (3) when communication with the infidel party is impossible because of the barbarous and warlike nature of the region where the infidel party is residing,[101] or also (4) when the infidel party, upon becoming acquainted with the plan of his converted spouse and the purpose of the interpellations, deliberately and purposely goes into hiding in order to deprive the baptized party or his agent of any and every opportunity to make the interpellations.[102]

The interpellations are to be considered *useless* when it is sufficiently established "[*absentem coniugem*] *monitum intra tempus in monitione praefixum suam voluntatem non significasse.*"[103] Further, by a number of authors it is held that, when there is a well-founded basis for suspecting the

[99] Vromant, *De Matrimonio*, nn. 357-358, pp. 320-321; Sego, *op. cit.*, pp. 157-166; Winslow, *The Apostolic Faculties*, p. 153; Payen, *De Matrimonio in Missionibus*, II, n. 2409; Paventi, *Brevis Commentarius*, p. 44; Vromant, *Facultates Apostolicae*, n. 80, p. 80.

[100] S.C.S. Off., 8 Iun. 1836; 18 Iun. 1884; Febr. 1891—*Collectanea*, nn. 848, 1620, 1746. Cf. Payen, *De Matrimonio in Missionibus*, II, n. 2413; Vromant, *De Matrimonio*, n. 357, p. 320.

[101] These circumstances are mentioned in the Constitution *Populis*. Cf. Sego, *op. cit.*, pp. 157-166, *passim*.

[102] Winslow, *The Pauline Privilege*, n. 67, p. 36; Conte a Coronata, *De Sacramentis*, III, n. 637, p. 891; Cappello, *De Matrimonio*, n. 780, p. 770; Sego, *op. cit.*, p. 165.

[103] Vromant, *De Matrimonio*, n. 359, p. 321; Vromant, *Facultates Apostolicae*, n. 80, pp. 80-81; Paventi, *Brevis Commentarius*, p. 44; Sartori, *Iuris Missionarii Elementa*, pp. 115-116; Vermeersch, "De Formulis Facultatum," *Periodica*, XI (1922), p. (140).

sincerity of the infidel party in his reply to the "*monitio,*" then there exists the uselessness of the making of the "*monitio.*"[104] A practical and valid example of the uselessness of the "*monitio*" is found when the infidel party has after a civil divorce entered a second civil marriage and in doing so has completely alienated himself from the former spouse who is now a Catholic.

Beyond the factors which connote the presence of some physical or moral condition of impossibility and uselessness of making the interpellations, it is further acknowledged that the Holy See may readily dispense from the obligation of making the interpellations in all cases wherein the fulfilling of the formality would be futile and therefore unnecesary. Now, the interpellations are futile whenever the infidel party is incapable of performing a human act in consequence of insanity, and this futility of making the interpellations is held equal to the uselessness of the same as far as the sufficiency of the cause for the use of the present Decennial Faculty is concerned.[105]

4. The Summary and Extrajudicial Investigation of the Case

The mere presence of a sufficient cause will not satisfy the condition required for the valid use of the present Decennial Faculty. The Holy See has continually warned bishops, vicars apostolic, and others who have the faculty of dispensing from the interpellations, whether by special grant or in consequence of the universal law, that they may not act upon an assumption no matter how well it may be

[104] Cappello, *De Matrimonio*, nn. 770 and 780, pp. 762 and 769; Doheny, *Informal Procedure*, p. 575; Woeber, *The Interpellations*, p. 117; Vermeersch-Creusen, *Epitome*, II, n. 437, p. 304; Conte a Coronata, *De Sacramentis*, III, n. 652, p. 911; Sego, *op. cit.*, pp. 167-168.

[105] S.C. de Prop. Fide, 5 Mart. 1787—*Collectanea*, n. 589, ad 1. Cf. Payen, *De Matrimonio in Missionibus*, II, n. 2413; Vromant, *De Matrimonio*, n. 363, p. 287; Paventi, *loc. cit.;* De Reeper, *A Missionary Companion*, p. 103.

founded,[106] and has consequently required that a summary and extrajudicial, but nevertheless careful, investigation be made concerning the sufficiency of the reasons which warrant the granting of the dispensation from the interpellations. Such a summary and extrajudicial investigation is prescribed expressly and in an unmistakable statement also in the case of the use of the present Decennial Faculty.

Before the baptized party can prove the impossibility, whether physical or moral, of making the *"monitio,"* inasmuch as the exact whereabouts of the infidel party is entirely unknown to him, he must first prove that he has used all diligence, as far as possible, including the publication of notices in the papers, in order to find the place where his infidel party is residing.[107] This condition, namely, to make at least a summary and extrajudicial investigation, originated in the Constitution *Populis* of Pope Gregory XIII, and thenceforth became a standard and accepted prerequisite for the use of the power of dispensing from the the interpellations. And such a summary and extrajudicial process of investigation is necessary for the validity of the dispensation from the interpellations by virtue of the present Decennial Faculty.[108]

The summary and extrajudicial investigation referred to in the Decennial Faculty will consist in ascertaining the

[106] S.C.S. Off., 23 Nov. 1796—*Fontes,* n. 825; *Collectanea,* n. 425; S.C.S. Off., instr., 11 Iun. 1760—*Fontes,* n. 811. Cf. Burton, *op. cit.,* p. 125, note n. 26; Gasparri, *De Matrimonio,* II, 224.

[107] Cf. (Private) S.C.S. Off. (Detroit), 22 Maii 1947—Prot. n. 1026/47 and Letter of Apostolic Delegate to Ordinaries of the United States, 17 July, 1935—No. 116/35. Cf. also Questionnaire for Application to Apostolic Delegate for Dispensation from Interpellations (Apostolic Delegation, U.S.) (Private), questions nn. 16-20 in Bouscaren, *Canon Law Digest,* III, 477.

[108] Vromant, *De Matrimonio,* n. 360, pp. 321-322; Vromant, *Facultates Apostolicae,* n. 81, p. 81; Conte a Coronata, *De Sacramentis,* III, n. 649, p. 907. Cf. S.C.S. Off., instr. (ad Superiorem Mission, Peguan.), 11 Iun. 1760—*Fontes,* n. 811. According to Sartori, the summary and extrajudicial process is necessary only for the lawfullness of the dispensation. See his *Iuris Missionarii Elementa,* p. 116.

facts of the case with all truthfulness relative to the physical or moral impossibility, the uselessness, or the futility, of making the *"monitio,"* after the use of all diligence on the part of the baptized party to find the infidel party, after a careful analysis of the attendant circumstances, and after a judicious appraisal of the statements regarding the alleged facts looking to the sufficiency of the reason for, and also to the necessity of, the granting of a dispensation from the making of the *"monitio."* When this summary and extrajudicial investigation has been completed, it should be reflected in writing, but this is required only for the lawfulness of the dispensation.[109] The written record of the investigation should be kept in the archives of the chancery of the residence of the convert to whose advantage the dispensation was granted.[110]

C. FACULTAS XXVI *in the* FORMULA MAIOR

1. The Relation of *Facultas XXVI* to the Preceding Decennial Faculty

The power granted in the Decennial Faculty XXVI in the *Formula Maior* is the same power which is granted in the preceding Decennial Faculty XXV in the sense that both faculties concern a grant of the power, as originally imparted in the Constitution *Populis,* for dispensing from the interpellations for the dissolution of a legitimate marriage between two infidels who subsequently have been separated, and one of whom is becoming a Catholic.

The basic difference between the two faculties lies in the fact that, while the power granted in the preceding faculty is operative in all *ordinary cases,* the power as granted in the present Decennial Faculty is to be used in *extraordinary cases,* which are described by means of the text *"siquidem*

[109] Vromant, *De Matrimonio,* n. 361, p. 322; Vromant, *Facultates Apostolicae,* n. 82, p. 81; Vermeersch, "De Formulis Facultatum," *Periodica,* XI (1922), p. (140).

[110] Vromant, *De Matrimonio, loc. cit.;* Vromant, *Facultates Apostolicae, loc. cit.;* Sego, *op. cit.,* p. 182.

certo constiterit . . . interpellationem fieri non posse sine evidenti gravi damni aut coniugi iam ad fidem converso (etsi nondum baptizato), aut christianis inferendi periculo." In other words, while the former faculty is operative in cases wherein physical or moral impossibility, or uselessness, or futility, in the making of the interpellations exists, the latter is operative in cases wherein the impossibility of making the interpellations derives solely from the danger of grave harm.

The condition that the converted party use all diligence to find the place where the infidel party is residing plays no role in the case of the present Decennial Facutly. In fact, it is supposed that the converted party knows the place where the infidel party is residing, and, further, knows that the danger of grave harm will certainly arise, if the infidel party be asked whether he is willing to live peacefully with the converted party. Another distinctive feature of the present Decennial Faculty is the fact that its power is also operative, by virtue of the phrase *"etsi nondum baptizato,"* even for non-baptized converted persons, who are still under instruction for their baptism and will certainly be baptized.

2. The Condition for the Use of *Facultas XXVI*

The condition for the use of the present Decennial Faculty is the impossibility of making the interpellations in view of the danger of grave harm. From the text of the present Decennial Faculty itself it is evident that the source of the grave danger of harm must arise from the very making of the interpellations, although it might proceed from the evil will of the infidel party himself, or from that of his relatives or associates.[111] The subject (or subjects) suffering the grave danger of harm is (or are) the converted party, even though he has not yet been baptized, or Christians in general. By those Christians are meant, not indeed all or even many of the Christians of the region where the

[111] Vromant, *De Matrimonio,* n. 363, p. 323; Sego, *Dispensation from the Interpellations,* p. 169.

converted party is residing, but simply any small number of Christians.[112]

For the application of the present Decennial Faculty, the said danger of grave harm must be seen to impend for positive manifest and evident reasons, and not merely as a matter of probable conjecture, or of some fear that lacks a foundation. However, it is not required that the grave harm itself be certain; it suffices that one be morally certain that the danger of grave harm is present.[113] The danger of the harm must be such as to be unavoidable, i.e., such as cannot readily be overcome or obviated.[114]

The grave harm envisioned in the present Decennial Faculty may be physical, or spiritual, or mixed in character.[115] The threatening danger which warrants the granting of a dispensation from the interpellations by virtue of the present Decennial Faculty would definitely be present if it imperiled life, but also a danger that threatens one's personal liberty or endangers one's personal fortune can be regarded as constituting a danger of grave harm.[116]

The danger of serious spiritual harm would exist when by answering affirmatively the infidel party sought either to prevent the convert from applying the favor of the Pauline privilege, or to resume the conjugal relationship with the convert for the purpose of using it as an occasion to work harm to the convert's (or Christians') faith or morals.[117] If the making of the interpellations would run the

[112] Vromant, *loc. cit.;* Sego, *loc. cit.;* Sartori, *Iuris Missionarii Elementa,* p. 117.

[113] S.C.S. Off., 23 Nov. 1769—*Fontes,* n. 825; 29 Nov. 1882—*Fontes,* n. 1075; *Collectanea,* n. 1581. Cf. Vermeersch, "De Formulis Facultatum," *Periodica,* XI (1922), p. (140); Sartori, *loc. cit.;* Vromant, *loc. cit.;* Paventi, *Brevis Commentarius,* p. 45; Sego, *op. cit.,* p. 170.

[114] S.C.S. Off., 11 Iul. 1886—*Fontes,* n. 996; *Collectanea,* n .1295. Cf. Paventi, *loc. cit.;* Winslow, *The Apostolic Faculties,* p. 157.

[115] Sartori, *loc. cit.;* Paventi, *loc. cit.*

[116] Doheny, *Informal Procedure,* p. 532; Sego, *op. cit.,* p. 169; Vromant, *loc. cit.*

[117] Payen, *De Matrimonio in Missionibus,* II, n. 2414; Vermeersch-Creusen, *Epitome,* II, n. 434, p. 300; Cappello, *De Matrimonio,* n. 781, p. 771; Sego, *op. cit.,* p. 169.

risk of promoting a general outbreak of persecution against the Christians of a given locality, this danger would stand as a sufficient reason for granting the dispensation from the interpellations in view of the danger of grave spiritual harm.[118]

The case involving a convert who has not yet received baptism would obtain when the making of the interpellations would precipitate an infidel husband's proposal or intent to sell or trade his wife, or give rise to a real danger of perversion for the Christian, who upon affirmative replies to the interpellations might be forced to return to cohabitation with the infidel party.[119]

3. The Summary and Extrajudicial Investigation of the Case

The mere existence of the impossibility of making of the interpellations in view of the danger of grave harm does not warrant the granting of the dispensation from the interpellations by virtue of the present Decennial Faculty. The impossibility must be proved to be real, manifest, evident, and unavoidable by way of positive reasons implemented through at least a summary and extrajudicial procedure.

Since for the use of the present Decennial Faculty it is supposed that the converted party well knows the place where the infidel party is residing, and the fact also that there exists the danger of grave harm from the same infidel party, the use of all diligence to find the place where the infidel party is residing, in order to ask him whether he is willing to live peacefully with the converted party, is not called for. Hence these two inquiries do not form part of the procedure preparatory to the application of the Decennial Faculty XXVI in the *Formula Maior*.

[118] Ayrinhac-Lydon, *Marriage Legislation*, p. 312; Sego, *loc. cit.*

[119] A. L. Eloy, *Compendium Theologiae Moralis* (3 vols., Hong-Kong, 1929). III, n. 619; Winslow, *The Apostolic Faculties*, pp. 157-158.

The proceedings in the summary and extrajudicial investigation, therefore, will comprise the following: the converted party and two witnesses are to appear before the ordinary, or the judge, or a duly delegated priest, and to make depositions in regard to the conversion of the party who asks this favor, the marriage which is to be dissolved, the existence, nature, and characteristics of the danger of harm to arise from the infidel party if the interpellations are made, etc. The converted party and his witnesses should under oath offer their despositions, which must be taken down by the notary. At the end of questioning they should sign their statements, and then take the oath *de veritate dictorum et de secreto servando.*[120] Upon a careful analysis of the depositions, of the circumstances related to the case, of the documents presented in the procedure, of the characters of the converted party, the infidel party, and the witnesses, etc., the ordinary (or the priest) should appraise the facts for their truthfulness and weigh the reasons for their sufficiency before he grants a dispensation from the making of the interpellations; when the ordinary or the priest has reached a judgment in favor of the converted party, he should issue a decree authorizing the converted party to omit totally the interpellations, and to proceed to the second marriage with a Catholic.

All the acts of the case together with the judgment of the ordinary or of the priest delegated by him should be committed to writing, and there should be listed briefly all the reasons that warrant the dispensation from the interpellations. The complete and authentic record of the entire case, signed by the ordinary or by the delegated priest and the notary, is to be filed in the archives of the diocese, and the proper notations are to be made in the baptismal and matrimonial registers.[121]

[120] Canons 1623, § 3; 1767, § 1; 1780. Cf. Doheny, *Informal Procedure,* p. 528; Woeber, *The Interpellations,* p. 79; Payen, *De Matrimonio in Missionibus,* II, n. 2362.

[121] Doheny, *loc. cit.;* Sego, *op. cit.,* p. 181.

Article IV. Dispensation from the Interpellations for the Dissolution of Marriages Contracted by Non-Baptized Polygamists

Section 1. *Nota ad Facultatem XXV* in the *Formula Maior*

In both *Formulae,* no faculty for dispensing from the interpellations for a dissolution of marriages contracted by non-baptized polygamists is included. There is, however, a *Nota ad Facultatem XXV* in the *Formula Maior,* which reads as follows:

> *Pro dispensandis infidelibus plures uxores habentibus, ut post baptismum quam ex illis maluerint, si etiam ipsa fidelis fiat, retinere possit, nisi prima voluerit converti, cfr. can. 1125.*[122]

Although this *Nota,* if considered in its context, is immediately related to the Constitution *Romani Pontificis* mentioned in canon 1125, commentators of the *Formulae* of the Decennial Faculties agree that in consequence of the present *Nota* two Constitutions which deal with the dispensing from the interpellations for the dissolution of marriages contracted by non-baptized polygamists and which are mentioned in canon 1125, i.e., the Constitution *Altitudo* of Pope Paul III and the Constitution *Romani Pontificis* of Pope St. Pius V, are drawn into the scope of the Decennial Faculties in both *Formulae,* the *Maior* and the *Minor.*[123] Missionaries who are canonically neither pastors nor quasi-pastors are not *ipso iure* competent in the cases which call for the use of the privileges granted in the Constitutions

[122] This is *Nota ad Facultatem n. 24* in the *Formula Minor.*

[123] Paventi, *Brevis Commentarius,* pp. 42-43; Sartori, *Iuris Missionarii Elementa,* p. 115; De Reeper, *A Missionary Companion,* p. 81; Vermeersch, "De Formulis Facultatum," *Periodica,* XI (1922), pp. (138)-(139). As a matter of fact, in consequence of the *Nota ad Facultatem XXV* all three Constitutions mentioned in canon 1125 are drawn into the scope of the Decennial Faculties in both *Formulae,* the *Maior* and the *Minor,* but *Facultas XXV* itself grants the very faculties imparted in the Constitution *Populis,* which likewise receives mention in canon 1125.

that receive mention in canon 1125.[124] Thus, missionaries who enjoy *Facultas XXV* in the *Formula Maior* or *Facultas* n. 24 in the *Formula Minor* enjoy also the faculties granted in the Constitutions mentioned in canon 1125, but they must use these faculties in the light of the Decennial Faculty (n. XXV in *Formula Maior*, or n. 24 in the *Formula Minor*) and its *Nota*.

As to the nature of the *Nota ad Facultatem XXV* in the *Formula Maior*, it is by no means constituted as a new faculty in the *Formula*, different from the privilege contained in the Constitution *Romani Pontificis*, to which the *Nota* is immediately related. This is clear from its form of incorporation in the *Formula* and from the text itself. Being a mere *Nota*, it does indicate the *mens* of the Sacred Congregation, which is the immediate source of Decennial Faculty n. XXV in the *Formula Maior*, and thus it cannot change substantially the nature, the essential favors, and the conditions attaching to the use of the privilege granted to the Constitution *Romani Pontificis*.

SECTION 2. THE CONSTITUTION *Altitudo* OF POPE PAUL III[125]

The beneficiaries of the privilege recounted in the Constitution *Altitudo* are the baptized converts who before conversion had many wives. These wives are defined in the text of the Constitution as those who according to the custom of the people of a given region are considered to be, or at some time to have been, wives in the true sense. Hence all other than wives, i.e., concubines who are legally and socially recognized as such in certain regions, or women who publicly or secretly cohabit with a man without the consent essential to true marriage, etc., are excluded from the scope of the term "wives."[126]

[124] Code Comm., resp. 26 Ian. 1919—*Sylloge*, n. 66. Cf. Burton, *A Commentary on Canon 1125*, pp. 35-37; 49-53; 172-176.

[125] For the text of this Constitution, see *Codex Iuris Canonici, Documentum VI;* for the detailed historical background of the issuance of this Constitution, see Burton, *A Commentary on Canon 1125*, pp. 30-44.

[126] Cf. Burton, *op. cit.*, pp. 38-39.

The converts who before their conversion had many wives were in all likelihood simultaneous polygamists, but in practice the Constitution makes no distinction between simultaneous and successive polygamists.[127] By reason of the equity inherent in law, the Constitution is applicable also for baptized women converts who before their conversion simultaneously or successively had many husbands.[128]

The actual privilege granted in the Constitution *Altitudo* consists in the fact that the polygamist convert can take from among his wives the one whom he wishes, in order to contract marriage with her. The latter can be any of his present or previous wives, even though she is, and wants to remain, pagan, and although perhaps another of his wives is willing to receive baptism. For such a marriage, a dispensation from the impediment of disparity of cult is not necessary, since it is granted through the Constitution itself,[129] and likewise no necessity exists for any dispensation from the interpellations.[130] Even if the woman whom the convert has selected for his wife be related to him in the third degree of consanguinity in the collateral line, he can marry her without the need of any separate dispensation.[131]

The essential condition for the application of the privilege granted in the Constitution *Altitudo* is the fact that the polygamist convert is unable to recall whom he married first (*"qui ante conversionem plures iuxta eorum mores habebant uxores, et non recordantur quam primo acceperint"*). This is a condition which is postulated for the valid application of the privilege to the extent that a marriage

[127] S.C. de Prop. Fide, 14 Ian. 1806—*Collectanea,* n. 685. Cf. Vromant, *De Matrimonio,* n. 341, p. 304; Conte a Coronata, *De Sacramentis,* III, n. 647, p. 904.

[128] S.C.S. Off., 5 Sept. 1855—*Collectanea,* n. 1117.

[129] S.C.S. Off. (Private reply), 30 Iun. 1937—Bouscaren, *Canon Law Digest,* III, 480-481. Cf. Vromant, *De Matrimonio,* n. 343, p. 305.

[130] Wernz-Vidal, *Ius Matrimoniale,* n. 633, pp. 826 ff.; Vromant, *loc. cit.*

[131] Canon 1076. The Constitution also mentions the third degree of affinity in the collateral line, but this degree no longer involves the presence of any matrimonial impediment. Cf. canon 1077.

contracted under the pretext of this privilege between the polygamist convert and any of his wives other than the first is null if he can unmistakably recall whom of the various wives he married first.[132] Thus, when the polygamist convert recalls whom he married first, he is to retain her and dismiss the others, unless the circumstances in any particular case will permit the application of the privilege stated in the Constitution *Romani Pontificis* of Pope St. Pius V.[133]

With the reference to his marriage with the wife he has chosen, the Constitution requires that the convert marriage *per verba de praesenti* with the chosen woman, i.e., the marriage must take place just as a new marriage, with the formal exchange of the matrimonial consent in the due canonical form.[134]

In the Constitution no specific procedure is prescribed for authorizing the valid and licit application of the privilege. However, the ordinary or the priest must have moral certainty of the fact that the polygamist convert is unable to recall whom he married first, after employing all possible reasonable means to establish it. In order to establish this moral certainty, the ordinary or the priest may interrogate the polygamist convert himself, his wives, and their relatives, separately, check the marriage registers in the civil courts or offices if there be any, etc. The authorization of the application of the privilege may be given orally or in writing.

When the second marriage by virtue of the privilege granted in the Constitution *Altitudo* becomes a disparate marriage, the *cautiones* or the *guarantees* normally prescribed for such a marriage in canons 1061 and 1071 are not required for the validity of the marriage,[135] but the

[132] Conte a Coronata, *De Sacramentis*, III, n. 647, p. 904.

[133] Also cf. canon 1127.

[134] Conte a coronata, *loc. cit.*

[135] S.C.S. Off., 18 Dec. 1872—*Collectanea*, n. 1392; S.C.S. Off., 9 Dec. 1874—*Collectanea*, n. 1427; Bouscaren, *Canon Law Digest*, III, 480-481.

divine law itself requires, for licitness, moral certainty that there will be no danger of perversion on the part of the infidel party,[136] and the convert must before his baptism acknowledge the obligation, though he need not furnish any formal guarantees.

After the marriage, the application of the privilege of the Constitution *Altitudo* is to be recorded in the parish baptismal and matrimonial registers.

SECTION 3. THE CONSTITUTION *Romani Pontifiicis* OF POPE ST. PIUS V[137]

The Constitution *Romani Pontifici* of Pope St. Pius V, under date of August 2, 1571, was not specifically addressed to the bishops of any determined territory, but rather it had reference to the class of converts who could be included under the general term *"Indi."*[138] This Constitution sought to simplify the procedure which was required for the dissolution of the marriages of polygamous converts.[139]

The beneficiaries of the privilege granted in the Constitution *Romani Pontificis* are the polygamist converts who in their infidelity have been allowed by law or by the custom of the region to have several non-baptized wives, and who are now converted to the faith and intend to marry one of their wives who has also been baptized with them (*"ut baptizati, et in futurum baptizandi, cum uxore, quae cum ipsis fuerit batpizata et baptizabitur, remanere valeant tamquam cum uxore legitima . . ."*). The polygamist mentioned in this Constitution is a person involved either in polygamy

[136] Bouscaren-Ellis, *Canon Law,* p. 601.

[137] For the text of this Constitution, see *Codex Iuris Canonici, Documentum, VII.*

[138] For the meaning of *"Indi,"* see Burton, *op. cit.,* pp. 49-53.

[139] For the study of this Constitution, cf. Woods, *The Constitutions of Canon 1125;* Burton, *op. cit.;* Wernz-Vidal, *Ius Matrimoniale,* nn. 633-638, pp. 826-840; *Periodica,* XX (1931), pp. 108* ff.; *Periodica,* XXVII 1938), pp. 295 ff.; *Periodica,* XXVIII (1939), pp. 24-52; Winslow, *The Pauline Privilege,* pp. 62-75; Winslow, "The Application of the Pauline Privilege," *The Jurist,* X (1950), 304-333; Vromant, *De Matrimonio,* nn. 340-345, pp. 301-312.

or in polyandry,[140] regardless of the fact that this polygamy is simultaneous or successive.[141]

The substance of the privilege as granted in the Constitution *Romani Pontifici* can be summed up thus: Without the need of making the interpellations the polygamist convert can remain licitly and validly in marriage with one of his past or present wives who receives baptism with him, if it prove harsh for him to be separated from this baptized wife. In consequence of this marriage, the natural bond of the other marriages becomes dissolved.

The special conditions postulated for the application of the privilege granted in the Constitution *Romani Pontificis* are conversion and baptism of the polygamist convert's prospective wife, and the serious hardship a separation of the two would entail. As to the first condition, the prospective wife must be one of the convert's several wives with whom he exchanged matrimonial consent in their infidelity; the prospective wife must be the one who has been baptized or will receive baptism along with the polygamist convert ("... *cum uxore, quae cum ipso fuerit baptizata et baptizabitur*").[142] But, it is not necessary that the prospective wife receive her baptism at the very time the polygamist convert receives his, for it suffices that her baptism take place before the marriage which she can enter by virtue of the privilege granted in the Constitution *Romani Pontifiicis.*

The second condition postulated for the application of the privilege granted in the Constitution *Romani Pontificis* is present when it is very harsh for the polygamist convert to be separated from his wife who has received baptism with him.[143] There is no specification of the source from

[140] Conte a Coronata, *De Sacramentis,* III, n. 648, pp. 904-905; Vromant, *De Matrimonio,* n. 344, p. 307; Burton, *op. cit.,* p. 152.

[141] S.C. de Prop. Fide, 14 Ian. 1806—*Collectanea,* n. 685. Cf. Vromant, *loc. cit.;* Burton, *loc. cit.;* Vermeersch-Creusen, *Epitome,* II, n. 436, p. 307; Conte a Coronata, *loc. cit.;* Bouscaren-Ellis, *Canon Law,* pp. 602-603.

[142] Cf. Vromant, *De Matrimonio,* n. 344, ad b), p. 308.

[143] Puthota Rayanna, "De Constitutione S. Pii Papae V *Romani*

which the hardship must arise. The hardship of a separation between the two converts could result in view of the especial love that exists between them, in consideration of the children born of them and the absence of children in the other unions, the husband's abhorence for his first wife in such a manner that his cohabitation with her would bar his conversion or keep him from embracing the means of salvation, etc.

Thus, when the two conditions are verified, i.e., a valid baptism on the part of the polygamist convert's prospective wife and the presence of the serious hardship of a separation between the two converts, of which conditions the former is absolutely required for the valid application of the privilege here in consideration, the ordinary or his delegate can declare the right for the contracting of a valid and licit marriage between the two converts, absolutely and apart from all use of the interpellations.[144]

It has been a controverted problem whether the privilege enunciated in the Constitution *Romani Pontificis* is applicable also in cases wherein the polygamist convert well knows whom among his wifes he married first, knows too that he can interpellate her, and knows finally that she likewise sincerely wishes to receive baptism and to live with him, but there exists at the same time a serious hardship for him to separate from the one, other than the first wife, who is to receive baptism with him.

When this case is considered in the light of the text of the Constitution itself, it could logically be concluded that

Pontificis, (3 [2?] Augusti,1571)," *Periodica*, XXVIII (1939), 199-202; Burton, *op. cit.*, pp. 155-156; Doheny, *Informal Procedure*, p. 554; Vromant, *De Matrimonio*, n. 344, ad 3, p. 307; Conte a Coronata, *loc. cit.*

[144] S.C. de Prop. Fide (Private), 1924; *Primum Concilium Sinense, Vota et Postulata*, n. 12, p. 273. Cf. de Léry, *Le Privilège da la Foi*, p. 108; Cappello, *De Matrimonio*, n. 787, p. 776; Burton, *op. cit.*, pp. 156-157; note 14; Vromant, *De Matrimonio*, n. 345, p. 309. Cf. also S.C.S. Off. (Private), 27 Martii 1952; S.C.S. de Prop. Fide, 8 Apr. 1951—Prot, n. 341/51; Bouscaren, *Canon Law Digest*, III, 478-479.

since no restriction is spefiically invoked, there is also not present any reason for considering the privilege inapplicable in such a case. From this interpretation of the privilege granted in the Constitution *Romani Pontificis* authors such as Cappello, Conte a Coronata, Doheny and Rayanna further assert that even if the first wife of the polygamist convert spontaneously declares her will to receive baptism or has already been baptized, the polygamist convert can avail himself of the privilege granted in the Constitution *Romani Pontificis,* provided that he cannot without serious hardship separate from the one of his wives, other than the first wife, who is to receive baptism with him.[145] But the authorities in the missions who can declare the use of the privilege granted in the Constitution *Romani Pontificis* should follow the *mens* of the Holy See which is expressed in the terms of a *Nota ad Facultatem* XXV, in the *Formula Maior.* The *Nota,* which reads: *"Pro dispensandis infidelibus plures uxores habentibus, ut post baptismum quam ex illis maluerint, si etiam ipsa fidelis fiat, retinere possint, nisi prima voluerit converti, cfr. can. 1125,"* is immediately related to the Constitution *Romani Pontificis,* and thus does indicate the *mens,* i.e., a directive force in the applying of the privilege here in consideration, especially in view of the controverted question. Hence, by the force of the clause: *"nisi prima voluerit converti,"* when the first wife of the polygamist convert has already been baptized or sincerely wishes to receive baptism and to live with him, the polygamist convert should accept her as his lawful wife after his baptism, even if there exists the hardship for him to be separated from the one, other than the first wife, who is to receive baptism with him.[146]

[145] Cappello, *De Matrimonio,* n. 787, ad 4, pp. 776-777; Conte a Coronata, *De Sacramentis,* III, n. 648, p. 906; Doheny, *Informal Procedure,* p. 556, ad 8; Rayanna, "art. cit.," *Periodica,* XXVII (1939), 50-52.

[146] Vromant, *De Matrimonio,* n, 345 *bis,* pp. 311-312; Vermeersch-Creusen, *Epitome,* II, n. 436, p. 307; Wernz-Vidal, *Ius Matrimoniale,* n. 635, note 87, p. 830; Burton, *op. cit.,* pp. 158-162; Payen, *De Matri-*

However, the polygamist convert is not bound to make the interpellations as a means of ascertaining whether or not his first wife wants to be converted and to be baptized, in order to avail himself of the privilege granted in the Constitution *Romani Pontificis.* For, in the light of the Constitution as they are set, the interpellations are not required at all for the application of the privilege. Hence, if there is no spontaneous expression of her desire for baptism on the part of his first wife, the polygamist convert may on his own initiative make use of the privilege without any interpellation.[147]

The verification of the baptism of the two, i.e., the polygamist convert and his prospective wife,[148] and, in the event that the latter is not the former first wife, of the absence of baptism on the part of the first wife,[149] are required for the valid use of the privilege granted in the Constitution *Romani Pontificis.* In addition to the foregoing, there should be inquiries on the presence of any serious hardship in consequence of the separation of the two, and on the absence of the first wife's desire to receive baptism. No fixed form of procedure in this matter is anywhere prescribed. However, in consideration of the procedure prescribed in the Decennial Faculties nn. XXV, XXVI, and XXVII, the summary and extraordinary procedure is recommended as a means to be used preparatory to the application of the privilege here in question.[150]

In all cases, whether the spouse of the polygamist convert is his first wife, or one of his wives other than his first, the renewal of a proper matrimonial consent must be made

monio in Missionibus, II, n. 2407; Sartori, *Iuris Missionarii Elementa,* p. 115; Paventi, *Brevis Commentarius,* p. 43.

[147] Winslow, *The Pauline Privilege,* n. 124, p. 72; De Reeper, *A Missionary Companion,* p. 92-93; Vromant, *eD Matrimonio,* nn. 345-345 bis, pp. 309-312.

[148] Conte a Coronata, *De Sacramentis,* III, n. 648, p. 906.

[149] "Non est locus applicationi Constitutionis, si prima sit iam baptizata aut rite interpellata declaret se velle baptizari."—Vromant, *De Matrimonio,* n. 345 *bis.* pp. 311-312.

[150] Vromant, *De Matrimonio,* n. 345 *bis,* p. 312.

according to the required canonical form, and prior to this renewal all other former wives are to be dismissed. A proper record must be entered in the baptismal and matrimonial registers in the parish or quasi-parish or mission residential station, and a record of the case should be properly made and kept in the diocesan or quasi-diocesan archives of the polygamist convert's local ordinary.

CHAPTER VIII

FACULTAS XXVIII: FACULTY TO IMPART THE SOLEMN NUPTIAL BLESSING OUTSIDE OF MASS

> *Impertiendi benedictionem nuptialem extra Missam aut preces recitandi iuxta formulas quae in Appendice Ritualis Romani continentur.*

This is a faculty by virtue of which the mission ordinary and his missionaries, when the latter are properly subdelegated, may impart the solemn nuptial blessing outside of Mass, or recite certain prayers in place of the solemn nuptial blessing, according to the formulae prescribed in the Appendix in the *Rituale Romanum*. This is *Facultas n. 27* in the *Formula Minor*, in both *Formulae* allows of subdelegation. The Quinquennial Faculties, *Formula IV*, contain a similar faculty, which is granted by the Congregation of Sacred Rites, and reads as follows:

> 5. *To bless marriages outside of Mass, or recite prayers over the couple, according to approved formulae with power to subdelegate.*[1]

SECTION 1. *Ex Iure*

The laws in the Code governing the solemn nuptial blessing are stated in canons 1101 and 1108, of which the former rules on the duty of the pastor to give the solemn nuptial blessing, on the forms and the manner for the imparting of the solemn nuptial blessing, and on the competence required for the imparting of the solemn nuptial blessing, and the latter, on the season and days when it is not allowed to impart the solemn nuptial blessing.

According to the rules prescribed in canon 1101, the solemn nuptial blessing is to be imparted only at Mass, either

[1] Bouscaren, *Canon Law Digest*, IV, 77.

in the votive Mass *pro sponsis* or in the Mass of the day with the observance of the special rubric, except during the forbidden time; it is imparted as a rule at the Mass for the marriage, but it could still be imparted even after the couple has lived a long time in the married state. The pastor should see to it that the parties of the marriage receive the solemn nuptial blessing at their marriage; the solemn nuptial blessing can be imparted by that priest alone who can validly and licitly assist at the marriage, either in person or through his delegate.

As to the form of the solemn nuptial blessing, there are two ordinary forms and an extraordinary form. The first ordinary form of the solemn nuptial blessing is imparted during the votive Mass *pro sponsis,* and consists of the votive Mass prayers and three additional prayers, of which two are said by the priest standing at the Epistle side of the altar, facing the bride and groom immediately after the *Pater noster;* and the third at the center of the altar, facing the bride and the groom, after the *Benedicamus Domino.* The second ordinary form has to be used when a Mass other than the votive Mass *pro sponsis* must be said according to the rubrics, and consists of exactly the same prayers, the oration, secret, and postcommunion of the Mass *pro sponsis* being added to those of the day *sub unica conclusione,* and the three special prayers being said in the same way as above described for the first ordinary form, except that the last one follows the *Ite, Missa est.*[2] The extraordinary form is used when by virtue of an apostolic indult the solemn nuptial blessing is imparted outside of Mass. It consists of Psalm 127 and of two prayers entirely different from those of the ordinary forms, as found in the *Rituale Romanum.*[3]

Besides the foregoing forms of the solemn nuptial blessing, there is a substitute form for the solemn nuptial bless-

[2] Cf. J. B. O'Connell, *The Celebration of Mass,* pp. 86-87; Bouscaren-Ellis, *Canon Law,* pp. 574-575.

[3] Tit. VIII, *De Sacramento Matrimonii,* cap. 4, *Benedictio Nuptialis Extra Missam pro Sponso et Sponsa* (1952 ed.).

ing which in virtue of an apostolic indult may be used when the bride is a widow who received this blessing in her former marriage,[4] or when the marriage is celebrated during the forbidden time and without the ordinary's permission to give the solemn nuptial blessing at Mass.[5] In the *Rituale Romanum* the form is entitled *"Preces Recitandae extra Misam super Coniuges."*[6]

According to canon 1108, § 2, only the solemn nuptial blessing of marriage is forbidden from the first Sunday of Advent until the Feast of the Nativity of Our Lord inclusive, and from Ash Wednesday until Easter Sunday inclusive. But the local ordinary may, in compliance with the liturgical laws, permit the solemn nuptial blessing even during the aforesaid time, for a just cause, the while he notifies the parties of the marriage that they should abstain from execessive pomp and ceremony.[7]

Thus, outside of the forbidden time, and if the permission of the local ordinary be obtained for its use, then also during the forbidden time, either of the ordinary forms of the solemn nuptial blessing at Mass can be used, in full accordance with the liturgical laws.

According to liturgical law, the votive Mass *pro sponsis* cannot be said, even outside of the forbidden time, on the following days: Sundays and feast of obligation, even suppressed;[8] doubles of the first and second class; days within the privileged octaves of Easter and Pentecost; the privileged vigil of Pentecost, and All Souls' Day. The votive Mass *pro sponsis* is likewise not permitted when an obligatory conventual Mass cannot otherwise be said, and when only one Mass is said in connection with the procession on the days of the Major or Minor Litanies. Even if the per-

[4] Canon 1143.

[5] Canon 1108, § 3.

[6] Tit. VIII, *De Sacramento Matrimonii,* cap. 4, *Benedictio Nuptialis extra Missam pro Sponso et Sponsa* (1952 ed.).

[7] Canon 1108, § 3.

[8] For a list of these days see *AAS,* XII (1920), 42; Bouscaren, *Canon Law Digest,* I, 254.

mission of the local ordinary be granted for the solemnization of marriage at Mass, during the forbidden time the votive Mass *pro sponsis* cannot be said on the following days: Sundays and feasts of obligation, though suppressed; doubles of the first and second class; the privileged vigil of Christmas; the privileged ferial days, i.e., Ash Wednesday and the first three days of Holy Week.[9]

SECTION 2. *Ex Facultate*

By virtue of the present Decennial Faculty, the solemn nuptial blessing can be imparted outside of Mass in the prescribed form, i.e., the extraordinary form, whenever by virtue of a special authorization of the local ordinary[10] the solemn nuptial blessing can permissibly be imparted at Mass in either of the ordinary forms of the solemn nuptial blessing both outside of and within the forbidden time. The present Decennial Faculty relaxes the prescription of canon 1101, § 1, which rules that the parties of the marriage receive the solemn nuptial blessing *only at Mass,* and indeed outside of the forbidden time.

Moreover, by virtue of the same Decennial Faculty, the "*Preces Recitandae extra Missam super Coniuges*" can be said outside of Mass by the mission ordinary or his missionaries if these be subdelegated, over the couple when the bride is a widow who received the solemn nuptial blessing in her former marriage, or when the marriage is celebrated on a day during the forbidden time and the permission of the local ordinary to impart the solemn nuptial blessing has not been obtained.[11] The faculty to recite the "*Preces Reci-*

[9] S.R.C., 14 Iun. 1918—*AAS,* X (1918), 332; Bouscaren, *Canon Law Digest,* I, 547-548. Cf. Bouscaren-Ellis, *Canon Law,* pp. 575-577; J. B. O'Connell, *The Celebration of Mass,* pp. 84-87.

[10] Canon 1108, § 3.

[11] Vromant, *Facultates Apostolicae,* n. 87; Winslow, *The Apostolic Faculties,* pp. 162-163; Paventi, *Brevis Commentarius,* p. 46; Sartori, *Iuris Missionarii Elementa,* pp. 118-119; Bouscaren-Ellis, *Canon Law,* pp. 574-577.

tandae extra Missam super Coniuges" depends for its use on an indult, as postulated in canon 1108, § 3.

The present Quinquennial Faculty is entirely the same with the present Decennial Faculty, not only in its content and scope, but also in the matter of allowing of subdelegation on the part of the local ordinary.[12]

[12] Cf. Eagleton, *The Diocesan Quinquennial Faculties, Formula IV*, pp. 134-135.

CONCLUSIONS

(1) Similar to the practice obtaining in the jurisprudence of the Roman Law, *"facultas"* was taken for *"potestas," "licentia," "permissio," indultum," "privilegium,"* etc., and *"facultates"* for *"possessiones,"* until the *Quinque Typicae Formulae Facultatum* were formulated in 1637. (Pp. 1-13). However, the concept of the apostolic faculties was being formulated during the period between the thirteenth century and the sixteenth centuries, during which period the Holy See issued numerous bulls in which it granted apostolic faculties to the Dominican and Franciscan missionaries (Pp. 9-17).

(2) A definition of *"facultas"* was formulated by canonists only at the end of the nineteenth century, yet it was not a finally decisive one (Pp. 31-32). A faculty can be defined as the power which an ecclesiastical superior, having jurisdiction in his respective forum, personally grants to one who is in some way his subject for the performance of an act that belongs to the granting superior himself, either by its very nature, or by way of postitive reservation, so that the grantee likewise can do it validly, lawfully, or at least safely, in the internal forum only, or in the external forum also. In its nature, a faculty implies an ability to participate in the ecclesiastical power of governing, sanctifying, or administering, conceded for the good of the faithful or of the Church, to one who is otherwise without competence (Pp. 33-34).

(3) All apostolic faculties which were granted in the forms of ordinary formulae or extraordinary formulae were declared to be habitual faculties (now the Decennial Faculties for ordinaries in quasi-dioceses as well as the Quinquennial Faculties for ordinaries in dioceses are such habitual faculties) (Pp. 25-30; 37-45).

(4) Since the promulgation of the Code of Canon Law, all habitual faculties in their juridical status are by virtue

of canon 66, § 1, considered as privileges outside the law, regardless of the fact that some Decennial or Quinquennial Faculties may have the juridical characteristics of simple dispensations, or licenses, or permissions, or privileges contrary to the law, or of a mere declaration of jurisdiction (Pp. 37-40). Accordingly Decennial and Quinquennial Faculties are favorable privileges, deserving of a liberal interpretation (Pp. 40-42).

(5) All Decennial Faculties are real and muneral privileges, and hence they cannot be renounced nor do they cease with the death of the physical ordinary of the place, but they remain or continue to be exercised with the same juridical activity on the part of the successor in office, to whom they automatically are transferred (Pp. 42-45).

(6) The source of the Decennial Faculties for ordinaries in quasi-dioceses is the Sacred Congregation for the Propagation of the Faith, while that of the Quinquennial Faculties for ordinaries in dioceses is multiple, i.e., the faculties are granted by various Roman Congregations through the channel of the Sacred Consistorial Congregation (Pp. 46-60).

(7) The Decennial Facutlies incorporated in the *Formula Maior* are granted to bishops who are ordinaries in the missions, to their vicars general in the missions *de facto, sed non de iure,* and to their vicars delegate in the missions *de facto et de iure, exceptis excipiendis.* The Decennial Faculties incorporated in the *Formula Minor* are granted to prefects apostolic and their prefects delegate. Now, by a specific declaration of the Holy See, missions *sui iuris* enjoy an equivalent juridical status with prefectures apostolic. And thus the superior of a mission *sui iuris* and his mission delegate have equal competence in the use of the Decennial Faculties (Pp. 67-85).

(8) The power given to ordinaries in quasi-dioceses by *Facultas III,* in the *Formula Maior,* namely to depute one or two of their priests as extraordinary ministers of confirmation, differs from the power which is granted in the Decree "*Spiritus Sancti Munera*" (Pp. 98-104).

(9) Mission ordinaries, by virtue of *Facultas IV*, in the *Formula Maior*, can grant permission to their missionaries to say Mass on a portable altar, even on shipboard. Now the use of the *Antimensium latinum* is available to missionaries, but for the use of this very special faculty the missionaries must apply to the Sacred Congregation for the Propagation of the Faith (Pp. 127-128).

10) The faculty to celebrate Holy Week ceremonies in the short form, i.e., to use the *Memoriale Rituum* (*Facultas X* in the *Formula Maior*) has become entirely unnecessary, because of the recent reorganization of liturgical law. At the present the use of the *Memoriale Rituum* is supplanted by the Simple Rite of the Restored Order of Holy Week, which requires no particular faculty for its use (Pp. 149-155).

(11) By virtue of *Facultas XII* in the *Formula Maior*, the ordinary in the missions can permit priests in his territory who are losing their sight, or whose sight is so weak, either accidentally or habitually, that they can read only very coarse type, or who are suffering from some infirmity such as nervousness, or from some defect such as stammering, and therefore are unable to read the Masses occurring each day in the *Missale Romanum*, to celebrate the votive Mass of the Blessed Virgin on all feasts and Sundays, and the *Missa quotidiana defunctorum*, on ferial days. Those who use the said faculty must follow the Instruction given on September 3, 1942 (Pp. 161-166).

(12) The new discipline on the Eucharistic fast of the sick is much more generous than *Facultas XVIII* in the *Formula Maior*. Thus the said faculty no longer stands as a favor granted for missionaries (Pp. 181-185).

(13) By virtue of *Facultas IV* in the *Formula Maior*, the mission ordinary can subdelegate to his missionaries the faculty to celebrate Mass "without a server." The phrase "without a server" (*sine ministro*) may be accepted as meaning "without anyone being present at all," or "with

no one present at all" during the celebration of Mass (Pp. 130-131).

(14) Missionaries, if they are not canonical pastors or quasi-pastors, do not *ex iure* enjoy the faculty given to pastors and quasi-pastors in canons 1044 and 1045. However, if they have *Facultas XXII*, in the *Formula Maior*, they can dispense from each and every one of the matrimonial impediments of ecclesiastical law, diriment as well as prohibitive, of major degree as well as of minor degree, multiple as well as individual, not only occult but also public, except from the three impediments which arise: 1) from the sacred priesthood; 2) from affinity in any degree of the direct line when the marriage has become consummated, and 3) from nonage, when the male party to the marriage has not yet completed his fourteenth, or the female her twelfth year (Pp. 231-234). The condition postulated for the use of the said faculty is neither an "*urgens periculum mortis,*" nor the "perplexing situation," but any ordinarily occurring circumstances attended with a sufficient canonical cause for a dispensation (Pp. 224-231).

(15) By virtue of *Facultas XXII*, in the *Formula Maior*, missionaries can dispense from the impediment of disparity of cult also when it exists between a Catholic and a Jew, or between a Catholic and a Mohammedan (Pp. 243-244).

(16) In the missions, now, either formal guarantees or equivalent guarantees may be requested for the granting of dispensations from the impediments of disparity of cult and of mixed religion. However, a special faculty from the Holy Office is necessary for the use of simply equivalent guarantees (Pp. 239-242).

(17) To the mission ordinary a power is given by *Facultas XIII*, in the *Formula Maior*, which can be subdelegated to his missionaries, to grant the *sanatio in radice* for very marriage invalid on account of one or more diriment impediments of the ecclesiastical law, with the same exceptions, however, that receive mention in *Facultas XXII*, in the *Formula Maior* (see Conclusion n. 14) (Pp. 258-266).

(18) By virtue of *Facultas XXIV*, the mission ordinary is empowered to grant, with the power also to subdelegate this faculty, the *sanatio in radice* for attempted marriages when in addition to the presence of either the impediment of mixed religion or of disparity of cult the union was contracted outside the Church as an invalid union (Pp. 269-272).

(19) Missionaries who are not canonical pastors or quasi-pastors also enjoy the faculties granted through the three Papal Constitutions mentioned in canon 1125, if they enjoy *Facultas XXV* of the *Formula Maior* (Pp. 317-318). The faculty granted in the Constitution *Populis* is not simply an extension of the scope of the Pauline privilege (Pp. 296-303). Faculties granted in *Facultas XXV* and *Facultas XXVI* are broader than the ones which derive from the Constitution *Populis* (Pp. 303-316).

(20) In the missions, a dispensation from the interpellations for the dissolution of marriages contracted by non-baptized polygamist converts can be given either by virtue of the Constitution *Altitudo,* or by virtue of the Constitution *Romani Pontificis,* but these Constitutions must be interpreted in the light of the *"Adnotatio ad Facultatem n. XXV,"* in the *Formula Mairo* (Pp. 323-325).

(21) In the missions, a dispensation from the interpellations for the dissolution of marriages contracted by non-baptized monogamous converts can be given in four ways, i.e., by virtue of the Constitution *Populis* and by virtue of *Facultates XXV-XXVIII* in the *Formula Maior* (Pp. 295-316; 288-294).

(22) By virtue of *Facultas XXVI,* in the *Formula Maior,* a dispensation from the need of making the interpellations may be given even to non-baptized converted persons, though they are still under instruction for their baptism, if their baptism is certain to follow (Pp. 308-315).

(23) *Facultas XXVII* in the *Formula Maior* deals with the possible use of two powers, i.e., the power of dispensing from the prescribed temporal element in the making of the

interpellations, and the power of dispensing, not only from the prescribed temporal element but also from the very obligation of making any interpellations at all, so that the convert may make the interpellation even before his reception of baptism, or be freed of the obligation of making the interpellations completely, in any case of true necessity (Pp. 288-294).

BIBLIOGRAPHY

Sources

Acta Apostolicae Sedis, Commentarium Officiale, Romae, 1909—

Acta, Decreta, Normae et Vota Primi Concilii Sinensis (1924), Zi-Ka-Wei, 1929.

Acta et Decreta Sacrorum Conciliorum Recentiorum, Collectio Lacensis, 7 vols., Friburgi Brisgoviae, 1870-1892.

Acta Sanctae Sedis, 41 vols., Romae, 1865-1908.

Annuario Pontificio, Città del Vaticano: Typografia Poliglotta Vaticana, 1958.

Bibliothèque des Écoles Francaises d'Athenes et de Rome, 2° ser.: *Les Registres de Gregoire IX (1227-1241). Recueil des Bulles de ce Pape, Publiées ou Analysées d'après les Manuscrits Originaux du Vatican*, 4 vols., Vols. I-III, ed. Lecien Auvray, Paris: Librairie Thorin et Fils, 1896-1918; Vol IV, ed. Vitte-Clémencet et Louis Carolus-Barré, Paris: E. De Boccard, Éditeur, 1955; *Les Registres d'Innocent IV (1243-124). Recueil des Bulles de ce Pape, Publiées ou Analysées d'après les Manuscripts Originaux des Archives du Vatican et de la Bibliothèque Nationale*, 4 vols., Vols. I-III, ed Elie Berger, Paris: Ernest Thorin, Édit., 1884-1897; Vol. IV (Index), (1911); *Les Registres de Benoît XI (1303-1304). Recueil des Bulles de ce Pape publiées ou Analysées d'après les Manuscrits Originaux des Archives du Vatican*, ed. Ch. Grandjean, Paris: Albert Fontemoing, 1905.

Bouscaren, T. Lincoln, *The Canon Law Digest*, 4 vols., Milwaukee: The Bruce Publishing Co., 1934-1958.

Breviarium Romanum ex Decreto Sacrosancti Concilii Tridentini Restitutum, S. Pii V Pontificis Maximi Iussu Editum, Aliorumque Pontificum Cura Recognitum, Pii Papae X Auctoritate Reformatum, editio juxta typicam vaticanam, 4 vols., Neo-Eboraci: Benziger Brothers, Inc., 1941-1942.

Bullarium Franciscanum, seu RR. Pontificum Constitutiones, Epistolae ac Diplomata Ordinibus Minorum, Clarissarum, Paenitentium Concessa, 8 vols., Vols. I-III, ed. Ioannes Hyacinthus Sbaralea, Romae, 1759-1764; Vol. IV, ed. Rossi, Romae, 1768; Vols. V-VIII, ed. C. Eubel, Romae, 1898-1904; Nova series, ab anno 1431, ad annum 1478, ed. primo ab U. Huentemann et secundo ab I. M. Pau y Marti, Ad Claras Aquas, 1929–1949.

Bullarium Ordinis Eremitarum S. Augustini, ed. L. Empoli, Romae, 1628.

Bullarium Ordinis Fratrum Praedicatorum, edd. Th. Ripoli et A. Bremond, 8 vols., Romae, 1729-1740.

Bullarum, Diplomatum, et Privilegiorum Sanctorum RR. PP. Editio Taurinensis, Augustae Taurinorum, 1857-1872.

Codex Iuris Canonici Pii X Pontificis Maximi Iussu Digestus, Benedicti Pape XV Auctoritate Promulgatus, Praefatione, Fontium Annotatione et Indice Analytico-Alphabetico ab Emo Petro Card. Gasparri Auctus, Reimpressio, Westminster, Md.: The Newman Press, 1954.

Codicis Iuris Canonici Fontes, 9 vol., Vols, I-VI, ed. cura Emi Petri Card. Gasparri, Romae, postea Civitate Vaticana: Typis polyglottis Vaticanis, 1923-1932; Vols. VII-IX, ed. cura et studio Emi Iustiniani Card. Serédi, 1935-1939.

Collectanea Constitutionum, Decretorum, Indultorum, ac Instructionum Sanctae Sedis ad Usum Operariorum Apostolicorum Societatis Missionum ad Exteros, 1. ed., Parisiis: Typis Georges Chamrot, 1880; 2. ed., Hongkong, 1905.

Collectanea S. Congregationis de Propaganda Fide, 1. ed., 2 vols., Romae: Typographia Polyglotta S.C. de Propaganda Fide, 1893; 2. ed., 2 vols., Romae: Typographia Polyglotta S.C. de Propaganda Fide, 1907.

Corpus Iuris Canonici, ed. Lipsiensis II, post Aemelii Ludovici Richteri curas instruxit Aemelius Friedberg, Lipsiae: Ex officina Bernhardi Tauchmitz, 1879-1881; ed. anastatice repetita, 1928.

Corpus Iuris Civilis, Institutiones, ed. sterotypa 15., quas recognovit Paulus Krueger; *Digesta*, ed. sterotypa 15., quae recognovit Theo. Mommsen, retractavit Paulus Krueger; *Codex Iustinianus*, ed. sterotypa 10., quem recognovit et retractavit Paulus Krueger; *Novellae*, ed. sterotypa 5., quas recognovit Rudolfus Schoell, absolvit Guilelmus Kroll, 3 vols., Berolini: Apud Weidmannos, 1928-1929.

Decreta Authentica Congregationis Sacrorum Rituum, ex actis eiusdem collecta eiusque auctoritate promulgata, 7 vols., Vols. I-IV, sub auspiciis Ss. Domini Nostri Leonis Papae XIII, Romae, 1898-1901; Vol. VI, Appendix, sub auspiciis Pii Papae X, Romae, 1912; Vol. VII, Appendix, sub auspiciis Pii Papae XI, Romae, 1927.

Decretales Gregorii IX cum Epitomis, Divisionibus, et Glossis Ordinariis, Romae, 1582.

Decretum Gratiani, Emendatum et Notationibus Illustratum cum Glossis, Gregorii XIII, Pont. Max., Iussu Editum, 2 vols., Romae, 1582.

De Martinis, Raphael, *Ius Pontificium de Propaganda Fide*, prima pars 7 vols., Romae, 1888-1897; seconda pars, Romae, 1909.

Directorium Commune Missionum Coreae, Iussu Concilii Regionalis 1931 Editum, Hongkong, Imprimarie de Nazareth, 1932.

Gardellini, Aloysius, *Decreta Authentica Congregationis Sacrorum*

Rituum, ex Actis Eiusdem Collecta, 3. ed., 4 vols., Romae, 1856-1858.

Harduinus, J., *Acta Conciliorum et Epistolae Decretales ac Constitutiones Summorum Pontificum*, 12 vols., Parisiis, 1714-1715.

Litterae Apostolicae Gregorii Papae XIII, Quibus Gratias et Facultates Societatis Jesus Declarantur, et Extenduntur, et Aliae de Novo Conceduntur in Forma Brevis, Romae: Apun Sanctum Petrum, 1575.

Jaffé, Philippus, *Regesta Pontificum Romanorum ab Condita Ecclesia ad Annum post Christum Natum MCXCVIII*, 2. ed., correctam et auctam sub auspiciis G. Wattenbach curaverunt S. Loewenfeld, F. Kaltenbrunner, et P. Ewald, 2 vols., Berolini, 1885-1888.

Mansi, Joannes, *Sacrorum Conciliorum Nova et Amplissima Collectio*, 53 vols. in 60, Parisiis, 1901-1927.

Migne, Jacque Paul, *Patrologiae Cursus Completus, Series Latina*, 221 vols., Parisiis, 1844-1855.

Missale Romanum, editio III juxta typicam Vaticanam amplificata, Neo-Eboraci: Benziger Brothers, Inc., 1944.

Ordo Hebdomadae Sanctae Instauratus, edition typica, Romae: Typis Polyglottis Vaticanis, 1956.

Pontificale Romanum Summorum Pontificum Iussu Editum, a Benedicto XIV et Leone XIII Pontificibus Maximis Recognitum et Castigatum, Ratisbonae-Neo-Eboraci-Cincinnati: Pustet, 1891.

Potthast, Augustus, *Regesta Pontificum Romanorum inde ab Anno post Christum Natum MCXCVIII ad Annum MCCCIV*, 2 vols., Berolini, 1874-1875.

Rituale Romanum Pauli V Pontificis Maximi Iussu Editum, Aliorum Pontificum Cura Recognitum, atque Auctoritate Pii Papae XI ad Normam Codicis Iuris Canonici Accommodatum, editio iuxta typicam Vaticanam, Neo-Eboraci: Benziger Brothers, Inc., 1944.

Sacrae Romanae Rotae Decisiones seu Sententiae quae . . . Prodierunt ab Anno 1909—, Romae: Typis Vaticanis, 1912—

Sylloge Praecipuorum Documentorum Recentiorum Summorum Pontificum et S. Congregationis de Propaganda Fide necnon Aliarum SS. Congregationum Romanarum ad Usum Missionariorum, Typis Polyglottis Vaticanis, 1939.

Waddingus, Lucas, *Annales Minorum seu Trium Ordinum a S. Francisco Institutorum*, 27 vols., 3 ed., curavit Joseph Maria Fonseca, Ad Claras Aquas (Quarrachi), 1931-1935.

Reference Works

Abbo, John-Hannan, Jerome D., *The Sacred Canons*, rev. ed., 2 vols., St. Louis: B. Herder Book Co., 1957.

Ayrinhac, H.-Lydon, P. J., *Marriage Legislation in the New Code of Canon Law*, 3. ed., New York: Benziger Brothers, 1957.

Bartoccetti, Victorius, *De Regulis Juris Canonici*, Romae: Angelo Belardetti, Editore, 1955.

———, *Jus Constitutionale Missionum*, Taurini, L.I.C.E. 1947.

Bender, Ludovicus, *Potestas Ordinaria et Delegata, Commentarius in Canones 196-206*, Tournai: Desclée et Cie, 1957.

Benedictus XIV (Prospero Lambertini), *De Synodo Dioecesana*, 2. ed., 2 vols., Romae, 1806.

Beste, Udalricus, *Introductio in Codicem*, 4. ed., Neapoli: M. D'Auria, Pontificus Editor, 1956.

Blat, Albertus, *Commentarius Textus Codicis Iuris Canonici*, 5 vols. in 6, Romae: Ex Typographia Pontificia in Instituto Pii IX, 1919-1927.

Bouscaren, T. Lincoln-Ellis, Adam C., *Canon Law: A Text and Commentary*, 3. rev. ed., Milwaukee: The Bruce Publishing Co., 1957.

Brennan, James H., *The Simple Convalidation of Marriage*, The Catholic University of America Canon Law Study n. 102, Washington, D.C.: The Catholic University of America, 1937.

Brys, J., *De Dispensatione in Iure Canonico, praesertim apud Decretistas et Decretalistas usque ad Medium Saeculum Decimum Quartum*, Brugis: Beyart, 1925.

Burton, Francis J., *A Commentary on Canon 1125*, The Catholic University of America Canon Law Studies, n. 121, Washington, D.C.: The Catholic University of America Press, 1940.

Capobianco, Pacificus, *Privilegia et Facultates Ordinis Fartrum Minorum*, 3. ed., Romae: Pontificum Athenaeum Antonianum, 1956.

Cappello, Felix, *Tractatus Canonico-Moralis de Sacramentis*, 5 vols., Vol. I *De Sacramentis in Genere, de Baptismo, Confirmatione, et Eucharista*, 6. ed., 1953; Vol. II, *De Poenitentia*, 6. ed., 1953; Vol. III, *De Extrema Unctione*, 3. ed., 1949; Vol. IV, *De Ordinatione*, 3. ed., 1951; Vol. V, *De Matrimonio*, 6. ed., 1950, Taurini-Romae: Marietti.

Cappiello, Linus, *De Ordinariorum Dispensandi Facultate ad Normam Canonis 81*, The Catholic University of America Canon Law Studies, n. 323, Washington, D.C.: The Catholic University of America Press, 1952.

Carberry, John J., *The Juridical Form of Marriage*, The Catholic University of America Canon Law Studies, n. 84, Washington, D.C.: The Catholic University of America, 1934.

Caron, Raymundus, *Apostolicus Evangelicus Missionariorum Regularium per Universum Mundum Expositus*, Antverpiae, 1653.

Carroll, James, *The Bishop's Quninquennial Report*, The Catholic University of America Canon Law Studies, n. 359, Washington, D.C.: The Catholic University of America Press, 1956.

Chelodi, Ioannes, *Ius Canonicum de Personis*, 3. ed., Vicenza, 1942.

Chelodi, I.-Ciprotti, Pius, *Ius Canonicum de Matrimonio*, Vicenza: Società Anonima Typografica Editrice, 1947.

Cicognani, A., *Canon Law*, 2. ed. rev., translated by J. O'Hara and F. Brennan, Philadelphia: The Dolphin Press, 1935; Reprint, Westminster, Md.: The Newman Bookshop, 1946.

Collins, Harold, *The Church Edifice and Its Appointments*, Philadelphia: The Dolphin Press, 1936; Reprint, Westminster, Md.: The Newman Bookshop, 1946.

Conte a Coronata, Matthaeus, *Institutiones Iuris Canonici*, 5 vols., Vol. I, *Normae Generales, De Clericis, De Religiosis, De Laicis*, 4. ed., 1950; Vol. II, *De Rebus*, 4. ed., 1951; Vol. III, *De Processibus*, 4. ed., 1956; Vol. IV, *De Delictis et Poenis*, 4. ed., 1955; Vol. V, *Index*, 3. ed., 1951, Taurini-Romae: Marietti.

———, *Institutiones Iuris Canonici, De Sacramentis Tractatus Canonicus*, 3 vols., Vol. I, *Praenotationes, De Baptismo, Confirmatione, Eucharistia, Poenitentia, et Extrema Unctione*, 2. ed. emendata et aucta, 1951; Vol. II, *De Ordine*, 2. ed., revisa et emendata, 1949; Vol. III, *De Matrimonio et de Sacramentalibus*, 3. ed. aucta et emendata, 1957, Romae: Marietti.

Daniel-Rops, Henri, *Cathedral and Crusade: Studies of the Medieval Church 1050-1350*, translated by John Warrington, London: L. M. Dent and Sons Ltd., 1956.

D'Annibale, Josephus, *Summula Theologiae Moralis*, 3 vols., 5. ed., Romae, 1908-1909.

De Camillis, Josephus, *Intitutions Iuris Canonici*, 2 vols., Parisiis, 1868.

De Gubernatis, Dominicus, *Orbis Seraphicus: Historia de Tribus Ordinibus a Seraphico Patriarcha S. Francisco Institutis, deque Eorum Progressibus et Honoribus per Quatuor Mundi Partes*, 6 vols., Romae: Typis Stephani Caballi, 1682.

De Reeper, J., *A Missionary Campanion*, Westminster, Md.: The Newman Press, 1952.

Descamps, Baron, *Histoire Générale Comparée des Missions*, Paris: Librairie Plon, 1932.

DeSmet, Aloysius, *De Sponsalibus et Matrimonio*, 4. ed., Brugis: Carolus Beyaert, Editor Pontificius, 1927.

Diederichs, Michael F., *The Jurisdiction of the Latin Ordinaries over their Oriental Subjects*, The Catholic University of America Canon Law Studies, n. 229, Washington, D.C.: The Catholic University of America Press, 1946.

Doheny William, *Canonical Procedure in Matrimonial Cases*, 2 vols., Vol. I, *Formal Judicial Procedure*, 2. ed., 1948; Vol. II, *Informal Procedure*, 2. print. 1948, Milwaukee: The Bruce Publishing Co.

Donohue, John F., *The Impediment of Crime*, The Catholic University of America Canon Law Studies, n. 69, Washington, D.C.: The Catholic University of America, 1931.

Dziadosz, Henry J., *The Provisions of the Decree* "SPIRITUS SANCTI MUNERA." *The Law for the Extraordinary Minister of Confirmation*, The Catholic University of America Canon Law Studies, n. 397, Washinton, D.C.: The Catholic University of America Press, 1958.

Eagleton, George, *The Diocesan Quinquennial Faculties, Formula IV*, The Catholic University of America Canon Law Studies, n. 248, Washington, D.C.: The Catholic University of America Press, 1948.

Ellard, G.-Prucha, F. P. *The Simple Rite of the Restored Order of Holy Week*, Milwaukee: The Bruce Publishing Co., 1958.

Eloy, O. L., *Compendium Theologiae Moralis*, 3 vols., Hongkong, 1929.

———, *Variae Quaestiones Practicae ad Matrimonium et ad Causas Matrimoniales*, 2. ed., Hongkong, 1915.

Epistolae Praepositorum Generalium ad Patres et Fratres S. J., Antwerpiae: Apud Joannem Meursium, 1635.

Eustace, Bartholomew, *Ritual for Small Churches*, New York: Joseph F. Wagner, Inc., Publishers, 1935.

Fair, Bartholomew F., *The Impediment of Abduction*, The Catholic University of America Canon Law Studies, n. 194, Washington, D.C.: The Catholic University of America Press, 1944.

Fang, Franciscus, *Dispensatio Matrimonialis Urgente Mortis Periculo et Instante Nuptiarum Contractu*, Romae: Officium Libri Catholici, 1946.

Feije, Henricus, *De Impedimentis et Dispensationibus Matrimonialibus*,, 3. ed., Lovanii, 1885.

Focher, Joannes, *Itinerarium Catholicum Proficiscentium ad Infideles Convertendos*, Romae: Apud Alfonsum Scribanum, 1574.

Fortescue, *The Ceremonies of the Roman Rites Described*, 7. ed., rev by O'Connell, London: Burns, Oates and Washbourne, 1947.

Frison, Basil, *The Retroactivity of Law*, The Catholic University of America Canon Law Studies, n. 231, Washington, D.C.: The Catholic University of America Press, 1946.

Fus, Edward A., *The Extraordinary Form of Marriage according to Canon 1098*, The Catholic University of American Canon Law Studies, n. 348, Washington, D.C.: The Catholic University of Press, 1954.

Gallagher, John F., *The Matrimonial Impediment of Public Propriety*, The Catholic University of America Canon Law Studies, n. 304, Washington, D.C.: The Catholic University of America Press, 1952.

Gannon, John Mark, *The Interstices Required for the Promotion to Orders*, The Catholic University of America Canon Law Studies, n. 196, Washington, D.C.: The Catholic University of America Press, 1944.

Gasparri, Petrus, *Tractatus Canonicus de Matrimonio*, nova ed. ad Mentem Codicis I.C., 2 vols., Romae: Typis Polyglottis Vaticanis, 1932.

Gérin, Marcel, *Le Gouvernement des Missions*, Les Thèses Canoniques de Laval, n. 1, Quebec: Faculté de Droit Canonique, Université Laval, 1944.

Goyau, George V., *Missions and Missionaries*, trans. by F. M. Dreves, London: Sands & Co., 1932.

Gregory, Donald, *The Pauline Privilege*, The Catholic University of America Canon Law Studies, n. 68, Washington, D.C.: The Catholic Univesrity of America, 1931.

Grentrup, Theodorus, *Ius Missionarium*, Tom. I, Steyl, Holland: Typographia Domus Missionum a S. Michaele Arch. nuncupatae, 1925.

Hannon, James, *Holy Viaticum*, The Catholic University of America Canon Law Studies, n. 314, Washington, D.C.: The Catholic University of America Press, 1951.

Harrington, Robert J., *The Radical Sanation of Invalid Marriages*, The Catholic University of America Canon Law Studies, n. 116, Washington, D.C.: The Catholic University of America Press, 1938.

Henrion, Le Baron, *Histoire Générale des Missions Catholiques depuis XIII* Siècle jusqu'à Nos Jours, Paris, 1847.

Hilling, N., *Codicis Juris Canonici Supplementum*, Friburgi Brisg.: Apud J. Waibel Bibliopolam, 1925.

Hinchius, Paul, *System des katholischen Kirchenrechts*, 4 vols., Berlin, 1869-1897.

Holboeck, Carolus, *Tractatus de Jurisprudentia Sacrae Romanae Rotae*, Graetiae-Vindobonae-Coloniae: In Officina Libraria "Styria," 1957.

Holzapfel, Herbert, *The History of the Franciscan Order*, trans. by A. Tibesar and G. Brinkmann, Tentopolis, Ill.: St. Joseph Seminary, 1948.

Huber, Rapahael, *A Documented History of the Franciscan Order—1182-1517*, Milwaukee-Washington, D.C.: O.F.M. Conv. Press, 1944.

Hueber, Fortunatus, *Menologium seu Brevis et Compendiosa Illustratio Sanctorum, Beatorum, Miraculorum, Incoruptorum, Extraticorum, Beneficorum, et Quocumque Sanctomoniae, vel Virtutis Fulgore, Illustrium, Singularium, aut Praecellentium Famulorum Famularumque Dei Martyrum, Confessorum, Virginum,*

Viduarum, Poenitentium, Romae: Typis Joannis Lucae Straubii, 1698.

Iglesias, Antonius, *Brevis Commentarius in Facultates Quas S.C. de Propaganda Fide Dare Solet Missionariis*, Taurini-Romae: Marietti, 1924.

Institutum Historicum FF. Praedicatorum, *Momumenta Ordinis Fratrum Praedicatorum*, 10 vols., Romae: Ad S. Sabinae, 1883-1894.

Institutum Societatis Jesus, 2 vols., Florentiae: Typographia Ss. Conceptionis, 1892.

Jaeger, Leo A., *The Administration of Vacant and Quasi-Vacant Episcopal Sees in the United States*, The Catholic University of America Canon Law Studies, n. 81, Washington, D.C.: The Catholic University of America, 1932.

Joyce, George, *Christian Marriage: An Historical and Doctrinal Study*, 2. ed., London: Sheed and Ward Publishing Co., 1948.

Kearney, Francis P., *The Principles of Canon 1127*, The Catholic University of America Canon Law Studies, n. 163, Washington, D.C.: The Catholic University of America Press, 1942.

Kearney, Raymond, *The Principles of Delegation*, The Catholic University of America Canon Law Studies, n. 55, Washington, D.C.: The Catholic University of America, 1929.

Keene, Michael J., *Religious Ordinaries and Canon 198*, The Catholic University of America Canon Law Studies, n. 135, Washington, D.C.: The Catholic University of America Press, 1942.

Kekumano, Charles A., *The Secret Archives of the Diocesan Curia*, The Catholic University of America Canon Law Studies, n. 350, Washington, D.C.: The Catholic University of America Press, 1954.

Konings, Antonius-Putzer, Joseph, *Commentarium in Facultates Apostolicas*, 5. ed., Neo-Eboraci-Cincinnati-Chicagiae: Benziger Fratres, 1898.

Kubik, Stanislaus J., *Invalidity of Dispensations According to Canon 84, § 1*, The Catholic University of America Canon Law Studies, n. 340, Washington, D.C.: The Catholic University of America Press 1953.

Kurtscheid, Bertrandus, *Historia Iuris Canonici: Historia Institutorum*, reimpr., Romae: The Catholic Book Agency, 1951.

Kurtscheid, P. B.-Wilches, F., *Historia Iuris Canonici: Historia Fontium et Scientiae Iuris Canonici*, Romae: The Catholic Book Agency, 1943.

Laymann, Paulus, *Theologia Moralis*, 2 vols., Venetiis: G. Valentini, 1630.

Léry, Louis Ch. de, *Le Privilège de la Foi*, Montréal: Ex Typis Collegii Maximi Immaculatae Conceptionis, 1938.

Leurenius, Petrus, *De Episcoporum Vicariis Eorumdemque Coadiutoribus*, Venetiis, 1709.

Liguori, St. Alphonsus, *Theologia Moralis*, 4 vols., ed. Gaudé, Romae, 1905-1912.

Litterae Apostolicae, Quibus Institutio, Confirmatio et Variae Privilegia Continentur Societatis Jesus, Antwerpiae: Apud Joannem Meursium, 1635.

Loenertz, Raymond, *La Société des Frères Pérégrinants: Étude sur l'Orient Dominicain*, Dissertationes Historicae, n. 7, Romae: Institutum Historicum FF. Praedicatorum, 1937.

Ly-Yuh-Wen, Petrus, *Vicarius Delegatus in Territorio Missionis*, Romae: Typografia Poliglotta "Cor Mariae," 1944.

Mahoney, E. J., *The Priest as Minister of Confirmation, The Decree* "SPIRITUS SANCTI MUNERA," *14 September, 1946, with a Commentary*, London: Burns, Oates and Washbourne Ltd., 1952.

Mahoney, E. J.-McReavy, L., *Priests' Problems*, New York: Benziger Brothers, Inc., 1958.

Mann, Horace K., *The Lives of the Popes*, 18 vols., in 19, Vols. I-XII in 13 2. ed., 1925; Vols. XIII-XVIII, 1925-1932, St. Louis, Mo.: B. Herder.

Maroto, P., *Institutiones Iuris Canonicii ad Normam Novi Codicis*, Vol. I, 3. ed., Matriti, 1921.

Matulenas, Raymond A., *Communication, A Source of Privileges*, The Catholic University of America Canon Law Studies, n. 183, Washington, D.C.: The Catholic University of America Press, 1943.

McCarthy, Eduardus A., *De Certitudine Morali quae in Juricis Animo ad Sententiae Pronuntiationem Requiritur*, Romae: Officium Libri Catholici, 1948.

McDevit, Gilbert Joseph, *Legitimacy and Legitimation*, The Catholic University of America Canon Law Studies, n. 138, Washington, D.C.: The Catholic University of America Press, 1941.

McKenzie, Eric F., *The Delict of Heresy in its Commission, Penalization, Absolution*, The Catholic University of America Canon Law Studies, n. 77, Washington, D.C.: The Catholic University of America, 1932.

Mergentheim, L., *Die Quinquennalfacultaeten* PRO FORO EXTERNO. *Ihre Entstehung und Einteilung in Deutschen Bistuemern*, 2 vols., Stuttgart, 1908.

Michiels, Gommarus, *Normae Generales Juris Canonici*, 2 vols., Parisiis-Tornaci-Romae: Typis Societatis S. Joannis Evangelistae, Desclée et Socii, 1949.

———, *Principia Generalia de Personis in Ecclesia*, 2. ed., Parisiis-Tornaci-Romae: Typis Societatis S. Joannis Evangelistae, Desclée et Socii, 1955.

Miscellanea-Vermeersch, 2 vols., Romae: Pontificia Universita Gregoriana, Soc. Tipogr. A. Macioce & Pisani, 1935.

Moeder, John M., *The Proper Bishop for Ordination and Dimissorial Letters*, The Catholic University of America Canon Law Studies, n. 95, Washington, D.C.: The Catholic University of America Press, 1935.

Monin, Arthur, *De Curia Romana, Eius Historia ac Hodierna Disciplina iuxta Reformationem in Pio X Inductam*, Lovanii: Universitatis Catholicae Typographus, 1912.

Motry, Hubert L., *Diocesan Faculties According to the Code of Canon Law*, The Catholic University of America Canon Law Studies, n. 16, Washington, D.C.: The Catholic University of America, 1922.

Naz, Raoul (Editor), *Traité de Droit Canonique*, 4 vols., Paris: Letouzey et Ané, 1948-1949.

O'Connell, J. B., *The Celebration of Mass*, 4. ed., Milwaukee: The Bruce Publishing Co., 1956.

———, *Symplifying the Ruberics of the Roman Breviary and Missal*, Milwaukee: The Bruce Publishing Co., 1956.

O'Dea, John Coyle, *The Matrimonial Impediment of Nonage*, The Catholic University of America Canon Law Studies, n. 205, Washington, D.C.: The Catholic University of America Press, 1944.

Oesterle, Geraldus, *Consultationes de Iure Matrimonii*, Romae: Officium Libri Catholici, 1942.

O'Keefe, Gerald M., *Matrimonial Dispensations: Power of Bishops, Priests, and Confessors*, The Catholic University of America Canon Law Studies, n. 45, Washington D.C.: The Catholic University of America, 1927.

O'Mara, William A., *Canonical Causes for Matrimonial Dispensations*, The Catholic University of America Canon Law Studies, n. 96, Washington, D.C.: The Catholic University of America, 1935.

O'Neill, William H., *Papal Rescripts of Favor*, The Catholic University of America Canon Law Studies, n. 57, Washington, D.C.: The Catholic University of America, 1930.

Paventi, Xaverius, *Brevis Commentarius in Facultates S. Congregationis de Propaganda Fide*, Romae: Officium Libri Catholici, 1944.

———, *Breviarium Iuris Missionis*, Romae: Officium Libri Catholici, 1952.

Payen, G., *De Matrimonio in Missionibus ac Potissimum in Sinis Tractatus Practicus et Casus*, 2. ed., 3 vols., Zi-Ka-Wei: Typographia T'ou-se-we, 1935-1936.

———, *Monita Nankinensia*, 2. ed., 2 vols., Zi-Ka-Wei: Typographia T'ou-se-we, 1933.

Petrovits, Joseph, *The New Church Law on Matrimony*, The Catholic University of America Canon Law Studies, n. 6, Washington, D.C.: The Catholic University of America, 1919; 2. ed., Philadelphia: J. J. McVey, 1926.

Pirhing, Ernricus, *Ius Canonicum*, novissima ed., Dilingae, 1722.

Quigley, A. M., *A Summary of the Canon Law on Matrimonial Impediments and Dispensations*, 4. print., Lancaster, Pa.: The Dolphin Press, 1954.

Quinn, John S., *The Extraordinary Minister of Confirmation According to the Most Recent Decrees of the Sacred Congregations*, Romae: Officium Libri Catholic, 1951.

Quinn, Joseph, *Documents Required for the Reception of Orders*, The Catholic University of America Canon Law Studies, n. 266, Washington, D.C.: The Catholic University of America Press, 1948.

Regatillo, Eduardus, *Interpretatio et Iurisprudentia Codicis Iuris Canonici*, 3. ed., Santander: "Sal Terae," 1953.

Reiffenstuel, Anacletus, *Ius Canonicum Universum*, 4 vols., Venetiis, 1735; 5 vols., in 7, Parisiis, 1864-1870.

Reilly, Edward M., *The General Norms of Dispensation*, The Catholic University of America Canon Law Studies, n. 119, Washington, D.C.: The Catholic University of America Press, 1939.

Rice, Patrick W., *Proof of Death in Prenuptial Investigation*, The Catholic University of America, n. 123, Washington, D.C.: The Catholic University of America Press, 1940.

Rodrigo, Lucius, *Praelectiones Theologico-Moralis Comillenses*, Tom. II. *Tractatus de Legibus*, Santander: "Sal Terrae," 1944.

Roelker, Edward G., *Principles of Privilege According to the Code of Canon Law*, The Catholic University of America Canon Law Studies, n. 35, Washington, D.C.: The Catholic University of America, 1926.

Romani, Sylvius, *Institutiones Iuris Canonici*, Vol. I, *De Fontibus, de Normis, de Personis*, Romae, 1941; Vol. II, Pars II, *De Matrimonio*, Romae: Editore "Iustitia," 1945.

Ruddy, James, The Apostolic Constitution *Christus Dominus*, The Catholic University of America Canon Law Studies, n. 390, Washington, D.C.: The Catholic University of America Press, 1957.

Ryan, Thomas, *The Juridical Effects of the Sanatio in Radice*, The Catholic University of America Canon Law Studies, n. 355, Washington, D.C.: The Catholic University of America Press, 1955.

Sadlowski, Erwin L., *The Sacred Furnishing of Churches*, The Catholic University of America Canon Law Studies, n.315, Washington, D.C.: The Catholic University of America Press, 1951.

Sanchez, Thomas, *De Sancto Matrimonii Sacramento*, Antwerpiae, 1626.

Sartorii, Cosmas, *Ius Missionarii Elementa*, Romae: Secretaria Missionum Ord. Fr. Minorum, 1947.

———, *Enchiridion Canonicum*, 8. ed., Romae, 1947.

Schell, Odoricus, *Compendium Sacrae Liturgiae*, 4. ed., Yen-Chow-Fu, Shantung: Typographia Missionis Catholicae, 1936.

Schenk, Francis J., *The Matrimonial Impediments of Mixed Religion and Disparity of Cult*, The Catholic University of America Canon Law Studies, n. 51, Washington, D.C.: The Catholic University of America, 1929.

Schmalzgrueber, Franciscus, *Ius Ecclesiasticum Universum*, 5 vols. in 12, Romae, 1843-1845.

Schmidt, Herman A.,*Hebdomada Sancta*, 2 vols., Vol. I, *Contemporanei Textus Liturgici, Documenta Piana et Bibliographia;* Vol. II, sects. I-II, *Commentarius Historicus*, Romae-Friburgi Brisg.-Barcinone, 1956-1957.

Schmidt, John R., *The Principles of Authentic Interpretation of Canon 17 of the Code of Canon Law*, The Catholic University of America Canon Law Studies, n. 141, Washington, D.C.: The Catholic University of America Press, 1941.

Schmidlin, Joseph, *Catholic Mission History*, Trans. by Matthias Braun, Techny, Ill.: Mission Press of S.V.D., 1933.

Schuhler, Ralph V., *Privileges of Regulars to Absolve and Dispense*, The Catholic University of America Canon Law Studies, n. 186, Washington, D.C.: The Catholic University of America Press, 1943.

Schulte, A. J.-O'Connell, J.B., *Benedicenda, The Rite Observed in Some of the Principal Functions of the Roman Pontifical and Roman Ritual*, New York: Benziger Brothers, 1955.

Sego, Arthur A., *Dispensation from the Interpellations*, The Catholic University of America Canon Law Studies, n. 316, Washington, D.C.: The Catholic University of America Press, 1951.

Seumois, André V., *Introduction à la Missiologie*, Schoeneck-Beckenreid, Suisse: Administration der neuen Zeitschrift fuer Missionswissenschaft, 1952.

Sipos, Stephanus, *Enchiridion Iuris Canonici*, 6. ed., edited by L. Galos, Romae: Orbis Catholicus-Herder, 1954.

Slafkosky, Andrew, *The Canonical Episcopal Visitation of the Diocese*, The Catholic University of America Canon Law Studies, n. 142, Washington, D.C.: The Catholic University of America Press, 1951.

Stickler, Alphonsus, *Historia Iuris Canonici Latini*, Vol. I, *Historia Fontium*, Augustae Taurinorum: Apud Custodiam Pontif. Athenaei Salesiani, 1950.

Stiegler, M. A., *Dispensation, Dispensationswessen und Dispensationsrecht im Kirchenrecht geschichtlich dargestellt*, 3 vols., Mainz, 1901.

Stanghetti, G., *Prassi della S. C. de Propaganda Fide*, Romae: Officium Libri Catholici, 1943.

Streit, R.-J. Dindinger, J.-Rommerskirchen, J., *Bibliotheca Missionum*, 11 vols., Friburgi: Caritas Druckerei, 1916-1939.

Suarez, Franciscus, *Opera Omnia*, 28 vols., Parisiis, 1856-1861.

Taunton, Ethelred, *The Law of the Church, A Cyclopedia of Canon Law for English Speaking Countries*, St. Louis, Mo.: B. Herder Co., 1906.

Tremblay, Roland, *La Pouvoir de Dispense de Empêchements Matrimoniaux en Pays de Mission*, Les Thèses Canoniques de Laval, n. 2, Quebec: Faculté de Droit Canonique Université Laval, 1944.

Thomassinus, Ludovicus, *Vetus et Nova Ecclesiae Disciplina circa Beneficia et Beneficiarios*, 3 vols., Venetiis, 1730.

Van der Stappen, *Sacra Liturgia*, 3. ed., 5 vols., Mechliniae: H. Dessain, 1911-1915.

Van Hove, A., *Commentarium Lovaniense in Codicem Iuris Canonici*, Vol. I, Tom. I, *Prolegomena*, 2. ed., Mechliniae-Romae: H. Dessain, 1945; Vol. I, Tom. V, *De Privilegiis, De Dispensationibus*, Mechliniae-Romae: H. Dessain, 1939.

Vermeerch, A. Creusen, J., *Epitome Iuris Canonici*, 3 vols., Vols. I-II, 7. ed.; Vol. III, 6. ed., Mechliniae-Romae: H. Dessain, 1946-1954.

Vlaming, T. N., *Praelectiones Iuris Matrimonii ad Normam Codicis Iuris Canonici*, 3. ed., 2 vols., Bossum in Hollandia, 1919-1921.

Vromant, G., *Facultates Apostolicae*, 3. ed., Paris: Desclée de Brouwer, 1947.

———, *Facultates Apostolicae Quas S. Congregatio de Propaganda Fide Dare Solet Ordinariis Missionum, Supplementum ad Commentaria in Formulam Tertaim*, Louvain, 1930.

———, *Ius Missionarium, De Matrimonio*, 3. ed., Paris: Desclée et Brouwer, 1952.

———, *Ius Missionarium, Introductio et Normae Generales*, Louvain, 1934.

———, *Ius Missionarium, De Personis*, Bruxelles: Dewitt, 1929.

Viau, Roger, *Doubt in Canon Law*, The Catholic University of America Canon Law Studies, n. 346, Washington, D.C.: The Catholic University of America Press, 1954.

Wahl, Francis X., *The Matrimonial Impediments of Consanguinity and Affinity*, The Catholic University of America Canon Law Studies, n. 90, Washington, D.C.: The Catholic University of America, 1934.

Welsh, Thomas J., *The Use of the Portable Altar,* The Catholic University of America Canon Law Studies, n. 305, Washington, D.C.: The Catholic University of America Press, 1950.

Wernz, Franciscus X., *Ius Decretalium,* 6 vols., Vols. I-IV, 2. ed., Romae-Prati, 1906-1913.

Wernz, F. X.-Vidal, Petrus, *Ius Canoncium,* 7 vols., in 8, Vol. I, *Nomae Generales,* 2, ed., 1952; Vol. II, *De Personis,* 3. ed., 1943; Vol. III, *De Religiosis,* 1933; Vol. IV, Partes I-II, *De Rebus,* 1934-1935; Vol. V, *Ius Matrimoniale,* 3. ed., 1946; Vol. VI, *De Processibus,* 2. ed., 1949; Vol. VII, *Ius Poenale Ecclesiasticum,* 2. ed., 1951 Romae: Apud Aedes Universitatis Gregorianae.

White, Robert J., *Canonical Ante-Nuptial Promises and the Civil Law,* The Catholic University of America Canon Law Studies, n. 91, Washington, D.C.: The Catholic University of America, 1934.

Winslow, Franciscus, *Vicars and Prefects Apostolic,* The Catholic University of America Canon Law Studies, n. 24, Washington, D.C.: The Catholic University of America, 1924.

———, *A Commentary on the Apostolic Faculties,* New York: Field Afar Press, 1946.

———, *The Pauline Privilege and the Constitutions of Canon 1125,* New York: Field Afar Press, 1948.

Woeber, Edward M., *The Interpellations,* The Catholic University of America Canon Law Studies, n. 172, Washington, D.C.: The Catholic University of America Press, 1942.

Woods, F., *The Constitutions of Canon 1125 and their Applications in the United States,* Milwaukee: The Bruce Publishing Co., 1935.

Wouters, Ludovicus, *Manuale Theologiae Moralis,* 2 vols., Brugis, 1933.

Woywod, S.-Smith, C., *A Practical Commentary on the Code of Canon Law,* first printing of combined Vols. I-II, New York: Joseph Wagner, Inc., 1952.

Ziolkowski, Thaddeus S., *The Consecration and Blessing of Churches,* The Catholic University of America Canon Law Studies, n. 187, Washington, D.C.: The Catholic University of America Press, 1943.

Zitelli, Zephyrinus, *De Dispensationibus Matrimonialibus,* Romae, 1884.

ARTICLES

Aguire, Ph., "Annotationes," *Periodica,* XXXII (1943), 103-110.

Allen, William F., "The Insincerity of the *Cautiones*—Disparity of Cult," *The Jurist,* XVI (1956), 59-86.

Arendt, Gullielmus, "Dispensatio a Forma Matrimonii in Casu Perplexo," *Periodica,* XVI (1927), 1*-17*.

Bartoccetti, Victorius, "Animadversiones circa Evolutionem Iuris Missionum," *Jus Pontificium,* XIV (1934), 263-265.

Bender, L., "Cautiones non Sincerae," *Monitor Ecclesiasticus,* LXXX (1955), 320-323.

———, "Dispensatio de Impedimento Dubio," *Ephemerides Iuris Canonici,* VIII (1952), 75-81.

Bernhard, J., "L'Explication Juridique de la Rétroactivité de la 'Sanatio in Radice' dans la Doctrine Canonique Moderne," *Ephemerides Iuris Canonici,* VII (1951), 80-88.

Bouscaren, "An Inquiry into the Practical Application of Canon 1125 outside Mission Territories," *Miscellanea-Vermeersch,* I (1935), 279-302.

Bride, A., "Marriage entre Catholique et non-Catholique et Education Religieuse des Enfants," *L'Ami du Clergé,* LXVII (1957), 263-266.

Cappello, Felix, "De Impedimento Publico Matrimonii," *Periodica,* XXI (1932), 285-286.

———, "De Separatione Coniugum," *Periodica,* XXI (1932), 286-288.

———, "Facultas Concessa Infirmis," *Periodica,* XXIV (1935), 18*-29*.

Carberry, John J., "Legal Relationship as an Impediment to Marriage," *Ecclesiastical Review,* XC (1934), 394-401.

Che, V. Chenn-Tao, "De Normis Iuridicis Continuitatis Regiminis Missionum Tuendae," *Commentarius pro Religiosis et Missionariis,* XXXVI (1957), 56-70.

Connolly, J. F., "The Emergency Powers of Canons 1043, 1044, 1045," *The Jurist,* V (1945), 20-53.

Conway, W., "Convalidation of Marriage by Confessor," *The Irish Ecclesiastical Record,* 5. series, LXXVII (1952), 292-295.

Crisci, G., "De Delegatione a Iure in Iure Canonico Vigente," *Apollinaris,* X (1937), 513-535.

Daniel-Rops, H., "Les Origines des Missions au Moyen Age," *Revue de l'Université de Laval,* VI (1952), 777-794.

De Smet, A., "Circa Dispensandi Potestatem apud Ordinarium," *Ephemerides Theologicae Lovanienses,* II (1925), 55-59.

Golubovich, P., "De Locis Fratrum Minorum et Praedicatorum in Tartaris," *Archivum Fratrum Praedicatorum,* II (1932), pp. 73-74.

Gutierrez, A., "De Linteo Benedicto Loco Altaris Portatilis pro Missionariis," *Commentarium pro Religiosis et Missionariis,* XXXIV (1955), 288-290.

Hanrahan, P. J., "Insincere Guarantees and Mixed Marriages," *Clergy Review,* XL (1955), 742-746.

Hilling, N., "Die neuen Quinquennalfacultaeten vom Jahre 1923," *Archiv fuer katholisches Kirchenrecht,* CIV (1924), 287-297.

Huerth, F., "Notae Quaedam ad Privilegium Petrinum," *Periodica,* XLV (1956), 371-391.

Jarré, Cyrillus, "De Iis Qui Vicariatum vel Praefecturam Ap. Sede Vacante vel Impedita Regunt," *Antonianum,* III (1928), 191-212; 321-332.

Kelly, Norbert, "Insincere *Cautiones* in the Light of Recent Decisions," *The Jurist,* XII (1953), 33-56.

Larraona, A., "Ius Missionarium," *Commentarium pro Religiosis Missionariis,* XVI (1935), 228-232; XVII (1936), 85-87.

Lee, Ting-Pong Ignatius, "Praefectus Missionis, Praefectus Apostolicus," *Commentarium pro Religiosis et Missionariis,* XXVI (1957), 51-55.

Loenertz, Raymond, "Les Missions Dominicaines en Orient au XIVe Siècle et la Société des Frères Pérégrinants pour le Christ," *Archivum Fratrum Praedicatorum,* II (1932), 1-83; III (1933), 5-55.

MacKenzie, E. F., "Insufficient Canonical Causes for Matrimonial Dispensations," *The Jurist,* X (1950), 54-72.

Mahoney, E. J., "Dissolution of Marriage '*in Favorem Fidei,*'" *The Clergy Review,* XXXVI (1951), 375-376.

Moreau, Ed. de, "La Papauté et les Missions," *Nouvelle Revue Théologique,* LX (1933), 193-212.

Oesterle, G., "Privilegium Paulinum in Sua Applicatione," *Apollinaris,* XXIX (1956), 395-412.

Paventi, Xaverius, "Origo Congregationis Urbanianae super Facultatibus Missionariorum," *Commentarium pro Religiosis et Missionariis,* XXIV (1943), 85-86.

———, "Quaestiones de Iure Missionali," *Ephemerides Iuris Canonici,* III (1947), 243-254.

——, "Adnotationes ad Facultates," *Monitor Ecclesiasticus,* LXXV (1950), 371-382.

———, "Epistola Qua Renovantur Particulares Facultates Ordinariis Missionum Americae Latinae," *Monitor Ecclesiasticus,* LXXV (1950), 562-565.

Pauwels, I., "Annotationes" [ad Ritum et Formulam Breviorem in Consecratione Altarium Quae Amiserunt Consecrationem, *AAS,* XII (1920), 450], *Periodica,* IX (1920), 237.

Pugliese, Augustinus, "De Missione Sui Iuris Eiusque Praelato," *Commentarium pro Religiosis et Missionariis,* XVIII (1937), 37-44; 175-184.

Rayanna, Puthota, "De Constitutione S. Pii Papae V Romani Pontificis,, 3 Augusti 1571," *Periodica,* XXVII (1938), 295-331; XXVIII (1939), 24-52; 112-134; 190-209.

Reckers. K. S., "De Favore Matrimonii inter Infideles Contracti," *Ephemerides Iuris Canonici,* VIII (1952), 140-173.

Roelker, Edward, "The Use of the Term '*Dispensatio*' in the Code of Canon Law," *The Jurist,* X (1950), 138-151.

———, "The Strict Interpretation of Law," *The Jurist,* X (1950), 9-34.

Schaaf, Valentine, "Dispensation from the Interpellations," *Ecclesiastical Review,* LXXXVI (1932), 533-537.

Uyttenbroeck, C., "Le Droit Pénitentiel des Religieux de Boniface VIII à Sixte IV," *Études Franciscaines,* XLVII (1935), 171-189; 306-332.

Vermeersch, Arturus, "De Munere et Officiis Vicarii et Praefecti Apostolici secundum Praesens Ius," *Periodica,* IX (1920), (19)-(34).

———, "Adnotationes," *Periodica,* X (1921), 200.

———, "Historia de Origine Formularum Facultatum," *Periodica,* XI (1922), (33)-(144).

———, "De Canone 1125 Eiusque Vi Extensiva," *Periodica,* XX (1931), 1*-5*.

———, "Facultates Quinquennales, Formula III, Quae Ordinariis Europae Anno 1932 Conceduntur," *Periodica,* XXI (1932), 220*-223*.

———, "De Disparitate Cultus," *Periodica,* XXIV (1935), 41*-42*.

———, "De Matrimonio in Missionibus," *Periodica,* XXIV (1935), 42*-43*.

Vromant, G., "De Natura Potestatis Vicarii Delegati in Territorio Missionum," *Jus Pontificium,* X (1930), 19-26.

———, "De Dispensatione ab Interpellationibus in Ordine ad Privilegium Fidei," *Periodica,* XX (1931), 108*-117*.

Wasner, Franciscus, "De Authenticitate 'Libelli Responsionum' Beati Gregorii Magni Papae ad Sanctum Augustinum Angliae Apostolum Animadversiones," *Jus Pontificium,* XVIII (1939), 174-185; 293-299.

Winslow, Francis J., "The Application of the Pauline Privilege and Constitutions of Canon 1125 in the United States," *The Jurist,* X (1950), 304-333.

Periodicals

American Ecclesiastical Review, The, Vols. I-XXXII, Philadelphia, 1889-1905; from 1905: *The Ecclesiastical Review,* Vols. XXXIII-CIX, Philadelphia, 1905-1943; from 1944: *The American Ecclesiastical Review,* Washington, D.C., Vol. CX, 1944—

Ami du Clergé, L', Langres, 1878—

Antonianum, Romae, 1926—

Appollinaris, Romae, 1928—

Archivum Fratrum Praedicatorum, Romae: Institutum Historicum FF. Praedicatorum, 1931—

Archiv fuer katholisches Kirchenrecht, Innsbruck, 1857-1861; Mainz, 1862—

Clergy Review, The, London, 1931—

Commentarium pro Religiosis, Romae, 1920-1934; *Commentarium pro Religiosis et Missionariis,* Romae, 1935—

Ephemerides Iuris Canonici, Romae, 1945—

Ephemerides Theologicae Lovanienses, Brugis, 1924—

Il Monitore Ecclesiastico, Romae, 1876-1948; *Monitor Ecclesiasticus,* Romae, 1949—

Irish Ecclesiastical Review, The, Dublin, 1864—; 5. series, 1913—

Jurist, The, Washington, D.C., 1941—

Jus Pontificium, Romae, 1921-1940.

Nouvelle Revue Théologique, Tournai, 1869—

Periodica de Religiosis et Missionariis, Brugis, 1905-1919; ab anno 1920: *Periodica de Re Canonica et Morali utilia praesertim Religiosis et Missionariis,* Brugis, 1920-1927; ab anno 1928: *Periodica de Re Morali, Canonica, Liturgica,* Brugis, 1928-1936, et Romae, 1937—

Revue de Droit Canonique, Strasbourg, 1951—

Sal Terrae, Santander, 1912—

Dictionaries

Dictionnaire de Droit Canonique, commencé sous la direction de A. Villien et E. Magnin, continué sous la direction de A. Amanieu, publié sous la direction de R. Naz, Paris: Letouzey et Ané, 1924—

Dictionnaire de Droit et de Pratique, Contenant l'Explication des Terms de Droit, d'Ordonnance, et Coutûmes et de Pratique avec les Jurisdictions de France, 2. ed., revue, corrigée et augmentée par Claude-Joseph de Ferrière, Paris: Chez Durand, Libraire, 1762.

Encyclopedic Dictionary of Roman Law, ed. by the American Philosophical Society, Philadelphia, 1953.

Gemma Legalis, ed. Bartolus a Saxoferrato, 11 vols., Venetiis: Apud Iuntas, 1590-1595.

La Grande Encyclopedie, Inventaire Raisonnée des Sciences, des Lettres et des Arts, ed. par la Société de Savants et de Gens de Lettres, 31 vols., Paris: H. Laminault et Cie, Editeurs, 1886-1902.

Law Dictionary, ed. by John Bouvier; 3. rev. ed. by Francis Rawle, 2 vols., Kansas City, Mo.: Vernon Law Book Co., 1914.

Vocabularium Iurisprudentiae Romanae, auspiciis Instituti Savigniani inchoatum et ex auctoritate Academiae Scientiarum Borussicae compositum, Berolini: Typis et Impensis Walter de Gruyter Co., 1933.

Vocabularium Iuris Utriusque, 2. ed. auctior atque emendatior a Philippo Vicat, 4 vols., Neopoli: Sumptibus Joannis Grevier, 1760.

Repertorium, a Ioanne Bertachino Firmano, 5 vols., Venetiis: Apud Bevilaquam et Socios, 1570.

ABBREVIATIONS

AAS—*Acta Apostolicae Sedis.*

Arch. f. k. KR—*Archiv fuer katholisches Kirchenrecht.*

ASS—*Acta Sanctae Sedis.*

B.O.P.—*Bullarium Ordinis Fratrum Praedicatorum.*

CpRM—*Commentarium pro Religiosis et Missionariis.*

Collectanea (1893)—*Collectanea S. Congregationis de Propaganda Fide*, ed. 1893.

Collectanea—*Collectanea S. Congregationis de Propaganda Fide*, ed. 1907.

Collectanea Sanctae Sedis—*Collectanea Constitutionum, Decretorum, Indultorum ac Instructionum S. Sedis ad Usum Operariorum Apostolicorum Societatis Missionum ad Exteros*, prima ed., 1880.

Collectanea Sanctae Sedis, Hongkong—*Collectanea Sanctae Sedis*, 2. ed., Hongkong, 1905.

Collectio Lacensis—*Acta et Decreta Sacrorum Conciliorum Recentiorum, Collectio Lacensis.*

Decreta Authentica—*Decreta Authentica Congregationis Sacrorum Rituum.*

Fontes—*Codicis Iuris Canonici Fontes.*

Jaffé—*Regesta Pontificum Romanorum ab Condita Ecclesia ad Annum post Christum Natum MCXCVIII.*

Mansi—*Sacrorum Conciliorum Nova et Amplissima Collectio.*

MPL—Migne, *Patrologia, Series Latina.*

Periodica—*Periodica de Re Morali, Canonica, Liturgica.*

Potthast—*Regesta Pontificum Romanorum inde ab Anno post Christum Natum MCXCVIII ad Annum MCCCIV.*

Primum Concilium Sinense—*Acta, Decreta, Normae et Vota Primi Concilii Sinensis (1924).*

ALPHABETICAL INDEX

BIOGRAPHICAL NOTE

Peter Byong-Bo Chyang was born March 30, 1922, in Yong-Chon, Kyong-Puk, Korea. He was graduated from Yong-Chon Public Primary School in 1934, and was received into the Catholic Church on August 19, 1935. In April, 1938, he entered Tong-Song Commerical School (St. Nicholas' Minor Seminary), in Seoul, from which he was graduated after five years. In 1943 he entered the Catholic Theological College, where he completed his philosophical studies, and in 1946, he entered the Holy Ghost College (former Catholic Theological College), where he completed his theological studies. On April 15, 1950, he was ordained to the Sacred Priesthood, and on the same day was appointed rector of the Immaculate Conception Church, in Chin-Hae, Kyong-Nam. In August, 1953, he was sent by the late Most Rev. John B. Choi, Ordinary of the Vicariate Apostolic of Taegu, Korea, to the Catholic University of America, Washington, D.C., and enrolled in the School of Social Science at the University, where he received the degree of Master of Arts in 1956. In September of the same year he entered the School of Canon Law at the University and from it he received the degree of Baccalaureate in Canon Law, in June, 1957, and the degree of the Licentiate in Canon Law, in June, 1958.

CANON LAW STUDIES*

402. Chyang, Rev. Peter B., M.A., J.C.L., Decennial Faculties for Ordinaries in Quasi-Dioceses.
403. Gossman, Rev. Francis J., A.B., S.T.L., J.C.L., Pope Urban II and Canon Law.
404. Love, Rev. Paul L., A.B., J.C.L., The Penal Remendies of the Code.
405. McLeaish, Rev. Donald C., A.B., S.T.L., J.C.L., The Laws of the State of Texas Affecting Church Property.
406. Rodriguez, Rev. Manuel J., Ph.B., S.T.L., J.C.L., The Laws of the State of New Mexico Affecting Church Property.
407. Sampon, Rev. Robert G., Ph.B., S.T.L., J.C.L., A Comparative Study of the First Provincial Council of Milwaukee and the Code of Canon Law.
408. Schreiber, Rev. Paul F., A.B., J.C.L., Canonical Precedence.
409. Welsh, Rev. Maurice L., M.A., J.C.L., The Laws of the State of Nevada Affecting Church Property.

* For a complete list of the available numbers of this series apply to the Catholic University of America Press, 620 Michigan Ave., N.E., Washington 17, D.C., for a general catalogue.

www.ingramcontent.com/pod-product-compliance
Lightning Source LLC
LaVergne TN
LVHW050300080826
844660LV00012B/661

* 9 7 8 0 8 1 3 2 2 5 6 2 3 *